LOVE OF ORDER

JOHN BARNWELL

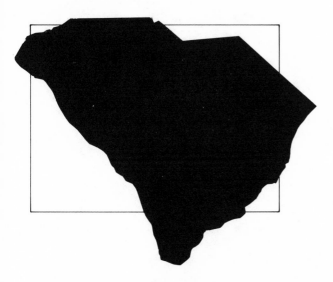

Love of Order

South Carolina's First
Secession Crisis

The University of North Carolina Press   Chapel Hill

For Beth and Lucy

© 1982 The University of North Carolina Press

All rights reserved

Manufactured in the United States of America

Library of Congress Cataloging in Publication Data

Barnwell, John, 1947–
  Love of order.

  Bibliography: p.
  Includes index.
  1. South Carolina—Politics and government—
1775–1865. 2. Secession. I. Title.
F273.B28 975.7′03 81-11441
ISBN 0-8078-1498-9 AACR2

CONTENTS

Preface   ix

ONE   SOUTH CAROLINA, *SUI GENERIS*

I.   Of Numbers and Anxieties   3

II.   Of Government and Its South Carolina Uses   20

III.   Legacies of Nullification   32

TWO   SOUTH CAROLINA, "A FIRESHIP IN THE UNION"

IV.   A Territorial Imperative   53

V.   "In the Hands of the Compromisers"   86

VI.   "Rouse Up to the Strife"   121

VII.   "The Love of Order"   155

         Appendix   191

         Notes   201

         Bibliography   237

         Index   251

MAPS AND TABLES

Maps   South Carolina Districts, 1860   xi

South Carolina Congressional Districts, 1851   182

Tables 1. Negroes as a Percentage of South Carolina's Negro   7
and White Population, 1703–1860

    2. Free Negroes as a Percentage of South Carolina's   10
Negro and White Population, 1790–1860

  A-1. Percentage of South Carolina's Population Slave (s), 192
Free Black (fb), and White (w) by District, 1790

  A-2. Percentage of South Carolina's Population Slave (s), 194
Free Black (fb), and White (w) by District,
1800–1820

  A-3. Percentage of South Carolina's Population Slave (s), 196
Free Black (fb), and White (w) by District,
1830–1860

  A-4. Percentage of Total Votes Cast for Secessionists and 198
Cooperationists by Congressional Districts

PREFACE

In the short space of thirty years, South Carolina "nullified alone and seceded first."[1] These dramatic manifestations of the Palmetto State's unique political culture have fascinated successive generations of historians. From a South Carolina perspective, the nullification movement and the secession crisis of 1860 have been examined most recently in William Freehling's *Prelude to Civil War* and Steven Channing's *Crisis of Fear*. Both works were honored with the Allan Nevins Prize, and both are crucial to our understanding of South Carolina's march along the political path which ended in disruption of the Union. But South Carolina's secession crisis of 1850–51, which served as a rehearsal for disunion, has received little attention. Philip Hamer's *Secession Movement in South Carolina, 1847–1852*, the only book-length treatment of this subject, is now over half-a-century old. Articles on this topic are also scanty and for the most part dated. In the following study, therefore, I have tried to explain the origins of South Carolina's political militance in the 1840s and early 1850s; and I have attempted to chronicle the Palmetto State's secession crisis of 1850–51 more fully and more accurately than previous writers.

This study could not have been undertaken, much less completed, without the assistance of many librarians, archivists, and manuscript curators. Carolyn Wallace and Dick Shrader of the Southern Historical Collection shared their time and knowledge with me. And I am indebted to Isaac Copeland for his special graciousness. E. L. Inabinett and Allen Stokes of the South Caroliniana Library were courteous and helpful to me during many visits to Columbia. My thanks are due also to the staff members of Wilson Library at the University of North Carolina, the Manuscripts Division of the Library of Congress, the Manuscript Department of Duke University Library, the South Carolina Historical Society, and the Virginia Historical Society. I must thank Rosalie Radcliffe and Claudia Price, typists and copy editors of remarkable skill and good humor, for their work on the manuscript.

For encouragement in many ways, I am grateful to George Cuttino and Becky Loveless. Harry McKown, Bob Martin, Gaines Foster, Bill and Ann Coulter, and Paula Wallace aided me immensely on various occasions. Wayne and Fran Mixon have proved friends in all seasons, and Wayne made numerous improvements in my manuscript. I must acknowledge, too, the generosity of Grady and Jo Goldston, who often provided me with food and liquor, yet never asked for a progress report in return.

For much intelligent advice and criticism, I am indebted to Frank Ryan, Joel Williamson, and Peter Walker, all of the University of North Carolina. I thank Frank Klingberg, my mentor and colleague, for his continued support. I benefited from the patience and understanding of Bill Abbot and Dorothy Twohig, editors of the Papers of George Washington. And I am grateful to John Livingston and the University of Denver for a grant which helped me complete the manuscript.

My mother, Lucy Ann Woolf Barnwell, knows my incalculable debt to her. My wife Beth not only endured my long obsession with antebellum South Carolina, but also criticized, corrected, and typed the original manuscript. She has my thanks more than I can say.

South Carolina Districts, 1860

"The heavens themselves, the planets and
    this center,
Observe degree, priority and place.
Insisture, course, proportion, season, form
Office, and custom, in all line of order."

Troilus and Cressida

PART ONE

SOUTH CAROLINA, SUI GENERIS

And by that destiny, to perform an act
Whereof what's past is prologue.
The Tempest

CHAPTER I

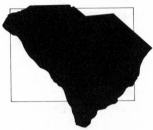

Of Numbers and Anxieties

1

The low country of South Carolina is crisscrossed by dark, almost black, rivers flowing sluggishly to the sea. Live oaks of incredible age still flourish in the naturally swampy terrain. Throughout its history the swamp has nurtured beauty but also disease and death. In colonial and antebellum times the mosquitoes of the swamp carried malarial parasites. Of these the deadliest strain (*falciparum*) was probably not indigenous but imported from West Africa, and it added heavily to the price white planters paid for exploiting alluvial soil and African slaves. The climate of "lowland South Carolina has," in brief, "more in common with the West Indies than with much of the Atlantic seaboard."[1] The colonial regimes of South Carolina and the West Indies had something else in common: both were peopled with black slaves who vastly outnumbered the white inhabitants. In South Carolina, both as colony and state, a white minority would rule, but "of all human factors determining the nature of the Carolina Society, the silent influence of the black African was the most subtle, the most forceful, the most pervading, and the most lasting."[2]

2

Gentlemen from Barbados, who proved so influential in Carolina's early history, were the prime movers in acquainting the new colony with Negro slavery. The Barbadians were accustomed to hereditary slavery, and they were also inured to an economic regime that worked slaves to death: replacement was cheaper than maintenance.[3] Moreover, each black slave imported to Carolina entitled his owner to 150 acres of land (exactly the same headright granted to masters of indentured servants). The slaveholder had the advantage of permanent title to laborer as well as land.[4]

In Virginia, Maryland, New York, and New England, white settlers by an "unthinking decision" consigned blacks to slavery. Before 1670 slavery in British mainland colonies had grown without design, and slavery as a lifelong, hereditary condition reserved for blacks appeared gradually; customary usage had preceded legal enactment. But in Carolina hereditary Negro slavery was deliberately transplanted and cultivated.[5]

As exceptionalism marked the origins of South Carolina slavery, so too it characterized the pattern of slavery's growth and development there. The slaves shipped to northern mainland colonies came in small lots from the West Indies. Southern mainland colonies received some slaves directly from Africa. Initially, the proportion of slaves arriving in southern colonies directly from Africa was quite low. This was true of the Virginia and Maryland trade, which dated from the seventeenth century, and of Georgia's experience, which began more than a century later. But South Carolina "was a direct importer from Africa at an early date, and its eighteenth century development was the closest mainland approximation to the West Indian plantation pattern."[6]

Slaves, although an important element in Carolina from its founding, did not outnumber whites in the first generation of settlement. With the coming of profitable rice production in the two decades after 1695, however, there emerged in Carolina a situation unprecedented and never duplicated in England's North American colonies: blacks outnumbered whites. The black majority probably first appeared in 1708. It increased rapidly and by 1720 slaves "outnumbered the free whites by roughly two to one." By that date slaves were predominant also in "pace of immigration and"—departing from the Caribbean pattern—"rate of natural increase."[7] By 1720, Peter Wood has estimated, blacks constituted a majority in eight of

South Carolina's eleven parishes and equaled the number of whites in Charlestown (St. Philip's Parish).

In the two decades after 1720, the natural increase of the black population fell to almost zero. Yet the absolute number of blacks increased because of increased importation of slaves, especially during the 1730s when the rate of this forced immigration reached its peak. The huge demand for slaves in the 1730s swamped efforts to foster white settlement and to reduce the ratio of blacks to whites. Noting the frenzied buying of slaves, a contemporary critic of the situation captured it in a violent and prophetic image: "*Negroes* may be said to be the Bait proper for catching a *Carolina* Planter, as certain as Beef to catch a Shark."[8]

After the Stono Rebellion in 1739, South Carolina's ruling whites decided to reduce the black majority by levying prohibitive duties on imported slaves. Beginning in July 1741 and continuing for three years, duties of one-hundred, fifty, and twenty-five pounds currency were applied to "adults, Negroes of medium height and . . . children."[9] This period coincided with war between Great Britain and Spain (the War of Jenkins's Ear) and the overlapping, larger War of the Austrian Succession, which lasted until 1748. Duties and war combined to reduce the slave trade to South Carolina. Nevertheless, in 1749 Governor James Glen reported that the number of Negroes in his colony increased rather than declined during the preceding nine years.[10] During the 1740s the black-white ratio fell from two-to-one to three-to-two, but there it held steady for two decades.

In 1751 small but permanent duties were placed on slaves of various ages. For three years beginning in January 1766, a prohibitive surtax of one-hundred pounds current money was added to the regular duty on each imported slave. The strength of the 1766 tax was sapped, however, by the lag between enactment and effective date; merchants and planters scrambled to make their transactions in the interim.[11] When the surtax expired, planters quickly indulged in an orgy of buying: "5,438 Negroes in the first eleven months of 1769." After another "spasmodic restriction during 1770," the influx continued. In five months during 1773 more than a fifth as many slaves entered South Carolina as had been imported during the previous twenty years.[12] Three-fifths of the revenue generated by the permanent duty on slaves funded bounties for white settlement, but these incentives made no headway against the seemingly insatiable desire for slaves.

During the colonial period, South Carolina's commitment to slav-

ery had set her apart demographically. Of the original thirteen
states, only Virginia entered the American Revolution with more
slaves than South Carolina. None of the other states, including
Virginia, approached a black majority, much less the 60-percent-or-
greater proportion of slaves that had prevailed in South Carolina's
population for more than half a century. Of the two Carolinas, the
older colony, with more slaves, had experienced a much slower rate
of growth than her northern neighbor and ended the colonial period
with a smaller total population.[13]

For its duration the American Revolution closed the trans-
Atlantic slave trade to Britain's embattled former colonies. And
four years later, in 1787, South Carolina's legislature banned the
foreign slave trade for five years; periodic extensions stretched the
ban to a total of sixteen years.[14] In the same period white immigration down backcountry valleys from Pennsylvania and Virginia to
the South Carolina up-country, notable since the 1750s, reached its
peak. By 1790, as a result of this flood of white newcomers, South
Carolina's black majority became a minority, and so it remained
from 1800 to 1810. South Carolina's dominant planters, however,
had not renounced slavery or the increase of their slave population.
The low-country gentry, who controlled the South Carolina legislature, consistently supported the same principle: "the right to import
slaves when it suited them. It did not suit them in 1787."[15]

The reasons for South Carolina's sixteen-year prohibition of the
foreign slave trade were diverse and complicated. Issues of economic
class and attitudes toward debt and credit were involved, but the
main cleavage was sectional. With a three-to-one ratio of slaves to
whites in 1790, low-country whites had all the slaves they wanted,
and, with the foreign supply cut off, this investment in slaves appreciated. In 1790 the up-country had a slaves-to-whites ratio of one-to-
four, and planters there demanded more black labor. The well-known
expansion of the up-country's short-staple cotton industry following
the introduction of the Eli Whitney type of cotton gin and the lesser-
known burgeoning of long-staple cotton culture in the sea islands of
the low country generated ever increasing pressure on the legislature to rescind the ban on imported slaves.[16] In 1803 South Carolina
resumed the Atlantic slave trade for four years and closed it just
before the 1808 federal deadline for ending this traffic.

The vast majority of these slaves were bound for up-country
owners, and the white preponderance in the up-country revealed by
the First Federal Census had been halved by the Third. Although
the low country exported some slaves by sale and more by migration

with their masters to the up-country or to other states, the low country's black population increased by about 24,000 between 1790 and 1810, while its white population remained almost constant.[17] From 1800 to 1810 more whites left South Carolina's up-country than entered it. In the same decade forced black migration to the up-country continued and increased. Sometime during the second decade of the nineteenth century, a black majority reappeared in South Carolina, and with each passing decade its size increased.[18]

From the early colonial period through Reconstruction, for two centuries in fact, the South Carolina low country contained a black majority. Only the extraordinary expansion of the up-country between 1790 and 1810 had produced the state's brief white majority. As the plantation regime moved up the rivers, black majorities appeared in up-country districts.[19] Slavery—and interests based on

Table 1

*Negroes as a Percentage of South Carolina's
Negro and White Population, 1703–1860*

1700	1710	1720	1730	1740	1750	1760	1770	1780
44.12[a]	50.12[b]	64.45	66.67	66.19	60.94	60.95	60.51	53.89

1790	1800	1810	1820	1830	1840	1850	1860
49.08[c]	42.93[d]	48.41	52.77	55.63	56.41	58.93	58.59

Source: Computed from statistics in Wood, *Black Majority*, p. 152, U.S. Bureau of the Census, *Historical Statistics of the United States, Colonial Times to 1970* (Washington: Government Printing Office, 1975), Part 2, p. 1168, and the First through Eighth Federal Censuses (titles and publishers vary; they will be cited only by number).

a. 1703.

b. 1708.

c. An arithmetical error in the First Federal Census understated slaves in South Carolina by 13,864. A smaller error appeared in the sum of South Carolina's total population. These errors were not corrected in subsequent compendia, hence the above figure is greater than the 43.7 percent usually cited in census publications, e.g., United States Bureau of the Census, *Negro Population of the United States, 1790–1915* (Washington: Government Printing Office, 1918), p. 51.

d. Arithmetical errors in the Second Federal Census produced totals that would yield a percentage of 43.2.

slavery—in the two sections of South Carolina grew less and less distinguishable. By 1850 black majorities existed in all but four of the seventeen districts on or below the fall line. Above the fall line black majorities had appeared in six of the twelve districts. By the mid-nineteenth century South Carolina was a slave society throughout its extent; in distribution, as in aggregate statistics, the black majority pertained to the entire state.[20]

Although South Carolina's black majority increased during the antebellum period, by 1850 the state's black population was only half again as large as it was in 1820. Population growth during the antebellum period, among blacks at least, was achieved solely by natural increase.[21] An annual birth rate of 2.5 percent, however, would have doubled this population in less than thirty years. The average natural increase of the South's black population was in the range of 2.5 percent annually during this thirty-year span. And South Carolina's black population showed no evidence of departing from this pattern.[22]

The reason for slower growth in South Carolina's black population vis-à-vis those of states in the deep South lay, obviously, in forced black migration from South Carolina to those states. For the 1810–60 period one estimate placed net black emigration from South Carolina at nearly 179,000. The 1830–40 decade that saw the smallest percentage increase in the black population also witnessed the largest percentage of net emigration. But large as was the number of slaves born in South Carolina who left the state, the number of whites who emigrated was even larger.[23]

Within South Carolina, the low country remained a region apart: the black majority was greatest there, the largest slaveholdings and the wealthiest slaveowners were concentrated there. Excluding the city of Charleston, all of the low country's districts contained black majorities of two-thirds or more during the antebellum period. Among the tide-washed parishes, the proportion of blacks was even higher.[24] The great rice-growing district of Georgetown was "virtually a closed system . . . continuity of plantation ownership discouraged buying and selling of slaves." Slaves "present on the plantations in 1850 had been handed down generation after generation from father to son. After the decade of the 1780s very few slaves had been brought in from outside the district." In 1850 slightly over a quarter of all southern slaveowners held ten or more slaves; in Georgetown District nearly one-half of the slaveowners held ten or more slaves. Of southern masters, 0.5 percent owned more than a hundred slaves; 17 percent of the slaveholdings in Georgetown were over a hundred. The low country was preeminently the region of master and bondsman.[25]

During the antebellum period two states other than South Carolina contained black majorities: Louisiana and Mississippi. In Louisiana, however, the black percentage of the population declined slightly during the fifty years before the Civil War. With Louisiana's high percentage of free Negroes, moreover, a slave majority was reported during Louisiana's statehood by only three of six decennial censuses.[26] In South Carolina, by contrast, the percentage of blacks in the population increased steadily, and five of the last six antebellum censuses revealed a slave majority. In Mississippi slaves constituted a majority of the population for a single generation before the Civil War (a black majority first emerged there in the mid-1830s).[27] At mid-nineteenth century South Carolina's isolated possession of a black majority had barely vanished; the duration of her experience with a black majority remained unique. South Carolina politicians labored under the weight of this historical experience as they observed and participated in the national struggle over slavery's fate.

3

The free Negro population of South Carolina was as remarkably small as the slave population was large. The Negro Act of 1740 tried to make emancipation of slaves a legislative prerogative. While the legislature probably did not enforce its monopoly on manumission, South Carolina masters were generally loath to part with their slave property, and "Negroes of free status do not appear ever to have exceeded one percent of the black population when South Carolina was a royal colony."[28]

As the egalitarian thrust of American Revolutionary ideology gathered momentum, emancipation and antislavery activity in the Upper South, particularly in Virginia, increased. Masters in the Lower South, however, were immune to such infectious ideas. In South Carolina through the first decade of the nineteenth century, a few, a very few, courageous voices were raised against slavery. These native critics were shouting not so much into the wind as into a void. Slavery was so overwhelmingly secure that no one bothered to reply. By 1800 antislavery sentiment in the Upper South was waning. But during the quarter century following the American Revolution, "the free Negro population of the Upper South grew darker through indiscriminate manumission and the addition of many black fugitives, that of the Lower South remained light-skinned. A crack, which would widen during the antebellum years, appeared in the ranks of the growing free Negro caste."[29]

Another gap, one of numbers, had also appeared and would widen in each prewar decade. In 1790 Virginia's free Negroes, to take an Upper South example, constituted 4.2 percent of the state's Negro population; by 1860 they represented 10.6 percent of the Old Dominion's black population. In South Carolina during the same period the free proportion of the Negro population increased from 1.5[30] percent to 2.4 percent. Ironically Negro refugees from a slave revolution were responsible for the largest duodecennial increase in South Carolina's free Negro population. South Carolina in common with the Lower South had quickly barred nonwhite refugees from war-torn Santo Domingo. Yet substantial numbers of the island's free people of color evaded the ban and entered Charleston and Savannah, where they remained.[31] These West Indian fugitives, however, had only a tiny impact on South Carolina's population. During the antebellum period free Negroes constituted less than 2 percent of the state's total population.

The proportion of free blacks in the black population was always smaller in South Carolina than in the South at large. Through 1840 the South Carolina figure was smaller even than the figure for the Lower South. By 1860 Alabama, Arkansas, Florida, Georgia, Mississippi, and Texas had smaller percentages of free blacks in their black populations than did South Carolina. But among states where slavery became rooted during the colonial period, only Georgia had a smaller proportion of free blacks in the black population than South Carolina.

Table 2
Free Negroes as a Percentage of South Carolina's
Negro and White Population, 1790–1860

1790	1800	1810	1820	1830	1840	1850	1860
0.72	0.92	1.10	1.36	1.36	1.39	1.34	1.41

Source: Computed from returns of the First through Eighth Federal Censuses.

4

By almost any index South Carolina whites had a larger stake in slavery than their counterparts elsewhere in the South. In Carolina "slave ownership quickly became a means for Englishmen to establish status distinctions," and during the colony's early history "local officials were among the largest individual importers of slaves."[32] Questions of status aside, the direct economic interest of South Carolina whites in slavery became—and remained—immense. Taking the antebellum period as a whole, South Carolina had more slaveholders (in proportion to its total white population) than any other southern state. Too, the average number of slaves per owner was higher in South Carolina than in the rest of the South.[33] "The largest slaveholdings in 1850 were clearly in South Carolina, with Louisiana a rather distant second." By 1860 Louisiana had surpassed South Carolina in the number of planters with more than a hundred slaves. "However, holders of the very largest numbers of slaves still resided on the South Carolina rice coast."[34] Although the Palmetto State's largest slaveholders remained concentrated in the low country, the discrepancy between the average size of slaveholdings in the low country and in the up-country diminished steadily during the antebellum years. By the 1820s a statewide planter community had emerged—a fact of crucial importance in the state's subsequent political history.[35]

As the number of slaveholders in South Carolina's population made it distinctive in the Old South, so too did the extraordinary migration of whites born in South Carolina to other southern states. The net outflow of whites began shortly after 1800. In the first two decades of the nineteenth century, the heaviest emigration came from up-country districts with small slave populations: "substantial numbers of nonslaveholding whites were leaving South Carolina at an early date." The expansion of the plantation system into and later throughout the up-country produced "displacement and further emigration of small farmers—a characteristic effect of the plantation system wherever it has existed."[36]

The peak of white emigration came during the 1830s when virgin soil and boom times in the Southwest coincided with soil exhaustion and economic stagnation in South Carolina. In that decade the state experienced a net emigration of more than 65,000 whites. From 1820 to 1860 the total net emigration of whites was approximately 200,000, a figure that represented "nearly half of those born in the state after 1800." In the 1850s the mid-Atlantic states from Delaware to South Carolina all suffered a net loss of slaves and whites through migration, but South Carolina's loss was greatest. In that last antebellum decade the number of slaves emigrating from the Palmetto State finally surpassed the number of whites.[37] But the net loss of whites in the 1850s combined with the cumulative loss in earlier decades meant that the black majority remained the same.

By 1860 the lack of immigration to South Carolina had produced a white population that was 96.6 percent South Carolina born. Hence, the state and its governing class were little influenced by outsiders from other states or abroad. In 1850 and 1860, respectively, 91.8 and 93.0 percent of the Palmetto State's legislators had been born in South Carolina. These percentages were by far the highest in the Lower South.[38]

By 1860 for every white resident of South Carolina who had been born in another state, there were fourteen native South Carolinians living in other states, and the typical white emigrant from South Carolina cast his lot in the deep South. Of whites born in South Carolina and living in other states at mid-nineteenth century, 70 percent resided in Georgia, Alabama, or Mississippi. By 1860 these three states still accounted for 63 percent of all South Carolina out-migrants, but South Carolinians were responding to the tug of fresh land; the states that showed the largest gains in South Carolinians at the end of the 1850s were Texas and Arkansas.[39]

In 1854 an observer of this migration noted proudly that the alumni of South Carolina College included twelve governors, "seven of South Carolina and five of other states, while of twenty-one graduates who had become judges of law and equity, eleven were in South Carolina and ten elsewhere."[40] Contemporary accounts and subsequent interpretations of the political implications of the great migration from South Carolina have varied widely. Delineating with certainty the impact on other states, particularly identifying South Carolina's ethos as the source of opinions expressed by expatriate South Carolinians, would seem a murky business at best. One commentator suggested that uneasiness over nullification doctrines contributed to the remarkably high white emigration from South Carolina during the 1830s. A more commonly endorsed interpretation held that the "sowing down of the whole South from the Savannah to the Rio Grande with South Carolinians in the forty or fifty years before the . . . [Civil War] had its part in spreading South Carolina politics and ideals throughout the South."[41] If some South Carolina migrants helped push other states toward secession, a variation on this theme may be even more plausible: the migration increased the commitment to slavery among those South Carolinians left behind. Overrepresentation of nonslaveholders among the migrants increased the proportion of slaveowners in South Carolina's population and concentrated the state's interest in preserving slavery.

5

Living in the midst of black slaves held to hard labor, white South Carolinians had ample cause to be anxious about their safety. But during the early eighteenth century the internal menace seemed subordinate to external dangers. For more than sixty years South Carolina was the English colony most exposed to Spanish attack; Indians, forced progressively inland by the colony's expansion, constituted another foreign threat. Carolina's black slaves were pressed into service against both of these enemies.

Faced with the Yemassee Indian War, the South Carolina legislature provided for a "standing army of 1200, including 400 Negroes or other slaves." Whites were of two minds concerning the wisdom of an armed body of slaves, however, as "suggested by the request in February, 1716, that they be disbanded." In 1742, only three years after Stono's bloody example of slave revolt, the threat of Spanish invasion prompted South Carolina to mobilize 240 Negroes. But external enemies were neither sufficiently strong nor persistent enough to give South Carolina whites the "experience with armed blacks . . . [that] the Brazilians," for example, gained by necessity. "Yet the comparison with the situation in Brazil suggests that if the foreign threats had been grave, perhaps a quite different attitude toward blacks might have been encouraged in South Carolina."[42]

Between Brazil and South Carolina, however, there was a more important difference that explained a great deal about the rigor with which South Carolina debased blacks, individually and collectively, free and slave. Slaveholders in South Carolina and elsewhere "in the United States viewed the free Negro as a potential threat to the slave system, [but] their counterparts in Brazil envisioned the free Negro as a veritable prop to the system of slavery." In Brazil race and skin color did not become as completely identified with slave status (and its train of pejorative connotations) as they did in the United States. In Brazil free people with varying amounts of

African ancestry could, and on occasion did, ally themselves with whites.[43] In South Carolina the possibility of such tacit alliances never arose.

This difference was in part a function of numbers. During slavery the proportion of free Negroes in South Carolina's black population scarcely increased and never reached 3 percent. By contrast during the 1817–18 period, Brazilian free Negroes and mulattoes constituted about one-fourth of the colored population, and by 1872 they represented more than two-thirds of Brazil's colored population. Brazilians were willing "to manumit slaves much more freely than North Americans" because they did not fear "free blacks in great numbers, regardless of the fears they may have entertained about slave uprisings." But in South Carolina where by overwhelming odds a dark skin indicated slave status, whites found it extremely difficult, perhaps impossible, "to believe that free blacks could side with white *free* people over enslaved *black* people."[44]

As early as the 1720s South Carolina whites revealed that their anxiety was turning from external foes to the enemy within—the black majority. From 1721 until the end of slavery, control of the black population was one function of South Carolina's militia, and suppressing a slave revolt rapidly became a more probable task for the militia than repelling a foreign invasion. In the 1720s the colony passed laws that implied a natural and obvious relationship between the size of the militia and the number of "potential black enemies."[45]

In the 1730s, while their colony's slave majority was increasing rapidly, South Carolina whites followed newspaper accounts of slave rebellion in the Caribbean, most notably the Maroon War in Jamaica, which raged sporadically from 1734 to 1738. In 1737 Lieutenant Governor Thomas Broughton expected a Spanish attack but considered South Carolina's slaves "more dreadful to our Safety than any Spanish invaders."[46] The priority of Broughton's fears was prophetic. In 1739 came the bloody climax of a decade-long increase in black resistance to slavery—the Stono Rebellion.

The participants in the Stono Rebellion intended to march to Florida and kill any whites who blocked their path. In the process they raised the most successful slave revolt in South Carolina history. The ruling whites, shaken and sobered, took counsel among themselves on how to avoid similar uprisings. They had feared that slaves fresh from Africa might be the most dangerous to the slave system; the Stono Rebellion proved that was no idle suspicion. Thereafter white South Carolinians took care that the proportion of newly imported Africans in the slave population should never again rise to the level that had prevailed in the 1730s.

South Carolina's "first generation of slaveholders" had believed that their greatest security lay in the diversity of the slaves' native languages. But among newly imported Africans the will to resist transcended language barriers. Moreover there emerged in the sea islands of South Carolina a unique Afro-American dialect—Gullah —that reminded whites that, despite their efforts to destroy the slaves' African heritage, fragments from the African past still survived. And South Carolina officials would remind each other that they had "already felt the unhappy Effects of an Insurrection of our slaves . . . (an intestine Enemy the most dreadful of Enemies) which we have just Grounds to imagine will be repeated."[47]

Thus the governing gentry of South Carolina were continually aware that a black Cataline might be numbered among their slaves; should one appear they were determined to act swiftly and ruthlessly. Their retribution was and would be purposely horrible, but it was free from hysteria. After the Stono Rebellion contemporary observers "considered it notable that the planters 'did not torture one Negro, but only put them to an easy death.'" In South Carolina, "the only colony seriously threatened" by slave revolt, authorities used the execution of slave rebels as object lessons; this behavior contrasted with the indiscriminate retribution New York officials visited on blacks after slave conspiracies in 1712 and 1741. South Carolina's gentry "seemed under no compulsion to invent slave conspiracies; they were sufficiently acquainted with the real thing."[48]

The era of the American Revolution, like the period it succeeded, brought sufficient threats to South Carolina's system to promote a healthy fear among the planters of slave revolt. During the American Revolution, South Carolina rejected all suggestions to emancipate slaves who enlisted and served against the British. White South Carolinians preferred to rely on other methods to counteract British attempts to induce slave defection or rebellion. The planters of the new Palmetto State did not want to see either Negro veterans or an increase of free Negroes within their borders.

In 1791 on Santo Domingo the most successful slave rebellion in the Western hemisphere began in earnest. Witnessing it from afar Governor Charles Pinckney of South Carolina was moved to write Santo Domingo's colonial assembly, observing that since "a day may arrive when . . . [southern slaveholders] may be exposed to the same insurrection, we cannot but sensibly feel for your situation." White refugees from Santo Domingo recounted scenes of slaughter and pillage, which were added to the stock of horrors South Carolinians visualized in slave revolution. Santo Domingo had been "the most lucrative colony in modern world history," and the impoverished state of many refugee planters, who were pouring into Charleston, reminded South Carolina's gentry of the wealth they too might lose.[49]

In December 1803—a month before the successful black revolutionaries of Santo Domingo officially proclaimed their new nation Haiti—the South Carolina gentry exercised the dangerous right their representatives had won at the Constitutional Convention: the right to import slaves before 1808. South Carolina not only reopened the trade but imported more than 39,000 Africans in the next four years.[50] Thus, at the start of the nineteenth century as during the eighteenth, South Carolina held more African-born slaves (and held them in a smaller geographical area) than her co-venturers in republican government.

In the antebellum period South Carolina's legislative efforts to perfect the security of slavery were continuous. But the multiplication of laws did not end slave plots or remove completely the specter of black revolution. Plots were detected near Columbia in 1805, at Ashepoo in 1816, "and in June of that year another of more serious character near Camden," which ended in the execution of six blacks. Finally in 1822 Charleston was the scene of "the most carefully planned antebellum Negro conspiracy."[51]

Although ruthlessly and efficiently crushed, the Vesey Conspiracy remained during the nullification crisis "and long thereafter a searing reminder that all was not well with slavery in South Carolina." Troubled times in Charleston did not expire with Denmark Vesey. For six months during 1826 the city was plagued by arsonists almost nightly; three blacks were convicted. Other real or supposed plots were discovered around the state during the 1820s and early 1830s and other rebellious blacks were executed by local authorities.[52]

To some of the South Carolina gentry, however, a massive slave revolt seemed a horrible fantasy. More immediate (and believable to all) were acts of sabotage by disgruntled individuals or small groups. Passive resistance could flare into sudden violence. "I suppose you have already heard," wrote James Louis Petigru to Hugh Swinton Legaré, "of poor Bull's fate—massacred by his negroes at Willington." South Carolina masters believed firmly in the loyalty of their own slaves and considered incidents of slave violence toward owners rare, but such incidents caused spasms of doubt. The slaveholders "could never be quite certain that they had established unquestioned control."[53] As a group the South Carolina gentry learned this lesson and applied it well enough to avoid "poor Bull's fate."

Sporadic incidents of overt resistance to slavery in South Carolina continued as long as the institution lasted, but the peak of violent resistance came in the 1820s. After that decade "never again did the slaves conspire so shrewdly, so widely, so often." After 1830 the gentry increasingly devoted their time to perfecting public measures and private techniques for slave control, and "attempted insurrections and rumors of slave plots declined in the generation before secession." In reaction to the slave unrest of the 1820s and the rise of militant abolitionism in the 1830s, South Carolina "strengthen[ed] the bonds of slavery and the penalties for insubordination on the one hand, while elaborating the public lie of slave contentment on the other."[54]

South Carolina's safety required more than individual watchfulness. This at least was the message delivered during times of political crisis by the state's officials. South Carolina's leaders feared above all a two-front war in which an external opponent of their regime could also strike from within by inciting the slaves. During South Carolina's first confrontation with the federal government, James H. Hammond suggested an old expedient: the use of one potential enemy against another. He would "turn over his male slaves for military labor, though they should be armed only in the 'greatest extremities.'" After the nullification crisis had passed, Governor Robert Hayne boldly opined that a "State of military preparation must always be with us a state of perfect domestic security. A period of profound peace and consequent apathy may expose us to the danger of domestic insurrection."[55]

But as the antebellum period wore on, the South Carolina gentry did not cherish constant tension from outside sources as a preservative of domestic security. Rather they came to believe that only the malign action and influence of enemies beyond their borders could produce widespread insurrection within them. Northern antislavery recruits became more numerous and more insistent, and South Carolina's gentry became preoccupied with external threats to their slave system. They nerved themselves to isolate their economic and political system from abolitionist enemies within the Union and, as they increasingly feared, from a federal government dominated by abolitionists.

"I must compliment you and your associates on the great skill and ability with which you have conducted your warfare on the South," wrote James Hammond to Lewis Tappan in the summer of 1850. "It is obvious that you have brought the entire non-slaveholding portion of the Union into line and arrayed them against us.... [But] the slaves *themselves* ... seem to grow more and more docile and are more easily managed now than ever heretofore.... You will never free a negro, I give you the most solemn assurance, save those you may cause to run away from us, which is a very small business, and those you may bring to the gallows."[56] To the enemies of slavery, Hammond always presented a bold front, while among intimates he frequently lapsed into gloom when discussing the prospects for slavery's survival. But Hammond's letter to Tappan accurately reflected a change in the gentry's anxieties; South Carolina's planter-politicians had come to believe that the abolitionists were more formidable enemies of slavery than the slaves themselves. "Whereas in the 1820's slave insurrection was very real ... and abolitionism remained for most a distant drum, the order in this scale appeared to change in the later antebellum years. By 1850 fear of a general abolition of slavery was the paramount racial concern.... And apprehension of Negro rebellion remained inextricably caught up in this fear."[57]

Abolitionists, then, became foreign Jacobins who would seek out and inflame domestic ones. Abolition, the South Carolina gentry were convinced, meant race war as surely as massive slave rebellion did. Negroes released from slavery (by whatever means) would not work, could not govern themselves much less a complex political economy, and would inevitably relapse into predatory barbarism.[58] By sheer force of numbers blacks might then reduce all of South Carolina to the same condition. Freedom for blacks conjured in the minds of whites a world dominated by the poorest, most ignorant, most debased portion of society: the black majority. Abolition would have the same consequences as successful black revolt: "an appalling world turned upside down, a crazy nonsense world of black over white, an anti-community which was the direct negation of the community as white men knew it."[59]

The South Carolina gentry foresaw the end of slavery leading inevitably to the end of law, the end of property, the end of material and moral progress. They roused themselves to preserve slavery for their children because they perceived it as an essential, indivisable part of civilized life in the South. As Congress debated the Compromise of 1850, South Carolina politicians had already despaired of any compromise with antislavery forces. Robert Barnwell Rhett demanded speedy action—secession—as the only hope for the South. South Carolinians, he was certain, were prepared to venture this course, and during the summer and fall of 1850, Rhett and the South Carolina secessionists proclaimed their gospel. "If you secede now," Rhett told a Georgia audience, "consolidation must try its vaunted strength, whilst yet we are strong and able to vanquish it. . . . Twenty years hence, you may not dare to talk of resistance; and if you resist successfully blood alone can cleanse your polluted liberties. If you fail, your only recourse may be in flight leaving country and home to become an African wilderness."[60]

The South Carolina secessionists were not alone in deploring the specter of "an African wilderness." It was also a stock image in the speeches of South Carolina cooperationists, who feared that premature and isolated secession would not preserve their state's social hierarchy but destroy it. Even the state's few procompromise, pro-Union politicians believed their course offered the greatest safety for slavery. During the secession crisis of 1850–51, South Carolina's gentry quarreled bitterly over the best means of preserving their world, but by December 1860 they were in agreement. Among the benefits of secession—in the eyes of the gentry—was that it promised a solution to the changing but ever-present problem of rebellion by the black majority.

CHAPTER II

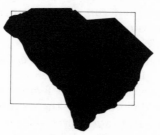

Of Government and Its
South Carolina Uses

1

"The Government of So. Ca. is that of an aristocracy," opined James Hammond in December 1850. The haughty master of Silver Bluff Plantation proceeded to sketch a government in which the "Legislature has all power. The Executive has none. The people have none beyond electing members of the legislature, a power very negligently exercised from time immemorial." But "should the people become thoroughly disgusted with the Legislature and its managers," they would support "the sweeping changes in the Constitution" which reformers advocated: "They will demand the Election of Governor, of Presidential Electors, and perhaps of Judges to be given to them. They will probably break down the Parish Representation and thus crush the Low Country with its rotten borroughs. . . . They will increase the power of the Governor and make him and the Public Officers responsible . . . [to the electorate]." Hammond and like-minded planters had opposed these changes "and arrested them thus far."[1]

Hammond did not live to see South Carolina's organic law subjected to "sweeping changes"; these came only after the state's attempt to preserve slave society lay finally in ruins. Until Reconstruction, South Carolina's gentry maintained both their power and its legal basis, the Constitution of 1790, substantially intact. During the last two antebellum decades, the dominant planter-politicians argued that democratic reforms would distract the voters and their representatives from a more fundamental political obligation—the preservation of slavery—on which all social order depended. Thus in South Carolina the defense of slavery became both the ultimate object of statecraft and the ultimate rationale for planter hegemony.

2

Under South Carolina's colonial and revolutionary regimes, the tidewater gentry had severely limited the participation of backcountry, or up-country, residents in government because, as one planter explained, they were "strangers to our interests, our customs, and our concerns." Central to those interests, customs, and concerns was slavery. But even as they were voiced, fears of the up-country's potential hostility to "certain fundamental institutions" were rendered obsolete by the inland march of slavery. By 1790 one-sixth of South Carolina's slave population was held in the up-country. Within the next fifteen years the spread of cotton culture and slavery, economic twins, reassured low-country planters that their peculiar institution would not be "confined and ultimately smothered."[2]

South Carolina's constituent convention of 1790 framed a constitution that distributed representation more equitably than did the constitutions of 1776 and 1778. But, as William Schaper observed about representation under South Carolina's first three constitutions, "no principle had ever been followed, unless it was that of giving the low country a good, safe majority."[3] Dissatisfied with apportionment under the Constitution of 1790, up-country leaders demanded and, in 1808, won a special legislative session to amend the constitution.[4] This session established a systematic basis for representation that endured as long as slavery.

The Compromise of 1808 created a senate with 45 seats and a house with 124. The low country's parishes remained election districts; and, since election districts in the up-country were larger and comparatively fewer, the low country retained control of the senate. In the house seats were apportioned according to the white population of the districts and the taxes paid by each. In effect one-half of the house represented the state's white population; the other half represented the state's taxable property.

In 1808 the up-country commanded a majority in the house, and

the low country enjoyed a narrow majority in the senate. If, however, the tidewater area and the adjoining districts that contained
black majorities were considered "the low country writ large," then
this black belt mustered majorities in both the senate and house.[5]
And with each passing decade, these majorities increased as the
black belt spread across and above the fall line.[6]

Two years after amending representation, the legislature altered
the constitution's franchise provision. Suffrage was extended to
virtually all adult, white males, with the exception of paupers and
United States soldiers beneath officer rank.[7] By contemporary stan-
dards this was a liberal suffrage provision, but its effects were confined within South Carolina's narrow range of popularly elected
state officials. The line drawn in the Constitution of 1790 between
those qualified to vote and those qualified to govern was not erased
until Reconstruction. By joint ballot the legislature chose presidential electors as well as the governor, lieutenant governor, secretary
of state, commissioners of the treasury, surveyor general, and virtually all other executive officers. By 1850 the lawmakers had granted
to local voters the right to elect their sheriffs, probate judges, court
clerks, tax collectors, and commissioners for the poor.[8] But the
choice of most other local officers remained with the legislature.

The legislature created and filled all judicial positions in the
state's separate equity and law jurisdictions; it kept South Carolina's judges few and overworked. Neither independent nor presti-
gious as a branch of government, the judiciary could not challenge
legislative decisions on issues of state or federal law.

James Hammond wrote from the bitter wisdom of experience
when he described the governorship as powerless. South Carolina's
governor could not veto legislation; he could make only interim
appointments to fill vacant executive posts. Although he was commander in chief of the militia, he could appoint few of its officers and
those few occupied auxiliary positions. On "extraordinary occasions"
the governor could convene a special session of the legislature to
deal with a perceived crisis. In "no other state of the region did the
governor have fewer powers than in South Carolina." Those who
aspired to or had held the office thought of it more in terms of prestige than of power, and "[n]owhere in the lower South did governors
occupy a higher social position than in South Carolina."[9] The governorship was an honor that the gentry bestowed on one of its own.

The Constitution of 1790 had not only retained property qualifications for the offices of governor, lieutenant governor, senator, and
representative, but it had also "revised [those qualifications] dras-

tically upward."[10] And by mid-nineteenth century the permanence of South Carolina's property qualifications had helped to make the state's legislators a wealthier lot than their counterparts in the deep South. But it was in terms of slave ownership that South Carolina's legislators were most distinctive: "the majority . . . [of them] belonged to the landed gentry." In 1850 the state's legislature ranked first in its ratio of slaveholding members (more than four out of every five). Most Palmetto legislators were not only slaveholders but also members of the planter class. In the deep South, during the last antebellum decade, the percentage of planters in most legislatures increased, but "in only one legislature—South Carolina['s]—was there a planter majority."[11] In South Carolina the legislature ruled the state, and the gentry ruled the legislature.

Before the secession convention of 1860, the South Carolina legislature had called two state conventions: the first had met (November 1832 and March 1833) to resolve the nullification crisis, the second had convened (April 1852) as a coda to the secession crisis of 1851. Constituent conventions in form, they were nevertheless malapportioned in precisely the same fashion as the legislature, their agenda were dictated by the legislative acts that called them, and their decisions were never submitted to popular ratification. Thus South Carolina's planter class shaped extraordinary as well as routine policymaking institutions. By mid-nineteenth century this government-by-the-gentry had combined uniquely with the state's commitment to slavery. In defense of South Carolina's particularistic society, the state's leaders prepared to march away from the Union on what they envisioned as an older and truer republican path.

3

When South Carolina's constitution was written, property tests for voting, higher property qualifications for holding office, exceedingly powerful legislatures, and other provisions based on Whig ideas were common. "Nor were such ideas easily abandoned. They lingered on . . . into the nineteenth century, helping to account for the many 'undemocratic' features of the state constitutions." In 1790, therefore, South Carolina's skewed process of constitution making and denial of popular ratifications were not unusual.[12] But, during the next seventy years, the lack of change in South Carolina's constitution and the success with which the gentry defended the old Whig ideas that were implicit in it were highly unusual.

After 1810 there were no alterations in the constitution's substantive provisions. By contrast the antebellum period witnessed a flurry of new constitutions in other southern states. In addition the other South Atlantic states experienced nearly continuous and largely successful agitation for constitutional amendments, as groups little-blessed with political power enlarged their constitutional rights and increased their participation in government.[13]

The South Carolina gentry viewed with disdain constitutional changes in other states and suspected that a South Carolina constituent convention, regardless of its original purpose, might arrogate the power to reform state government.[14] Consequently both of South Carolina's antebellum state conventions were carefully restricted to specific topics: federal relations and nullification during 1832–33, federal relations and secession during 1851–52.

Robert Barnwell, a leader of the cooperationist faction, proposed that the state convention meeting in April 1852 should amend South Carolina's constitution to permit secession by a two-thirds vote of two consecutive legislatures. But Langdon Cheves, the cooperationists' senior statesman, feared that the convention ("an infernal machine") might break its traces and plunge state government into fearful changes. As chairman of the steering committee of twenty-one that controlled the convention, he moved to suppress any proposals touching the powers of state government and guided the convention to adjournment in four days. Afterwards Barnwell ruefully observed that "it was a strange contradiction to say that the Convention could throw off the United States and the Federal Constitution adopted by South Carolina, and yet not be able to alter or change the State Constitution!" Contradictory it may have been, but it was not strange for South Carolina's gentry to shun any precedent for change in the state's organic law.[15]

From 1836 until the Civil War, Greenville's Benjamin Franklin Perry waged a valiant, if sporadic and futile, campaign to reapportion representation in the legislature. Perry's introduction of a bill to give "the election of electors of President and Vice-President to the People" became a perennial legislative event in the 1840s and early 1850s. In 1844 and 1846 Perry forced the issue to a vote in the senate but lost. In 1847 Perry's allies in the house narrowly succeeded in passing the bill, but it failed again in the senate. In 1848 Perry's temporary coalition brushed victory as their bill was stopped only by a senate vote of twenty-three to twenty-one. Low-country legislators, despite an increased trickle of defectors, had staved off the change. After 1848 support for this reform declined steadily. In 1851, preoccupied by what they conceived to be the far more crucial issue of secession, the Committee of the Whole House reported their "opinion that it is inexpedient, at this time, to agitate the State by any attempt to change the present mode of electing Electors of President and Vice-President." The house agreed to the report by a vote of sixty-six to forty-eight. Perry continued his efforts from year to year, but he was supporting a lost cause.[16]

The movement for popular election of presidential electors had stirred the gentry's fears of widespread changes in South Carolina's government. The popular election of other officials might follow in unchecked and fatal succession. Surveying "the changes in our own time in So Ca even," James Hammond feared that his state might duplicate the terrible experiments taking place in the North; New York, for example, had given "the election of Judges to the miscreant rabble whose necks they perhaps ought to stretch—*but never can now.*" Allowing popular "election of the judiciary," observed another gentry commentator, would be the "last step to anarchy." And the first step was popular election of presidential electors. In "other States . . . it [had] been the entering wedge that . . . [had] riven asunder the government to its very pediment." The "incessant struggle on the part of the Northern people to usurp all the powers" had produced dire results: "labor and capital [were] beginning to be confronted." The gentry were determined to prevent "this antagonism of classes, this war of the poor upon the rich, and of the rich upon the poor" from reaching the Palmetto State. By preserving the electoral system unchanged, the gentry hoped to "keep away from the soil of South Carolina . . . [the] rank and noisome growth of the vices of popular government."[17]

4

In defending property qualifications for officeholding, granting representation to property, and restricting the range of popularly elected officers, South Carolina's planter-politicians may have "had a better right than their opponents to claim to be the legitimate heirs of the Whig constitution makers of the revolutionary era."[18] Certainly the gentry thought of themselves as true heirs of the Revolution. According to them only the precise republican balance of South Carolina's government made its democratic parts workable. Democracy was an addictive drug, demanded by ever larger majorities in ever larger doses until orderly government was inevitably destroyed. And the gentry quickly learned that the institution of slavery was, in the words of Nathaniel Beverley Tucker, "a perfect antidote" for democracy in poisonous doses.[19]

Given the close relationship between property and liberty in Whig ideology, South Carolina's gentry also saw themselves as waging the good fight against an abolitionist threat to the foundation of all liberty—the right to the free enjoyment and disposition of one's property. Too much democracy distracted and divided the citizenry and made an effective defense of slavery difficult, if not impossible. "Seeking to defend an institution under attack, . . . [the gentry] continued to conceive of politics as the defense of liberty. Attempting to maintain their position of leadership in a political system which grew increasingly anachronistic as the rest of the nation became more democratic they invoked the Colonial ideal of the independent man of property who unselfishly devoted himself to the public weal."[20] And the South Carolina gentry believed, as Robert Barnwell put it, "that unless slavery is upheld as a political institution essential to the preservation of our civilization and therefore to be maintained in the same high strain as liberty itself we must become a degraded people."[21] Thus South Carolina's lawmakers saw themselves as uniquely qualified to preserve both liberty and its vital prerogative in the South—slavery. They did not intend to abdicate their responsibilities.

In governmental policy on most social issues, the gentry insured that the Palmetto State did not move with unseemly haste. Francis Lieber, the German-born political economist who taught at South Carolina College for twenty years, acidly observed that "[e]very son of a fool here is a great Statesman mediating on the relations of State sovereignty to the United States government; but as to roads, common schools . . . as to cheerily joining in the general chorus of progress, what is that for Don Ranudo de Colobrados of South Carolina. . . ? Does he not belong to the chivāl'ry?"[22] B. F. Perry was less caustic; nevertheless in 1849 he lamented that the legislature "opposed . . . all improvements in law, politics, morals and physics . . . [because South Carolina's] quarrel with the general government for the last twenty years has absorbed all our thoughts and energies." Two years later, noting the South's general acceptance of the Compromise of 1850, Perry warned that South Carolina's defense of slavery had become an *idée fixe* which distorted all political perception. "Ought it [the South's acceptance of the Compromise] not to satisfy us that we are under some delusion in regard to this matter? We have been deceived by the disunionists in South Carolina . . . We have been kept so constantly and so long in a state of alarm that . . . to guard against these . . . dangers which have been conjured up in South Carolina, but can be seen nowhere else, it is proposed as a remedy that the state shall secede."[23]

A South Carolina secessionist, sketching the consequences of popular elections in the South after the Compromise of 1850, decried the process by which other southern voters, "accustomed to party strifes, are ready to be arrayed against each other." Nothing promoted this disunity "half as well as a Gubernatorial or Presidential election." Popular elections had converted Georgia and Mississippi, "the warmest resistance States a few months since . . . into the most submissive." The Palmetto State had maintained its militant objections to "a 'Compromise' act despoiling and degrading the whole South," solely because South Carolina's "political habits and structure" differed from those of her neighbors.[24]

Privately the gentry spoke more plainly about the relationship between their domination of government and the preservation of slavery. "I do not apprehend that our [political] institutions in So Ca will ever degenerate into tyranny," wrote James Hammond. But he did "fear that their overthrow will introduce anarchy. . . . As to Slavery its fate is not yet unveiled. My only hope for it is in keeping the actual slaveholders not only predominant but *paramount* within its circle. It is weakened by every accession of administrative and creative power to the masses, even here."[25]

While they used the machinery of government to defend slavery, South Carolina's planter-politicians did not view slavery as an institution separate and apart from government. Slavery was part of well-ordered republicanism. "My visit here [to Europe] has made me neither a monarchist nor aristocrat," wrote Hammond to Congressman Francis W. Pickens. "I go for a Republican government based on the institution of slavery." Pickens too was an ardent exponent of the South Carolina style of republicanism. By 1850 the proposition that "republican government can not exist without slavery" had become a political commonplace, a suitable topic for students at South Carolina College to use in practicing rhetoric and composition. According to the prevailing ideology of their elders, South Carolina defended proper republicanism as much as it defended slavery.[26]

State representative David Flavel Jamison, who vehemently opposed popular election of South Carolina's governor or presidential electors, was nevertheless "in favor of a popular form of government, because I have been born and reared under one." But as a political theorist he was "not so impressed with its advantages as to force it upon all men." James Hammond agreed. He knew "full well that all the blessings of our government and of all modern governments arise from the degree of power which the people have at length assured to themselves," but he was also persuaded "that the next cycle of barbarism will be consummated by their overturning all existing establishment." He theorized, "A Republican Government develops more fully than any other the energy of its people and calls into exercise the character and talents of the underclasses beyond any other political organization." But a "Democratic republic . . . in which universal suffrage is adopted and offices are open to all" tended to become worse than "despotism, because it is itself a despotism . . . of the monster multitude . . . of the low-bred [and] ignorant instead of the high-bred and enlightened, of passion instead of policy." As much as Jamison and Hammond desired secession in theory, Alfred Huger and his low-country Unionist friends William J. Grayson and William Elliott dreaded it, but they could at least agree with most secessionist-minded members of the gentry on the issue of excessive democracy. A properly organized government made a "distinction between an immoral and unlawful 'freedom' and a well restrained and Constitutional 'liberty.' "[27]

The gentry also espoused the eighteenth-century doctrine that, in a republic, certain decisions could be competently made by the people at large and other decisions could be competently made only by their representatives. Hammond believed strongly in this proposition and used it as his chief argument against the popular election of presidential electors: "The people should not hold any power, especially should [not] hold any elections which could be as well executed and managed by responsible agents, already chosen." Legislators included, "in theory at least, and for the most part in practice . . . a concentration of the popular intelligence." Legislators were "elevated . . . upon a more commanding position and . . . [could] better . . . observe and determine" a state's most urgent concerns and formulate policy accordingly.[28] Some Anglophiles among the gentry, notably Hammond and Huger, privately expressed a whimsical attraction to government by an aristocracy such as England's—an aristocracy which, "in conjunction with . . . the whole better part of the people, wield[ed] the political, social, moral and intellectual power of the nation."[29]

In southern states other than South Carolina, the increase in popular elections became a powerful argument for better public education: political welfare demanded a literate electorate. In South Carolina, however, this argument was occasionally used in reverse: momentous political decisions should not be vested in an electorate containing a large number of illiterates.[30] Citing Charleston elections in particular, planter John Berkley Grimball argued that the "principle of Universal suffrage as it prevails in So. Ca. was never more clearly proved to be wrong." Northern states were "corrupt by a thousand causes," wrote Alfred Huger, while government was corrupt in South Carolina and the South chiefly, if not exclusively, because "the Elective Franchise . . . [had been] equalized in that monstrous perversion, we call a 'general suffrage.'"[31]

On the whole the state's planter-politicians questioned the judgment of South Carolina voters rather than their honesty. Charges of vote-buying were confined almost exclusively to Charleston. The South Carolina gentry prided themselves that, under their management, political conduct remained pure and disinterested. Believing that their politics were pure, they professed disdain for soliciting votes and "treating" the voters. "I scorn to degrade myself by electioneering for the office, yet I will take all proper occasions to speak out" was a standard protestation among South Carolina candidates for office.[32]

Even while South Carolina politicians were preoccupied with the Compromise of 1850, a number of Barnwell District gentry directed their attention away from federal relations long enough to organize against the "treating of voters" and other forms of electioneering "destructive to the purity of elections." Speeches "on stated occasions" were proper, but "any cornering of voters, or private special pleading with him [sic], is improper and derogatory to the public good." By September 1850 Charleston too had an association opposed to treating or other "corruption[s] of the elective franchise." In December of that year South Carolina's legislators enacted a bill making it illegal to "bet or wager . . . upon any election in this state." During February each year the gentry gambled considerable sums on the Jockey Club races in Charleston, but they did not consider elections to be sporting propositions.[33]

In this secession movement of the early 1850s, the proper role of voters was to endorse policies conceived by their betters, "for the multitude know nothing about the matter. As little did they understand the questions of the stamp-act and tea tax; but they followed the lead of those who did." For the fall of 1851 the South Carolina legislature had scheduled an election for delegates to a proposed Southern Congress. The election became, in effect, a referendum on secession. As viewed by the gentry it was truly an issue "essential to Liberty." Robert Barnwell expressed confidence to Congressman James L. Orr that "the people" would adequately discharge their responsibility. But as Barnwell, his fellow cooperationists, and their secessionist opponents constantly made clear, Carolina's statesmen would determine the issues, debate them, and offer their decisions. The sole responsibility of the people was to choose between rival leadership groups. In their attitude toward the function of voters in determining state policy, South Carolina's leaders had changed little, if at all, since the nullification crisis. As James Hamilton, Jr., had remarked then, "The people expect that their leaders in whose . . . public spirit they have confidence will think for them—and . . . they will be prepared to *act* as their leaders think."[34]

In his vigorous defense of the Old South's political democracy, Fletcher M. Green conceded that the Palmetto State withstood the rising democratic tide. Yet, he concluded that by 1860 the South's planters "constituted a social not a political aristocracy." They enjoyed wide influence, "but they did not possess that influence because of special political privileges."[35] The gentry's political privileges in South Carolina and elsewhere in the South, however, rested on more than the bare legal framework of constitutional rights and responsibilities. Social and political influence were embedded in the same matrix, as recent interpreters of the role of deference in American politics have shown. "Fundamentally, deference meant the acceptance of the view by the whole of society that, whether by choice or simply by habit, people would naturally delegate power to a select minority." Richard Buel and, especially, J. R. Pole have argued that eighteenth-century "deferential attitudes continued to modify democratic tendencies . . . into the early part of the nineteenth century." And South Carolina in particular "maintained for an unusual length of time the deference of less fortunate whites toward the more privileged planter class."[36]

Although unsuccessful, nettlesome challenges to the gentry's political habits of thought were frequently directed to the legislature in the form of petitions and grand jury recommendations. Gentry politicians considered certain citizens of Lexington District to be particularly obstreperous. There the grand jury in 1849 made so bold as to suggest "that all elections from Constable up to President should be decided by the people." Two years later "sundry citizens of Anderson District" also petitioned the legislature to amend the constitution "so as to give the election of all civil officers of the State to the people." Mindful that "sweeping changes" might lie in store if voters became thoroughly disenchanted with their representatives, South Carolina politicians consistently paid verbal homage to the ultimate sovereignty of the people; but only occasionally and with specific limitations did they subscribe to "the Democratic doctrine of 'instruction.'"[37]

In practice gentry politicians molded popular instruction and then graciously accepted back their own views. When William Elliott's constituents, for example, did not share his opposition to nullification, he resigned and published a pamphlet hot with irritation "that *hoi polloi* . . . [had] shown the poor grace and judgment not to follow the local squire whose family leadership had not heretofore been questioned." With most offices in the gift of the legislature, ambitious planter-politicians had to court the favor of their social and economic peers, not the general electorate. While seeking the governorship, James Hammond wrote his wife, "I am called the Aristocratic Candidate & c & c. . . . I am happy that no more serious charges have been made." Hammond lost the prize not because he was the "Aristocratic Candidate" but because Calhoun and the dominant legislative faction opposed his candidacy; two years later, from the hands of these same men, Hammond received the office.[38]

South Carolina's antebellum legislative and congressional campaigns "rested on a democratic electoral base, but the state's political system remained, as it always had, in the hands of an oligarchy." The state's planter-politicians certainly believed that their leadership merited deference. The extension of popular elections had produced in the North "a very low order of *demogogues.* . . . The statesmen of the golden age of the Republic were trained in a different school," which the gentry believed remained in session only in South Carolina. With government so centralized in the legislature, gentry politicians spent long hours administering all manner of local affairs, and they took pride in their "guardianship of the social order."[39] According to their ideology, statesmanship demanded that they give most of their remaining time to the most urgent public issue: the defense of slave-based republican government. Their ideology was neatly tailored to maintaining both their interest in slavery and political control of the state. Interest preceded ideology. Still, the South Carolina gentry held their political faith with sincerity and conviction. They were true believers.

CHAPTER III

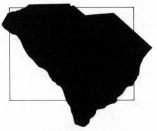

Legacies of Nullification

1

The South Carolina gentry's commitment to slavery, which had surrounded whites with a black majority, bred in turn "South Carolina's morbid sensitivity to the beginnings of the antislavery campaign." As early as the 1820s, members of the Carolina gentry began to detect "signs of a worldwide antislavery attack." Girding themselves to meet this attack, South Carolinians began to argue for slavery as a positive good and to develop proslavery propaganda.[1]

The depressed prices and high tariffs that together afflicted South Carolina's short-staple cotton industry in the late 1820s coincided with the gentry's anxiety about present and, especially, future attacks on slavery. South Carolina nullifiers began to see more than a chronological coincidence between the enactment of protective tariffs and the birth of abolitionism. They came to see high tariffs as "not only an inherently onerous economic burden but also an integral part of a pattern of sectional exploitation which would lead to slave revolts, colonization schemes, and ultimately the abolition of slavery." By 1833 when the tariff crisis was resolved, the nullifiers had developed a critique of the federal government (and of hostile forces operating through it) which would make secession seem more attractive with each passing decade. At the reassembled Nullification Convention, in his bold, alarmist style, R. B. Rhett presented that critique: "A people, owning slaves, are mad, or worse than mad, who do not hold their destinies in their own hands. . . . Every stride of this Government, over your rights, brings it nearer and nearer to your peculiar policy [slavery]. . . . It is not the Tariff—not Internal Improvement—nor yet the Force Bill, which constitutes the great evil which we are contending. . . . These are but the forms in which the despotic nature of the Government is evinced—but it is the despotism which constitutes the evil: and until this Government is made a limited Government . . . there is no liberty—no security for the South."[2]

The nullification movement gave to South Carolina an enduring political creed—among other legacies. The nullification movement left nullifiers with a determination to render the state's Unionist minority politically impotent. The movement bestowed on South Carolina a reputation for political extremism that isolated the state in 1832–33 and hindered its efforts thereafter to unite the South in defense of slavery. And the nullification movement endowed participants with a fierce pride in their state and strengthened the nullifiers' subsequent belief in South Carolina's proslavery mission.

2

For South Carolina Unionists, the immediate legacy of the nullification crisis was a bitter, two-year struggle with the nullifiers. During 1833–34 an intrastate civil war seemed possible. Nullifiers demanded and Unionists resisted a series of test oaths, requiring all state officials to give their primary allegiance to South Carolina.[3] The crisis within the state was resolved as the crisis with the federal government had been—by compromise. James L. Petigru and James Hamilton, friendly enemies and former law partners, agreed to support a committee report defining the allegiance clause of the proposed amendment to the state's constitution. In a triumph of ambivalence, their wording declared that "the allegiance required by the oath . . . is the allegiance which every citizen owes to the State consistently with the Constitution of the United States." Under this formula Unionists and nullifiers could take the same oath and yet cling to their vastly different conceptions of South Carolina's relationship to the Union. Unionist leaders, except for Perry, readily accepted the compromise, but Hamilton was hard put to win over the nullifiers. In the end the settlement required all his prestige as a low-country aristocrat and former governor as well as his formidable skills as a political tactician.[4]

While the Unionists were fighting against test oaths, they were steadily losing political offices and political power. The congressional elections of 1833 (deferred from the previous fall) produced only one Unionist among the state's nine congressmen. Until Reconstruction that representative (James Blair of Lancaster) was the only outspoken Unionist sent from South Carolina to the United States House. In 1834 the Unionists' best hope for a congressional champion—B. F. Perry from the district including Greenville, Pickens, and Anderson—was defeated by nullifier Warren Davis; Congressman Davis died the following year, and in the contest for his vacant seat, Perry lost to nullifier Waddy Thompson.[5] South Carolina's senators were, of course, chosen by the nullifier-dominated legislature.

"However desirable it may be that harmony and good fellowship should be restored," wrote planter John B. Grimball, as he surveyed the political campaigns of 1833, "it is much too soon for union men to come forward as candidates for office. . . . The wounds of party are too recent, the sayings and doings of the Submission men are too fresh in our memories. Let them remain for a while in obscurity, and time may cast his mantle over their sins." In 1834 nullifiers still subscribed to this opinion, and they strengthened their already tight grip on the legislature. Dominance in Columbia meant dominance in local offices across the state. "The foremost champion of states rights had made scarcely any provision for county rights. . . . There were no autonomous local offices in South Carolina where Union men could entrench themselves and live out the storm of the nullification controversy. The party that gained control over state government was able to deprive its opponents of nearly every office and instrument of power." Personally many nullifiers maintained warm social relations with Unionists; politically the nullifiers were determined to keep even Unionist friends in exile.[6]

Leading those nullifiers who neither forgave nor forgot the sins of the Unionists was George McDuffie. Following the compromise on the test-oath amendment in December 1834, McDuffie had been elected governor. Unionist legislators had, as a peace gesture, cast their ballots with the nullificationist majority; they soon had cause to regret their votes. James L. Petigru, believing that Unionists and nullifiers had concluded a "treaty of peace," was appalled by McDuffie's inaugural address, a speech with "nothing like peace in [it]."[7]

In the spring of 1835 McDuffie dedicated his administration to increasing South Carolina's military preparedness. At militia reviews and encampments, Governor McDuffie exhorted the troops to preserve Carolina's liberties against external foes or internal traitors. McDuffie's activities led Petigru to "fear for the Soundness of our Governor's intellect." In May 1835 Petigru noted that the governor, since his inauguration, had "been . . . worrying the unfortunate militia with strategy, and the mimickry of military discipline." Petigru dismissed much of the governor's campaign as comic. B. F. Perry saw more danger in the governor's activities than did the satirical Petigru. At the Pickensville encampment the Greenville Unionist "saw Governor McDuffie acting as drill sergeant to a squad, [and] . . . was more than ever convinced that the leading Nullifiers were plotting dissolution of the Union and establishment of a Southern confederacy."[8]

By mid-1835, while radicals like McDuffie nursed their past grievances against Unionists, more reflective nullifiers pondered the lessons that the nullification movement held for the future defense of slavery. And the nullifier who pondered most deeply was John C. Calhoun. Senior among the state's active politicians by 1835, Calhoun had secured undisputed leadership of the South Carolinians who had advocated nullification. He had by that date no one to rival him as a theoretician or a party manager. Robert J. Turnbull was dead, Thomas Cooper was enmeshed in a vain struggle to retain the presidency of South Carolina College, and James Hamilton and Robert Hayne were largely retired from Carolina politics. George McDuffie had been reared by Calhoun's family and loyally acknowledged himself a Calhoun protégé. Among younger leaders, Francis W. Pickens and Armistead Burt were related to Calhoun by blood or marriage; Robert Barnwell Rhett and James Hammond, in 1835, equalled Calhoun in ambition but lacked his statewide prestige and his national recognition. Profoundly impressed by South Carolina's isolation during 1832–33, Calhoun and his lieutenants knew that the forging of a united South would require much preparation. As a necessary first step, Calhoun directed the nullifiers toward a reconciliation with the minority in their own state.

A bridge between Unionists and nullifiers had always existed in their common commitment to a slave society. Although he deplored the nullifiers' extreme critique of the threats to South Carolina's slave economy, Congressman William Drayton, a leading lowcountry Unionist had "expressed quite clearly the sense of slavery as an absolute" in the Palmetto State. Slavery, he conceded, had become as inherent to South Carolina as "the miasma of our swamps and the rays of our burning sun."[9] And as early as 1830 B. F. Perry declared that, if Congress authorized a subsidy for the American

Colonization Society, "we may well begin to 'calculate the value of this Union'.... As dearly as we love this Union ... we love still more dearly our rights, our liberties, and our preservation."[10]

After mid-summer 1835 the circulation of abolitionist literature by mail produced heavy traffic on the bridge between Unionists and nullifiers. "The abolitionists' assault was more effective in unifying South Carolina than a thousand test oaths would have been." In early September, Beaufort District Unionists Benjamin Allston and William Elliott were active in a public meeting called to protest congressional reception of abolitionist petitions and "to discuss plans for protection against anti-slavery agitation." In the up-country Perry witnessed with misgivings the efforts toward nullifier-Unionist rapprochement. Perry's distrust of the nullifiers still overbalanced his contempt for the abolitionists. He feared that nullifiers were making political capital from the new abolitionist tactics. The safety of slavery, Perry observed, was "the only thing that will unite the whole South in opposition to the North."[11]

In 1836 the increasing number of petitions asking Congress to end slavery and the slave trade in the District of Columbia produced an opportunity to further Unionist-nullifier reconciliation. South Carolina's congressional delegation, following the lead of Calhoun and Hammond, argued that Congress had no jurisdiction over slavery in the District, that the petitions were therefore unconstitutional, and that Congress must refuse to receive such petitions. This argument called into question not only the issue of federal authority but also the right of petition. Henry L. Pinckney, knowing that his colleagues' stand had no chance of congressional endorsement, decided to take another position on abolitionist petitions.[12]

Pinckney, with the blessing of the Van Buren administration, offered in the House the resolutions that became known collectively as the gag rule. The Pinckney resolutions denied that Congress had any authority over slavery in the states and asserted that Congress "ought not to interfere in any way with slavery in the District of Columbia." Pinckney's plan called for a select committee (chaired by him) to receive the petitions and report on them with his resolutions. After this report the House would automatically table abolitionist petitions. On the crucial Pinckney resolution—which branded congressional interference with slavery in the District as inexpedient but implied that it was constitutional—southern congressmen divided almost equally; the Pinckney resolutions passed. Carolina radicals were incensed.[13]

A few of South Carolina's Unionists agreed with Pinckney's rationale: his resolutions were the best that could be obtained from Congress. Far more agreed with the rest of South Carolina's representatives: the South should never concede, even indirectly, that Congress had authority over slavery in the District. They saw it as a fatal precedent that would inevitably be extended. The nullifiers turned on Pinckney with a vengeance and decreed that he must no longer represent the Charleston district in Congress. After consulting with Joel R. Poinsett and other Charleston Unionists, Calhoun arranged to have nullifiers support Hugh S. Legaré as Pinckney's replacement. Congressman Legaré proved orthodox on issues relating to slavery and abolition.[14]

During 1839–40 the direction of abolitionism took a new turn. Abolitionists sought power through a political organization, the Liberty party. Calhoun had fearfully prophesied such a development, and he moved to combat it by furthering the political unity of South Carolina and consolidating his control over the state's politics. He largely achieved these goals by supporting an erstwhile Unionist for governor. This ploy probably also involved Calhoun's presidential ambitions, and it certainly involved Rhett's desire to increase the power of his political faction and advance his senatorial ambitions.[15]

With Calhoun's approval the scheme was managed by the Rhett-Elmore clique, headed by R. B. Rhett, who was in Congress at the time, and former Congressman Franklin H. Elmore, the president of South Carolina's bank.[16] Early in 1840 Rhett informed John P. Richardson that the nullifiers desired a complete reconciliation with the Unionists, that the Rhett-Elmore faction would support Richardson for governor, and that Richardson's candidacy would have Calhoun's blessing. The *Mercury* promptly hailed Richardson as the next governor of South Carolina.[17]

Rhett's expectation that he would shortly ascend to the Senate was frustrated by a coalition whose members disliked the Rhetts and the methods of the Rhett-Elmore clique. However the merger of Unionists and nullifiers in defense of slavery proceeded apace with the increase of abolitionist sentiment among northern politicians. In 1842 Calhoun gave notice of his retirement from the Senate and approved of Daniel Elliott Huger (who had vigorously denounced Calhoun during the nullification controversy) as his successor. Three years later Huger willingly resigned so that Calhoun could resume his accustomed seat.

Despite Governor Richardson's inaugural shibboleth ("We are all nullifiers, we are all Union men"), men of his stripe, who were elected to office under Calhoun's auspices, soon sounded more like nullifiers than Unionists. Within a decade of his gubernatorial term, Richardson matched Rhett in demanding immediate secession. In the late 1840s Richardson and Huger supported Calhoun's movement for a southern party and the establishment of a newspaper in Washington to represent a proslavery, prosouthern viewpoint.[18]

In 1846 David Johnson, Richardson's erstwhile colleague in Unionist and judicial circles, was elected governor. Twelve years before, sitting on South Carolina's Court of Appeals, Johnson had authored one of the opinions that overturned the nullifiers' test oath.[19] The nullifiers had once vilified Johnson for his views; by the mid-1840s, however, Johnson's views had changed substantially. The political distance he had traveled since the nullification movement was measured by his last message as governor. He predicted that, if slavery were excluded from the territory acquired from Mexico, other southern states "would readily unite with us in any measure promising relief. With our united, moral, and physical strength, in a just and honorable cause, we can successfully oppose any power that can be brought to bear upon us."[20]

Some Unionists in the up-country and in Charleston adhered to their early faith. But they did not constitute an effective or unified party. Perry and his Greenville lieutenants were Democrats, while Whigs predominated in the Charleston circle of Petrigru-Legaré-Grayson. These disparate groups agreed on the value of the Union but disagreed on other issues. In the legislature a number of Unionists and former Unionists (particularly in Charleston's very large delegation) continued to represent their localities. Unionist legislators often enjoyed high reputations for personal charm and parliamentary skill, but the legislative majority did not trust state or national office to men whose political values were not congruent with those of the nullifiers.

Unionists won no recruits among South Carolina's younger leaders; Unionist ranks, therefore, were steadily thinned by death. Those ranks were also thinned, if not by outright desertion, by increasing doubts about the Union as an absolute good. Loyalty to the federal government became more and more conditional. During 1832–33 the Unionists had styled themselves the "State Rights and Union" party. They had believed it absurd for a state to remain in the Union and yet disobey its laws, but a number of them had never denied a state's abstract right to withdraw from the Union.[21] Thus many Unionists embraced Calhoun's terminal-compact interpretation of the constitution; most did embrace Calhoun's defense of slaveholders' rights under the constitution. In the context of a militant abolition movement and the growing political appeal in the North of antislavery views, South Carolina's Unionists emphasized state rights more and federal authority less.

During 1832–33 Unionists and nullifiers had not differed on the need to preserve slavery in Carolina. By 1850 Unionists and nullifiers had also reached agreement on the benign nature of southern slavery and on the multiple reasons why slavery should be preserved. This accord was well-illustrated in the careers of William John Grayson and William Gilmore Simms, the most literary of South Carolina's many contributors to proslavery polemics.

Grayson was one of the very few South Carolinians to travel from the camp of the nullifiers to that of the Unionists. In 1832 Grayson was elected to Congress as a nullifier. Drawn in part by his continuing loyalty to the Whig party and his Unionist-Whig friends, Grayson broke with Calhoun and the nullifiers. By the late 1840s Grayson was a confirmed Unionist. But as his political faith in the Union increased so did his already strong commitment to slavery; his literary interests also burgeoned. "Of the fifteen essays that he is known to have written on Unionism, slavery, finance, and other miscellaneous subjects, excluding his reviews of numerous books, six are wholly concerned with . . . [the] defense of slavery." Grayson was intimately familiar with the proslavery works of William Harper and James Hammond. Despite their political differences, Grayson and Hammond corresponded on the merits of the latest proslavery pamphlets; "few of our people understand . . . [slavery] in its philosophical and economic bearing," the Beaufort native lamented.[22] By 1850 Grayson had come to believe in the Union largely as the guarantor of slavery. He reasoned that, in a world hostile to her institutions, Carolina's particularistic society could best be protected by the power of the Union, whose grand charter sanctioned slavery.

With his prolific pen Gilmore Simms became to "the world outside the South . . . above all things the champion of the South." Of his "large list of fiction only one book, *Southward Ho!* [1854], confront[ed] directly the theme of slavery and secession." But at least as early as 1835 Simms was turning characterizations and subplots to proslavery purposes. In *The Yemassee*, for example, faithful, black Hector chose slavery as a happier condition than freedom.[23] Moreover, Simms poured his defense of slavery into numerous articles and essays, most notably the material he contributed to *The Pro-Slavery Argument*.[24] The agreement between Simms and Grayson in their *apologiae* for slavery belied their divergent political careers.

As a Unionist editor during the nullification period, Simms had endured a mob attack by nullifiers. Moving in a direction opposite to Grayson's, by 1850 Simms was espousing "secession by a unified South."[25] Although Simms became a secessionist and Grayson a Unionist, both were seeking a governmental entity that afforded slavery the best protection from its enemies.

A legacy of nullification slowly poisoned the viability of a Unionist party in South Carolina. Unionists were first branded as traitors and then largely proscribed from office. In the context of increasing northern hostility to slavery, nullifiers promoted harmony in South Carolina by offering a reconciliation to the state's former Unionists. Those who returned to power had, in effect, renounced primary loyalty to the federal government. The Unionist leaders who remained at odds with the gentry majority did not accept the proposition that Union and slavery were, or might become, mutually exclusive. Their political faith rested largely on the belief that slavery was better protected within the existing federal structure than outside of it.

3

Through the twists and turns of successive interpretations of the nullification movement, commentators have agreed on at least one point: in the final crisis South Carolina found herself utterly alone.[26] After 1828, as the nullifiers demonstrated an increasing appetite for confrontation, their extreme state-rights philosophy attracted only scattered, ineffective support outside South Carolina. Yet, despite the mounting evidence that throughout the slave states planters opposed nullification, South Carolina radicals cherished the hope that Georgia, at least, shared their principles as well as their plight and might stand with the Palmetto State against the federal goverment.

Along the Georgia coast and in a few piedmont counties, cotton planters staged rallies protesting tariff levels. Of all southern states, Georgia most nearly duplicated the unique "combination of internal unity, heavy concentration of slaves, and new experience with economic depression" that had spawned nullification in South Carolina.[27] But opposition to the tariff in Georgia produced less militancy than in her neighbor across the Savannah River. Richard Habersham, a Georgia friend of William Elliott, thought the South Carolina Unionist was too optimistic about reducing the tariff through normal congressional channels, but Habersham was certain that Georgians would not pursue the path of nullification. "The majority of our people are in favor of a State Convention whose proceedings are to be ratified by the people . . . but which course the Convention ought to advise or recommend, is one about which we are still more divided. Some think they ought to endeavor to obtain a convention of the Southern States, some that a protest would be sufficient, some to open a correspondence with the other aggrieved states, and a very few are in favor of Nullification. This last," he emphasized, "is rather an unpopular name in our State and few are willing to acknowledge themselves to be such without giving it some qualification."[28]

Georgia's conflict with the federal judiciary over Cherokee Indian lands inspired an eleventh-hour hope among nullifiers for joint resistance—if the federal government tried to enforce national law in either state. Through the end of 1832 Georgia continued to defy the Supreme Court's decision in *Worcester* v. *Georgia*, which had asserted the federal government's exclusive jurisdiction in the Cherokee nation's territory. Convicted and jailed under Georgia law, Samuel A. Worcester and Elizur Butler, New England missionaries, continued to deny Georgia's authority over their actions in Cherokee country and pursued a second, decisive appeal to the Supreme Court. In the context of these events, if "the President should ask for legislation permitting the use of force against South Carolina, he might also be given unwanted authority to coerce her neighboring state. Such . . . [action by Congress] would destroy the administration's hopes of isolating South Carolina."[29]

Georgia's Governor Wilson Lumpkin strongly rejected South Carolina's theory of *de jure* nullification but just as strongly refused to end Georgia's *de facto* nullification of federal law regarding the Cherokees. Lumpkin's position placed Martin Van Buren, Jackson's consummate manager of party politics, in a dilemma. "A bolt of his Georgia partisans, if the President used force in the *Worcester* case, would completely wreck the New Yorker's dream of an alliance between the 'Southern planters and the plain republicans of the North'; while the failure of the administration to aid the Court would cost him support in New England and the Middle States."[30]

Van Buren threw himself and his Albany Regency into an effort to resolve the conflict. Georgia's former governor who was then a junior senator, John Forsyth, joined Secretary of War Lewis Cass and Van Buren in entreating Lumpkin, the missionaries, and their sponsor (the American Board of Commissioners for Foreign Missions) to terminate the case. Georgia Unionists visited the missionaries and pressed the argument that "any attempt by the federal government to use force to release them would cause Georgia to side with South Carolina in the nullification controversy." The missionaries abandoned their appeal, and Lumpkin pardoned them. "On January 16, two days after the release of the missionaries, President Jackson sent his message to Congress asking for powers to use coercive measures against the Palmetto State."[31]

Disgusted by Lumpkin's proclamation that the Cherokee dispute had ended in victory for Georgia, the nullifiers saw another political implication: Jackson "had wit enough to take no step like 'the military force bill,' till he had got the Georgia case out of his way." While their hopes for Georgia's official support turned to ashes, unofficial expressions of sympathy for South Carolina's type of nullification also flickered to an end. The "Milledgeville [Georgia] Convention has proved an abortion," James L. Petigru rejoiced to Hugh Swinton Legaré. "[Senator] Troop [Troup] has published a letter telling them to beware of conventions of all sorts, and there is no such constitutional remedy as they are in search of." Moreover, Georgia's John Forsyth was acting as the administration's floor leader in the Senate.[32] The chance, always remote, that Georgia would aid South Carolina in a fight with federal forces had vanished.

For nullifiers the news from Georgia was bad; the news from Tennessee was worse. Two powerful and previously rival factions in Tennessee politics saw their common opposition to nullification as an opportunity to join forces. The results of this alliance were soon apparent. In October 1832 Mitchell King, representing South Carolina Unionists, presented a message to the Tennessee legislature. This message sparked lively debate on the issues posed by the Palmetto State's dispute with the federal government. But during the debate, reported the Nashville *Banner*, "not a voice was raised even in palliation of the absurdities and ruinous tendencies of state nullification."[33]

Both the majority and the minority reports presented by the legislature's joint committee on the question denied that nullification was constitutional, and both condemned nullification as a threat to peace. The minority report "had a more conservative, states'-rights orientation," regretted that the federal government had sought to enlarge its powers, and decried the current tariff as "'extremely oppressive on the people of the south and west' but not unconstitutional." On October 22, 1832, Tennessee's legislature chose the majority report "by a unanimous vote of those present" in the senate and by a vote of twenty-two to six in the house. Tennessee's stand against nullification was official.[34]

After South Carolina adopted the Nullification Ordinance, Union rallies were organized throughout Tennessee and were staged from December through February. Jackson's wishes were clearly reflected in Nashville's Union rally of December 29, and his lieutenants may have directed others, but "both Jackson and anti-Jackson partisans played important roles at the various rallies." The rallies condemned nullification, sometimes in language borrowed from Jackson's Nullification Proclamation. In the rallies Tennesseans acknowledged their antipathy for current tariff levels, but demonstrated their much stronger determination to separate nullification from state-rights principles, which they vigorously affirmed. Finally, in measured phrases, the rallies "generally consented to the use of force if necessary, since the preservation of the Union was paramount to all other considerations."[35]

"If we are to have a civil war in S.C.," wrote Jackson's friend and political ally John Catron, "I wish to see over-whelming military force at once brought out to suppress the Rebellion." Governor William Carroll, anxious to improve his relations with Jackson, offered to place at the president's disposal ten thousand Tennessee volunteers equipped from the state arsenal. Tennessee legislator James W. Wyly posed a more imaginative solution: "The old chief [Jackson] could rally force enough if necessary, upon two weeks notice from other States to Stand on the Saluda Mountain and piss enough . . . to float the whole nullifying crew of South Carolina into the Atlantic Ocean." The numerous other suggestions for military campaigns and offers of military service were more orthodox. The message to South Carolina's nullifiers was clear: Tennesseans were willing to fight against them. Forty years later W. J. Grayson, in writing his autobiography, bitterly recalled that President Jackson "began, in Tennessee, to prepare his battalions for war."[36]

The radicals among South Carolina's nullifiers had accepted the necessity of forcing other southern states to choose between supporting South Carolina belligerency or supplying troops to suppress it. They had anticipated that, in the final test of wills, slave states would dare not sacrifice one of their own. As William C. Preston predicted: "The slave question will be the real issue—All others will be absorbed in it." But independent-minded Langdon Cheves, who rejected nullification as unworkable, had asked: "What apology can we make to the other states and to posterity, if we shall put at hazard these great questions on our own single strength and they shall be doomed by our weakness and rashness to fail?" He had also warned that a South Carolina attempt to force its own definition of issues and its own solution on the rest of the South would produce fierce resentment.[37]

Cheves's prophecy was fulfilled. In the crucial months of November and December, 1832, evidence of the unpopularity of "Carolina Doctrines" and of South Carolina's isolation mounted steadily.[38] The Alabama legislature denounced nullification as "unsound in theory and dangerous in practice"; Georgia lawmakers called it "rash and revolutionary"; and Mississippi deplored South Carolina's "reckless precipitancy." By early February 1833 Palmetto State Unionist James L. Petigru was encouraged that "[i]n all the other states it has been the same way." Referring to Benjamin W. Leigh's mission to South Carolina, Petigru noted that only Virginia had offered help and that consisted of "advice to get out of the scrape."[39]

The nullifiers got out of the scrape by compromising on the tariff, a course they had scorned for two years. They had not forced Congress to abandon the principle of protection, and they had to accept not only higher rates but also far slower reduction of those rates than the November session of the Nullification Convention had demanded. The convention, which reconvened in March, repealed its ordinance and, in a gesture of defiance, nullified the Force Bill. "Leading nullifiers had entered the crusade partially to win a weapon with which they could avoid an encounter with the abolitionists. And nullification had been irretrievably smashed."[40] Nullification as a tactic was placed in an honorable, if increasingly dusty, niche in their political armory. The state's dominant planter-politicians, however, never abandoned the creed developed during the nullification movement. That episode strengthened their resolve to do battle against "the despotic nature" and the centralizing tendency of the federal government—a government that might claim supreme authority over slavery as it had asserted supreme authority over the tariff.

John Randolph, believing that the "slave interest has the knife at its throat in the hands of fanatics and rogues and fools," had written Jackson that nullification "was a question of 'Slavery versus Anti-Slavery.'" The president had also received this counsel from sources closer and friendlier to his administration. But the old Tennessean did not accept the genuineness of the nullifier's fears; he "missed the vital connection between nullification and the South's defense of

slavery." Instead he loudly blamed nullification on the disappointed
political ambitions of a South Carolina faction and persistently
identified Calhoun as the directing force behind the movement, despite Joel R. Poinsett's eyewitness reports of Calhoun's moderating
influence.[41]

Jackson's twin themes—that nullification was secession and that
it was motivated by selfish political ambitions—were disseminated
by the administration's organ, the Washington *Globe*. After the
crisis had been resolved, the *Globe* continued to proclaim "that the
nullifiers [had] used the tariff as a screen, not for the defense of slavery but for the pursuit of power." Jackson declared that "the nullifiers' dire accounts of northern hostility to slavery were a 'false
tale,'" and the *Globe* deplored South Carolina's "alarms which have
not the slightest hold even on the imaginations of those who origi-
nate them." Jackson's denunciations of the abolitionists as dangerous fanatics appeared in the *Globe*'s columns, as did Negrophobic
editorials. Thus the administration's own antiabolitionist, antiblack
credentials comforted southern planters outside South Carolina and
made the administration's interpretation even more plausible to
them.[42]

To the *Globe*'s barrage, Duff Green's short-lived *United States
Telegraph* replied that the nullifiers' "heedlessness of federal office
and patronage" proved that they sought only sectional justice not
political rewards. In this national propaganda battle, however, the
nullifiers were hopelessly outgunned. Jackson may have "mistak-
enly fit nullification into a concept of republicanism that explained
radical dissent as a product of base political motives and conspira-
torial ambitions."[43] But Jackson's concept, mistaken or not, proved
tenaciously effective in isolating South Carolina long after the nullification crisis.

During the twenty years following 1832, South Carolina's spokesmen repeatedly sounded the alarm against antislavery influence in
the federal government and tried to rally the South to combat it.
Legacies of nullification hampered each attempt. The nullification
movement had endowed South Carolina with a reputation for arro-
gance, for extremism, and for pursing her own course regardless of
its impact on her neighbors. Warnings from the Palmetto State
about dangers to slavery were commonly discounted. South Carolina's demands for action aroused evil memories of nullification, and
the motives of South Carolina leaders remained powerfully suspect
among other southern politicians. Fears of "South Carolina dicta-

tion" helped frustrate efforts to unite the South behind radical measures as South Carolinians, to their dismay, learned time and again.

In Georgia and Tennessee candidates who had associated themselves with Jackson's stand on nullification swept to victory in 1832 and 1834. During 1835–36 South Carolina officials were incensed at the prospect of abolitionist literature moving through the South via the United States mail. When Calhoun's legislative remedy for "incendiary publications" reached the Senate floor, Georgian John P. King voted for the bill, but only after he "took sharp issue with Calhoun's constitutional reasoning and accused the South Carolina Senator of playing politics."[44]

When the Wilmot Proviso, barring slavery in any territory acquired from Mexico, passed the House in 1846 and again (in stronger form) in 1847, the nullifiers' ominous prophecies no longer seemed fantastic. Southern politicians were alarmed and aroused, but they were still not prepared to place their faith in the Palmetto State's leadership. Most South Carolinians, however, could neither restrain themselves nor their great champion from proclaiming a new crusade. In March 1847 Calhoun called on southerners to abandon party distinctions, to boycott the national nominating conventions, and to unite in a single proslavery party. "Let us profit by the example of the abolitionist[s] . . . [and] make the destruction of our institutions the . . . issue," he told a cheering crowd in Charleston.[45]

Undoubtedly that stern Calvinist could see no one more fitted by providence to save both the Union and slavery than himself. The initial response to a southern party and Calhoun's leadership of it pleased both the old Carolinian and his disciples.[46] But southern enthusiasm for the program of Calhoun and his South Carolina protégés quickly waned. As Hammond had foreseen, despite the vast changes in the political climate since nullification days, South Carolina could "do nothing if she puts herself foremost but *divide the South* and insure disastrous defeat." Old suspicions about South Carolina reappeared as did the theme of Calhoun's unholy, unquenchable ambitions. President James K. Polk "entertain[ed] a worse opinion of Mr. Calhoun than . . . ever. . . . He is wholly selfish. A few years ago he was the author of Nullification and threatened to dissolve the Union on account of the tariff. . . . [Currently,] he selects slavery to agitate the country." The Raleigh *North Carolina Standard*, an inveterate enemy of South Carolina extremism, attributed the new crusade to Calhoun's lust for the presidency. "Many southern journals, like the Jackson *Mississippian"* joined the "de-nunciation of the Squire of Fort Hill for 'courting collision upon this deprecated, awful and monstrous' slavery issue." Many other south-ern newspapers dismissed South Carolina's apocalyptic visions as premature.[47] By summer 1848 the southern party conceived by South Carolinians had died *in utero.*

In December 1848, when the second session of the Thirtieth Con-gress convened, Calhoun requested a caucus of all southern senators and representatives. His purpose was to present an "Address of the Southern Delegates in Congress to their Constituents." Knowing that the current Congress must grapple with the issue of permitting slavery in the huge area officially acquired by the Treaty of Gua-dalupe Hidalgo, Calhoun had drafted his Southern Address as a manifesto of slaveholders' rights in the new territory. If slavery should be confined to its present limits, the address warned, the majority power of the free states would soon be sufficient to "eman-cipate our slaves under color of an amendment to the Constitution." With Calhoun heatedly demanding that all southern legislators endorse his address, southern Whigs began interpreting the docu-ment less as a surety for slavery and more as a death decree for their party. When the issue was forced in January 1849, Calhoun ob-tained the signatures of only two Whigs. "We have completely foiled Calhoun in his miserable attempt to form a Southern party," boasted Georgia's fiery Robert Toombs.[48]

To South Carolinians in the late 1840s it sometimes seemed that not only Georgia Whigs but also that Georgians generally disliked the Palmetto State and all its works. Referring to a speech William Gilmore Simms had given, James Hammond offered his "congratu-lat[ions] . . . on having won laurels in Georgia, where very thing Carolinian is received with such bitter prejudice." And James Ham-ilton, Jr., who had established his family in Savannah, Georgia, while he pursued ventures in Texas, complained that "Georgia came to dislike us . . . more than the people of Massachusetts."[49]

North Carolinians, too, harbored ill-feelings toward South Caro-lina and characteristics regarded as peculiarly South Carolinian. In February 1849 James Johnston Pettigrew came to Charleston to read law in the office of James L. Petigru and Mitchell King; young Pettigrew, scion of a prominent Whig family in North Carolina, dreaded his "sojurn in a state of disunionists and conceited fellows." He rapidly came to respect Petigru and King, who had been active Unionists during the nullification movement, but he found "the remainder . . . [of South Carolinians] fast degenerating, devoting their time to Slavery Meetings[,] disunion speeches, and subjects of a like unprofitable nature."[50]

James C. Johnston, an old family friend of the Pettigrews, also confessed a dislike for the inhabitants of "Mr. Calhoun's Plantation." Johnston claimed to be "a little surprised that with your [Pettigrew's] strong anti-nullification feeling you are suffered to go about Mr. Calhoun's Plantation so much *without a pass*." Finally, noting there had "been a great meeting on the subject of the Wilmot Proviso" in Charleston, the North Carolinian suggested that the city's "military parade of an armed force [the slave patrol] is kept up to scare the Government of the United States as well as the negroes."[51]

As 1849 wore along, however, the political strength of antislavery opinions in the North and the congressional impasse on sectional issues produced increasing southern support for the militant posture South Carolina had long advocated. The movement for a southern convention (largely inspired by South Carolina) culminated in Nashville and was followed by South Carolina's attempt to organize the concerted secession of two or more states. Hostility to "South Carolina dictation" again dogged the efforts of South Carolina radicals. Ten years later the final chapter of South Carolina's antebellum extremism concluded with shell bursts over Fort Sumter. In the midst of that crisis South Carolina's feisty reputation was not forgotten, as Mrs. Chesnut learned, when Thomas Clingman told her that Virginia and North Carolina would come to the rescue of "a poor, little, hot-blooded, headlong, rash and troublesome sister State."[52]

The nullification movement left an increased hostility in other states toward South Carolina. But within South Carolina the nullification movement imparted a different legacy: an increased pride in the state and its proslavery cause. The gentry's confidence that South Carolina was "certainly beyond her Sister States of the South in the perfect appreciation of those political truths on which the great sectional questions hinge" placed them in a dilemma when they sought to educate the rest of the South. On the one hand they felt that South Carolina must lead, because only she saw the threats to slavery with sufficient clarity; on the other they knew that "South Carolina dictation" would be resented and might abort a new proslavery initiative. Thus the gentry were torn between a policy of forcing the issue of secession by their own action and one of waiting "Cassandralike" until other southerners shared their vision and were prepared to act with them.[53]

Frustrated by the rejection of their views and their programs, South Carolina's leaders bewailed "how ignorant and supine" the southerners were. The gentry who advocated separate secession described Georgia as a "Submission—Yankee state" and Virginia as "craven." Seccessionist leader Maxcy Gregg disgustedly wrote that he regarded a "consolidation with Georgia and Tennessee . . . as only not quite so great an evil as a consolidation with New York and Ohio."[54] With considerable justice other southerners regarded South Carolinians as being devoted more to South Carolina nationalism than to southern nationalism. The proud provinciality of South Carolina's gentry was a self-imposed obstacle to their sporadic efforts to achieve Southern political unity.

PART TWO

SOUTH CAROLINA,
"A FIRESHIP IN THE UNION"

no simple man that sees
This jarring discord of nobility,
This shouldering of each other in the Court,
This factious bandying of their favorites,
But that it doth presage some ill event.
I Henry VI

CHAPTER IV

A Territorial Imperative

1

On Saturday, August 8, 1846, President James K. Polk submitted an appropriation request to the House of Representatives. With the first session of the Twenty-Ninth Congress scheduled to end the following Monday, the usual preadjournment turmoil prevailed, and Polk hoped that the busy legislators would grant his request with a minimum of congressional fuss. The United States had been at war with Mexico for three months, and Polk was seeking two million dollars to be used in negotiating a peace. Mexico might make "a cession of territory," said the President's message explaining his request, "[and] we ought to pay them a fair equivalent" for it. Polk had publicly acknowledged what had long been privately known: his administration wanted to expand the United States's domain at Mexico's expense.[1]

House Democratic leaders scheduled the desired appropriation bill for consideration in the evening session. During that hot, uncomfortable August night, New York's Hugh White and Massachusetts's Robert C. Winthrop, Whigs both, denounced Polk's message as disingenuous. The purpose of the appropriation, they charged, was to buy or bribe land from Mexico, and the administration's "ulterior purpose was to extend the area of slavery." Two proadministration Democrats followed White and Winthrop. Polk's floor managers found this opposition and support entirely routine, even predictable. But the next speaker changed all that. With the House sitting in Committee of the Whole, a young Democrat from Pennsylvania obtained the floor and offered an amendment to the pending appropriation bill, which "*Provided,* That as an express and fundamental condition to the acquisition of any territory from the Republic of Mexico by the United States, by virtue of any treaty which may be negotiated between them, and to the use by the Executive of the moneys herein appropriated, neither slavery nor involuntary servitude shall ever exist in any part of said territory except for crime, whereof the party shall first be duly convicted."[2] The Wilmot Proviso had entered America's political vocabulary; and, although the proviso was never enacted, it altered irrevocably the political struggle over slavery.[3]

The rebellion of northern politicians was measured in the House's first ballot on the proviso: it passed by a vote of eighty to sixty-four. Only three congressmen from the free states voted against Wilmot's amendment. In a stronger version introduced by Van Burenite Preston King, the proviso passed the House the following year.[4] Although the Senate never approved it, fourteen of the fifteen free-state legislatures adopted resolutions in favor of the proviso. Moreover it catalyzed the formation of the Free-Soil party, a coalition of former Democrats, former Whigs, and Liberty party men who, despite their differences, agreed that slavery should not be extended.[5] For many northerners, debate on the nonextension of slavery produced or intensified their perception of an ominous and aggressive political enemy: the slave power. This perception of a slave power—not sympathy for enslaved blacks—would awaken vast northern animosity toward the slaveholding South.[6]

Ironically the South Carolina gentry had not been inclined to choose the territories that were increasingly certain to be annexed from Mexico as advantageous battlegrounds for slavery. Despite northern suspicions that southern planters had fomented the Mexican War to expand the area of slavery, the prevailing opinion among the South Carolina gentry was that the territory in question was unsuitable for slave labor. While extreme proponents of Manifest Destiny, flushed with excitement by military victories, demanded the incorporation of Mexico into the United States, South Carolina's leaders staunchly opposed the all-Mexico movement. They saw in it deadly threats to their slave system and to their concept of republicanism. Although few South Carolina politicians believed that slavery could flourish in the territory Polk proposed to annex, they fully appreciated the proviso's symbolic importance, and they prepared the Palmetto State to meet this new challenge.

Enactment of the proviso would have stigmatized slavery in the law of the land—a stigma that the framers of the constitution had consciously omitted. The South Carolina gentry feared that the proviso would have grave practical as well as moral consequences. They saw its introduction as the opening maneuver in an offensive against slavery, a maneuver that would surround the peculiar institution with hostile states. Federal power, invoked to prohibit slavery in the territories, would soon be turned on slavery in the states. South Carolina politicians were determined to check this attack at the outset.

In the controversy over the Wilmot Proviso, as in other controversies that have cut deeply into the fabric of American society, questions of policy gave "place to questions of power; questions of wisdom to questions of legality. Attention shift[ed] to the Constitution itself,"[7] and South Carolina's objections to the Wilmot Proviso, like her objections to the Tariff of 1828, were soon couched in constitutional terms. The proviso rested on the belief that the constitution empowered Congress to prohibit slavery in territory owned by the United States. Calhoun and Rhett developed a counterinterpretation, asserting that the constitution denied Congress the power to prohibit slavery in the territories. The triumph of the proviso, South Carolinians declaimed, would justify secession.[8]

While controversy over slavery in the territories escalated in constitutional terms, it also intruded in the forthcoming presidential race. Led by Lewis Cass, Democrats who remained loyal to their party espoused a compromise position. Loyal Whigs chose a politically naive champion, Zachary Taylor, and strove to evade the issue entirely. Free-Soilers agreed on Martin Van Buren as their standard-bearer. Calhoun and his South Carolina followers had meanwhile attempted, with little success, to organize a Southern party to meet antislavery men of all stripes in a death struggle. Following the collapse of this effort and of Calhoun's feeble candidacy, a number of influential South Carolinians, believing that Zachary Taylor's planter status would determine his future policies, touted his election as the South's best hope. By the fall of 1848, however, Taylor's political counselors and his second Allison letter had disenchanted many of the general's erstwhile advocates in South Carolina. With party lines holding strongly elsewhere in the South, South Carolina's planter-politicians were forced to decide whether Cass or Taylor represented the lesser evil.

In December 1848 and January 1849, following hard on congressional attempts to limit slavery's expansion, came proposals to abolish the slave trade in the District of Columbia and even a proposal to abolish slavery there. The House passed Daniel Gott's resolution instructing the Committee for the District of Columbia to report a bill, "prohibiting the slave trade in the . . . District."⁹ By late spring southern Whigs were appalled to see their slaveholding president choosing antislavery Whigs as his principal advisors. In the last half of 1849 South Carolina's long effort to unite the South against threats to slavery gained sudden momentum. Mississippi planters seemed especially anxious to mobilize their colleagues throughout the slave states. And South Carolina's leaders diligently promoted the movement for a southern convention that would answer threats with concerted action.

2

Relations between the United States and Mexico had deteriorated rapidly after Texas entered the Union. Polk's zeal in claiming the Rio Grande as the border between the new state of Texas and Mexico produced a frail but serviceable casus belli. Northerners who interpreted the Mexican War as part of a proslavery conspiracy saw the annexation of Texas as the first step in the conspirators' grand design for expanding slavery. The slave power had known that war with Mexico (and the acquisition of yet more land for slavery) would inevitably follow the annexation of Texas—so ran the conspiracy theory. By such reasoning South Carolinians were guilty members of the slave power and John C. Calhoun was the archconspirator: South Carolinians had demanded that Texas be incorporated into the Union, and Calhoun, as secretary of state, had presided over the process.

Many of the South Carolinians who migrated to Texas maintained their ties with kin in the Palmetto State. South Carolina natives, moreover, played major roles in the creation of the Republic of Texas.¹⁰ South Carolinians also felt a strong ideological concern for Texas and her political fate. As early as 1837 the Charleston *Mercury* had urged annexation on the grounds that the "slaveholding interest, wherever spread, must join forces and stand in a body, or they will be hewn down and trampled underfoot."¹¹

The South Carolina gentry feared most of all that an alliance between Great Britain and Texas (which seemed possible) would give British abolitionists a dangerous new base from which to spread their doctrine. Proannexation rallies in South Carolina typically warned of "the insidious attempts of these missionaries of blood and of evils, the British and Northern Abolitionists" to establish themselves in Texas. Acting in his official capacity, Secretary of State Calhoun wrote to Richard Pakenham, British minister in Washington; in this letter Calhoun argued, in effect, that British diplomatic activities in Texas posed a threat to slavery which justified United States annexation of Texas as a measure of self-defense.[12]

Calhoun's letter, denounced as a grossly sectional misuse of his office, contributed to the defeat of the treaty of annexation that he had helped negotiate.[13] But territorial expansion in general and Texas's annexation in particular were sustained as programs of the Democratic party. In congressional divisions on the Texas issue "attitudes toward expansion played a greater role in determining voting than did attitudes toward slavery." The Cleveland *Plain Dealer*, a Democratic organ, "put the expansion issue into perspective [for loyal Northern Democrats] by saying that the United States could 'better endure the evils of slavery for a season than British domination forever.'"[14]

With the annexation of Texas accomplished, South Carolinians saw no threats to slavery on the institution's southern or western frontiers. The Republic of Mexico was weak and riven with internal problems. It had neither Great Britain's inclination nor power to pursue an antislavery foreign policy. During 1844–45 northern Democrats had sought the fulfillment of Manifest Destiny; South Carolina planters had sought to protect slavery. In the case of Texas's annexation, these ends converged, but in the case of the Mexican War, they did not.

Throughout the winter and spring of 1846, Calhoun had suspected that the Polk administration was courting war with Mexico, a war that the Carolinian believed was needless. In May the president asked for men and money to wage war, which—he said—already existed between the two nations because of a Mexican attack on United States troops. In the House, Congressmen Rhett and Holmes (among others) objected to Polk's request; only Congress could declare war, these critics noted, and the president's request ignored this constitutional requirement. Calhoun raised this objection in the Senate and proposed that Congress grant the president supplies and men only "to repel invasion." But with remarkable speed and by a large final margin, the original request was driven through Congress, and the president had his war.[15]

In South Carolina as elsewhere citizens jumped to the flag; most newspapers denounced the Mexicans as perfidious and roared with appropriate bellicosity. The Charleston *Mercury* alone anticipated and stood by Calhoun's position. There "would have been no war if the United States had left the narrow and worthless valley of the Río del Norte [Río Grande] to Mexico," editorialized the *Mercury*. A few days later its editors suggested that the United States should offer peace as soon as Mexican troops were driven south of the Río Grande and warned that "a love of conquest . . . is the enemy of liberty and law." Nevertheless Calhoun's popularity in the Palmetto State as well as in the South temporarily declined. The senator's South Carolina correspondents advised him that his constituents appreciated and would sustain his constitutional objections to the war's origin but that, for the moment at least, Carolinians wanted to see the Mexicans chastised.[16]

Only a small group of the state's politicians, led by Francis Pickens, challenged Calhoun's stand more or less openly.[17] Although Pickens had powerful allies in Edgefield District, including Preston S. Brooks, Milledge L. Bonham, William F. Durisoe (editor of the Edgefield *Advertiser*), and various members of the Butler family, Calhoun forced this "Edgefield Junto" to abandon their unqualified support for the administration's war policies. In correspondence and at least one interview with Calhoun, Pickens vainly protested his loyalty to his old mentor; the Edgefield speeches and resolutions that Calhoun found offensive had been made and moved, Pickens claimed, after he had left the rally. Nevertheless "Pickens was forced into [political] retirement in November 1846."[18]

James Hammond also was inclined to support the Polk administration. But Hammond's support for the administration's management of the war was far less consistent than his resentment and criticism of Calhoun's opposition to it.[19] Hammond and his admiring protégé Simms did not dare, however, to challenge Calhoun publicly over his stand on the Mexican War. "It will not do for me to urge my own claims—my own fitness—in the teeth of two notices to quit— [one] so immediately after the other," Simms conceded in December 1846, after he was defeated for a state legislative seat and for the lieutenant governorship.[20]

Hammond, who greatly desired the United States Senate seat vacated by McDuffie's resignation, lost it to A. P. Butler. Hammond's jealousy of Calhoun's power—a jealousy nurtured since Calhoun had crushed Governor Hammond's bid to revive the Bluffton Movement —was increased by Calhoun's support of Butler for the Senate.[21] Hammond's involvement in a scandal, which the Hampton family threatened to reveal if Hammond persisted in seeking national office, increased the former governor's frustration. His political exile and his diminished political influence during the period that coincided with the Mexican War chaffed Hammond badly.[22]

By the winter of 1846–47 enthusiasm for the Mexican War had flagged in South Carolina. "Many now begin to see that I was right in opposing [the war]. . . . There is no seeing when or how it is to be ended," wrote Calhoun to his daughter. As far as South Carolina was concerned, Calhoun's serene confidence that his position would be recognized as correct seemed justified. Doubts about the war's origins and results were displacing the desire for glory. The annexation of Texas would not have led to war, wrote former state senator James Gregg to Calhoun, "had it not been for Mr. Polk's utter lack of judgment and unaccountable indiscretion." Francis Lieber, South Carolina College's German-born, German-educated political economist, concluded that "cabinet wars" were possible in democracies as well as in monarchies: "Here we have in spite of Republic, public press, Congress, Constitution and all, as regularly built a cabinet war as ever the war of the Spanish succession or the Seven Years war was—it is emphatically Mr. Polk's war!"[23]

In February 1847 Waddy Thompson, who had served as "Envoy Extraordinary and Minister Plenipotentiary" to Mexico during the Tyler administration, detailed his opposition to the war. Denouncing it as unprovoked, bloody, and expensive, Thompson proposed that the "United States should establish defensive border posts and cease operation beyond that line." His article reflected the attitude of southern Whigs and conservative northern Whigs, who hoped to avoid the issue of slavery in new territories by opposing territorial acquisitions and concentrating their criticism on "the fraud and the aggressiveness of the war."[24]

Four days after Thompson's article had appeared in the *National Intelligencer,* Calhoun delivered a major speech, defining his own position on the war. The United States had repelled Mexican forces and established the Río Grande as the southern boundary of Texas, he noted. To achieve the government's only other announced aim ("indemnity for the claims American citizens had against the Mexican Government"), he suggested that the United States need only defend part of the territory its forces already held. Calhoun proposed holding "the Río Grande to the line of 32° of north latitude, thence along that parallel to the Gulf of California, and down the gulf to the sea." (In private, Polk had earlier indicated to Democratic leaders that all of the territory he wished to acquire from Mexico lay north of that line.) Calhoun warned that launching and sustaining an invasion of Mexico from Vera Cruz, as the Polk administration intended, would prove costly in blood and money. The outcome of such an invasion was far from certain, he continued, but the continuation of offensive operations would surely burden the United States with a huge war debt and might create new pressures for a high tariff policy.[25]

Before and during the winter of 1846–47, Calhoun had hinted at this "'defensive line doctrine' . . . [to] South Carolina's political and press leadership so that he might receive full coverage and complete endorsement once his speech was delivered." Both press and politicians reacted as expected. A. P. Butler supported his senior colleague; Congressmen James A. Black, Richard F. Simpson, Joseph A. Woodward, and Isaac E. Holmes also backed Calhoun. Rhett had been "baying after Polk's promise of additional territory." But, alarmed by the reintroduction of the Wilmot Proviso and sensitive to a possible tariff increase, Rhett changed his tack and "cooperated with Calhoun in opposing the continuation of the war." Only Congressman Alexander D. Sims of Darlington favored Polk's efforts to conquer a peace.[26] During the remainder of 1847, the isolation of Sims's position became increasingly apparent.

Locally powerful gentry in Columbia and Charleston, fall-line districts and low-country districts endorsed Calhoun's policy. Charleston-Unionist Joel R. Poinsett advocated an early end to the war. Up-country Unionist Perry, glad to find himself at last in agreement with the state's most powerful figure, vigorously supported the defensive-line policy. Governor David Johnson, whose political ties with the up-country were strong, followed Calhoun's advice on the war. Mouthing the senator's arguments Johnson "protested against [Polk's war policy] . . . as unwise and unjust."[27] Hammond and Simms continued their private colloquy on Calhoun's selfish motives for breaking with the Polk administration; Calhoun's dominance continued to frustrate the ambitions of younger men.[28] But South Carolina's planter-politicians overwhelmingly agreed that offensive war in Mexico was unnecessary and that its continuance would breed dangers for slavery in the United States.

In South Carolina as elsewhere, attitudes toward the war were linked inextricably with attitudes toward expansion. The Polk administration's desire for territorial expansion had sparked the Mexican War, and military successes during the war stimulated the appetites of expansionists for yet more territory. During the war the dispute between expansionists and nonexpansionists became increasingly complicated but remained more a function of party than of section; the Whigs "were hesitant about promoting United States expansion at the expense of her neighbours, the Democrats were eager exponents of it." When antislavery forces charged the Democrats with supporting a war designed to extend slavery, northern Democrats simultaneously removed that political incubus and remained expansionist by embracing the Wilmot Proviso. Nor did southern Democrats abandon territorial ambitions; they refused to concede that the extension of slavery was "incompatible with the ideal of diffusing democracy." Democratic institutions, they believed, involved the liberties of whites only and included the right of southern whites to emigrate with their slave property to new United States territories. Antislavery Whigs wanted to limit the area of slavery; proslavery and conservative Whigs wanted to avoid the issue of slavery in new territories, an issue that they believed would divide their party and endanger the Union. Both groups believed they could achieve their ends by preventing territorial expansion.[29]

Standing largely outside the party system, South Carolina's dominant politicians ruled their attitudes toward territorial expansion according to its perceived effect on slavery. Their nonpartisan abolitionist enemies did the same. South Carolina planters favored and abolitionists opposed the annexation of Texas for the same reason: both believed that annexation would strengthen slavery in the South. The movement to annex all of Mexico, however, led to a reversal that stood the slavepower-conspiracy interpretation of the Mexican War on its ear. The abolitionist *National Era* endorsed and the proslavery Charleston *Mercury* denounced the annexation of Mexico for the same reason: the belief that the Mexican provinces south of the Río Grande contained a climate and a population hostile to slavery. Hence, they concluded, these provinces would enter the Union as free states, circumscribing the area of slavery and weakening the political power of slaveholders.[30]

Iteration of the theory that slavery had reached its natural geographical limits played an obvious role in the growing popularity of the all-Mexico movement with northern voters. "Increasing numbers" of these voters, during the fall of 1847, "were becoming convinced that the Wilmot Proviso was not an indispensable prerequisite for the addition of free territory to the Union." Avid expansionists began to characterize the Wilmot Proviso as a distraction, a fraudulent device intended to prevent territorial acquisition. By January, 1848, endorsement of the annexation of Mexico came from such diverse northern sources as the Illinois *Globe* and the *National Era*, but their operative reasons differed. Democratic and expansionist, the *Globe* complained that "Mr. C[alhoun], with a great portion of the slave influence, have [*sic*] no doubt determined to oppose the extension of our borders. Our country is coming to a pretty pass between the Abolition Wilmot humbuggers and the slaveholders of the South." The nonpartisan, abolitionist *National Era* editorialized that the annexation of Mexico would "establish Freedom as the fundamental and unchangeable Law of the North American continent." Annexation would be "a most formidable Anti-Slavery measure."[31]

The South, too, had expansionists who coveted Mexico, but in South Carolina the men in power saw little to covet and much to fear in the conquest and assimilation of Mexico's population. William Gilmore Simms's romantic visions of a slaveholding confederacy extending deep into Central America were exceptional in the Palmetto State. He suggested that "beyond the Río Grande, what we once acquired would enure to the South & to the South exclusively." To Calhoun, Simms "threw out the hint that the Anglo Norman race would never forgive the public man who should fling away territory."[32]

While Simms dreamed dreams of slavery prospering in Central America, however, South Carolina's active politicians saw no possibility of establishing slavery there. They also foresaw disaster for slavery where it already existed, should Mexico be annexed. In his speech calling for an end to offensive operations south of the Río Grande, Calhoun proclaimed "Mexico . . . forbidden fruit, and the day that we consume it, the penalty will be almost the political death of our nation." On February 19, 1847, he "predicted that annexation" of Mexico in addition to the territory already in United States possession "could eventually result in the addition of fourteen non-slaveholding states." This would completely destroy the balance between free and slave states in the Union and lead to "political revolution, anarchy, civil war and widespread disaster."[33]

The South Carolina gentry echoed Calhoun on the danger of annexing territory that would become free soil. The Wilmot Proviso, wrote South Carolina House member William Ford DeSaussure to James Hammond, "has brought up that horrid question, the spectre of which is always haunting the South . . . the acquisition of territory becomes a curse to us." From the rostrum and with his pen, Waddy Thompson warned his fellow South Carolinians that cultivation of the South's staple crops would be impossible in Mexico; moreover Mexico's terrain was such "that there is not and never can be the means of transportation." There was, finally, for South Carolinians a definitive argument against the annexation of Mexico: "It is nakedly a proposition to add fifteen or twenty non-slaveholding states to our union—woe to the Southern man who lends his aid in doing that."[34]

When the regular session of the South Carolina legislature convened in November, 1847, Governor David Johnson observed that Mexico was not "worth what it would cost in dollars and cents to conquer her." Furthermore, he prophesied, the annexation of Mexico would produce in the Union a conflict over slavery "more disastrous than the [present] war." In January, 1848, Calhoun delivered another major plea for his defensive-line policy and against the all-Mexico movement. Warnings from George Hatcher, a Presbyterian clergyman and a northerner who wished to acquaint Calhoun with "the *real* state of things at the North," must have confirmed the South Carolinian's fears. Abolitionists as well as "that large portion of anti-Slavery men at the North who do not belong to Abolition organizations technically so called" were "fast becoming converts to the idea of *extensive annexation*. In their view the *more extensive* the better." These men, wrote Hatcher, believed that if Mexico were annexed slavery eventually "would be between two fires. Besides, the facilities for the escape of slaves would be greatly multiplied. Thus the South would be like a barrel tapped at both ends."[35]

South Carolina's representatives both in Washington and Columbia believed they were well advised to maintain a steady opposition to the all-Mexico movement. For a variety of reasons most of the gentry were pessimistic about the possibility of extending slavery into Central America. Their great concern and their great goal, in any case, was to protect and preserve slavery and government as these institutions existed in South Carolina. South Carolina's planter-politicians saw the annexation of Mexico as "a threat to the state's social order."[36] Hence, in March 1848, they welcomed the Treaty of Guadalupe Hidalgo (which precluded United States territorial expansion south of the Río Grande) as at least a partial victory for their cause.

3

In the summer of 1846 South Carolina's political leaders had been aware of northern Democrats' disenchantment with the Polk administration and of their reluctance to cooperate with southern colleagues on programs that would redound to slavery's benefit.

"The West has but to say," declared the Cleveland *Plain Dealer* in late June, "that *no more slave territory shall be annexed to the Union* and the dark tide of slavery will be stayed. . . . Let the motto be written on the back of every man's vote when the question arises— 'No More Slave Territory.'"[37] Yet Wilmot's introduction of the proviso "did not appear to increase interest in the issue during 1846." The initial reaction of South Carolinians was mild. They did not foresee the galvanic effect the proviso would have on northern public opinion nor the divisive effect it would have in future congressional sessions. "Even in the South Carolina legislature . . . during November and December, 1846, the question of slavery extension caused no discussion."[38]

In the second session of the Twenty-Ninth Congress, however, South Carolina's representatives quickly learned that the proviso would not fade away. On January 4, 1847, Preston King of New York moved that the proviso be attached to Polk's renewed request for funds (increased to three million dollars) to facilitate negotiations with Mexico. "The fact that King was one of the principal lieutenants of Martin Van Buren meant that the northern Democrats had now embarked on a deliberate and continuing revolt." King accompanied this reintroduction of the proviso with a reformulation of the issue it addressed: "If slavery is not excluded [from the territories] by law, the presence of the slave will exclude the laboring white man." Thus "defined as a struggle between free white labor and slave plantation labor in which the freedom, dignity, and opportunities of the white laboring man were at stake . . . the Proviso became an immediate [and compelling] issue" for masses of northerners.[39] For South Carolina's planter-politicians, the proviso had become not only a malign doctrine but also a dynamic one that required an equally powerful counter-doctrine.

In the course of debate on a bill to organize the Oregon Territory, Rhett outlined South Carolina's legal reply to the proviso. United States territories, he contended, were "the common property of the states, as co-owners, not of the United States as an entity." In administering this common property the federal government was merely the agent or trustee for the states. Since it was merely an agent, the federal government could not "discriminate in any way among the various states [the coowners] or among their citizens. It must admit into the territories and protect there as property anything, slaves, for example, which a citizen" legally owned in his native state. The federal government had, in brief, no constitutional power to prohibit (or establish) slavery in any territory, but the government had both the power and the duty to protect the property rights of slaveholders in the territories. A majority of the House of Representatives, however, did not accept this "ingenious dualism." On the day after Rhett's speech, the House approved the organization of Oregon as a free-soil territory.[40]

On February 15, 1847, the House passed the proviso in a revised form that prohibited "slavery . . . in any territory on the continent of America which shall hereafter be acquired by or annexed to the United States . . . in any manner whatever." Four days later Calhoun delivered South Carolina's definitive reply to the proviso. Calhoun framed that answer in terms of constitutional propositions, which he offered as a set of resolutions. He affirmed the common-property-of-the-states interpretation of the territories and asserted the right of slaveholders to emigrate "with their property [slaves], into any of the territories of the United States." He acknowledged "that a people, in framing a [state] constitution . . . [had] the unconditional right to prohibit slavery." He declared, finally, that no "condition is imposed by the Federal Constitution on a [prospective] State, in order to be admitted into this Union, except that its Constitution shall be republican; and that the imposition of any other [condition] by Congress would . . . be in violation of the Constitution."[41]

Prohibition of slavery in United States territories began, of course, with the Northwest Ordinance, adopted by the Continental Congress while the Constitutional Convention was in session and re-enacted by Congress after the constitution was ratified. Congress "included the same prohibition, in virtually the same language, in a series of five territorial acts, from 1800 to 1838, and in the Missouri Compromise of 1820."[42] But Congress had also accepted from North Carolina and Georgia land cessions stipulating that slavery not be prohibited in the ceded territories. Nevertheless, before 1846–47, the authority of Congress to legislate on slavery in the territories had not "been seriously challenged."[43]

But, "while the Wilmot Proviso represented a merely conventional step constitutionally, politically it was the most radical of measures." The proviso thrust aside a customary practice dating from 1789 by which Congress organized free and slave territories (and admitted free and slave states) in rough balance. When the House abandoned this custom by passing the proviso, Calhoun and his followers responded by reexamining the constitutional warrant for federal legislation on slavery in the territories. Their conclusion might have been "a radical constitutional innovation," but, in view of the brevity and ambiguity of the most applicable constitutional text (art. IV, sec. 3), they could defend their interpretation and cite no less an authority than Madison in support of it. Moreover, appealing to the constitution was a familiar tactic for southerners, especially South Carolinians. In the words of Calhoun: "I see my way in the constitution. . . . A compromise is but an act of Congress. It may be overruled at any time. It gives us no security. But the constitution . . . is a rock. . . . It is a firm and stable ground, on which we can better stand in opposition to fanaticism, than on the shifting sands of compromise."[44]

The issue of slavery in the territories is inseparably linked in American historiography with the question of whether slavery could have prospered or even functioned there. A contemporary allegedly remarked that the "whole controversy over the Territories . . . related to an imaginary negro in an impossible place."[45] That observation anticipated and wryly paraphrased the later argument of revisionist historians who saw the issue of slavery in the territories as an entirely unnecessary cause for civil war. Their view rested on the argument, most systematically advanced by Charles W. Ramsdell, that slavery had reached its "natural limits" and (regardless of the Wilmot Proviso) could not have expanded into the territories.[46]

Critics of Ramsdell's thesis have attacked his argument "for virtually equating slavery extension with the extension of cotton cultivation" and have emphasized slavery's adaptability to a variety of climatic and industrial conditions. This argument had been anticipated by participants in the debate on the proviso. Supporters of the proviso noted that in the territories Polk proposed to annex slavery had in fact existed until prohibited by Mexico in 1824. Northerners who hoped for the ultimate, if gradual, extinction of slavery were hardly reassured by the knowledge that the slave states admitted since 1789 vastly exceeded in area the states where slavery had flourished in the original Union. "As David Wilmot concluded, 'the whole history of the settlement of this continent' proved that not one of the vast territories of the United States had been saved from slavery without a prohibitive enactment of the federal government."[47]

A reexamination of congressional debate on the possibility of slavery's expansion into the territories found "the arguments on either side were more sophisticated than has been remembered." But this study emphasized "that the majority of Congressmen who discussed slavery extension did so in moral or constitutional terms." Of those congressmen who "discussed slavery in the territories between August 1846 and March 1849, only 11% expressed an interest in the limits question"; most congressmen chose to make a stand on principle rather than probability. Many northern congressmen who subscribed to the belief that natural geographic laws barred slavery from the territories in question still "seriously considered supporting the Wilmot proviso." It was apparent, too, "from the fact that even those southern politicians who were convinced that slavery could not exist in the territories were unalterably opposed to the Proviso, that the issue had a great deal more meaning for the people than the practical question which was involved, and it was this meaning which gave the Proviso its importance."[48]

Thus it was hardly surprising that South Carolina's leaders—who took principle and precedent very seriously—saw in the Wilmot Proviso an intolerable threat to the rights of slaveholders and to the future of slavery. In January, 1847, shortly after the proviso had been reintroduced, the Charleston *Mercury* warned that enactment of the measure would make the South "a portion of the Union to be tolerated only—not to be cherished, not to be held as sharing in joint sovereignty the empire of the continent. Our increase is to be stifled, our state institutions to be denounced in legislative acts in Washington and like a caged debtor we are to give bonds not to go out of the jail bounds."[49] Passage of the Wilmot Proviso would simultaneously record the federal government's disapproval of slavery and its power to act on that disapproval.

The proviso, South Carolinians believed, would unleash further assaults on slavery through federal legislation. "Its adoption would mean that the [northern] majority would thereafter wield its power without regard to" the South's interests in slavery. Calhoun feared that the existing free states, with the aid of others created after passage of the Wilmot Proviso and dedicated to its free-soil spirit, would in time amend the "Constitution to abolish forever the peculiar institution of the South." Calhoun "for one . . . would rather meet any extremity upon earth than give up one inch of our equality—one inch of what belongs to us as members of this great republic." Not only in South Carolina but throughout the South slaveholders subscribed to his interpretation of the proviso as a device "designed solely for the purpose of destroying that equality of political power to which the Southern States are entitled under the Constitution."[50] Calhoun's counterdoctrine to the Wilmot Proviso rapidly became the standard position for southern politicians.[51] But they did not embrace his program for political counteraction.

By the fall of 1847 South Carolina's grim prophet saw the continuing "appeals to the [free-soil and antislavery] prejudices of the

Northern people as well as to their sectional and selfish feelings" as
the inevitable result of that rejection. In 1848 South Carolinians
believed their fears about the Wilmot Proviso were being realized.
They saw its dread spirit bring to life "A new party [the Free Soil
party] . . . to [slaveowners] the most formidable that has ever yet
existed—a party founded upon avowed hostility to the South, and
whose professed purpose is to prescribe us to our present limits, and
to bring its whole moral influence and that of civilized Europe . . . to
bear against us. . . . We have no longer vulgar abolition to contend
with. The party now forming occupies a higher position, and oper-
ates on an infinitely wider basis."[52]

4

During the second session of the Twenty-Ninth Congress,
debate on slavery in the territories had filled the air with threats
and counterthreats. Northerners "will establish a cordon of free
States that shall surround you," Columbus Delano of Ohio told representatives from the South, "and then we will light up the fires of
liberty on every side, until they melt your present chains, and render all your people *free*." South Carolinians were not the only southerners who replied that they would dissolve the Union rather than
endure such a fate.[53] Determined to begin his Southern party while
free-soil threats were fresh in southern memories, Calhoun addressed a carefully prepared Charleston audience on March 9 (less
than a week after Congress had adjourned).

Dividing northern voters into four classes, he estimated that
5 percent of northern voters were "abolitionists proper—the rabid
fanatics," that another 5 percent were proslavery, and that 70 percent "regard[ed] slavery as an evil, and . . . [were] disposed
to aid in restricting and extirpating it, when . . . [that could] be done
consistently with the constitution, and without endangering the
peace or prosperity of the country." The final 20 percent consisted of
"the political leaders of the respective parties, and their partizans,
and followers" who espoused whatever position was most likely to
gain them a presidential victory and its patronage rewards. The
South's only hope, Calhoun suggested, was to abandon party ties
and to form a single, proslavery, Southern party. To win the presidency, Northern party leaders would then be forced to court this
Southern party and appeal to the northern majority's constitutional

scruples and pro-Union sentiments rather than to their antislavery opinions.[54]

He envisioned the disruption of the national parties and an end to national nominating conventions. However, the mechanism by which Calhoun expected the people to select and support him as the presidential candidate of "a real honest conservative party based on broad constitutional grounds" remained vague even to the South Carolinian's most ardent disciples.[55]

Critics of Calhoun's scheme characterized it as counterproductive or chimerical. It meant "if anything . . . a party for . . . [the South, with] all other interests merging in that of Slavery, to the exclusion & defiance of the North, unless where individuals from that region choose to lose themselves in ours—a proposition which at once forces a corresponding organization upon the North—a result which leaves us in rather worse condition than before." When southerners "do organize a Party and act in concert," observed James Hammond, "we must strike a far higher key note. We must place our rights on the Constitution and not . . . on the occupant of the Presidential chair. . . . It is mean and contemptible to think of going to the ballot box with the fanatics on such a question."[56] Although hailed briefly outside of South Carolina, the Southern party was soon denounced by the manifold enemies (new and old) of Calhoun and his state. By the fall of 1847 both the Southern party and Calhoun's presidential candidacy had expired.[57]

"Even before the Carolinian had recognized defeat . . . his friends had been attracted by the candidacy of Zachary Taylor," and Carolinians were not alone in their admiration for the general. His early victories in the Mexican War (Palo Alto and Resaca de la Palma) had "made an instantaneous impression upon the popular mind."[58] In September 1846 Taylor won the Battle of Monterrey, but the terms he granted to the defeated Mexicans aroused Polk's displeasure. While relations between the president and the general continued to deteriorate, Whig leaders John J. Crittenden and Thurlow Weed, among others, took an increasing interest in Taylor. He was a popular hero with an apolitical past; his political innocence was such, in fact, that he had never voted. Whig politicians looked forward to molding the general's ideology. Moreover they correctly assumed that popular clamor for a Taylor presidential candidacy coupled with his grievances against the Democratic administration would make him amenable to Whig overtures.[59]

To southern Whigs, Taylor seemed a godsend: a southern slaveholder who could nevertheless unite the party, attract Democratic votes (especially in the South), and win the presidency. Alexander H. Stephens of Georgia initiated a movement to draft Taylor. In December, 1846, Stephens formed a "Taylor-for-President" club among Whig congressmen. The charter members included Georgia's Stephens and Robert Toombs, three Virginians, an Alabaman, and two northerners (Abraham Lincoln and Truman Smith), who provided the club with "a necessary nationwide touch." Taylor's unexpected victory at Buena Vista in February, 1847, gave a dramatic boost to his candidacy. Southerners were especially attracted to the general, "because," in the words of the New Orleans *Bee*, "his nomination affords us a . . . chance of electing a Southern man to office. . . . When it is considered that both . . . parties at the North court the antislavery faction . . . the importance of placing at the head of the Government one who from birth, association and conviction, is identified with the South and who will uphold her rights . . . cannot fail to strike every candid mind."[60]

"Calhounites everywhere flocked to . . . [Taylor's] banner; some of Calhoun's friends even suggested an open alliance." A number of Carolinians persuaded themselves that Taylor, as a Louisiana cottonplanter owning more than a hundred slaves, perforce shared their concerns and would readily accept their advice on governmental policies. "I presume he [Taylor] is very little more of a Whig than you and I are Democrats," wrote Hammond to Simms, who concurred. "The more South Carolina delays in declaring herself with respect to . . . [Taylor's] nomination, the less naturally will be her influence upon his administration."[61]

Calhoun's Charleston speech, with its denunciation of party ties, furthered the notion that southerners regardless of party could rally to Taylor and make him the savior of southern interests. By late July, Calhoun believed that Taylor would "be the popular candidate, in opposition to the caucus nominees," and the South Carolinian toyed with the idea of supporting Taylor's candidacy. In May, Calhoun had "congratulated [Taylor supporter H. W.] Conner on redirecting [the Charleston] *Mercury*'s policy toward Taylor," and in August the senator "told Conner to consult with Ker Boyce and Franklin Harper Elmore on the strategy for organizing a Southern Taylor movement."[62]

Noting Taylor's "fair chance for . . . election by both parties or against both" and the general's apparent lack of "fixed political principles," Franklin Elmore was not enthusiastic about embracing Taylor's candidacy. If the hero ascended to the presidency "without a safe and steady and strong counsellor in his cabinet to keep him straight," the United States would have "exchange[d] the corruptions of party usage . . . for almost if not quite as dangerous a condition." Rhett, believing that the "Kentucky Whigs, with Crittenden at their head," would rule Taylor's administration, was even more skeptical about the general's desirability as a candidate.[63] But those South Carolinians who believed that Taylor's candidacy offered salvation for southern slavery did not recant. Taylor's reluctance to espouse Whig programs cost him support among party regulars.[64] Among the South Carolina gentry, however, Taylor's stock rose in inverse proportion to its decline with the Whig faithful.

During August and September, in letters that were both numerous and vaguely worded, Taylor piously reiterated his devotion to nation rather than party. In a letter to Dr. F. S. Bronson of Charleston, the general characterized himself as "a whig, not an ultra partisan Whig, but a decided Whig." However he also repeated "his determination to run only as a candidate of the people." Taylor's campaign for the remainder of 1847 allowed supporters to cherish different (and often contradictory) notions about the candidate's political beliefs. In December, John A. Campbell, who had supported Calhoun, still believed that southerners "must find a man who will not accept a party nomination. General Taylor is that man."[65]

In December the leading Democratic presidential candidate, Lewis Cass, officially launched his campaign and unveiled his solution to the problem of slavery in the territories. Cass also intended his doctrine of popular sovereignty as a compromise formula for reuniting the Democratic party. Senator Daniel S. Dickinson of New York, a Cass supporter, presented the popular sovereignty doctrine in resolutions for congressional approval. Dickinson's resolutions suggested that Congress's power over slavery in the territories was doubtful at best, that slavery was a "domestic policy" best decided by the inhabitants of the territories concerned, and that these inhabitants, acting through their territorial governments, could decide to establish or prohibit slavery.[66]

Senator Dickinson's political background should have inspired South Carolinians with a measure of confidence in his resolutions. He was a member of New York's Hunker faction, which had attacked the Barnburner faction's extreme advocacy of the proviso. Throughout 1847 the two groups had feuded. Barnburners characterized their rivals as "sycophants" and "southern mercenaries"; Hunkers replied that Barnburners were "African Democrats" and "factious agitators." Moreover, in embracing popular sovereignty as an alternative to the Wilmot Proviso, the Hunkers and other Cass supporters were embracing a modification of state-rights doctrine.[67]

But Calhoun and the rest of South Carolina's spokesmen pronounced popular sovereignty heresy. They believed that the distinction between territories and states was a crucial one. The power of inhabitants to ban slavery *during* the territorial stage was, according to the South Carolinians, not popular sovereignty but squatter sovereignty. The people who would decide slavery's fate were "pioneer settlers, adventurers, and those of Spanish and Mexican origin already on the ground, and there were few if any slaveholders among them." Therefore "in operative terms the Dickinson proposals would produce a free-soil result, quite as much as the Wilmot Proviso."[68]

Calhoun called for South Carolina "papers . . . [to] come out against Dickinson's resolutions," and the Charleston *Mercury* soon obliged him with "an almost hysterical attack against" the New Yorker's position. Lewis Cass's exposition of popular sovereignty (contained in a pro forma letter to A. O. P. Nicholson) was published in late December. Unlike Dickinson, Cass "did not specify at what stage of their political evolution the people of a territory were entitled to regulate slavery."[69] But South Carolina's politicians found popular sovereignty as unacceptable in the Nicholson letter as in the Dickinson resolutions.

Through the winter and spring of 1848 Taylor enjoyed far more popularity in South Carolina than Cass, but many of the state's politicians found Taylor's ideology (or lack of one) suspect; outside Charleston few were willing to endorse the Louisianan publicly. Congressman Armistead Burt warned Charleston's Democrats-for-Taylor that an organized movement for Taylor in the Palmetto State was both premature and divisive. Still Taylor's continuing pronouncements against party discipline and strict party ties and his endorsement by independents in Louisiana, Kentucky, and Mississippi heartened his South Carolina supporters to stand their ground. Taylor's political viability in the state survived publication of his letter to John Stadler Allison dated April 22, a carefully worded avowal of Whiggery that the general's political advisors had insisted was a sine qua non for the Whig nomination.[70]

In May the Democratic party proceeded, as expected, to nominate Lewis Cass as its candidate. Southern Democrats, again ignoring South Carolina's example, participated in the national convention. During that convention William Lowndes Yancey offered resolutions incorporating the "Alabama Platform," a pledge to support only a candidate who expressly "repudiated the idea that either Congress or a territorial legislature could exclude slavery from a territory." The assembled Democrats chose instead to repudiate Yancey's resolutions, and he stalked out of the convention. On his way home from Baltimore, Yancey "stopped at Charleston, where he delivered a passionate indictment of the Democratic nominee, whom he charged with holding Provisoist opinions." A number of South Carolinians already feared as much. The "refusal by the North and partly by the South and West to adopt Mr. Yancey's resolutions really looks as if the interests of *party* are to be the only tests and guaranty that we are hereafter to have," observed South Carolina House member William W. Harlee. "Is not Genl. Cass in favour of the Wilmot proviso upon principle?" Harlee asked Calhoun. "Outside South Carolina," however, "Yancey received a cool reception" from southern Democrats. "Many who had once [supported the Alabama Platform] . . . now roundly condemned his course."[71]

The national Democratic convention precipitated the Barnburners' official renunciation of their party and began the final series of maneuvers that led Barnburners, militantly antislavery Whigs, and Liberty party members to the Free Soil Convention at Buffalo. The Barnburners had long nursed intraparty grudges unrelated to the issue of slavery in the territories. The national convention's endorsement of popular sovereignty rather than the Wilmot Proviso was as much the occasion as the cause for the Barnburners' revolt.[72] Their separate convention, held in June at Utica, New York, was privately concerned with revenge, but publicly it called for northerners to vote an end to slavery's expansion.

The Barnburners' stand attracted the close attention of groups primarily concerned with restricting slavery but lacking the Barnburners' electoral power: "conscience Whigs" in Massachusetts, supporters of Joshua Giddings and George Julian in the Midwest, and those Liberty party leaders who were anxious to expand their electoral strength, even at the risk of diluting their abolitionist principles.[73] Barnburners, antislavery Whigs, and Liberty party men overcame their mutual (and well-founded) dislike for each other and achieved coalition. Early in August they formed the Free-Soil party with a ticket that offered arch-Barnburner Martin Van Buren for president and conscience-Whig Charles Francis Adams for vicepresident. The platform borrowed liberally from Liberty party doctrines and asserted that "the national government ought to abolish slavery whenever such action became constitutional."[74]

Meanwhile congressional attempts to reach a compromise settlement on the territories had ended in failure. The Clayton Compromise—which, in effect, banned slavery in Oregon and referred a final decision on slavery's legality in the Mexican cession territories to the Supreme Court—passed the Senate but failed in the House. Both free-soil and proslavery congressmen feared that the judicial branch would decide against them. Moreover the impending presidential election overshadowed congressional activity. The Whigs, enjoying more unity than the Democrats, sensed victory for their standard-bearer in the fall and "had no desire to help the Democrats achieve a triumphant solution of the sectional impasse." On August 12 Congress narrowly succeeded in establishing Oregon as a free-soil territory; adjournment followed two days later, and Whigs and Democrats rushed home to join electoral battle in earnest. The "attitude of the candidates toward slavery extension, an issue that both major parties would have preferred to avoid, quickly and inexorably came to dominate the discussion of each candidate's merits."[75]

On the issue of slavery extension, the Whigs, by heroic effort, managed to surpass the Democrats in evasion and ambiguity; while the Democrats had adopted a platform endorsing popular sovereignty, the Whigs had adopted no platform at all. South Carolinians were especially frustrated by the ensuing confusion. They distrusted both Cass and his popular sovereignty doctrine. But the support that Taylor enjoyed from such antislavery politicians as Seward, Lincoln, and Benjamin Wade hardly inspired the Carolinians with confidence in Taylor's soundness on slavery. Cass was "exceedingly obnoxious to a So. Ca. republican . . . when considered as the representative of the radical democracy of the North," observed Ephraim M. Seabrook, a state representative from St. John's, Colleton. But he also found "strong objections to General Taylor . . . his ignorance of politics and therefore his liability to be made the tool of bad and designing men."[76]

Hoping that disenchantment with both candidates prevailed elsewhere in the South, Calhoun sought to revive the Southern party movement. He concentrated his attack on Cass, whose popular sovereignty doctrine offered the Carolinian a more substantial target than Taylor's patriotic homilies. Outside South Carolina, however, the strength and vitality of the traditional party organizations quickly put an end to Calhoun's dreams; southern politicians and their constituents generally remained loyal Whigs or Democrats. Realizing this James Hammond delivered an acid critique of Calhoun's actions: "Mr. C. as some others think that . . . [one has] but to say nigger to the South to set it afire. . . . no man having any pretensions to the Presidency would or could take his ground, and he hoped to be thus made an independent Slavery Candidate. But you see, three fourths of the negro country have repudiated it. Why persist in it?"[77]

On July 20 Charleston's Democrats-for-Taylor proclaimed their formal existence. By early August they were publishing their own organ (*The Palo Alto*), with Simms, among others, contributing editorial advice and copy. The group's leaders intended to appropriate Taylor as the candidate of the South rather than of the Whigs. Accordingly their ticket was composed of Taylor and William O. Butler of Kentucky (the regular Democratic nominee for vice-president). The "political maneuvering of the Taylorites centered not on Taylor's Southerness but on the general's usefulness" in clearing the way for a southern party. Charleston's Taylorites planned "to avoid absorption in the 'Great Democratic party of the North—who . . . desert us when in power. . . . and instead of going to the Wigs [*sic*] . . . ultimately [to] bring the Southern Wigs to us and produce . . . [unity] in the Slave States.' "[78]

"Neutrality on your part," wrote Taylorite James Gadsden to Calhoun, "will distract" the state. Despite this and other such pleas, on September 1 Calhoun announced that he could not choose between Taylor and Cass. A pro-Cass rally had already been staged in Charleston, and Calhoun's neutrality declaration accelarated a South Carolina reaction against Taylor which had been fueled by the belief that he represented "all the hated Whig 'consolidationist' heresies." With Calhoun's restraining hand removed, the campaign also provided the state's politicians with a rare opportunity to choose sides for the sake of indulging personal rivalries and settling old scores.[79]

Rhett decided, after all, that the Democrats (with the Barnburners removed from their ranks) were a lesser evil than the Whigs. South Carolina's Hotspur, therefore, assumed leadership of the state's anti-Taylor forces. He had vigorous allies in the up-country in Burt and Perry. Senator Butler and Congressman Richard F. Simpson also declared Cass to be less objectionable than Taylor and worked for the regular Democratic ticket.[80]

Early in September the state's anti-Taylor leaders were immeasurably aided by the publication of two documents: Taylor's second Allison letter and Millard Fillmore's ten-year-old letter to the Erie County Antislavery Society. In the first the Whig presidential nominee superseded the numerous "letters or scrapes of letters" implying his independence from party with a final and definitive assertion of

Whiggery. In the second the Whig vice-presidential nominee had indicated his support for abolishing slavery in the District of Columbia and for "exercising all the constitutional power . . . [Congress] possesses to abolish the internal slave trade between . . . [southern] states." Taylor's refusal to pronounce an opinion on the Wilmot Proviso and his pledge to eschew "the coercion of the veto" worried many South Carolina leaders; Fillmore's letter gave them visions of a Free-Soiler or worse in the White House.[81]

By contrast with Whig possibilities, Cass's attitude toward the proviso seemed much less obnoxious than it once had. Replying to an inquiry from Elmore, Cass noted that for "thirty years . . . [prohibitions of slavery were] successfully applied to our territorial governments, and no one had a doubt respecting . . . [them], north or south." But, Cass claimed, soon after the Wilmot Proviso's introduction, "I opposed . . . it. . . . Not on the ground of its unconstitutionality. . . . But because I considered it inexpedient and injurious." He added that he still thought so.[82]

The October elections for the state legislature revealed a victory for the Taylorites in Charleston but nowhere else in South Carolina. The "Southern State Rights Republican Party," as the Taylorite group was styled, "died quietly in its infancy." When the legislature met to choose presidential electors, the representatives from Pendleton (Calhoun's home district) suggested that "South Carolina . . . [could not] consistently with her long cherished principles . . . vote for either Gen. Cass or Gen. Taylor." Opting finally for expediency rather than principle, however, the legislators divided between Cass and Taylor: Cass electors were chosen by a vote of 129 to 27.[83] The Electoral College chose otherwise, and South Carolina waited with misgivings to learn the president-elect's policy on slavery in the territories.

5

The failure of Calhoun's call for a Southern party in 1847 tempered but did not destroy South Carolina's determination to confront the North's hardening antislavery opinions and multiplying antislavery enactments—opinions and laws that the proviso symbolized. Calhoun and his lieutenants considered a plan to organize Southern Rights Associations throughout the South, but the region's lack of enthusiasm forced temporary abandonment of this idea. From September through November, however, at Edgefield, Darlington, Anderson, Laurens, Greenville, and elsewhere, South Carolina bristled with public meetings denouncing the proviso. The Darlington and Anderson meetings called on southern representatives to withdraw from Congress and return to their home states for consultation if the proviso became law. At the Greenville meeting Waddy Thompson warned that passage of the proviso would make the "alternatives before you . . . resistance at all hazards . . . to this insulting, degrading and fatal measure, or the conversion of the South into black provinces." B. F. Perry had asked Calhoun to dictate resolutions on the proviso for this meeting; following Calhoun's guidance Perry drafted and presented the resolutions adopted at Greenville.[84]

In July, Perry had decided to run for Congress, and in the fall he began his campaign "by speaking against the Wilmot Proviso in the principal towns of the congressional district, which now included Laurens as well as Pendleton and Greenville election districts." In Pickens judicial district, where slaveowners were relatively few, Perry's speech emphasized racial rather than economic consequences of the proviso. While it would "cut off all out let for . . . [slave] property, and make it valueless," the proviso would also embolden "Northern abolitionists [to attempt] to place the Southern Slave on an equality . . . with the white man. He is to go with him to the polls and vote, to serve on juries . . . to meet the white man as his equal . . . intermarry with his children, and form one society and one family!"[85]

Perry subscribed to Calhoun's analysis of abolitionism's impact on Northern party politics as well as the senator's classification of northern voters. The Greenville native was confident that a demonstration of southern unity against the proviso would restore in the North a due respect for the slaveholding rights guaranteed "by plain express provisions in the Federal Constitution." And Perry supported a convention of the slaveholding states to warn the North against encroaching on those rights.[86]

Perry envisioned the convention as a temporary expedient. He noted "favorable symptoms" in the North: the antiproviso views of Secretary of State Buchanan and Vice-President Dallas, "[p]ublic meetings in opposition to the Proviso . . . in New York, Pennsylvania and other free States." His campaign stressed his attachment to Union *and* slavery. Perry eventually lost his bid for a congressional seat, but his effort was not hampered by timidity in denouncing the proviso. In 1847–48 Perry was willing to "declare that any interference, on the part of the Federal Government, with our Slave property, will be the cause of an immediate dissolution of this great and hitherto glorious Union."[87]

Governor David Johnson, Perry's erstwhile Unionist ally, bewailed at length the increasing affinity between northern state legislatures, free-soil politicians, and antislavery groups, but he was unwilling to risk another southern reaction against Palmetto extremism; regarding federal relations his message to the legislature recommended only a reassertion (in language already endorsed by several other states) of the Wilmot Proviso's unconstitutionality and a pledge to resist it. A resolution instructing the governor to convene the legislature immediately upon congressional approval unanimously passed the senate, but it failed in the house. In order that a presidential veto "may continue to be available," concluded W. F. DeSaussure, chairman of the South Carolina House's Committee on Federal Relations, "it is manifest that we must look well to the Presidential election."[88]

With the rest of the South preoccupied by the presidential contest, South Carolina became increasingly, if reluctantly, involved in the debate over which candidate offered greater security for slavery. But calls for other solutions to the free-soil threat continued in the midst of the presidential campaign. Burt and Johnson swelled the echo for a southern convention. "How long," Johnson wondered, "will Maryland, Western Virginia, Kentucky, Eastern Tennessee and even the Western part of No. Carolina feel it their interest to retain slaves." Even without them, he decided, "there will be yet strength enough in the remaining states to make their rights respected if they can be brought to act in concert. A Southern Convention is the only means of accomplishing this." H. W. Conner agreed that "any separate or independent action of the state—at least . . . until all efforts for a joint action of the Slave States . . . [fail, would be] fatal to the very object we were all driving at."[89]

Rhett, however, did not believe a southern convention could be organized; even if it could, it might "only breed confusion and weakness in the South." Rhett was for action "by the States—the parties to the Constitutional compact. . . . Let [them] instruct their Senators, and request the representatives, to leave their seats in Congress immediately . . . should Abolition in any of its forms prevail in . . . Congress." Warmed by his words Rhett suggested that if necessary "South Carolina, unaided and alone . . . can compel the alternative—that the rights of the South be respected, or the Union be dissolved." The Charleston *Evening News* opposed Rhett's ideas, while the *Mercury* soon supported them.[90]

Assailed by conflicting advice, the legislature assembled for the annual session of 1848. Rice-planter Robert F. W. Allston anticipated a "stormy session; differences of opinion as to our Federal Relations," he wrote his wife, "are about to divide us again into two parties." Among numerous other proposals resolutions envisioning independent action by South Carolina were offered by Charleston's John Carew (editor of the *Mercury*) and Lawrence Maissillon Keitt, a young fire-eater from Orange Parish. But a caucus of all legislators agreed on a single, moderate resolution pledging South Carolina's willingness to cooperate with other slave states in resisting the proviso. In making this decision the legislature followed the advice of Calhoun and Governor Johnson. The governor's message, which issued yet another call for a southern convention, pointed a moral of the nullification movement: "No . . . State can reasonably hope for success, when acting alone [and] in opposition to the opinions of all the others."[91] Radicals, however, could take comfort from the gubernatorial election; the victor was Whitemarsh Benjamin Seabrook, the candidate whom Blufftonites had supported for governor in 1844.

While the South Carolina legislature called for a united southern front, Calhoun worked to achieve one among the South's representatives in Washington. By Calhoun's lights the South's response to the proviso between December, 1846, and December, 1848, had not been promising. Southern politicians outside South Carolina "were strongly enough opposed to the Wilmot Proviso to accept Calhoun's constitutional objections to it, [but] they did not view it as a northern gambit to a full-scale assault on" slavery as Calhoun and his followers did.[92] Except in South Carolina, the slave states' politicians "tended to focus [their] attention on the specific issue raised by the Wilmot Proviso rather than the slavery question as a whole." Thus the Virginia legislature in March, 1847, promised to resist the Wilmot Proviso "at all hazards and to the last extremity." The language of the "Virginia Resolutions" was quickly appropriated by legislatures, state-party conventions, and local political rallies across the South.[93]

But the best efforts of Calhoun loyalists did not destroy the South's confidence that slavery could be protected through existing party mechanisms; nor did those efforts assuage hostility toward South Carolina politics and politicians. Georgia Whigs in particular "appealed to the traditional . . . feeling against the neighboring state" and ridiculed the "mighty warriors of Palmettodom." The Savannah *Republican* prophesied "that Georgia will not become an appendage of this political comet [South Carolina]—which is ever ready to dash into the midst of our glorious constellation of stars and destroy the harmony of their orbits."[94]

When a series of antislavery measures climaxing with Daniel Gott's resolution appeared early in the second session of the Thirtieth Congress,[95] Calhoun "made his supreme effort" to achieve southern unity in Congress. He intended to cement this alliance and state its goals with the Southern Address. The possibility of a southern bloc, however, began to dissipate during the southerners' first caucus. The Whigs had just elected Zachary Taylor president and were in no mood to hamper the incoming administration. Too, a number of northern congressmen abandoned the Gott resolution. In December the House had passed it by a vote of 98 to 88; in January the House reconsidered it by a vote of 119 to 81. "Fundamentally, however, neither the tactical retreat of the free-soilers nor the southern distrust of Calhoun would have neutralized . . . [his] movement if most southerners had not believed that . . . a Louisiana slaveholder would solve their problems. They regarded Taylor as their man."[96] Beverley Tucker captured both this faith in Taylor and the distrust of Calhoun in one of his elegant images: "It is especially desirable that General T[aylor] . . . by manifesting . . . [his] loyalty to the South . . . will give the deadliest blow to that mischievous faction of which C[alhoun] is the head, and Rhett the tail (it is you know a sort of political amphisbaena and sometimes goes tail foremost)."[97]

Southern Whigs suffered moments of uncertainty about Taylor's attitude toward the proviso, but they suppressed their doubts and dismissed his association with antislavery Whigs on grounds of his political inexperience. "Only gradually did they learn that they had played an incredible trick on themselves." Taylor's brief, noncommittal inaugural address hardly reassured southern planters that the president had their interests at heart. James Hammond did "not like the inaugural *nor the appointments*. Altogether they look[ed] very much as if Taylor had surrendered entirely to . . . the rabid— Whigs. I fear he will . . . throw cold water on our side of the Slave question."[98]

Less than a month after Taylor took office, William H. Seward (a man southern Whigs regarded as extremely antislavery) emerged as the president's most influential advisor. Seward's influence seemed clearly evident in Taylor's decision to encourage Californians to apply directly for statehood, bypassing the territorial stage and avoiding the question of slavery's legality under a territorial government. California's newly discovered gold had drawn thousands of immigrants to the West Coast, making the lack of government there an acute problem—and this increased the likelihood that California would eventually become a free state. Taylor was persuaded that a free-soil government in California was far better than no government at all; in April 1849 he sent Thomas B. King to speed California's government-making process. Taylor's continuing reliance on antislavery Whigs, first openly demonstrated by the King mission, "precipitated a very severe, even violent, reaction in the South."[99]

Southern state legislators and local groups of planters "had responded to Calhoun's [Southern] Address . . . far more heartily than had the southerners in Congress, whose party ties, both Whig and Democratic, made them reluctant to act in a context which separated them from their northern affiliates." In January 1849 the Virginia legislators had requested the governor, if Congress passed either the proviso or legislation hostile to slavery in the District of Columbia, to convene the legislature immediately so that Virginia could make an appropriate response. During the winter and early spring, denunciations of the proviso and promises of cooperative resistance came from North Carolina, Florida, and Missouri—states with a reputation for moderation on issues involving slavery. And in organizing resistance to federal measures, South Carolina was once again far ahead of the other slave states.[100]

In November 1848 a group of Fairfield District planters met at Winnsboro and revived Calhoun's idea of creating local Southern Rights Associations. The Fairfield association instructed its committee of correspondence, chaired by John H. Means, to encourage the establishment of similar associations throughout the South. In the winter and spring of 1849, these associations blossomed across the Palmetto State. The Sumter organization called for delegates from each association to meet in Columbia and establish a Central Committee of Safety. Seconding this proposal, Richland's association invited delegates to meet in the capital city on May 14. On that Monday, Daniel Huger presided over an assembly of 109 delegates, representing 29 Southern Rights Associations.[101]

In acknowledging the invitation to Georgetown's association, R. F. W. Allston replied that there was "much difference of opinion amongst us here as to . . . policy," adding that he hoped "respective differences may be harmonized throughout the State" by the convention. Calhoun, aware of the convention's potential for dissonance as well as harmony, had advised the planners to concern themselves with perfecting an organization rather than recommending any

immediate or direct action; that advice was reflected in the decisions
made at the convention. Its resolutions were restrained: an approval
of the Virginia legislature's January actions, a recommendation
that the South Carolina legislature follow suit, and the appointment
of a five-member Central State Committee of Vigilance and Safety.
Even B. F. Perry could (and did) hail the convention's call for "concerted and united measures . . . with other Committees and persons
in . . . other States."[102] And, in fact, an opportunity for interstate
cooperation had just been presented by a convention in Mississippi.

On May 7 a group of prominent Mississippians, including Governor Joseph W. Matthews and Chief Justice William L. Sharkey of
the state's supreme court, met at Jackson to protest the trend of
antislavery agitation in Congress and northern state legislatures.
This group proposed that a statewide convention meet in October.
Delegates to the October convention were to be equally divided
between Whigs and Democrats and were to be selected by public
meetings in each county. Leaders of the Mississippi movement corresponded with South Carolina officials, and Governor Seabrook
asked Congressman Daniel Wallace to serve as his envoy and observer at the October convention. Wallace eagerly accepted the
mission.[103]

In South Carolina, Seabrook initiated plans to strengthen defensive fortifications and increase military preparedness. On these and
other matters, South Carolina's Central Committee of Vigilance
and Safety acted as a quasi-official advisory body to the governor.
Franklin Elmore, chairman of the central committee, cautioned
Seabrook against hasty decisions on the kinds and quantities of
arms to purchase for the state. Elmore suggested that a stronger
guard on the United States arsenal in Charleston was a more immediate need. If security was not improved, he warned, the city's
black draymen, carriage drivers, and hostlers might easily convert
themselves into cavalry: "Denmark Vesey's plan in 1822 was based
on this very class of men."[104]

Seabrook, again in consultation with the central committee, questioned southern governors about the willingness of their states to
join in cooperative resistance to the proviso. In addition to these
written inquiries and the projected mission of Daniel Wallace, Elmore advised the governor to send Christopher Memminger to
confer with Kentucky officials (a trip Memminger himself had suggested). Elmore also urged the governor to exploit the propaganda
apparatus of the "South Carolina associations." While suspicious of
the southern Whigs, Elmore believed that Taylor's policies would

soon force them to abandon his administration. The chairman of the central committee was optimistic about prospects for southern unity despite some discouraging replies.[105]

The first of these came from Governor W. D. Mosley, who could not "*warrant* the co-operation of Florida in such measures as are . . . alone calculated to give security to the South." The "chief obstacle to unanimity," the Florida governor opined, was the tendency of "many Southerners to . . . [view the Proviso either] as a mere abstraction . . . [or as a boon to] the prospective welfare of the poor or non-slaveholding portion of the Southern People." From Tennessee, Calhoun received word that a "large party . . . [was] disposed to cater for Northern support. Mr. [John] Bell stands at the front, having . . . [admitted] the constitutionality of the Wilmot proviso. . . . Bell carries with him nearly all of the leading Whigs of the State." Herschel V. Johnson, Calhoun's senate colleague from Georgia, reported that his state's Democratic convention "went a little further on the doctrine of noninterference than any other convention in the South (except Carolina) has gone." But, despite "much excitement . . . upon the slavery question" among Georgia Democrats, Johnson "seriously feared that the people of the South . . . [were] not properly awake to the danger—not thoroughly nerved to united resistance." Wilson Lumpkin could not muster even such qualified optimism.[106]

Yet the South Carolinians were not discouraged. They were receiving unexpected (and unintentional) aid from Taylor, whose speeches during a northern tour drove Whigs of the deep South into despair. Except for Rhett, Palmetto leaders were willing to wait for the southern convention that they confidently expected to be the outcome of Mississippi's bipartisan, state convention in October.[107]

Collin S. Tarpley, one of the organizers of that convention, had asked Calhoun to suggest an agenda for the convention. Calhoun replied that a southern convention was essential. The time, place, and representational scheme for such a convention should be proposed by the Mississippians. "No state could better take the lead in this great conservative movement than yours. It is destined to be the greatest of sufferers if the Abolitionists should succeed; and I am not certain but by the time your convention meets, or at furthest your Legislature, that the time will have come to make the call." In late September, Senator Henry S. Foote informed Calhoun that leaders "of both the two great political parties in Mississippi, have promised me at our approaching Convention, to act upon your suggestion relative to the recommendation of a Southern Convention."[108]

Enthusiasm for a southern convention remained high because the divisive question of its exact purpose had been muted. Southern Unionists, both Whigs and Democrats, were determined to secure guarantees of slaveholders' rights and were confident that they could succeed in this. Perry, for example, believed that a show of southern unity would "preserve the Constitution, the Union and . . . [the slave states'] own honor and rights." He did not anticipate a "dissolution even on the subject of slavery. It will be settled like all great questions have, since the organization of our government." Mississippians Sharkey and Foote were of a like mind. Calhoun was more pessimistic but did expect, at the least, that a southern convention "would have a powerful effect on Congress." If the convention failed to elicit adequate federal safeguards for slavery, the South would accept disunion as its only alternative.[109]

During the first week of October, the Mississippi convention transacted its public business. The convention's resolutions, notable for militant language rather than novel argument, culminated with a call for delegates from the slaveholding states to meet in Nashville, Tennessee, on June 3, 1850 "to devise and adopt some mode of resistance to . . . [antislavery] aggressions." To insure representation of both Whigs and Democrats at Nashville, the convention chose twelve delegates (twice the total of Mississippi's congressional delegation) and invited the other states to adopt this ratio in selecting their delegates. Seemingly, the Mississippians had provided "[a]ll that Calhoun and his South Carolina followers had wanted . . . without the hindering factors of jealousy and distrust."[110]

In fact the consensus displayed at the October convention was tenuous. A number of Whigs suspected that Daniel Wallace had attended the convention to impose a South Carolina plan upon it or to influence Mississippi's gubernatorial election. The South Carolina congressman, therefore, abandoned his hopes of addressing the convention. Although his movements were "closely watched," Wallace did arrange interviews with Justice William Sharkey, Governor Joseph Matthews, and Democratic gubernatorial candidate John Quitman.[111]

Sharkey, who presided over the convention, declared that Mississippi "could not exist as a political community without the institution of Slavery." Impressed by such rhetoric Wallace believed that Sharkey was "thoroughly roused and most *thoroughly Southern* on the subject" of defending slavery and that Mississippi Whigs would be "*obliged to follow his lead.*" In conversation with Wallace, Governor Matthews pledged to seek an immediate constituent convention if Congress passed the Wilmot Proviso (a course of action suggested in one of the convention's resolutions). Quitman took pride in the Whig accusation that he was "ultra on all questions of Federal policy . . . *a Nullifier of 1832, and in a word . . . a politician of the South Carolina School.* . . . Should I be elected," he told Wallace, "Mississippi will make common cause with the Slave States who go for resistance."[112]

According to Matthews and Quitman, Mississippi would support resistance measures, but neither would assert, before the fact, that Mississippians would support any and all actions that South Carolina might take. Wallace failed to obtain for Seabrook's use an official "declaration of the course of action . . . [the Mississippi governor] intended to pursue" during the remainder of his term (which expired January 1, 1850). The South Carolina congressman was appalled by the "extent of . . . prejudice against South Carolina, on account of the Doctrines of 1832." He conceded that Mississippi's "Democrats were driven to their utmost skill, to keep the Whigs in the right place, and in order to do this, it was a part of their policy to *keep South Carolina as much out of sight as possible.*" Wallace was assured, however, that because South Carolina "had not assumed the lead . . . Mississippi would wheel up into line more willingly." And he was encouraged to find "the people of Mississippi warmer upon the subject [of defending slavery] than any people . . . [he had] met." He was "fully persuaded that . . . [Mississippi will be] with us when the hour of struggle comes."[113]

South Carolinians were encouraged, too, by state elections during the late summer and fall of 1849. In Kentucky, Tennessee, North Carolina, and Georgia, candidates who emphasized loyalty to slavery and section triumphed over less militant southerners. In Georgia, where Democrats captured the governorship and won control of the legislature, party organs in the middle and lower part of the state "hailed . . . [the elections] as a victory for southern-rights over Whig 'submissionism'." In Alabama, Governor Reuben Chapman planned to recommend "that provision be made for convening the [Alabama] legislature immediately upon the passage of the proviso or any similar measure, or the admission of California as a state through the agency above alluded to."[114]

Cheered by events of the past several months, South Carolina's legislators eagerly assembled in late November. In a much different mood, the nation's legislators were also gathering. The men in Columbia and the men in Washington were facing a political crisis—and they knew it.

CHAPTER V

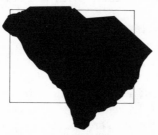

"In the Hands of
the Compromisers"

1

There would be no protection for southern rights, Governor Seabrook warned the South Carolina legislature on November 27, 1849, "when the Northern States, by territorial aggrandizement . . . shall have secured an undisputed ascendancy in the councils of the nation. To force on such a result is now obviously the aim of the enemy, and the non-extension of slavery furnishes a plausible plea to cover their real design." But he held out hope: "The South has at last been aroused from its criminal lethargy. . . . For the first time in our political history, party affinities are becoming merged in the higher obligation of cooperation for the sake of safety." Seabrook "hail[ed] with satisfaction the proposition of Mississippi for a Convention of the people of the Southern States, and ardently hope[d] that it . . . [would] meet with a warm and unanimous response."[1]

To prepare the Palmetto State for the crisis in federal relations, Seabrook had both political and military recommendations. He asked for statutory authority either to convene the legislature or "to issue writs of election for a Convention of the People, should [Congress pass] the Wilmot Proviso, or any kindred measure." He suggested the "reestablishment of Brigade Encampments," and he called for the organization of a new militia division composed of infantry, artillery, and a "Cavalry force . . . always ready for duty" (this new division would require more than six thousand men). Finally he requested a $50,000 appropriation for the purchase of arms and a $30,000 appropriation for the military contingencies fund.[2]

Seabrook, in keeping with strategy dictated by Calhoun, understated South Carolina's role in the convention movement and carefully avoided rhetoric that would justify charges of South Carolina dictation. Calhoun, in fact, feared that Seabrook's deferential tone might be overdone. Unless South Carolina quickly and enthusiastically accepted the Mississippi proposal, "other states will be backward to move. As jealous as they may be of us, they still look to us to give the signal. Nor . . . [did Calhoun] think that we should make the meeting depend on the coming of eight, or any other number of states." Calhoun urged Hammond to add his "influence to induce the members of our Legislature to appoint delegates." The senator had also moved speedily to quash an effort to make the Nashville Convention a Calhoun presidential vehicle.[3] The old Carolinian knew his health was failing, and he wanted nothing to disrupt his final bid for southern unity.

For four successive nights beginning on December 7, South Carolina's legislators met in caucus to arrange the state's representation at Nashville. They recommended that public meetings in each electoral district select delegates to conventions in the state's seven congressional districts; each of these conventions would choose two delegates to represent the district at Nashville. South Carolina would elect fourteen Southern Convention delegates by this process. And the legislators, in their final caucus, elected four delegates-at-large: Langdon Cheves, Franklin Elmore, Robert Barnwell, and James Hammond. "All were men who had served in Congress and enjoyed national reputations. It was a selection designed to show the South and the country as a whole that South Carolina would take the Nashville Convention very seriously."[4] The legislators empowered Seabrook to call them into session should Congress enact the proviso. They were not yet ready to fund his proposed military measures, but they did appropriate $7,500 more for the "Military Contengencies" fund than they had approved the previous year.[5]

Calhoun's letter to Hammond and Hammond's election as a delegate to Nashville indicated that the ambitious master of Silver Bluff was returning to political favor in the Palmetto State. Once again he was calculating his chances of representing South Carolina in the Senate. Although he privately moaned about receiving fewer votes than South Carolina's other delegates-at-large, Hammond relished his new opportunities to sway state and sectional councils. He heard with satisfaction the assurances of friends that he should take the lead in the movement for southern unity. "Ambition [should] look forward to the high rewards which popular favour is eager to bestow, at the end of any revolutionary movement, on those who began it," wrote Beverley Tucker pointedly. And by the end of December, Hammond boasted of "hav[ing] started the Georgia Constitutionalist and the Repubic agitating for a [Georgia] Convention to send Delegates to Nashville."[6]

2

Chaos prevailed in the House of Representatives during the opening weeks of the Thirty-First Congress; the sound of angry voices seemed the leitmotif of disunion. "Resourcefulness in invective waxed and waned while the impulse to invective only waxed."[7] The representatives assembled daily, but the House remained unorganized. After the rival factions had struggled for ten days over the speakership, Virginia's Richard K. Meade "said plainly what everybody knew—that it was no partisan question but a battle to control certain committees of the House."[8] It seemed typical of the House's problems that Meade's speech began with a plea against the continuing strife and almost ended in a fistfight.

At stake was the speaker's power to promote or obstruct crucial bills on slavery in the territories and in the District of Columbia, and no candidate could be found whose politics or promises were trusted by a majority of the House. Democrats enjoyed a narrow plurality, but Free-Soilers held the votes necessary to give either of the major parties victory. The situation was complicated by southern Whigs and southern Democrats who refused to support the nominees of their respective parties. According to Robert Toombs, he and fellow-Georgian Alexander H. Stephens had arrived in Washington and found "the whole Whig party expecting to pass the Proviso and that Taylor *would not veto it.*" When the Whig caucus refused to guarantee certain rights of slaveholders, Toombs, Stephens, and four other southern Whigs refused to vote for Massachusetts's Robert Winthrop, the caucus's nominee for speaker. Similarly South Carolina's Isaac Holmes led a small group of Calhoun partisans who adamantly opposed Georgia's Howell Cobb, the favorite of the Democratic caucus, because they considered him "merely a southern man with northern principles." The Free-Soilers, in turn, offered David Wilmot for speaker.[9]

On December 12 William J. Brown of Indiana, a Democratic substitute for Cobb, fell only two votes short of the necessary majority. Brown's total included the votes of six Free-Soilers; suspicious southerners quickly forced the Indianan to concede that he had promised to "constitute the committees on the District of Columbia, on the territories, and on the Judiciary in such a manner as shall be satisfactory to" David Wilmot and Preston King. "Indescribable confusion followed—threats, violent gesticulations, calls to order, and demands for adjournment were mingled together," the *Congressional Globe* reported. Brown's candidacy collapsed, and the struggle over the speakership continued. On December 23, after the House agreed to elect the speaker by a plurality, Cobb finally emerged as the victor.[10]

Robert Allston, president of the South Carolina Senate, hoped, meanwhile, that the speakership battle "and the excitement consequent upon it will serve to assure our Northern friends of the feeling which pervades the Southern Country on the subject of slavery. . . . Unless the Northern People now come to be reasonable people, Revolution will be unavoidable. It were better to settle the matter now than have to leave it to our children." But Cobb's election as speaker lessened Calhoun's chances for saving the Union on South Carolina's terms. According to the old Carolinian, Cobb "was forced on us by the Northern democrats as they call themselves, but free soilers as they should be called . . . and the only reason they rallied on him was, that he was the least true of all the Southern members . . . to the South."[11]

In Calhoun's analysis the "great, pressing, practical question of the session will be on the admission of California." The senator regarded California's entry into the Union, under the terms proposed by Californians, "as worse than the Wilmot Proviso. What the latter proposes to do openly the former . . . [will] do covertly and fraudulently." The *Mercury*, a faithful voice of Calhoun orthodoxy, began warning in late December of 1849 that "the real danger to the South lay neither in the Wilmot Proviso nor the moves against slavery in the District. The true danger lay in the pending admission of California to the Union; her constitution had been drafted by Whig-appointed antislavery agents."[12]

President Taylor's message to Congress, submitted January 21, 1850, proposed that the legislators do precisely what the South

Carolinians found most objectionable: admit California and New Mexico as soon as their residents petitioned for statehood.[13] Taylor expected California's application shortly, since a convention held at Monterey the previous fall had completed a state constitution—one that barred slavery. Moreover the civil government established by that constitution had begun operating on December 21. South Carolina's planter-politicians responded to the president's message by denouncing California's existing government as "manufactured . . . contrived and carried out by" Taylor and his agents. "California is first to be fraudulently introduced into the Union, and then to be used both as a precedent and a positive power for introducing the other Territories."[14]

Eight days after the delivery of Taylor's message on the territories, Henry Clay dramatically resumed his role as the Great Pacificator and stepped center stage. Having returned to the Senate after a seven-year absence, the old Kentuckian was eager to justify the title bestowed for his part in the Missouri Compromise of 1820 and the Compromise Tariff of 1833. Through January, Clay had watched and waited for the proper moment. In the House the sectional jealousies and tensions that had produced the speakership battle spilled over into skirmishes for minor offices, including the "exalted post of doorkeeper." In the Senate, however, the atmosphere in late January seemed more favorable to compromise.[15] Unsatisfied with Taylor's solution to the sectional impasse, Clay called on Webster, and the New Englander promised to support Clay's efforts. On January 29 Clay judged that the time was ripe for presentation of an "amicable arrangement of all questions in controversy between the free and the slave States, growing out of the subject of slavery."[16]

Clay's "amicable arrangement" was embodied in eight resolutions. The first called for California's admission to the Union without congressional preconditions regarding slavery—in effect California would be admitted as a free state. The second proposed that the remaining area obtained from Mexico—New Mexico and Deseret[17]—be organized under territorial governments that neither sanctioned nor prohibited slavery. The third would fix Texas's boundary far short of its claims in New Mexico; as compensation for surrendering these claims, the fourth resolution stipulated that the federal government would assume Texas's public debt.[18] The fifth resolution stressed the inexpedience of abolishing slavery in the District of Columbia, while the sixth provided for abolition of the slave trade there. The seventh resolution urged enactment of a new, more effective fugitive slave law, and the eighth asserted that Congress had no authority to interfere with the interstate slave trade. The Kentuckian's defense of his resolutions and of the Union began on February 5 and continued the next day. In his peroration, Clay "ask[ed] every senator . . . to examine the plan of accommodation which this series of resolutions propose[d], and not to pronounce against them until convinced after a thorough examination."[19]

It took the South Carolina gentry little time to pronounce Clay's plan not a compromise but a series of concessions by the South. Clay had promised to "go with the furthest Senator from the South . . . to impose the heaviest sanctions upon the recovery of fugitive slaves, and the restoration of them to their owners." Carolina radicals, however, believed that northern public opinion would make any fugitive slave law unenforceable. Moreover the "admission of California, with its present Southern boundary, and the surrender to Congress of the *right in any way* to legislate upon the slave trade in the District would be . . . an abandonment of the whole question." The District slave trade could not "be yielded without opening a door for the exercise of the same power wherever Congress claims a jurisdiction." There was, warned the *Mercury*, "*danger in any admission of* [congressional] *power*" over slavery. This was Calhoun's interpretation, and it was reiterated more violently by a number of favored correspondents: "Listen not to false hopes, or to those prophets who cry peace! peace! when there is no peace. But resist every encroachment on your just rights, by measures 'short, sharp and decisive.' Giving up an inch today is equivalent to a mile next year."[20]

Rather than give space to Clay's program, the *Mercury* preferred to concentrate first on the North's implacable hostility to slavery and slaveholders and secondly on the South's increasing unity. To document the first, the Charleston paper poured forth a stream of antislavery editorials and resolutions culled from the northern press and the records of northern legislatures.[21] The *Mercury* found impressive evidence of the second in a speech by Congressman Thomas L. Clingman, a Whig from western North Carolina where slaves were few. Clingman's demand that slaveholders share occupancy of the territories showed "how baseless . . . [were] the calculations of those who have supposed that . . . only the large slaveholders . . . care to resist the aggressions of Abolitionists and only they . . . would shrink from being placed on a level with emancipated negroes."[22]

Clay's plan, however, dominated the political copy of newspapers outside South Carolina, just as it dominated conversation in Washington. The press hardly reflected unanimous approval of Clay's measures, but they did win support from established journals. Clay and his longtime enemy Thomas Ritchie, editor of the Washington *Union* and still a power in the Democratic party, were reconciled; with modifications that Clay accepted, the Kentuckian's plan was vigorously espoused by Ritchie's newspaper.[23] In the Senate eight southerners immediately noted their objections to Clay's resolutions, and they developed their points after his speech of February 5 and 6. But Clay had focused debate and provided a starting point for sectional bargaining. Less than two weeks after his speech, Speaker Howell Cobb hosted a meeting of three northern and four southern congressmen (including Toombs and Stephens) who agreed to support a compromise package very similar to Clay's.[24] Clay had also rallied the support of the Lone Star State's creditors—and the holders of these rapidly appreciating Texas bonds included "some of the most widely known lawyers, bankers, brokers, and public men in America."[25] Clay's initiative had, in brief, irretrievably damaged Calhoun's chances of forging a politically united South, a South capable of dictating terms for the continuance of the Union.

Calhoun's reply to Clay came on March 4. Assisted to his senate seat by James Hamilton, Calhoun was too weak to deliver his final oratorical set piece, which was read by James Mason of Virginia. Its themes were familiar to listeners. The equilibrium existing between North and South in the early republic was destroyed by the increasing power of a central government that had been manipulated by the North for the benefit of its sectional interests. The exclusion of slaveholders from territory held in common—a process that stretched from the Northwest Ordinance through the organization of Oregon and that would be made perpetual by the Wilmot Proviso—was only one of the devices the northern majority had used to consolidate its power within the Union. Still white southerners would have accepted northern domination of the federal government —if their peculiar and vital institution had not been threatened. But northerners had chosen to attack slavery and to compass its eventual abolition.

Clay's compromise proposals were mere palliatives; they were grossly inadequate to cure the republic's disease. And that disease, according to Calhoun, was the North's disrespect for the constitution's protection of slavery, a disrespect flagrantly exhibited in fugitive slave cases. The South could safely remain in the Union only if the North would agree to accept a constitutional "amendment, which will restore to the South in substance, the power she possessed of protecting herself, before the equilibrium between the sections was destroyed by the action of this Government."[26] The decision on California's application for statehood would reveal northern intentions. If California were admitted as organized by Taylor's "Executive proviso," then southerners "would be blind not to perceive in that case, that your real objects are power and aggrandizement, and infatuated not to act accordingly."[27]

Since fourteen of the fifteen free-state legislatures had already endorsed the Wilmot Proviso, the intent of Calhoun's speech was not to win northern supporters.[28] His final effort was directed at southern doubters, but it gathered few converts. In fact the speech prompted Mississippi's senior senator to part company with Calhoun. Foote did not think a constitutional amendment was absolutely essential. To make this amendment an ultimatum, he suggested, would provoke disunion rather than avoid it. Alabama's Senator William King believed that "in some particulars [Calhoun's speech] met with no approval from a large majority of Southern men." Among southerners Foote and King were far from alone in believing that Calhoun's remedies were worse than the disease.[29]

In South Carolina, Calhoun's "ideas as to the precise course necessary at this exigency" were praised as the "only safe and sound ones." The Palmetto gentry agreed that the South "must act *now*, and *decisively*. We will be in a clear minority [in the Senate] when California comes in and in twenty or thirty years, there will be ten more free states West of the Mississippi. . . . Long before the North gets this vast accession of strength she will . . . proclaim freedom or something equivalent to it to our Slaves and reduce us to the condition of Hayti. . . . If we do not act now, we deliberately consign our children, not our posterity, but *our children* to the flames."[30]

When Calhoun's speech was finished, Daniel Webster scheduled his own remarks for March 7. A past master of theater, Webster made the most of his opportunity on that Thursday. Arguing that California's organization as a free state was a fait accompli and that climate barred slavery elsewhere in the Mexican cession, the New Englander saw no need for the Wilmot Proviso. He "would not take pains to reaffirm an ordinance of nature, nor to reenact the will of God." He supported Clay in calling for a new fugitive slave law and for federal assumption of the Texas debt. "What Webster uttered on March 7," in brief, "was tailored to southern, not northern, taste."[31]

"If he [Webster] should be sustained by his constituents and N. England generally," Calhoun wrote on March 10, "it is not improbable, that he will take still stronger grounds; and that the question may be adjusted, or patched up for the present, to brake [*sic*] out again in a few years. Nothing short of the terms I propose," Calhoun insisted, "can settle it finally and permanently." In the opinion of *Mercury* editor John Carew, Webster had given a "great speech; noble in language, generous and conciliating in tone, and . . . having one general, broad and powerful tendency towards the peaceable and *honorable* adjustment of the existing controversy." But the *Mercury* cautioned that only the prospect of imminent disunion had elicited Webster's stand; he would "certainly not escape denunciation . . . [by the] whole brood of factionists who live on the bitter fruits of abolitionism."[32]

And South Carolina's political oligarchy soon decided that Webster's attitude had been repudiated not only by New England but also by northern conservatives. The North's "strongest man . . . [was] incapable of maintaining himself on the smallest amount possible of concession to the South. . . . Can anything more clearly evince the utter hopelessness of looking to the North for support . . . ?" The North had rejected Webster's criticism of the "free-soil and anti-fugitive movements . . . [and] called him 'dough face.'" According to the *Mercury*, the North's few conservatives on issues relating to slavery were shouted down by "Free-soil rowdies." Virtually ignoring northern rallies and petition campaigns in support of Clay's compromise package, the *Mercury* stressed evidence of northern opposition to the return of runaway slaves and depicted the North as overwhelmingly hostile to slaveholders and southerners.[33]

Henry Foote, however, was favorably impressed by procompromise, pro-Union rallies in "every part of the republic." In the wake of Webster's speech, Foote sharpened his attack on Calhoun's position. Such criticism from an organizer of the southern convention movement boded ill for South Carolina's planter-politicians. Webster's words may not have "changed a single Senate vote," but "Webster, like Clay, was more influential in the country at large than on Capitol Hill," and the March 7 speech was a "valuable and undeniable encouragement to compromisers."[34] Virginian William Goode wrote to Senator Robert M. T. Hunter that the "chief injury to the South, resulting from Webster's speech, is the hesitation it has occasioned. This has given courage to all [southerners] who wavered in their resolution or who were secretly opposed to the" Nashville Convention.[35] The *Mercury* lamented that the Wilmington [North Carolina] *Commercial*, "on receipt of Mr. Webster's speech, gave way to the feeling that the danger was now over, and . . . [doubted] whether . . . the people of that state should . . . appoint Delegates to the Nashville Convention." Hammond, a delegate-at-large to that convention, bewailed the increasing likelihood of a compromise: "the party leaders will cry out 'victory' and the . . . people of the South, bigoted to party and to Union will applaud to the echo."[36] Events in Washington had overtaken and upset plans laid in South Carolina.

3

"The Nashville Convention remained uppermost in [John] Carew's mind throughout the progress of the congressional debate. Designed . . . [to crown] Calhoun's effort to solidify the South, the convention took precedence over all else in the *Mercury*."[37] This emphasis also reflected the wishes of Palmetto officials. Elections for South Carolina's remaining delegates to Nashville would not begin until April, and in the meantime the state's politicians worked cautiously to promote enthusiasm for the convention among other southern leaders, especially those in Georgia.[38]

By January the Georgia legislature (which had been in session since early November) seemed ready for a confrontation with the North on issues relating to slavery. "Georgia is an important state. You can do much there," wrote Calhoun to Hammond, "and I hope you will exert yourself, if it should be necessary, to induce her to be represented at Nashville." The *Mercury* praised George W. Towns, Georgia's recently elected governor, and reprinted his warning that the South must act swiftly to protect slavery, since "our adversaries are constantly growing stronger, and ourselves comparatively weaker in all the elements of power."[39]

Towns had requested a constituent convention in Georgia to consider "measures proper for . . . safety and preservation, in the event of the passage of the Wilmot Proviso, or other kindred measures." The tumultuous debate in Washington during December and January persuaded a majority of Georgia's legislators that the admission of California was akin to enactment of the proviso. By February 5 the legislature had mandated a state convention should any of four contingencies—including California's admission "in its present pretended organization"—occur; the legislators had also passed a Nashville Convention bill, providing for the election of two delegates from each of Georgia's congressional districts.[40]

During January even "Little Ellick" Stephens, who believed the disunionists were incapable of constructing as good a government as the one they proposed to destroy, "decided that secession was inevitable, sooner or later." Stephens advised his brother Linton, a state legislator, to present bills "for reorganizing the militia . . . the formation of volunteer companies, the creation of arsenals, of an armory, and an establishment for making gunpowder." Parties in Georgia seemed on the verge of realignment; the traditional organizations were giving way to Union and southern-rights groups.[41] Pleased by these developments, the South Carolina gentry assumed that Georgia's leaders would soon be with them "heart and hand in the cause."[42]

South Carolina's planter-politicians were also encouraged to see official approval of the Nashville Convention by the Virginia, Texas, and Mississippi legislatures and extralegal endorsement by Alabama legislators. Motives for sanctioning the convention, however, varied widely. Secessionist Beverley Tucker was "much afraid that . . . the Legislature of Virginia will *appoint* no deputies, but leave all to the people. In that case . . . [he had] little chance of being selected." Tucker's fears were realized; moreover the legislature characterized the convention as a means of preserving the Union by seeking redress for sectional grievances. In selecting their delegates Alabama legislators indicated that the convention should not be a forum for secession. In Texas the legislature's approval of delegate elections generated little popular enthusiasm. Only in Mississippi was official endorsement of the convention emphatic and unqualified. On March 6 Mississippi's legislature approved of sending delegates to Nashville and appropriated $20,000 for their expenses; the legislature also appropriated $200,000 for implementing measures to protect the "constitutional and sovereign rights of the states" in case of the Proviso's enactment.[43]

Although the *Mercury* reassured readers "that the movement of the people [was] resolutely onward," editorial interpretation could not conceal the South's increasingly partisan division over the Nashville Convention. In Tennessee the Whig-controlled senate defeated the Democratic house's attempt to sanction the election of delegates to the convention. With two exceptions (the Memphis *Enquirer* and the Trenton *Banner*), Tennessee's Whig newspapers opposed the convention movement. A similar situation prevailed in Kentucky. There the senate killed "resolution[s] appointing delegates to the Nashville Convention . . . by the decisive vote of twenty-six to nine. Only one Whig voted for them, only two Democrats against them."[44]

Still the Carolina supporters of the convention tried to maintain a bold front. Although Louisianans would not be represented in Nashville, the *Mercury* praised their governor's stand in favor of the convention. Events in Florida required the paper's editors to take a different tack. Although newly elected Governor Thomas Brown opposed the convention and refused to appoint delegates to it, the "people of Florida . . . [were] nearly unanimous for it. They . . . [would] appoint delegates themselves," the *Mercury* claimed, "as . . . [would] the people of Tennessee." Although the legislatures of Virginia and Georgia had approved the Nashville Convention, rallies opposed to it were staged in both states. And South Carolina's true believers were driven to the limits of their ingenuity in explaining the low voter turnout for the first stage of delegate elections in Georgia.[45]

By mid-March southern disunity both on the purpose of the Nashville Convention and on the wisdom of its meeting was apparent. This had a chilling effect on the hopes of South Carolinians. Disunion "is only a question of time and *now* is the *best* time," James Hammond had written in February. The Nashville Convention should not meet, he wrote in early March, unless it could "open the way to dissolution." He "had drawn up . . . resolutions . . . [calling for] the Slave States to send Delegates to a General Congress, empowered to dissolve the Union, form a new Constitution . . . [and] appoint a Provisional Government until the Constitution could go into operation." He had intended to offer these resolutions at Nashville, but by March 17 he had decided that they would receive little or no support there. By the end of March, Hammond was almost "inclined to wash . . . [his] hands of the whole matter."[46]

March brought still another misfortune to the supporters of the Nashville Convention: the death of its spiritual father. Calhoun had been ill and confined to his rooms in Hill's boarding house for most of February and March, but he had worked as best he could to rally Nashville Convention delegates to a common program. "It is . . . highly desirable, that at least two members from each of the [state] delegations, should visit Washington on their way to Nashville, in order to consult freely with the members of the South who are true to her," he wrote on February 16. On March 13, after a bitter exchange with his erstwhile supporter Henry Foote, Calhoun left the Senate for the last time. A South united behind his demands seemed once more beyond Calhoun's reach. He died on March 31.[47]

4

While tributes to the departed prophet filled the *Mercury's* black-bordered columns and preparations for his funeral dominated most public and private correspondence, Governor Seabrook moved quickly to select Calhoun's interim replacement. Speculation concerning Seabrook's choice centered on Rhett, Hammond, and Elmore.[48] The governor, however, offered the vacant Senate seat to James Hamilton, whose colorful and peripatetic career had led him far from South Carolina.

After retiring from Carolina politics in the mid-1830s, Hamilton had pursued numerous avocations: planter, president of the Bank of Charleston, railroad entrepreneur, and speculator in Alabama, Mississippi, and Texas real estate. In 1838 President Mirabeau Buonaparte Lamar of the Republic of Texas appointed Hamilton commissioner of loans. After the Mexican War, Hamilton planned to "repair to Washington and hold on *de die* and *en diem*, until some thing definitive shall be concluded in reference to the Texan Debt." A creditor of Texas to the amount of $210,000, he hoped that federal assumption of the Texas debt would enable him "to do a partial if not a total and plenary justice to" his own creditors, and payments to his South Carolina creditors were long overdue.[49]

On February 11, 1850, investors and speculators who held Texas securities assembled in Washington's National Hotel. The purpose of the meeting was, most probably, to establish "an effective bondholders' lobby." Hamilton was "[c]hief sponsor of the gathering . . . and attorney for owners of over half the bonds." Hamilton also received a fee as the agent of William S. Wetmore, a New York millionaire with a large interest in Texas paper.[50] Because of his "private engagements of an imperative character," Hamilton ended a movement by old friends in Carolina to draft him as a congressional candidate. His time was spent in "constant consultation with the Southern members [of Congress] in reference to . . . the pacification & assumption of the public Debt of Texas by the U.S. as an equivalent for a cession of . . . Territory."[51]

Obviously Hamilton welcomed Clay's third and fourth resolutions.[52] Whether reluctantly or not he embraced Clay's entire program. Believing that California's admission was inevitable, he argued that the South should demand a quid pro quo: the creation of two additional slave states within the existing boundaries of Texas, and he supported Senator John Bell's resolution to that effect.[53] Despite Hamilton's special interest in a compromise that promised him a large measure of financial relief, he proclaimed his sectional loyalty in extravagant terms. "I would sacrifice every farthing of the Debt Texas owes me and throw myself like a galley slave on the mercy of my creditors rather than give up one principle one security one right to which the South is entitled. In all my efforts & negotiations at Washington I kept this steadily in view." Hammond, among others, received such declarations from Hamilton with extreme skepticism.[54]

Nevertheless, on the day after Calhoun's death, Governor Seabrook offered Hamilton the "appointment of United States Senator from South Carolina." From the "character of . . . [his] private engagements," Hamilton had "great difficulty in determining whether . . . [he] could accept"; nevertheless he did, with the stipulation that he could "only serve during the present session of Congress." Before this reply reached Seabrook, however, the governor had written Hamilton that "doubts had been expressed" about the constitutionality of his appointment. On April 6, bowing to "even the shade of a doubt as to . . . [his] eligibility," the planter-politician who had turned lobbyist "return[ed Seabrook's] . . . letter of appointment and respectfully decline[d] the commission." With grateful haste the governor accepted Hamilton's reconsideration.[55]

The governor's doubts about Hamilton's appointment involved, ostensibly, the constitution's residency requirement for senators. In conversation with Seabrook, South Carolina Attorney General Isaac Hayne and Charleston lawyer Henry W. Perronneau questioned Hamilton's status as "'an inhabitant' of South Carolina, within the meaning of the Constitution." In 1848 Hamilton had sold his "legal habitation in St. Peter's [Parish], South Carolina." His wife's permanent home was in Savannah, Georgia, and Hamilton spent most of his time in Washington or Texas.[56] Widespread opposition to Hamilton's appointment was officially unmentioned, but it was certainly operative in the decision to seek another replacement for Calhoun. The gentry made plain to the governor their distress over Hamilton's interest in and promotion of Clay's compromise package.[57]

Having stumbled badly with the Hamilton appointment, Seabrook turned next to Langdon Cheves, whose credentials were impeccable. Cheves was Carolina's senior statesman; he had served as speaker of the House and head of the Bank of the United States; moreover he was a brilliant lawyer and a large planter. Cheves, however, declined the senate post with the plea that he was "nearly seventy four years of age and . . . [had] been for upwards of thirty retired from the public service."[58] Franklin H. Elmore, Calhoun's longtime confidante and advisor was Seabrook's third choice. Although reluctant to leave the Bank of the State of South Carolina even briefly outside his care, Elmore accepted the interim senatorship, but less than two months after his appointment, Elmore died. Seabrook turned finally to Robert Barnwell, who proved an orthodox spokesman for the South Carolina gentry during the remainder of the first session of the Thirty-First Congress. Before Barnwell took up his duties in Washington, he and his Palmetto colleagues centered their attention on the Nashville Convention.[59]

5

Well before the April 1 date recommended by South Carolina's legislative caucus, the first stage of delegate selection had been completed in a number of electoral districts. Following a pattern set by these early meetings, delegates to the congressional district conventions were appointed rather than elected.[60] The six men chosen "to cast the vote of Abbeville for Delegates from . . . [the Fifth] Congressional District to the Nashville Convention" solicited the opinions of potential nominees on a number of issues.[61] Most delegations from the electoral districts, however, were less methodical in appraising candidates for Nashville. Despite procedural differences, fourteen Nashville Convention delegates (two from each congressional district) had been named by early May. The list included former governor Johnson, former congressmen Rhett and Pickens, and South Carolina Senate President Allston; the remaining delegates also had well-established careers in South Carolina politics.[62]

Palmetto Unionists privately rejoiced over compromise efforts in Congress but offered them little public support. Francis Lieber, for example, feared to voice pro-Union opinions lest he jeopardize his career. A conversation with a like-minded colleague "on the all-engrossing subject of Union or no Union" moved Lieber to initiate a correspondence "more definite and more private than an exchange of ideas in the faculty room can be." A grateful Mathew J. Williams sympathized completely with Lieber's position. "I think much more on this subject than I speak or write. It is no inconsiderable relief to give even this slight expression of my feelings," he replied.[63] During the spring of 1850 even B. F. Perry, who had welcomed Clay's compromise program and no longer considered the Nashville Convention necessary, confined his opinions to his diary and to private letters.[64]

In Charleston a small group of old Unionists, including Charleston *Courier* editor Richard Yeadon, promoted Joel Poinsett as a Nashville Convention delegate. Unlike Yeadon, however, Poinsett vowed that he would never sanction secession under any circumstances. Yeadon and his friends concluded that Poinsett's "views would render his candidacy hopeless; and Poinsett, knowing that he could no longer pretend to represent the will of the people of his state, accepted their decision without question." The South Carolina gentry did not want their delegation to Nashville leavened by the presence of a Unionist.[65]

But South Carolina's preoccupation with the Nashville Convention was not shared by the rest of the South. Far from desiring militant spokesmen in Nashville, Georgia voters did not seem interested in choosing delegates at all. Georgians were scheduled to choose among the nominees on April 3, but the election proved "a complete and dismal failure for the plain reason that the great masses of both parties ignored it." A Forsyth County farmer explained this voter apathy by observing that he and his neighbors "could not see that Congress had yet *done* anything against them, and until it did they would behave themselves." In Virginia, also, interest in the Nashville Convention had waned; voters in "[m]ore than half . . . [of] Virginia['s] counties refused to choose their delegates."[66] In North Carolina there were no plans either to elect or appoint delegates to Nashville.

In Tennessee, Alabama, and even Mississippi, Whig opposition to the Nashville Convention grew louder. Of the Whigs who planned to journey to Nashville, many agreed with the rationale of Alabaman William M. Murphy: "if the object of the Convention is to dissolve the Union . . . no earthly power should prevent my attendance—to prevent that awful calamity." Tennessee (Nashville in particular) seemed, finally, an inauspicious location for the convention. The city and surrounding Davidson County were predominantly Whig in political sympathy, and the *Republican Banner and Nashville Whig* "suggested that Tennessee 'tell the plotters to assemble elsewhere.' "[67]

Publicly, at least, South Carolina's leaders tried to ignore the widening gap between themselves and other southern politicians on the possibility of sectional compromise; the Palmetto gentry hoped that the Nashville Convention might yet salvage a measure of southern unity and rally slaveholders behind certain minimum demands. "If I find a spirit favourable to *actual resistance*, I shall join in it warmly, no matter how mild the measure to begin with may be, so it is a *measure*," wrote Hammond to Edmund Ruffin. "Union in the South is the one thing needful and if there is a chance of obtaining it, almost everything should be sacrificed to it." The South Carolinian conceded that Virginia would scarcely be represented at Nashville, but he urged Ruffin "not [to] give up the fight." Hammond and his peers hoped that despite "Georgia's jealousy of So. Ca.," a common front might still be formed in the deep South. The convention was an unwieldy tool for this purpose, but it was the only tool available.[68]

While South Carolinians struggled to revive interest in the Nashville Convention, congressional supporters of compromise tried to steer Clay's proposals through a procedural quagmire. Henry Foote doggedly promoted the creation of a "select committee to pass upon the sectional problems and unite most or all of them in a single bill." Clay, Webster, and Douglass initially opposed both a select committee and an omnibus bill, but they grudgingly accepted both tactics in hopes of overcoming the inertia that had gripped all compromise proposals once they had been introduced. In late April the Senate approved and appointed a select committee of thirteen chaired by Clay. On May 8 the Kentuckian delivered the committee's report. It included statehood for California, territorial governments for New Mexico and Utah, and settlement of the Texas debt and boundary questions in a single bill. Kept separate from this omnibus measure were fugitive slave and District slave trade bills.[69]

The *Mercury*'s reaction to the select committee's report was both quick and violent. The paper denounced every provision of the omnibus bill and, of course, the bill to suppress the District slave trade. "The demand for the abolition of slavery in every spot subject to the control of the Federal Government would not be checked by these measures." Even the fugitive slave bill was unacceptable, "because notoriously heretofore the obstruction . . . [of] recovery has been the popular opinion at the North instigating . . . mob violence to prevent" the return of slaves.[70] Perry noted the gentry's complete agreement with the *Mercury*'s critique of the report: "The whole State of South Carolina is opposed to it, and a large portion of the state [is] for disunion *per se*!!" Robert Barnwell and R. F. W. Allston thought the report would pass the Senate but expected massive southern resistance if the House concurred. On the eve of his departure for Nashville, Allston predicted an attempt "to seperate [sic], in the House, the California measure from the rest and pass it by itself. Should this be attempted I think the House will be broken up in a general row, with perhaps bloodshed."[71]

6

On June 3 delegates from nine states rendezvoused in Nashville. The size of delegations varied immensely: a single delegate journeyed from Texas, while approximately one hundred came from Tennessee.[72] Of the eight Whigs elected in Georgia, seven had resigned; after Governor Towns appointed substitutes Georgia's delegation "consisted finally of eight southern-rights Democrats and three Whigs." Of the fourteen delegates chosen in Virginia, only six attended the convention. Mississippi mustered the "full number of delegates fixed by her October convention, but while every Democrat appointed by the legislature appeared, only three Whigs were present." Thus the delegates were hardly representative of their supposed constituents.[73]

But it was enough for the South Carolinians that the convention had met. R. F. W. Allston lauded "Judge Tucker of Va. half brother to John Randolph of Roanoke, Judge Colquite [Colquitt] of Geo. Genl McDonald of Geo. Judge Goldthwaite and Fitzpatrick and Walker, and Campbell of Ala. Judge Sharkey & Smith & Boykin of Miss. among many other gentlemen of worth and ability."[74] And South Carolina radicals were especially pleased to see secessionists Beverley Tucker, Henry L. Benning, and Charles J. McDonald numbered among the delegates.

Before the convention met the South Carolinians caucused to decide on their tactics. The delegation decided "to remain quiet. Pickens and Rhett were for speaking and being active. Judge Cheves, Barnwell and myself were opposed," Hammond recorded, "and most of the delegation went with us. . . . It was generally expected that So. Ca. would go . . . [to Nashville] violent for a dissolution of the Union and all [the Southern states] were prepared to resent [us] or nearly all. Our policy was to show that we were reasonable and ready to go as far back to unite with any party of resistance as honor and safety would permit."[75] Hammond urged his colleagues to "press for a vote by States." James Chesnut proposed the substitution of "delegations" for "states"; the caucus agreed "to this ruse." The

South Carolinians eventually achieved this procedural goal: the organizing committee of the convention apportioned one vote to each of the nine delegations.[76]

Denied the use of Tennessee's public buildings, the delegates assembled first in Odd Fellows Hall and moved on the next day to Old McKendree Church, where they met for the remainder of the convention. The delegates elected William L. Sharkey president of the convention, and the Mississippian's acceptance speech struck the keynote for the convention's moderates. The purpose of the convention, Sharkey declaimed, was to seek redress for "violations of the Constitution . . . and to perpetuate the Union, not destroy it." Sharkey's speech revealed both the conservative temper of Whig delegates and the potential schism between Whigs and Democrats at the convention. After informally polling delegates on whether secession was a constitutional right, a New York *Herald* reporter concluded that the "Democrats . . . gave the doctrine an unanimous endorsement." The Whigs did not.[77]

In dealing with business before the convention, the delegates agreed to vote by state delegations and to appoint a resolutions committee that was also empowered to "report on any other matter that . . . [the committee] thought necessary." Two members from each delegation served on this central committee to which resolutions were referred without debate.[78] Between June 5 and 8 resolutions aplenty were offered from every delegation except South Carolina's. Cheves sat "silent mostly" and even Rhett kept his peace; the Carolinians were, in brief, "'studious in yielding precedence' to others."[79]

The convention's secessionists centered their hopes on Henry L. Benning's set of twenty-three resolutions, which (among other items) asserted the right of secession and declared extension of the Missouri Compromise line to the Pacific a sine qua non for compromise. The central committee, however, chose to base its report on the more conciliatory resolutions offered by John A. Campbell. The Alabaman's resolutions espoused Calhoun's common-property-of-the-states interpretation of the territories, condemned the Wilmot Proviso, demanded that northern states observe more faithfully the constitutional injunction to return fugitive slaves, "but advised no method of resistance, in the confident hope that Congress would not adjourn without a settlement of the questions in dispute."[80]

The twenty-eight resolutions finally recommended by the central committee unveiled nothing new in political doctrine. Resolution eleven proposed a division of the territories acquired from Mexico along the Missouri Compromise line; this was presented as the

South's maximum concession on the issue of slavery's expansion. Resolution sixteen preached the South's duty to defend Texas from any loss of territory; resolution eighteen reaffirmed Texas's right to create "four new slaveholding States" within its borders. The resolutions included a demand for Congress "to provide effectual means of executing the 2nd section of the 4th article of the Constitution relating to the restoration of fugitive" slaves, and southerners were urged to support the Washington-based, southern-rights organ endorsed by a group of southern men in May. The last resolution pledged the convention to meet again at Nashville "the 6th Monday after the adjournment of" Congress.[81]

With these resolutions the committee submitted to the convention an "Address" written by Rhett. The address constructed a platform for the convention's anticompromise forces. After giving a synopsis of developments in the "sixteen years since the institution of Slavery in the South began to be agitated in Congress and assailed by our sister States," Rhett proceeded to attack Clay's compromise proposals one by one. The admission of California was a thinly veiled application of the Wilmot Proviso; the reduction of Texas's size was an "enormous wrong and a spoilation" of slave territory. If Congress yielded "to the prejudice against" the District slave trade, how long would it "be able to resist the greater prejudice . . . against the holding of slaves at all in the District of Columbia?" The proposed fugitive-slave bill was "quite inadequate to" return runaways to their owners. The Missouri Compromise line, Rhett concluded, was probably not constitutional, but it was hallowed by long acceptance. The South should accept the extension of that line to the Pacific "as a partition . . . between the two sections of the Union; and besides this, nothing but . . . the Constitution."[82]

The address won approval from the central committee and from the convention—but only by the hardest. Signers of the committee's minority report "were not prepared to say that the impending compromises might not be so altered as to make them acceptable." Once both majority and minority reports reached the convention floor, the South Carolina delegation broke its self-imposed silence. Hammond, who privately claimed full credit for obtaining committee endorsement of the address, defended Rhett's work in a sharp exchange with Sharkey. By the state-delegation method of voting, the address passed unanimously, but only with the disclaimer "that the delgates were not unanimous in approving its arguments." Dissenters demanded and received an opportunity to record their opposition to the address.[83]

The *Mercury* had high praise for the results of the Nashville Convention. Its recommendation to extend the Missouri Compromise line was a simple, "moderate and effectual" solution to the problem of slavery in the territories. Glossing over evidence to the contrary, the paper assured its readers that in the future the South could "meet in council with a precedent full of assurance . . . [of] the essential unity and mutual confidence of her people." Returning delegate Hammond, however, was less sanguine. A "great *Submission Party* . . . [was] in course of formation," he conceded; the "malcontents in the Convention . . . [were] of it. Cobb, Foote & c [*sic*] represent[ed] it in Congress." But he did believe that the convention's results would "strengthen the friends of the South" in Washington. And the convention's "great points . . . [were] that the South *ha[d] met*, ha[d] acted with great harmony in a nine days convention and above all *ha[d] agreed to meet again.*"[84] The Nashville Convention's message was uncertain, but South Carolina's radicals intended to interpret its meaning for the South.

7

"I feel that we did not attain the mark set for us by the people of this State," wrote D. F. Jamison ten days after the Nashville Convention adjourned, "but in seeking for more we might have obtained less . . . stronger measures might have been adopted, but . . . would have failed in securing that unanimity so necessary to all action by the South."[85] Still substantive "action by the South" depended upon the decision made finally by the first session of the Thirty-First Congress. On that point alone the delegates to the Nashville Convention had been truly unanimous. South Carolina's radicals, therefore, tried to anticipate the results of debate in Congress on Clay's proposals and to prepare the South for "ulterior measures" if Congress ignored the demands voiced at Nashville. Addressing himself to the probable course of events in Washington, South Carolina's preeminent secessionist began to warn southerners "not [to] be deceived, and thus weakened by false expectations."[86]

The occasion Rhett seized to begin his latest mission was a public meeting called "to receive the report" of Charleston's delegates to the Nashville Convention. Rhett was not a scheduled speaker; when the audience "loudly called for" him, however, he responded eagerly and "at much length."[87] He began by boosting the convention's importance and vastly exaggerating its harmony. Even this seemingly innocuous portion of his speech managed to alienate Tennesseans, because it implied that their delegates had been "brought into line" with the convention's radicals.[88]

Interpreting his address as the collective opinion of the delegates, Rhett claimed that the "Convention [had] repudiated and condemned the measures pending in the Senate of the United States, called 'the Compromise.'" He predicted that Clay's proposals, biased against slaveholders though they were, would not satisfy northern representatives and would inevitably fail in the "House . . . [where] the anti-slavery bigotry of the North most predominates." The Nashville Convention's notions of compromise stood even less chance of winning congressional sanction than did Clay's. If "all of these expedients of adjustment fail in Congress," Rhett asked, "where are we? We are in the beginning of a revolution." As his biographer has observed, Rhett's "wish . . . [was] father to the prophecy. He intended to make it come true."[89]

Warmed by the thought of revolutionary action, Rhett compared the South's status in the Union to the North American colonies' status in the first British Empire—an analogy Rhett had employed during the nullification movement and one he never relinquished. The "North [was] the exact counterpart of British statesmen in our Revolution, who would heed nothing and learn nothing, until the thunders of Revolution burst upon their heads." In regard to the federal government's policy on the tariff and internal improvement, the southern states were "colonies in a more . . . oppressive sense than the colonies of England . . . [were] to the mother country." Most tyrannical and dangerous of all was the North's relentless assault on slavery. As the American revolutionaries had gradually abandoned hope of reforming the empire, so Rhett had despaired of bringing the Union "back to the limitations of the Constitution." Thus he saw "but one course left, for the peace and salvation of the South—a dissolution of the Union."[90]

Having broached the alternative of secession, Rhett delivered a passage destined for national notoriety:

> There are some who will be ready to exclaim—Traitor! A Traitor to what and to whom . . . to the Constitution? The Constitution has no existence, under the construction of consolidation, and the base purposes of abolition, to which it is made to subserve. . . . But let it be, that I am a traitor. The word has no terrors for me. I am born of Traitors—Traitors

in England . . . in the middle of the seventeenth century . . .
Traitors again in the Revolution of 1776 . . . [and] I am surrounded by a host of Traitors ready to strike for equality and
independence against those . . . real Traitors who would convert
the Union into a bond of infamous degradation, or a cordon of
fire to consume the South.[91]

Briefly recalling the tactics South Carolina leaders had pursued
since the fall of 1849, Rhett allowed that his state would "join her
sister States of the South, or support any of them, in all expedients
for redress they may propose, and . . . [that South Carolina was]
content . . . to follow rather than to lead." Any impression of co-
operation and restraint, however, was erased by Rhett's closing
appeal for the Palmetto State, if abandoned by others, to "make
one brave, long, last, desperate struggle, for our rights and honor,
ere the black pall of tyranny is stretched over the bier of our dead
liberties."[92]

In South Carolina, Rhett's speech did not seem remarkable. Perry
sadly recorded that public opinion, even in the up-country district of
Laurens, was "for secession if the compromise" prevailed.[93] Hammond "concur[red] in every sentiment of Rhett's" but deplored the
timing of the Charleston speech. "We succeeded at Nashville in
overcoming the prejudice of the South against us as 'Hotspurs & c,' "
Hammond observed. He feared that Rhett's speech would isolate
South Carolina and preclude "another and a fuller meeting" of the
slave states. "Such men spoil all movements," Hammond lamented,
but he offered no public criticism of his rival's speech. Until South
Carolina's senatorial election was decided, Hammond would dance
to the tempo dictated by Palmetto politics, not to the slower beat
required for southern unity.[94]

The oratory produced at Fourth of July celebrations throughout
South Carolina lent support to Rhett's position. South Carolinians
dearly loved the spoken word, and the *Mercury* sated its readers
with a succession of toasts offered at Fourth of July picnics from
Whippy Swamp to Anderson. Toasts from the low country in particular breathed the same spirit as Rhett's treason speech,[95] and at
the dinner of Charleston's Seventy-Six Association, Henry L. Pinckney, Jr., raised his glass with the hope that the "Hon. R. Barnwell
Rhett . . . [would] soon return to the service of the State."[96]

In Beaufort on July 24, Rhett followed up his Charleston speech
with a consideration of the prospects for and the future of a southern
confederacy. The enthusiastic St. Helena's Parish planters gave him

a banner inscribed "Oh that we were all such Traitors." The *Mercury* aided Rhett's campaign by publishing denunciations of "Submissionists"—southerners who "counsel[ed] the South to trust to the action of . . . [the federal] Government for justice and security" and who hindered "every effort of the South to band for its own protection."[97] The paper warned that the serpent, Proviso, still lived; it proclaimed the South's unity in demanding an extension of the Missouri Compromise line; and it defended Rhett and the arguments used in his treason speech, when the fire-eater was attacked by Clay, Foote, Ritchie, and other critics.[98]

While Rhett heard the cheers of Carolina audiences, interim-Senator Barnwell found his southern colleagues unenthusiastic about joint action. Southern representatives viewed "their places here as very comfortable offices," he reported to Hammond; and in the new Senator's opinion, the Palmetto gentry could not "look to Washington for any lead [or] even for any . . . earnest co-operation in the just measure of redeeming the South." He was almost persuaded that South Carolina "must act alone, but hope[d for] *better* things." Cooperative action by the slave states, Barnwell wrote, depended upon the response of Georgia's "people . . . they must be brought up to the point of secession to make . . . [our movement] effectual."[99]

While Barnwell's reports from Washington were definitely pessimistic, Governor Quitman's letters from Mississippi were scarcely encouraging. Quitman's personal preferences had not altered since his interview with Daniel Wallace; the governor denounced congressional compromises and agreed with Rhett that secession was the South's only alternative, but the governor admitted that Mississippians were not united in that opinion. Senator Foote, who led the state's pro-Union forces, was a very able opponent. And the secessionists had to contend with apathy as well as opposition: "Prosperity . . . [made] the masses indifferent to the crisis," South Carolina's governor conceded in replying to the complaints of his Mississippi counterpart.[100]

In Georgia procompromise forces appealed to the "unparalleled prosperity" that the state had enjoyed under the aegis of the Union and implied that secession was merely the local and desperate remedy of South Carolinians for their own economic ills.[101] Georgia's Union Democrats were also quick to attribute disunion sentiment in their state to the influence of South Carolina natives who had migrated across the Savannah River. Unable to deny Georgia's relative prosperity and denounced as lackeys of South Carolina, Georgia's secessionists had finally to contend with the widespread opinion among southern-rights Democrats that slave-state political unity did not yet require secession.[102]

Nevertheless Georgia's proslavery radicals pursued their attack on Clay's compromise proposals. They published their views in the *Georgia Telegraph*, the *Muscogee Democrat*, the *Federal Union*, the Augusta *Constitutionalist*, and in the temporarily sympathetic Augusta *Republic*; and they organized a series of southern rights meetings. Directed by Charles McDonald, Andrew Dawson, and Walter Colquitt, this campaign was designed to culminate with a mass rally in Macon, where—they hoped—"Georgia would proclaim to the nation her readiness for secession." South Carolina secessionists also hoped for a great deal from the Macon rally that would call upon the oratorical talents of the South's two most famous fire-eaters: Yancey and Rhett.[103]

Rhett's speech in Macon began in soft tones, as he tried to avoid charges of South Carolina's interference in Georgia's affairs. He had ventured into Georgia only because the South faced a common fate and was engaged in a contest "as old as the first efforts for liberty and free government in the world." The northern majority's usurpations of power and violations of the constitution had begun the latest chapter in the long history of "struggle . . . between despotism and liberty—between the rulers and the ruled." Thus, invoking eighteenth-century Whig theories of history, Rhett proceeded to particulars.[104]

In their quest for aggrandizement the northern majority had ignored the spirit of the Missouri Compromise. They had embraced the goal of abolition and would eventually repudiate any compromise that barred the realization of that goal. Moreover the "proposed measures in congress on the subject of slavery, to calm the southern mind, touch[ed] but two points, slavery in our territories, and the recovery of fugitive slaves. The enemies of the South . . . [had], however, pending in congress, no less than six points, by which they assail[ed] . . . the institution of slavery." Rhett enumerated these six points of attack and explained the damage each would inflict on slavery. At times progress toward abolition might seem slow; abolitionists occasionally showed great tactical subtlety; but the "one great object of all these attacks on slavery in Congress . . . [was] to abolish . . . [slavery] in the States." And the "one great issue between the North and the South [was] *emancipation, or no emancipation by the General Government of the slaves of the South*."[105]

"No government was ever reformed by those who corrupted it," declared Rhett. Then he elaborated a possibility mentioned in passing in his treason speech: secession might lead to a restoration of the old, pure Union. Here was a lure for Georgians torn between the conflicting values of southern rights and Union. "Whether this secession . . . [would] be temporary or permanent . . . [would] depend on the Northern States. . . . We would require . . . new guarantees in the constitution, [and] the exclusion forever of the agitation of slavery in Congress" among other limitations on the power of the majority. If the North refused those conditions, the "Union [must] be permanently dissolved!" Rhett's glowing description of the government that would follow that dissolution made it plain that he already "cherished the abiding purpose of a permanent Southern Confederacy."[106]

The time to act had arrived; delay would only strengthen the North. Secession during 1850–51 would force "the frontier States of Virginia, Maryland and Kentucky" to join a southern confederacy, but within a few years they might "be Northern in their sympathies and interests."[107] The true Rhett was revealed in his peroration: "Let . . . [Georgia] fire the signal gun! and what State in the South but will move up to her side. . . . South Carolina will stand by Georgia in this great contest and triumph or perish with her. Whatever in the past has occurred to breed alienation between them she asks may be forgotten. . . . She extends to Georgia, her mailed hand, in friendship and support."[108]

Despite its array of secessionist speakers from Alabama, Georgia, and South Carolina, the Macon rally failed to justify its billing as a *mass* meeting. Georgia's southern-rights Democrats refused to march in the direction indicated by Rhett and his allies. Having feared such a reaction to Rhett's campaign, Hammond politely refused to contribute copy to the secessionist press in Georgia and declined invitations to speak in that state. Hammond overrated the significance of the Nashville Convention and the potential for building on its tenuous agreements, hence he exaggerated the damage to southern unity inflicted by Rhett's campaign. Nevertheless Rhett's husbandry seemed to be producing only bitter fruits. His treason speech had been "denounced throughout the Union and So Ca along with him. . . . [It had] given every one a handle to abuse So Ca and to . . . hold her up as the leader of the Southern Movement and its aim as disunion. For this the South . . . [was] not yet fully prepared and many . . . [might] be alarmed and kept out of . . . [the Movement] by this course."[109]

8

While Rhett and his secessionist allies labored to prepare South Carolina and the deep South for secession, South Carolina's representatives in Washington struggled to reshape the specific measures under debate or, failing in that, to defeat them. In this effort the Palmetto delegation followed Calhoun's dictum that California's admission was the key issue. The South Carolinians hoped to deal with that issue—as the Nashville Convention had recommended—by extending the Missouri Compromise line of 36 degrees 30 minutes to the Pacific Ocean. They supported the proposition that California should be organized into two territories divided along the 36 degree 30 minute line. And they demanded that slavery should be expressly permitted in California south of that line.[110]

In advocating extension of the Missouri Compromise line, Senators Barnwell and Butler carefully recorded their belief that any geographic restriction of slavery in the territories was "without any warrant from the Constitution." Nevertheless, they were willing to accept the "Missouri compromise . . . line of partition" because it was hallowed by experience, because it had resolved a past crisis over slavery, and because the survival of the Union "require[d] some similar arrangement." The South Carolinians generally conceded that they did not know whether "slaves would ever" be taken to Southern California much less whether slavery could be permanently established there. In demanding "an eligibility, a mere right" to enter California with slaves, the Palmetto delegation was concerned with precedent, with the future of slavery in their own region. Thus they drew "upon geopolitical thought . . . in a way that demonstrated their central concern for self-defense. They sought to maintain a 'balance of power' in the Union with which to check what they regarded to be the monistic urge of the free-soilers to complete dominion."[111]

Calhoun had warned that the dominance guaranteed to free states by the exclusion of slavery from the territories spelled eventual doom for slavery and the South's way of life. This prophecy sounded in the speeches of the Palmetto congressional delegation like a choral refrain. Their lamentations about northern attacks on slavery turned invariably to California's pending admission as a case in point, and their speeches opposing California statehood frequently included long and bitter digressions on the growth of abolitionist sentiment in the North and its impact on federal politics. The non-extension of slavery was "but the means by which the abolition of slavery" would be accomplished, explained Congressman Daniel Wallace, in "consider[ing] these subjects together, with the view to show the identity of their object and tendency." To Wallace and his colleagues, California's "admission into the Union" had become "a part of the scheme of non-extension, and therefore of ultimate abolition."[112]

If they could not secure the organization of Southern California as a slave territory, the South Carolinians hoped at least to delay statehood for the entire West Coast region. Quoting excerpts from correspondence between the War Department and General Bennett Riley, Congressman Colcock alleged that a collusive arrangement involving the executive department and the army commander in California had foisted an antislavery state constitution on California's inhabitants. Only because slavery was prohibited by California's "so called constitution," declaimed Congressman Wallace, was "this act of usurpation . . . tolerated" by the North.[113]

The South Carolinians charged not only that California's constitution-making process was irregular but also that her admission to the Union without prior territorial organization by Congress would be unprecedented and would subvert the constitution. Despite the number of states that had entered the Union without prior territorial governments created by Congress, the Palmetto delegation repeatedly stressed the lack of precedent for granting statehood to California. The most vigorous defense of this difficult position was undertaken by Senator Butler. "Kentucky, Tennessee, Vermont, and others," he explained, became states "by the previous consent of the States of which they formed a part, and by consent of Congress recognizing such arrangement and partition." The power of Congress over territorial organization had not extended to Texas, said Butler, since before entering the Union, Texas was a foreign country —not a territory belonging to the United States. California, however, was not part of an existing state, was clearly a territory belonging to the United States, and yet it had organized a state government without consent of Congress. To the South Carolina gentry, Butler's argument seemed sound.[114]

Other objections to statehood for California revealed perhaps more about the homogeneous world and oligarchic rule of the gentry in South Carolina than about the nature of society and government in California. The inhabitants of the region should "wait until the anarchy which prevail[ed] there . . . subside[d] into organic order" before attempting to assume "the dignity and rights of an independent State." California had no naturalization laws and "no legal impediment to . . . the four quarters of the globe . . . exercising the right of suffrage." California's inhabitants included transients, adventurers, and worse—"the floating population, of every color and nation."[115] In his final plea against California's admission to the Union, Robert Barnwell argued that such law and local government as California possessed exhibited "a lawless spirit, in the highest degree irregular, violent, and oppressive." Californians should "first learn to govern themselves in an orderly and quiet manner," he said, "before we admit them to govern us."[116]

Connected with the plan of the northern majority was "another scheme, [one] to dismember Texas, in order to restrict slavery, and swell the number of free States." If the "majority . . . succeed[ed] in annulling the claim of Texas to" the large area in dispute, annexed it to the soon-to-be-organized New Mexico Territory, and "admit[ted] it into the Union as a free State, they . . . [would] thereby perfect their whole non-extension scheme." The Texas boundary and debt bill would "purchase nearly one-third of Texas (acknowledged by Mr. Webster himself to be slave territory) with our own money." The Texas measure would establish the "precedent . . . that the Treasury of the United States . . . [might] be subsidized to abolish slavery wherever it exist[ed], or to bribe a State to give up the institution, as was done in the case of Portugal and Spain, by the abolitionists of England." The South Carolinians, therefore, demanded that the South "maintain . . . the rights of Texas and resist her dismemberment."[117]

In debate on the Texas boundary and debt bill, I. E. Holmes charged, finally, that the free states were trying to condemn the South to the Malthusian evils of time. Confined to the South the slave "population would soon press against available resources, drive down the value of labor, and at last compel the slaveholders to set the bondsmen free." Within fifty years, Holmes predicted, the South's slaves would number fourteen million. Cotton production, "encumbered by the support of so large a population," would become unprofitable, the slaves' labor would be valueless, and slavery perforce would be abolished. "All this," he warned, would "result from the exclusion of our negroes from the new lands."[118] The Texas boundary was the nominal topic of the South Carolinian's remarks, but the specifics of the bill under consideration were lost in his fears for the future of slavery; the word "Texas," in fact, never appeared in Holmes's speech.[119]

The South Carolinians were remarkably consistent in their voting pattern on procedural and substantive matters relating to the compromise measures,[120] and they were consistently among the minority when yeas and nays were counted. Late in June their solution to the California issue was pressed to a vote. Louisiana's Pierre Soule moved to amend the California bill so as to establish "between 36 degrees 30 minutes . . . [and the Mexican border] the Territory of South California," which would have no restriction regarding slavery and which, "when ready, able, and willing to become a State," would be admitted to the Union "with or without slavery as the people thereof . . . [might] desire." In the division on June 28 Soule's amendment attracted not a single senator from the free states and failed by a margin of 36 to 19.[121] The South Carolinians did not abandon their advocacy of 36 degrees 30 minutes, but its fate had been determined.

Although the cause of southern militants made little headway in Congress during June, it was espoused by a new Washington paper, the *Southern Press*, the first number of which appeared on June 17.[122] The senior editor of the *Southern Press* was Elwood Fisher, a Virginian who settled in Cincinnati and established himself as a successful lawyer and a vigorous partisan of state rights. Charleston-born Edwin De Leon, described by the Richmond *Times* as "an impulsive young Carolinian," served as Fisher's junior editorial colleague. Fisher and De Leon immediately established their position on policies as well as principles. The *Southern Press* "was not opposed to compromise, but the line of 36 deg. 30 min. to the Pacific . . . [was] the utmost concession to be made." The paper persisted "in its virtual ultimatum of the Missouri Compromise line," and its tone became more strident as passage of the compromise measures became more likely.[123]

While the issue of California statehood seemed to be moving inexorably toward settlement, the Texas–New Mexico boundary dispute suddenly approached the flash point. Since late March the administration's surrogates in Santa Fe, Lieutenant Colonel George A. McCall and Military Governor John Munroe, had labored intensively to promote statehood for New Mexico.[124] With Munroe's backing a constitutional convention met in May and produced a state charter that prohibited slavery and included within New Mexico's boundaries the large area in dispute with Texas. By the end of June this constitution was on its way to Washington. Southerners in general and Texans in particular were outraged.[125]

Texas Governor P. Hansborough Bell made plans to raise Texas troops, and even pro-Union Sam Houston "declared in the Senate that Texas would," if necessary, "fight the United States army to defend territory belonging to Texas." Georgia's Alexander H. Stephens warned that federal guns "illegally fired against the people of Texas . . . would signal 'freemen from the Delaware to the Rio Grande to rally to the rescue.'" Representatives from the South had interests apart from state rights for championing Texas's claims. As North Carolina Congressman David Outlaw, a procompromise Whig, observed, "The question of the boundary of Texas is so mixed up with the question of slavery, it might kindle a flame throughout the entire South." Southern Whigs, however, remonstrated with President Taylor in vain. He would not change his policy, and he pledged that armed resistance to federal authority in the disputed region would be subdued by superior force. As for "discontent at the South and fears excited by the Nashville Convention," Taylor tried "to persuade [Senator A. P.] Butler that there was nothing in it."[126]

The possibility of a clash between Texans and the federal garrison at Santa Fe, which had loomed so suddenly, was removed by Taylor's death on July 9. The possibility that New Mexico would enter the Union in the near future died with him. Taylor's death also removed from the White House the influence of "That arch-demagogue Seward [who had held the] Administration in the palm of his dirty hand." Viewing Seward as "the main pillar of Abolitionism," Whigs as well as Democrats from the slave states feared and distrusted him,[127] and the South Carolinians shared in the general relief southern politicians felt over the end of Taylor's territorial policy and Seward's fall from power.

Taylor's death also meant that the compromise package advocated by Clay and the Senate's select committee "had lost an unflinching enemy." Vice President Millard Fillmore and Senator Seward belonged to rival factions in New York politics; Fillmore's "nomination to the Vice-Presidency was a Clay triumph over the Sewardism that had selected Abbott Lawrence." As President, Fillmore sought the advice of Webster and Clay and soon took Webster into his cabinet. "Administration prestige and patronage were now thrown on the side of compromise."[128]

As the Senate moved toward a showdown vote on the select committee's omnibus bill,[129] the South Carolinians found themselves on the defensive: first the Nashville Convention and then Rhett came under fire. In deploring sectional attacks "founded not upon the conduct of the North and the South generally, but upon the conduct of" individuals or groups, Webster noted that the Nashville Convention had been "charged upon the South as a sort of exposition or homily of southern sentiment." Webster did "not believe a word of it." He refused "to impute to the South generally the sentiments of the Nashville Convention," and he decried the Nashville Address as "a studied disunion argument." Robert Barnwell defended the convention and denied that the address characterized disunion as inevitable. If northern interference with slavery ceased, Barnwell said, "We do not contend that there is any necessity whatever for a dissolution of the Union. If that interference is persisted in, it is the language of the address, and it is the belief, I believe, of a large portion of the southern people, that the Union cannot be made to endure." Webster, however, remained unconvinced that Barnwell interpreted the tone and substance of the Nashville Address as did its author.[130]

On July 22, five days after the exchange between Barnwell and Webster, Henry Clay denounced Rhett's activities and doctrines. The Kentuckian remarked that "only the other day . . . a member returned from the Nashville Convention, addressed . . . the people of Charleston, South Carolina, proposing to hoist the standard of disunion . . . [and] was applauded most enthusiastically . . . when he declared that, if the South did not join herself to this standard of rebellion, South Carolina would . . . fight this Union singly and alone!" Clay had "no patience for hearing this bravado." In reply Barnwell allowed that Rhett's "political opinions differ[ed] very widely from those of the Senator from Kentucky" but insisted that Rhett was not "very singular in the opinion . . . that the admission of California . . . [was equivalent to] the Wilmot proviso." Moreover "disunionist . . . [was] rapidly assuming at the South the meaning which rebel took when it was baptized in the blood of Warren at Bunker's Hill, and illustrated by the gallantry of Jasper at Fort Moultrie."[131]

Clay protested that he was not impugning the private "character of Mr. Rhett," but if he advocated disunion, Clay declaimed, and "if he follows up that declaration by corresponding overt acts, he will be a traitor, and I hope he will meet the fate of a traitor." This period drew vigorous applause from the galleries,[132] and Clay's stand won support from some southern representatives. "No arrangement which can or will be made will satisfy South Carolina," wrote David Outlaw, "and it is useless to attempt it. Her leading statesmen have satisfied themselves, that they made a bad bargain, by entering into the Union, and they are desirous of getting out of it. . . . The sooner we begin to war upon" such disunionists, the North Carolinian continued, "the sooner we shall put them down."[133] Among the South Carolina gentry and in the state's press, Clay's attack on Rhett became a minor cause célébre, but the episode won Rhett little or no sympathy elsewhere.[134]

On July 31 the omnibus bill came to a vote. A tactical error by the bill's floor manager, Senator James A. Pearce, contributed to its piecemeal destruction. First the Texas–New Mexico boundary provisions and then the provisions establishing New Mexico's territorial government were stripped away. The southerners who would have accepted California statehood "were afraid to do so before the other items had been voted, and California was also deleted." Only territorial government for Utah remained in "the onetime omnibus, and this pitiful remnant was permitted to pass 32 to 18." Poor management on the crucial day contributed to the wreck of the omnibus, but its design was chiefly at fault. As Clay's Kentucky colleague Joseph R. Underwood later conceded, "[Uniting] the various measures . . . in one bill . . . arrayed all the malcontents . . . into a formidable phalanx against the whole."[135]

Free-soil diehards had joined southern militants in opposition to the omnibus. Clay had often deplored this "extraordinary conjunction of extremes" and had warned that defeat of the omnibus would be "a triumph of ultraism." After venting his disappointment Clay left Washington to nurse his wounds in Newport. His place as pilot of the compromise was immediately taken by Stephen A. Douglas, who was committed to the same measures as Clay but whose tactics were different. He intended to exploit the voting blocs Clay had denounced. Douglas would combine the support of the senators who consistently favored compromise with support from one or the other of the sectional blocs. By these shifting alliances he intended to secure majorities for each of the measures.[136] Within two weeks Douglas proved his parliamentary virtuosity.

Douglas "discovered that he dared not promote New Mexico until after the Texas boundary and California measures had been passed." Accordingly he set Senator Pearce to work on a more attractive Texas boundary and debt measure, and the Marylander fashioned a revised bill that, among other items, provided for a $10,000,000 settlement between the federal government and Texas—a payment that would be applied to Texas's public debt. Sharing the enthusiasm of Douglas and Pearce for this bill and promoting it through the Baltimore *Sun* was "the journalist-bondholder" Francis J. Grund.[137]

The South Carolinians considered any monetary settlement in which Texas relinquished claims to territory as "a design of bribery and corruption." Congressman Daniel Wallace's pointed denunciations of the Texas bondholders and their agents finally drew from

James Hamilton a defense of bondholders and of lobbyists. Although their reputations in Carolina suffered badly, neither Hamilton nor Waddy Thompson renounced their lobbying efforts. As former congressmen both men had privileged access to the capitol, and both men were conspicuously present there. In the case of the Texas bill, the lobbyists were, in effect, Douglas's allies, and he hurried the measure to a vote on August 19. It passed by a 3 to 2 margin. A disillusioned Robert Barnwell lamented that "both the Georgia and Alabama Senators" voted in favor of the bill. "The ten millions of money to be paid to the Texas creditors carried the day. . . . I really do believe," wrote Barnwell to Hammond, "that this whole difficulty about the boundary of Texas was gotten up by Hamilton, Thompson and Clay and the Texas Senators and others interested in the Bonds of Texas."[138]

Statehood for California was next on Douglas's agenda. The South Carolinians, despite repeated failures, continued to support amendments to divide California into free and slave territories. On August 13 Sam Houston took occasion to ridicule the Nashville Convention's pretensions in making recommendations on California or any other subject. Houston charged, moreover, that the Nashville Convention movement had originated not in Mississippi but in South Carolina. Robert Barnwell, this time in conjunction with Jefferson Davis, defended the convention's legitimacy. This digression served only to postpone a decision that had become predictable. By a vote of 34 to 18, the Senate approved California's admission to the Union.[139]

Immediately after the vote on California, Douglas moved that the Senate take up the bill for territorial government in New Mexico. The South Carolinians, meanwhile, were discouraged not so much by defeat on the Texas and California measures as by their progressive loss of allies in the Senate. Moreover die-hard southern opponents of compromise were continually harassed by Mississippi's unpredictable senior senator. "That fellow Foote . . . has made the Senate the most intolerable deliberative body in which I was ever present," Barnwell complained. "No Southern man can open his mouth in defence of his section, that this bawling blackguard is not immediately up howling and ranting against disunion and traitors . . . nothing can so much annoy a minority as to have this incessant war made upon them by one of their own section, the majority sit by and enjoy it." On August 15 the New Mexico territorial bill, with the same provisions as the Utah measure, passed the Senate by a vote of 27 to 10.[140]

The next compromise measure taken up for consideration (and

the last one to pass the Senate during August) was the fugitive slave bill. In its earlier versions the Palmetto delegation had objected that even this supposed concession to the South abridged rights formerly enjoyed by slaveowners. A series of amendments, however, made the bill more to their liking. On August 23 Barnwell and Butler were among the majority who approved the fugitive bill for its final reading.[141] Early in September, South Carolina's junior senator gloomily reported on the progress of the compromise. Congress had passed the "land measures" that South Carolinians found so objectionable, and Barnwell feared that the House would not approve the fugitive slave bill "in the form in which" the Senate had "sent it to them." South Carolina was powerless in Washington, where her fate was "in the hands of the compromisers."[142]

CHAPTER VI

"Rouse Up to the Strife"

1

While Senator Robert Barnwell was lamenting the apparent victory of the compromise, some of its champions were lamenting the effects of their victory celebration. "This morg. Mr. Foote has diarrhoa from 'fruit' he ate," wrote naval surgeon Jonathan Foltz on Sunday, September 8. "Douglas has headache from 'cold' & c. No one is willing to attribute his illness to drinking or frolicking—Yet only last evg. all declared it was 'a night on which it was the duty of every patriot to get drunk.'" The compromisers had decided that passage of their final two measures was "a foregone conclusion."[1]

In the House, as in the Senate, the crucial struggle had come over the Texas boundary and debt bill. Democratic floor leaders coupled the Texas bill with the New Mexico territorial measure, and neither obstructive tactics by South Carolinians and others nor suspicions about the activities of Texas bondholders sufficed to halt the "little omnibus." On September 6, amid demands that lobbyists be removed from the House floor, the little omnibus passed by a vote of 108 to 98.[2] On the next day the House's approval of both the California and Utah bills precipitated the revelry that Foote and Douglas, among others, joined. On September 12 the House passed the Senate-sponsored fugitive slave bill, and within another five days both houses had sanctioned abolition of the district slave trade.[3] By September 20 President Fillmore had signed all the compromise measures into law.

"They have fired cannons in Washington and displayed lights as if for a great victory. Well, it is a victory over law and the Constitution . . . a victory . . . of the spirit of Abolition over all the Departments of Government. The burning of powder may not stop with Washington." So said the editors of the Charleston *Mercury*. The Nashville Convention's "moderate proposition for the settlement of the sectional dispute . . . [had] been rejected with derision by the united North." The *Mercury*, therefore, called for a new southern unity "and a full representation of the Southern people . . . [at] the second session of" the Nashville Convention. Some *Mercury* readers demanded a severing of all social as well as political ties with the North. One contributor, who called himself simply "A Carolinian," took Robert Barnwell to task for presenting the credentials of and acting "as gentleman-Usher to one of the Senators from that surreptitiously created State [California]. . . . It has been too much the fashion of late for Southern Representatives to regard themselves as bound to practice courtesy to our Northern enemies."[4]

Had "A Carolinian" seen Barnwell's private correspondence, however, he would have been comforted. South Carolina's junior senator was sending "1500 [copies] of Garnett['s pamphlet][5] into Georgia[,] 1500 or 2000 into Alabama, 500 . . . to Mississippi[,] 500 to Tennessee and 500 to Arkansas." He urged Hammond to work with Georgia's secessionists. "As for Nashville," Barnwell asserted, even "if South Carolina goes alone[,] she must go . . . expose these peace measures, advise a Congress of the Slaveholding States and . . . defend the right of secession. . . . [South Carolina] shall be a fire ship in the Union, if they [the northern states] do not let us go out of it."[6] And to Mississippi's Governor Quitman, Barnwell wrote: "If by action any state will give assurance of sustaining her, I should be decidedly for South Carolina seceding, thus forcing a Congress of slaveholding states to assemble. But I should think first to take counsel together in Nashville."[7]

Compromise "presupposes a desire on both sides to be at peace, when such is not the fact," Hammond had written in May.[8] The actions of Barnwell and his South Carolina colleagues in September supported that observation. Its truth was also illustrated in the response of militant antislavery partisans to passage of the compromise measures.[9] Consistent voting support from the procompromise bloc together with the parliamentary skill of its leaders had passed, in substance, the measures reported in May by the Senate's select committee. But "on all of the crucial roll calls by which the six measures of compromise passed in both the Senate and the House, only once in one house did a northern majority and a southern majority join in support of a bill." Thus the first session of the Thirty-First Congress produced "a truce perhaps, an armistice, certainly a settlement, but not a true compromise."[10]

The Fillmore administration was, nevertheless, determined to enforce the settlement that had been reached. Indeed, by the end of September 1850, the "politicians in Washington [had] made decisions that briefly but effectively removed the slavery issue as a source of partisan conflict between Whigs and Democrats." During 1850–51 the regular party organizations of Whigs and Democrats supported the compromise, and "pro-Compromise planks [were included] by both . . . [parties] in their 1852 national platforms."[11] But the Palmetto State stood outside the discipline of the party system, and South Carolina's planter-politicians immediately rejected the compromise. They argued that secession was the proper southern response, and they urged southerners to "rouse up to the strife."[12]

2

Before the last compromise measures could reach President Fillmore's desk, demands for a special session of the South Carolina legislature began to appear in the Charleston *Mercury*. Quoting the legislature's 1849 resolution that requested the governor "to call together the Legislature . . . should the Wilmot Proviso or any kindred measure become Law," avid secessionists claimed that California's admission was "not a 'kindred measure,' but the Wilmot Proviso itself."[13] Among others J. A. Leland, a confidante of Congressman Daniel Wallace, was discreetly urging the governor to convene a special legislative session. But Seabrook had decided to "await the movement of Georgia & that of one or two other slaveholding states before . . . committing So Ca." He argued that "a false step" by the Palmetto State, "at this time, would ruin her and the cause of the South." In another letter, one intended for publication, Seabrook wrote: "I am not certain that the best mode of making . . . resistance effective has been agreed upon. Let, then, the remedy . . . be the subject of ceaseless consideration. Let meetings be promptly

held in every District and Parish, in order that when . . . [the legislature meets in regular session,] it will be ready to act, and not to
deliberate merely."[14]

Seabrook's position derived from his hope for cooperative action
and from his correspondence with other southern governors, especially Governor Towns of Georgia. There were "satisfactory reasons
why South Carolina should move cautiously," wrote Seabrook to the
governors of Alabama, Virginia, and Mississippi. But, as soon as
two or more states "furnish[ed] some . . . evidence . . . of determined
resistance," the South Carolinian pledged that he would advocate
secession to his legislature.[15] In reply to a Seabrook inquiry, Governor Towns "suggest[ed] that no action whatever be taken in South
Carolina until after the election" of delegates to the state convention
mandated by Georgia's 1849 legislature.[16] But Seabrook could not
immediately quell agitation for a special meeting of South Carolina's
legislators. He felt compelled to sponsor counter-demonstrations in
support of his decision. Although he had prepared a summons for the
South Carolina legislature to convene on November 18, he withheld
it, lest that action weaken the Palmetto State's allies in Georgia.[17]

Agitation for an extra session of the legislature was only one out-
let for the gentry's anger over the compromise measures. Planters
also vented their dissatisfaction by boycotting northern shippers
and, especially, by organizing Southern Rights Associations. The
gentry's frenetic activities, however, were largely uncoordinated. A
number of vaguely formulated programs, occasionally couched as
mutually exclusive alternatives, competed for the gentry's approval
and the legislature's imprimature. Rhett's faction aimed for immediate disunion but possessed no institutional machinery for implementing its goal; and Rhett himself had no official standing—a
serious lack for any aspiring leader among such a legal-minded
people as the Palmetto gentry. With Calhoun gone the state was
temporarily without a political rudder, but if the South Carolina
gentry's dissent from the sectional truce was as yet undirected, it
was nonetheless vigorous.

In mid-August rice and sea-island cotton planters were exhorted
to cease transporting their products in Massachusetts-owned schoo-
ners and sloops. Paying the owners of these coasting vessels was
equivalent to paying "tribute . . . towards the support of the Abolition voters of Massachusetts," the *Mercury* editorialized. Late in
September seventy-three St. Helena's Parish planters responded by
pledging "never to employ any coaster owned by a citizen of the
North or manned by a Northern crew to take any part of our prod-

ucts to the city of Charleston or elsewhere." In October this form of
protest spread to Prince William's, St. Bartholemew's, and St. Luke's
Parishes. The boycott appealed to the planters' desire to borrow
tactics as well as rhetoric from the revolutionary era.[18] The boycott,
however, ran afoul of the planters' traditional marketing habits;
and, as the *Mercury* conceded, voluntary "non-intercourse resolutions will be evaded by dishonest men, while honest men will, at
personal sacrifices, adhere" to their promises.[19]

During 1848–49 Southern Rights Associations had been cultivated under Calhoun's supervision, and their Central Committee of
Vigilance and Safety had enjoyed a quasi-official relationship with
the state government.[20] In the fall of 1850, however, these associations germinated spontaneously. Expressing the views and venting
the emotions of their members, they remained autonomous, local organizations until 1851. Geographically, they frequently over-
lapped. By November, among other districts and towns, Abbeville,
All Saints, Barnwell, Beaufort, Bluffton, Charleston (St. Philip
and St. Michael), Chesterfield, Claremont, Clarendon, Columbia,
Darlington, Georgetown, Richland, St. Helena, and Williamsburg
boasted Southern Rights Associations. The parade continued during the winter and spring of 1850–51.[21] Each association typically
pledged itself "to promote concert of action among the citizens of this
and other Southern States . . . and to sustain the State authorities
in whatever measures South Carolina may adopt for her defence or
that of her sister States."[22] Within each association committees of
"Vigilance and Safety" and of "Correspondence" managed the work
of propaganda.

Each inauguration of a Southern Rights Association presented an
occasion for denouncing the compromise. Barbecues to fête candidates in the state legislative and congressional campaigns offered
still other opportunities for explaining South Carolina's grievances
and remedies. Finally public meetings (especially in the up-country)
were employed to rally public opinion against the recent decisions of
Congress.

Calhoun's home district of Pendleton was the site of a major effort
in this last category. Staged on October 1 the meeting was attended,
among other dignitaries, by Governor Seabrook, Congressman Burt,
and fifteen candidates for the state senate and house. Charleston's
highly respected Christopher Memminger was the featured speaker.
Twenty years before Memminger had opposed nullification; but if
"other Southern States should refuse to meet with us, and we are
brought to the alternative of SUBMISSION or RESISTANCE," he

reportedly declared at Pendleton on that Tuesday in October, "let us secede from the Union and abide our fate for better for for worse."[23]

On October 7 the "people of Spartanburg held a meeting . . . and went for resistance," B. F. Perry noted in his diary. "Union and Laurens for secession. Greenville has not yet spoken." When Greenville did hold a public meeting early in November, the results did not please Perry. Memminger was again among the orators. Opposing Memminger and defending the compromise was Waddy Thompson. who appealed to the audience's up-country prejudices: he expressed "astonishment at seeing a gentleman from Charleston brought there to enlighten the minds of the people of Greenville." Thompson "proceeded at much length to depict the disastrous and fatal consequences that would follow the measures recommended by Col. Memminger." The crowd hissed Thompson and showed little patience with Perry's remarks. "The audience seemed bent on disunion, not disposed to hear arguments on the other side," Perry confessed.[24] Perry's rival James L. Orr also advocated resistance to the compromise, as he toured his congressional district of Pendleton, Greenville, and Laurens, campaigning for reelection. "Let . . . [Mississippi] or any other State but lead, and South Carolina will follow and fear no evil," Orr told a Laurens District audience. "There is a providence that will . . . [direct] us—the same that guided the footsteps of our ancestors in the glorious revolution to triumphant success."[25]

In the wake of the compromise Rhett's call for repudiation of federal authority—by South Carolina's separate secession if necessary —won new converts. The case for separate secession was advocated regularly in the columns of the *Mercury*, and the organization of Southern Rights Associations presented militant secessionists numerous pulpits from which to spread their gospel.[26]

Late in August, Rhett returned from his foray into Georgia and continued his speechmaking in South Carolina. He was supported by Maxcy Gregg, a lawyer by trade, a southern nationalist by avocation, and a soldier by desire. In early October, Rhett spoke at the inaugural meetings of Southern Rights Associations in Charleston and in Barnwell District. At Barnwell Court House his program was also espoused by Congressman W. F. Colcock and Nashville Convention Delegate D. F. Jamison. Colcock "took the ground that disunion is our only remedy, that we must make up our minds to overthrow this government and form a new one, and held out little hope" that other states, acting officially, would aid South Carolina.[27] Later in October, Colcock presented these arguments to St. Helena's Southern Rights Association. On November 1 he spoke at a dinner in

Bluffton and was honored with this toast: "The Hon. W. F. Colcock our Guest—The Nullifier of '32; the Seceder of '50; the Patriot always."[28]

The low country responded enthusiastically to secessionist speeches and called for more. The Colleton Rifle Company volunteered its services to the state; Governor Seabrook accepted the offer "in the firm belief that South Carolina should be prepared, at a moment's warning for any emergency that may arise." The Winyah and All Saints Southern Rights Association denounced those who previously objected to its "recklessness" and saw in the "backwardness" of other states "no reason . . . why the State of South Carolina should fail in carrying out her declared intentions." The association's members were "in favor of separate State action" and resolved "that our Senator and Representatives to the Legislature be requested so to vote."[29]

For the Palmetto gentry during the autumn of 1850, the state's "harmony" remained a watchword. Cooperationists and separate secessionists were not sharply divided. Nearly every speaker who mounted a platform called for resistance to the compromise, but not all of them were eager to see South Carolina secede alone. Cooperationists usually professed a willingness for the state to secede, but they also professed the desirability, even the necessity, of proceeding to that remedy by gradual and deliberate steps. Invoking the example of nullification, they softly suggested that precipitate secession would leave the Palmetto State isolated and impotent. Separate secession, they believed, would damage, if not destroy, prospects for southern unity—and only a united South could successfully defend the peculiar institution.

Attorney General Isaac Hayne sketched the case for cooperation before the Charleston Southern Rights Association: "Let us prepare for that consultation and concert which alone can render action effectual . . . remember that other states are subject to the same grievance." South Carolina should "resort to any remedy that the other States" might approve. To his old friend James Hammond, Hayne wrote, "I think we should give them [Mississippi, Georgia, and Alabama] time to come up with us before we proceed to extremities."[30] Judge Edward Frost observed that South Carolina had tried to act alone in the nullification movement and had "backed out in disgrace." He remembered "the pain and agony which it cost him and . . . [would] not advise" a repetition of separate state action.[31] In print Senator A. P. Butler urged that violence be avoided in adjusting sectional differences and that a congress of southern states develop a common program of resistance; in private he advised Governor Seabrook that action by South Carolina should await Georgia's official response to the compromise.[32]

With attitudes ranging from grudging acceptance to secret applause, South Carolina Unionists had witnessed the making of the compromise. In May and June, writing to the Charleston *Courier* under the pseudonym "Caroliniensis," Francis Lieber had attempted a partial apology for Clay's compromise scheme. Professor Lieber then repaired to Washington, where he listened to the debates and collected materials for an essay denying the right of secession, but he had little appetite for publishing his arguments and then braving his reception in South Carolina.[33] Petigru, too, spent time in Washington offering moral support (if little else) to the Fillmore administration's advocacy of compromise.[34] During the summer of 1850 Perry's legal practice kept him, as usual, in South Carolina; in early August he encountered John O'Neall at a "Temperance Picnic" and was pleased to find the judge "in favour of Clay's compromise of the Slavery question."[35] Until October or later, however, the state's Unionists generally expressed support for the compromise only to friendly listeners.

For Perry, as demands for secession increased, the flaws of the compromise paled before the tragedy of disunion. Georgia "has ordered the Governor to call a convention in case California is admitted [as a free state]. . . . Secede say the ultras. What will she gain by that act of folly and madness? How much of California will she have after secession?" Perry ruminated in his diary. "The admission of California is wrong . . . but in it there is no violation of the Constitution or point of honor so far as the South is concerned."[36]

Disappointed by the initial success of secession agitation in the up-country, Perry jealously rejected an invitation to share the platform at Pendleton with advocates of disunion. Reelection to the South Carolina House by his faithful Greenville constituents helped Perry overcome his pique. At Greenville's public meeting on November 4, he defended the compromise and the Union. Although his speech was scarcely more popular than Waddy Thompson's, Perry's combative instincts had revived. He persuaded Thompson, Wesley Brooks, Benajah Dunham, Perry Duncan, and C. J. Elford to join him in contributing capital for a Unionist newspaper. Elford was soon "disposed to back out from the project of starting and editing the *Southern Patriot*." He thought "the prejudices of the community . . . so much excited that . . . [the] paper would do no good and could

not be sustained." But Perry's persistence renewed Elford's commitment. From Charleston Petigru "sent the money for twenty subscriptions," and by mid-November the *Southern Patriot*'s backers
were "scattering the Prospectus all over the Country. This is our
purpose," wrote Perry, "when the Paper starts to send it everywhere,
whether it is subscribed for or not."[37]

Outside Greenville, Perry had precious few allies. Poinsett,
leader of Charleston's Unionists during the nullification crisis, was
"seventy-one and feeble." He seemed "weary of statesmanship and
the life of a statesman."[38] Other nullification-era Unionist survivors
were dispirited or fatalistic about their ability to influence the
state's politics. In mid-September Petrigru hoped that the compromise had secured political peace for his lifetime. "I wish to leave
the world without more broils, happy that those I am to see are no
worse," he wrote from Philadelphia.[39] From New York, William Elliott observed that South Carolina's "political fever . . . rages worse
than the dengue . . . which I shall avoid—if I am not forced into it by
the intolerance and assumption of exclusive patriotism by the ruling
demagogery." Francis Lieber, having returned to his post at South
Carolina College, remained "a silent onlooker" until well into the
next year.[40] Only the sometime nullifier W. J. Grayson was eager to
wield a pen in defense of the Union.

At his own expense Grayson published as a pamphlet the twenty-
four-page "Letter . . . on the Dissolution of the Union," which refuted
charges against the compromise, denied that the federal government was oppressive, and cataloged the horrors that would follow
destruction of the Union.[41] Texas's senators had approved and her
citizens had accepted the boundary and debt settlement, Grayson
wrote. Why, then, should South Carolinians constitute themselves
"guardians of the persons and property of the good people of Texas?"
The territorial governments provided for Utah and New Mexico fulfilled Calhoun's demand that "Congress should include no provision
on the subject of slavery." California's admission with an antislavery
constitution was not congruent with the Wilmot Proviso; such an
argument was "a mere rhetorical flourish." For every southern emigrant "to California, one hundred or five hundred . . . go from other
countries. . . . Would the delay of a year, or ten years, have produced
a shade of change in her [antislavery] policy?" The new fugitive
slave law demonstrated the federal government's "disposition to
carry out the provisions of the Constitution," and, in enforcing that
law, Grayson trusted that "the friends of law and order" would prove

"more numerous and determined" than free "negroes and abolition-ists."[42] About abolition of the District's slave trade, Grayson chose to say nothing.

He rejected the analogy between the South's "relations with the General Government, and those of the Colonies with England at the time of the Revolution." Unlike the South's participation in the for-mation and subsequent operation of the federal government, the colonies "did not assist in forming [their central government] . . . they made no portion of it; they were without representation in either" the House of Lords or Commons. Within the Union the only problem facing the South, Grayson postulated, "is in the state of Northern Society; it is social, not political; it comes from the people of the North, not from the Government of the United States." The so-lution ought to be "directed against the people of whose sentiments and proceedings we complain, not the National Government which has done us no injury. . . . To the social wrong we . . . [should] apply a social remedy."[43]

To Grayson the evil consequences of dissolving the Union were as predictable as a proof in geometry. Achieved with difficulty and bal-anced with infinite care, the federal Union had resolved differences between states and sections, protected them from foreign interven-tion, and secured "unbroken internal peace . . . for seventy years." If the South destroyed the Union and attempted to establish another central government, Grayson asked, "Will the mountain region agree with the coast? Will the men . . . of East Tennessee, or West Virginia, consent to enjoy no greater political weight than the slaves of our rice and cotton-fields?" The secessionist prophecy "that all will be easy and smooth in the formation of a Southern Confederacy is a delusion and a snare. It will not be easy. Once break up the pres-ent Confederacy and the principle of voluntary cohesion is gone forever. In this as in every other movement of change or revolution men never go back. . . . [Disunion] will be followed by confusion and disorder first, and last by the forced combinations brought about by temporary interests, or military power."[44]

Grayson's effort inspired little literary support from fellow Union-ists. Separate and cooperative secessionists, however, penned nu-merous hostile reviews and replies. The Charleston *Daily Sun* denounced his "Letter." The *Mercury*'s editors received his views with "sorrow and amazement." Sadly noting the transmutation of Grayson's nullification-era loyalties, the *Mercury* found his pam-phlet "illogical and self-contradictory in the most material points."[45] The collector for the port of Charleston, his critics noted, had "a personal interest" in the continued existence of the federal government. "As to any effect which your opinions might have in our own State," he was assured, "we have no fears whatever, for we are united and prepared for the emergency of disunion."[46]

3

Watching for evidence that cooperative resistance to the compromise was possible, the Palmetto gentry saw discouraging signs on the South's western and northern flanks. In November the Texas legislature agreed to the boundary and debt settlement that Congress had tendered in the compromise: Texas had "accepted the bribe." The New Orleans *Picayune* hoped that "contentions and bickerings will cease, and harmony be again restored." Pierre Soule's lonely voice in opposition could scarcely be heard above the hum of business on Canal Street. Passage of the compromise measures returned North Carolina to her "accustomed and refreshing slumber" in which the state was content to "make her usual amount of Tar and Turpentine." Virginia's legislature "was to light up the fires of resistance on the passage of the Wilmot Proviso, or any kindred measure. . . . Alas!" lamented a *Mercury* correspondent, the Virginians "fulminated against the name not the substance." The South Carolinians could hope for support only from Georgia, Alabama, and Mississippi. They centered their attention first on Georgia.[47]

Governor Towns called Georgia's convention to meet in Milledgeville on December 10; election of delegates to the convention was scheduled for November 25. Anticipating Towns's proclamation, Robert Barnwell wrote Hammond: "Georgia is the first battlefield and we must fight gallantly there." Secessionists faced a difficult struggle in Georgia, Barnwell conceded; Whigs Toombs and Stephens and Democrats Cobb and Chappell were "foemen worthy of [their] steel."[48] Disunionists in Georgia had also to contend with the traditional hostility toward South Carolina, the economic rivalry between Charleston and Savannah, and the current prosperity of Georgia planters.

Despite Seabrook's official restraint "the old distrust of 'Palmettodom' persisted and grew in Georgia in proportion to the growing intensity of the secession controversy." Savannahians, especially, remembered that in 1847 "Charleston merchants, seeking to tap the export trade of the central Georgia cotton belt, [had] had the effrontery to petition the Georgia legislature for the incorporation of a trunk line that would have diverted the traffic of the Atlanta and Macon Railroad from Savannah to Charleston." The Palmetto gentry had good cause to fear that if South Carolina seceded "her ports would be blocked up—her trade would pass to Geo. and the appeal to Georgia cupidity . . . would be irresistible in keeping" Georgia in the Union.[49] Moreover "thirteen cents a pound for Cotton were powerful contributors to make civil war and revolution exceedingly distasteful to" Georgians.[50] As the Milledgeville *Federal Union* eventually admitted, some "large cotton planters . . . acted upon the principle openly acknowledged by one . . . give me my negroes for ten years, and cotton at thirteen cents, and then I shall be rich enough, and the negroes may go the d——l."[51]

Taking their tone from the governor's proclamation, Georgia's secessionists argued that slavery's very existence was at stake and openly advocated secession, but the unpopularity of this position forced them to modify their demands. "The issue of Union or disunion has been abandoned by most of those who are discontented with the late action of Congress," Stephens reported to Attorney General Crittenden, and "the more sagacious and cunning of the leaders now declare themselves not for disunion . . . but for some sort of resistance under the Constitution." The retreat of the radical Democrats, however, failed to recoup their popularity, nor did Whig Senator Berrien's plan to protest the compromise by economic "nonintercourse" with the North attract many of his old constituents; in the fall of 1850, Berrien was a leader without followers. The November 25 election confirmed the worst fears of the South Carolina gentry: procompromise, pro-Union candidates overwhelmed their opponents by a margin of nearly two-to-one.[52]

The response of Alabamans to the compromise was divided and difficult for South Carolinians to read. Senator William King seemed chiefly concerned with the well-being of his party; Whigs would sweep the next elections, he warned, if the Democratic label became synonymous with disunion. King's junior colleague Jeremiah Clemens was more forthright: he actively defended the compromise. William Lowndes Yancey, sometime congressman and full-time fire-eater, and John J. Seibels, editor of the Montgomery *Advertiser* who had been born in South Carolina, among other Alabama radicals, proclaimed that acquiescence in the compromise was treason to the South; they promoted the organization of Southern Rights Associations in the state. Unionists countered with rallies supporting the compromise and ridiculing secession. With public opinion deeply —and apparently evenly—divided, Governor Henry W. Collier proposed in late October that Alabama await the outcome of the re-assembled Nashville Convention and take no action until other southern states, particularly Georgia, Texas, and Virginia, ex-pressed their official attitudes toward the compromise.[53]

Unlike Collier, Mississippi's Governor Quitman had no use for delay. To Seabrook's circular letter of September 20, Quitman re-plied: "Before this reaches you, my proclamation of the 25th con-vening the Legislature . . . on the 18th Nov . . . will have conveyed a practical answer to . . . your letter." The recommendations Quitman would make to this special session were not in final form, he wrote, but "among them will be the call of a regular convention . . . with full powers to annul the Federal compact, establish new relations with other States, and adapt our organic laws to such new rela-tions."[54] Congressman Albert Gallatin Brown "heartily approved" of a special session; he "hoped it would call a State convention and that South Carolina, Georgia, Alabama, and Florida would 'meet us on a common platform, and resolve with us to stand or fall together.'" Except for Senator Foote, Mississippi's congressional delegation had resolutely opposed the compromise. Quitman's call for a special legislative session received strong support from that delegation, but his desire for speedy secession did not. Albert Brown and Jefferson Davis spoke for those Mississippi Democrats who were unterrified of disunion but who believed its time had not quite arrived.[55]

In the fall of 1850 Quitman was under federal indictment for violating the Neutrality Act of 1818 and was being pressed "to sur-render himself for trial or to submit to arrest," but he refused to be distracted from the pursuit of secession. Convinced that "the indict-ment was a maneuver to embarrass him," Quitman argued that, as governor, he was immune from prosecution; and he continued to exercise the powers of his office.[56]

In his message to the legislature, Quitman sketched the evils of the compromise and suggested that the "only effectual remedy . . . is to be found in the prompt and peaceable secession of the aggrieved states." The legislature responded by censuring Senator Foote for supporting the compromise.[57] Foote, however, was not without back-ers, especially among the state's Whigs. Outside the capitol's walls Mississippi's feisty senior senator addressed a procompromise rally, "called for the formation of a new Union Party and urged the crowd to 'censure the censurers.'"[58] Inside the legislative building, mean-while, Quitman's timetable for a state convention went awry. The bill he sponsored was "obstinately and ferociously opposed by a minority respectable in point of numbers." As a result the bill's supporters, Quitman confided to Rhett, provided for the convention to meet much later than the governor desired.[59] Nine months would pass before delegates would be elected and almost a year before the convention would assemble.

4

The potential of a reassembled Nashville Convention for promoting disunion had been considerably diminished by the South's early response to the completed compromise. However poor an opportunity to further cooperative secession, it was an opportunity South Carolina's leaders felt they must seize. James Hammond alone differed with the rest of the state's delegates "about the Nashville Convention. . . . If it meets under existing circumstances it will either split the South immediately or let it down to zero," he quietly predicted. The first session of the convention was not "recognized by the majority of the people of any state but ours and perhaps Mississippi as other than a self-constituted body and it was such to a very great extent. . . . It could be at the least a farce to repeat the experiment and I shall not attend it," he told Gilmore Simms.[60] Outside South Carolina Hammond's assessment was borne out by the attention given to the approaching second session of the convention: it was occasionally denounced but more often simply ignored.

William Sharkey, who had presided over the June session, was satisfied with the work of Congress and refused to summon the delegates to the November session.[61] Convention Vice-President Charles McDonald, however, agreed to act in Sharkey's place. A number of South Carolinians urged that the second session be held in Georgia to aid the campaign of secessionists there, but McDonald would not accept responsibility for changing the convention's site. Accordingly those delegates who still believed in the convention's importance gathered in Nashville on November 11. They numbered less than sixty; they represented, in some fashion, seven states; "and only the South Carolina and the Tennessee delegations were to any extent composed of the same men as in the June session." Except for the Tennesseans the convention's moderates did not attend in November. Disunionists would rule this rump session.[62]

"Thinking it possible that you may want your speeches (disunion) we send you copies," Elizabeth Rhett wrote her husband shortly before the convention reassembled. Disunion resolutions and speeches consumed most of the convention's time. The South Carolinians abandoned their sub-rosa tactics of the previous June, and Langdon Cheves, acting as principal spokesman for the delegation, offered a resolution that "secession, by the joint action of the slaveholding States is the only efficient remedy for . . . the enormous events which threaten them in the future, from the usurped and now unrestricted power of the Federal Government." He followed this resolution with an impassioned, three-hour speech. If Virginia, "the mother of the Southern States," led the movement for disunion, then secession could be accomplished peacefully, Cheves predicted. "Unite," he declaimed in an apostrophe to southern planters, "and your slave property shall be protected to the very border of Mason's and Dixon's line. Unite . . . and a tale of submission shall never be told!"[63]

By Saturday, November 16, the convention's resolutions committee had delivered its report. The Tennesseans, who had vainly urged conditional acceptance of the compromise, protested both the tone and substance of the committee's recommendations; "great as were Southern grievances," opined Gideon Pillow, "they did not justify such measures as the report contemplated." On November 18 further objections from the Tennesseans were quashed; A. O. P. Nicholson's attempt to address the galleries—galleries filled with "Yankee merchants, clerks and tradesmen, who . . . [were] Abolitionists at heart"—was ruled out of order. Secessionists ruthlessly invoked the previous question, and, with each delegation allowed one vote, the report was adopted six to one. Included among the report's resolutions was the recommendation that "the slaveholding States . . . meet in a Congress or Convention, to be held at such time and place as the States desiring to be represented, may designate, to be composed of . . . [delegates] entrusted with full power and authority to deliberate and act with the view and intention of arresting farther aggressions." Adoption of the report set off an impromptu pro-Union demonstration by the Tennessee delegation and the galleries, and amid noise and confusion the secessionist members of the Nashville Convention adjourned sine die.[64]

5

As the legislative session of 1850 drew nearer and nearer, the South Carolina gentry increasingly manifested a siege mentality. "For my part while I am no politician, but a Minister of Christ. . . . I think the alternative is secession or abolition. . . . I find myself unable to pray except as a *partisan*. I can not help feeling that we are in a contest, and praying that God would give *us* the victory," confessed John Adger to fellow clergyman James H. Thornwell. South Carolina's political warriors were eager for the clergy's blessing. The legislators unanimously proclaimed December 6 a "day of Humiliation and Fasting" on which the state's congregations should "ask divine guidance for the General Assembly." At St. Peter's Church the Reverend Mr. William Barnwell assured the faithful "that the State cannot and ought not to submit to the usurpations of the General Government. . . . Even those who would regard separate State-action as unwise . . . are ready to stand by the decision of the General Assembly at all hazards." Variations on this theme came from other preachers. The *Mercury*'s editors "rejoice[d] to see these solemn appeals to patriotism," which urged "Christians to act their part in preserving their own Government and social institutions from outrage and degradation."[65]

In 1849 the legislators had responded cautiously to Governor Seabrook's military recommendations; in 1850 they underwrote a program of military preparedness that exceeded the governor's requests. They established a "Board of Ordnance" to store, inspect, and purchase arms and ammunition for the state, and they revived "Brigade Encampments" to train the militia. Mindful of the state's dependence on the export trade, the legislators chartered the "South Carolina Atlantic Steam Navigation Company" and authorized a state loan of $125,000 to the company. Among other conditions the loan required that the company's vessels "be built . . . in such style and manner . . . as will make them available in an emergency for war purposes" and that, upon demand, the company be prepared to sell the state "all of the steam-vessels built under this Charter."[66]

The legislators' desire for military preparedness made for a substantial increase in the state's budget. In addition to routine military expenditures, the legislature appropriated $350,000 to be spent "as recommended in the Report of the Committee on the Military . . . and in" the act establishing the board of ordnance and requiring brigade encampments. To fund this increase the legislature, among other levies, raised taxes on slaves, agricultural land, town "lots, lands and buildings," stock in trade, business commissions, and professional fees.[67]

Robert Allston, newly elected president of the state senate, expected that the legislature would choose a new governor and senator by December 3 and proceed to "the excited—the stirring debate."[68] In fact debate on secession so preoccupied the legislators that successors to Governor Seabrook and interim-Senator Barnwell were not elected until the middle of December. The legislators anticipated a quick and easy decision in the gubernatorial contest and scheduled it first.

The leading candidates in the fall had been Robert Barnwell, Francis Pickens, and John H. Means. Barnwell, however, renounced all ambition for office.[69] Pickens's political career had only recently revived, but his prospects were boosted by his services as a Nashville Convention delegate.[70] Means's credentials as a defender of South Carolina's presumed rights were well-established and his commitment to secession was forthright. Senate President Allston considered Means "an untried man, fond of popular favor, and very successful in commanding it." The last judgment, at least, was accurate; Means handily defeated Pickens and was inaugurated governor on December 16.[71]

The principal contenders for Calhoun's senate seat were Hammond and Rhett. Just before the election Hammond confided to his diary that "with the help of God and Tolerable health, I could guide the State and the South through all their present difficulties. And if there is another man who can do it, I do not know him." Rhett was equally confident. Anointed as Calhoun's successor by the legislature, the victor would enjoy—at least temporarily—a measure of the moral authority Calhoun had wielded. On November 21, responding to an invitation from the Charleston City Council, Hammond delivered a "Eulogy and Funeral Oration" on Calhoun. One week later, addressing the legislature at Governor Seabrook's request, Rhett delivered his eulogy on Calhoun. Willingly or unwillingly the orators were pitted in a symbolic "contest for the crown."[72]

To intimates and political allies, Hammond "declared . . . against our State's seceding now as impolitic." The "aggressions of the abolitionists" would ultimately force the South to join South Carolina in secession, but "the true crisis" had not arrived. In the meantime the Palmetto State should concentrate on improving its logistical capacity to wage war rather than on "breaking openly with the Federal Government . . . or calling a Convention" or making vain gestures in response to the speeches at Nashville. Rhett, of course, viewed the situation differently. The constant prophet of secession "came to Columbia with the assembling of the legislature to throw all his strength" behind the demand for a secession convention. He came also to direct the final phase of his campaign for the Senate.[73]

On the first ballot Rhett led with 56 votes, followed by Hammond with 50, Barnwell with 27, James Chesnut with 15, and Joseph Woodward with 14; three other candidates received 2 votes each. On the fourth ballot Rhett won with 97 votes to Hammond's 46. Hammond's supporters attributed his defeat largely to his decision not to return to Nashville; Lewis Ayer added that Hammond's "enemies were more active the first week of the Session than . . . since. The fact is that the debates on our federal relations absorbed all attention." Hammond received the news of his defeat bitterly. He judged that the victory of Means, and especially of Rhett, meant that "the Legislature have given their approbation to *abortive violence*. For they are both of the violent, bugle blast section and neither of them capable of effecting any thing." James Petigru watched the election from the capitol gallery and interpreted the results quite differently: "There were but two candidates, Rhett and Hammond, and yet it required four ballotings. . . . The whole Legislature, with very few exceptions, are declared disunionists, yet they object to Barnwell Rhett because he was so violent. I infer from this that they are not so mad as they affect to be, and that with a great deal of real malice there is a good deal of acting." In commenting on the senatorial election, the *Mercury's* editors felt compelled to stress that the state's harmony—always so dear to Calhoun's heart—was undisturbed. According to the *Mercury*, Hammond and Rhett were "so nearly identical . . . in political faith, that the vote may be taken as an almost unanimous decision in favor of resistance."[74]

Before South Carolina's legislators were elected, separate secessionists had urged voters to "call on every candidate to answer, categorically, whether he will vote, if elected, for a Convention or not. . . . Let Convention or no Convention, where there is any difference of opinion on this measure, be the turning point of the election."[75] The structure and style of South Carolina politics, however, precluded such clear tests. The state's planter-politicians agreed that a constituent convention could ordain secession, but the legislative session of 1850 revealed a deep disagreement on when and under what circumstances that convention should meet.

Just before departing for Columbia, a disconsolate B. F. Perry predicted: "A convention of the State will be called. That convention will in all probability secede from the Union." Having taken his seat Perry estimated that "there were not more than four or five Union men in the house."[76] Some of the roll-call votes on convention proposals indicated that Unionists of all shades numbered perhaps twice Perry's figure.[77] But in any case they constituted a tiny minority of the 123 house members. From the gallery a South Carolina matron watched one of Perry's "*submission speech[es]*" and noted gleefully that "in the midst of it, some member gave a tremendous *yawn* which so discomposed Major P. that he took his seat and did not say another word." Since direct arguments against secession were futile, the Unionists supported measures that promised, at least, to delay secession. Hoping that the gentry's anger over the compromise would cool with time, Perry sponsored a resolution designed to channel that anger into yet another southern convention.[78]

The separate secessionists believed that South Carolina's goals must be "first, secession from the Union . . . and, secondly, the formation of a Southern Confederacy. To do either, or both of these things, there must be a convention of the State." Separate secessionists were willing to set the date for that convention as late as December 1851 (after Mississippi's convention had met and acted). They were willing to attend a Southern Congress—if one could be organized before South Carolina's convention met. But they were determined to call a constituent convention on a fixed date. Should Mississippi, or any other state, join South Carolina in secession that would be well and good; but, they argued, the Palmetto State must secede with or without promises of support. They accepted the probability that South Carolina must act first and alone. She would thus, they believed, "force into existence a Southern Confederacy."[79]

Cooperationists lacked the cohesiveness that the pursuit of an immediate and positive goal imparted to their secessionist colleagues. Like secessionists, however, cooperationists favored military preparedness measures; "An Act to Provide for the Defence of the State" constituted, if nothing else, an earnest of South Carolina's dissatisfaction with the Union. Some cooperationists would accept isolated secession—but only after initiatives to secure joint action had failed. Others argued that South Carolina should never secede alone, that successful resistance to the federal government would require collaboration among the slave states, and that even "*ten years*" of labor to achieve such cooperation would be "time *well spent*."[80] Cooperationists were finally united only in their unwillingness to embrace separate secession under the circumstances prevailing in December 1850. Their rallying point—and their counterproposal to the secessionists' demand for a state convention—was endorsement of the Southern Congress recommended by the Nashville Convention.

Secessionists enjoyed an overwhelming majority in the senate; they also commanded a majority in the house. Cooperationists, however, had able leaders who occupied influential house positions. Christopher Memminger, chairman of the Ways and Means Committee, was the cooperationists' chief tactician; his maneuvers were well-supported by John S. Preston, chairman of the Committee on

Federal Relations, and by James Chesnut, Jr., James H. Irby, and Edward McCrady, who were members of that committee. The cooperationists judged that their numbers were increasing as the session wore on. Although a bill to call a state convention in December 1851 won approval in the senate by 37 to 6 and in the house by 75 to 42, it failed because a two-thirds majority of the total membership of *each* house was required in order to call a constituent convention. Secessionists would not accept the cooperationist alternative— unless it also provided for a state convention on a fixed date. The impasse produced long amendments and short tempers. "We are not sufficiently united here," grumbled Robert Allston, "and there has been so much talking for ten days past in the other House, that time has been insensibly lost."[81]

On reconsideration of the cooperationists' "Bill to provide for the appointment of Deputies to a Southern Congress," John I. Middleton moved an amendment by which the bill would also provide for a state convention in February 1852. With 80 house members in favor and 32 opposed, Middleton's effort fell 2 votes short of the necessary two-thirds majority, but this suggested a way around the impasse. After a series of amendments compromise was achieved. The compromise bill endorsed the southern "Congress or Convention" recommended by the Nashville Convention and suggested that this congress meet in Montgomery, Alabama, on January 2, 1852. The bill stipulated that on October 13 and 14, 1851, each of South Carolina's congressional districts would elect two delegates to the proposed congress and that during its current session the legislature would designate four delegates-at-large. The bill also provided for a constituent convention in South Carolina. In this convention each electoral district was entitled to a delegation "equal to the whole number of Senators and Representatives" which the district sent to the legislature. Delegates to the state convention would be elected on February 10 and 11, 1851—but no date for the convention itself was fixed. That task was left to the next legislature. In the unlikely event that the proposed congress took place before the next legislative session, the governor was empowered to name the day on which the state's constituent convention would assemble.[82]

The compromise bill passed its crucial test in the house by a vote of 109 to 12. In the senate a final move to delete the Southern Congress portion of the bill failed by a vote of 37 to 5. On December 20 the bill became law, and the legislators elected Langdon Cheves, Robert Barnwell, John Richardson, and Wade Hampton delegates-at-large to the contemplated Southern Congress.[83] The next day the legislature adjourned, maintaining the tradition of completing public business in time for the members to spend Christmas on their plantations. They had enacted measures other than the convention bill. They had postponed—after a minor tempest precipitated by the clumsy diplomacy of British consul George B. Mathew—reassessment of the Negro Seaman Law. The session had fulfilled the *Mercury*'s prediction that "the proposed changes in the school system, the criminal law, the mode of granting charters of incorporation, and other matters, important in themselves, but not especially pressing" would be shunted aside in the effort to decide whether South Carolina would secede.[84]

6

In honor of the legislature's convention bill, a "grand salute of one-hundred guns was fired from the battery by the Washington artillery." The *Mercury* was certain that the "adoption of this decisive measure" would "be greeted in every district of South Carolina with equally cordial manifestations of approval." Favoring separate secession, the paper's editors chose to interpret the session's outcome as a triumph for the "resistance party" and asserted that the state's "true resistance men"—whatever their prior differences —would wholeheartedly support the constituent convention's decision on secession. Cooperationists were less inclined to minimize the gentry's division over separate secession; they expected that division to become a political fixture in 1851. "The truth is," wrote Hammond, "that Rhett and his set want confidence in the people . . . they determined to commit them *irretrievably at once*. Rhett himself told me in Charleston that the people would cool down unless we pushed onwards and kept them excited. Hence the calling of Conventions *now* which are not to meet until *after another session of our Legislature*." Hammond predicted that the proposed Southern Congress would never meet and that a reaction would "take place in this State against the puerile wild and injurious measures of the late session."[85]

B. F. Perry saw the legislature's convention bill as "the beginning of a Revolution or rather an attempt at Revolution." He, too, believed that such an attempt could end only in fiasco: "South Carolina alone is disposed to be dissatisfied and overturn the government. This she cannot do." He opined hopefully that the legislature's "prodigal appropriations and increase of taxes have produced a reaction in

Greenville in favor of the Union. Touching the purse of a patriot is touching him in a tender point and he feels it very quickly."[86]

Perry's dogged opposition to secession was slowly eliciting support from old-line Unionists. During the legislative session Poinsett wrote a public letter that defended the compromise and warned "of the fearful consequences of revolution." Noting that all his wealth was "vested in lands and negroes," Poinsett argued that the federal Union offered slavery its only safe refuge. A southern "Confederacy would present no barrier against the attacks of the Abolitionists of all the world. The sympathies of civilized Europe are against our institutions, and if they be not protected by the Constitution and the much despised Union, our slaves would not be worth ten years purchase." Separate secessionists mistook "violence for strength." A glance at "the map and . . . the census," Poinsett suggested, would demonstrate how easily "South Carolina might be prevented from inflicting any injury except upon herself."[87] With encouragement from Poinsett and a few others, Perry, meanwhile, was bringing to fruition his plans for *The Southern Patriot*, an organ dedicated to "the Rights of the South, the Federal Constitution, and the Integrity of the Union of the States."[88]

Unionists in South Carolina were heartened, too, by recent events in Georgia. On December 10 the delegates to Georgia's constituent convention assembled in Milledgeville. By December 14 they had framed a preamble and five resolutions that enunciated the state's official attitude toward the compromise. The preamble denounced extremists of both sections; it admonished northern Unionists to suppress attacks on slavery, and it pronounced secession a "decidedly unwise" and counterproductive response to the compromise. In addition the preamble stated (and the third resolution reiterated) the delegates' solemn pledge that Georgia, "whilst she does not wholly approve [of the compromise], will abide by it as a permanent adjustment of this sectional controversy." The fourth and fifth resolutions made that pledge a conditional one; the fourth enumerated possible congressional actions that Georgia "ought to resist even to a disruption of . . . the Union," and the fifth warned that the preservation of the Union depended "upon a faithful execution of the *Fugitive Slave Law*." The convention's product, soon dubbed the "Georgia Platform," was all that southern Unionists had wanted, all that South Carolina's leaders had feared. Secessionists and cooperationists both deplored the Georgia platform, but they drew different lessons from it.[89]

Initially the *Mercury* had kind words for the fourth and fifth resolutions being considered by Georgia's convention. The paper's Milledgeville correspondent, however, reported that in sum the convention's "action was as tame and submissive as the veriest Northern Compromisers could desire. The great object of its [the convention's] managers seemed to be to form a sort of National Union party." The *Mercury*'s editors concluded, finally, that Georgia was deservedly "called 'the New England of the South.' "[90] Palmetto secessionists argued that the Georgia platform merely added to the accumulating evidence that cooperative secession was unobtainable. The last and "the brightest hope of ultimate Southern Union was in the separate action of South Carolina." If the federal government responded to South Carolina's secession with force, "no member of the Federal Union . . . [could remain] neutral. . . . To follow our example, and take their places by our sides . . . [would] be the only mode by which our Southern brethren would escape from this war against us." The indefinite delay—which cooperationists seemed increasingly willing to espouse—would only "diminish both the chances of ultimate [southern] union and our ability to defend ourselves."[91]

Secessionists denied the possibility, raised by cooperationists, that the federal government could end a South Carolina experiment in independence by maintaining a bloodless blockade of her ports. That scheme could not "avoid the issue of war," because it would prove impossible to confine hostilities "to the act of blockade alone." Moreover Great Britain would not respect a federal blockade of South Carolina. Without "the cotton of the slaveholding South," Britain's "manufactories would be closed, and millions of her people reduced to pauperism . . . her laboring classes, driven to despair by want, would speedily involve her in revolution. All the dictates of interests," then, "would impel her" to support South Carolina's right "to secede at pleasure."[92]

Secessionists also argued that, "whatever may be the fears of many . . . on the score of coercion, blockades, dismemberment, and all the alarming *et ceteras*," South Carolina's course for the past two years had committed her to secession and South Carolina was bound by honor to secede, regardless of the military and commercial risks. The chief advocate of secession was quite prepared to undertake those risks. "Of course you will volunteer, if there is any prospect of the Govt. coercing South Carolina," wrote the state's new senator to his eldest son.[93]

The cooperationist minority in the legislature had fought a cunctative battle. In January 1851, when debate moved outside legis-

lative halls, cooperationists were again on the defensive; advocates
of separate secession dominated the South Carolina press. In mid-
January, however, the cooperationist cause began to find polemi-
cists. Denying that South Carolina's legislative resolutions and acts
of the last two years had committed the state to separate secession, a
cooperationist spokesman observed that the legislature had elected
Robert Barnwell and Langdon Cheves as "Delegates to the Southern
Congress . . . [and] they were both known to be utterly opposed
to South Carolina acting alone." Since "Virginia, North Carolina,
Florida, Georgia, Alabama, Arkansas, Louisiana have, either by
resolution or by their acts" accepted the compromise, since their
judgment was contrary to South Carolina's, was it probable they
would leave the Union "without a word to come to . . . [South Carolina's] relief?" The cooperationists answered, of course, that such an
expectation was "idle, vain, delusive."[94] Separate secession threatened South Carolina with a reprise of the nullification crisis: isolation. This became a constant theme of the cooperationists. Returning
from "sacred duties in Tennessee, Mississippi, Louisiana, Alabama,
and Georgia," Bishop William Capers of the Methodist Church
South opined that "three-fourths of the [southern] people would oppose . . . [secession] at the present time." South Carolina's secession
"at once, or at a future time, alone . . . [would] be to secede from
the other Southern States no less than from the Northern," Capers
warned. There was, finally, "no battle to be fought for glory, by secession, but a fearful struggle with poverty and high taxes, hard times,
without hope of improvement. . . . And may God grant us deliv-
erance."[95]

While secessionists presented their case through the press, they
also began to convert the machinery of Southern Rights Associations to their purposes. When Barnwell District's association met on
January 6, its secessionist members had prepared an agenda and
were present in force. Edmund Bellinger spoke for his colleagues
and presented, "by way of response to the action of the Legislature,"
a series of resolutions. The last of these declared the association's
opinion "That after all the proposed means of procuring . . . united
Southern action shall have failed," South Carolina should "alone
strike the blow" to dissolve the Union.[96]

Secessionist members of Southern Rights Associations in the parishes followed the pattern established at Barnwell. To the discom-
fort of its president Robert Barnwell, the St. Helena association
unanimously resolved "that in the crisis that has come" South Carolina must trust "under God, in herself" alone. The most extreme

manifesto came from St. Bartholomew's; there the association "disapprove[d] of the proceedings of the Legislature . . . touching the matter of State action . . . as productive of needless delay." St. Bartholomew's association "approve[d] of the increase" in taxes necessary to fund "defence against threatened aggression" and resolved that no candidate from that parish "should be entrusted with a seat" in the state convention unless he was "prepared to pledge his vote for separate State action." Cooperationists in Christ Church replied through the parish's Southern Rights Association that it was a "wiser course not to commit . . . [convention] delegates at this time to any specific measures." But cooperationists were generally slow to organize locally, and secessionists were winning control of most associations.[97]

The *Mercury* had proposed that Charleston's Southern Rights Association have a quasi-official role in selecting the city's delegates to the state convention. The St. Philip's and St. Michael's association should, it suggested, nominate a slate of candidates, "after having previously laid down a platform of political doctrine." The Charleston association was too evenly divided between cooperationists and secessionists to agree either on a platform or candidates, but a number of low-country associations besides St. Bartholomew's followed this formula. Secessionists also staged public meetings to instruct local candidates on how to vote and called for candidates to pledge themselves unequivocally for or against separate secession. As long as both instructions and pledges were limited to an issue carefully defined by gentry spokesmen, secessionist politicians saw no "impropriety in the People's requiring of those who represent them in this Convention, a distinct declaration of the course they design to pursue."[98]

Cooperationists accused their opponents of disrupting the "quiet and natural" course of debate, of trying to compel a premature decision on secession. Cooperationists deplored calls for binding pledges from state convention candidates. "It would be most unreasonable to suppose that any one, possessed of the proper qualifications, would pledge himself to any specific conduct during the session of a Convention, which will not take place until some time in the year 1852," wrote A. G. Magrath. Isaac Hayne, John Zimmerman, A. P. Aldrich, and other cooperationist candidates for the state convention entirely agreed.[99] When the votes cast on February 10 and 11 had been tabulated, the *Mercury* claimed that 127 of the 169 delegates chosen were in favor of separate secession.[100] Nevertheless the election was a questionable triumph for secession's generals. In Charleston their forces had been routed. Fifteen of the twenty delegates elected from Charleston had been included on the cooperationists' slate of candidates. Numbered among those victors were the state's most prominent cooperationists: Langdon Cheves, Robert Barnwell, Christopher Memminger, Daniel Huger, Senator A. P. Butler, Judges Edward Frost and Mitchell King, Chancellor Benjamin Dunkin, and Attorney General Isaac Hayne.[101] Secessionists fared dismally, too, in Greenville, where a slate of Unionists won. In slave-poor Horry District no polls were opened,[102] and more ominous for secessionists than local defeats was the low turnout of voters statewide.

In Charleston only 873 ballots were cast for convention delegates compared to the 2,743 for legislative candidates cast the previous fall—a decline in voting of nearly 70 percent.[103] Francis Lieber reported that in the February elections Richland District polled about 800 votes compared to "1400 votes at a late election for the Legislature." Even secessionists conceded that the state's aggregate vote total was low. A majority of the delegates elected were separate secessionists, but the remedy they espoused had hardly won massive endorsement at the polls. Secessionist leaders were haunted by the "general apathy among the people" noted by Hammond and other observers. Rhett's "game . . . [was] to commit the state as early and as deeply as possible. He feared a cooling down." Cooperationists devoutly hoped that February's light vote signaled such "a cooling down."[104]

On February 5 Elizabeth Rhett informed her husband that "the country is coming out bravely for secession; though the city [Charleston] still shews a craven spirit of doubt and fear." The Palmetto State's premier fire-eater had been able to take little, if any, part in the campaign that preceded the February elections. Since January 6 he had been serving as senator from South Carolina, an office that would soon cease to exist if Rhett had his way.[105] A month before Rhett arrived in Washington, President Fillmore had delivered a ringing defense of the compromise and asserted that it was "final and irrevocable." The New Yorker made plain his determination to enforce all provisions of the sectional settlement—including the Fugitive Slave Act. Senators on both sides of the aisle echoed Fillmore. But the fugitive slave issue continued to loom as the most immediate threat to the compromise's much proclaimed "finality." It was on the fugitive slave issue that the foremost champion of secession made his only major speech of the session.[106]

While the proviso "had dealt with a hypothetical slave who might never materialize," the Fugitive Slave Act dealt with real and visible people whose pluck and ingenuity had won them freedom. The Fugitive Slave Act mandated the return of past as well as future escapees, and it stipulated that northern citizens were required, under certain circumstances, to render physical assistance in the recapture of fugitives. "That obligation galled: it was a direct and personal challenge to the conscience."[107] Boston abolitionists pledged that the law would not be enforced in their city. In October 1850 they made good on that promise in the case of fugitives William and Ellen Craft. South Carolina's politicians had predicted that northern attitudes would make any fugitive slave law a dead letter, and Palmetto secessionists interpreted the episode involving the Crafts as a fulfillment of that prediction.[108]

In February 1851 Boston was the scene of another sensational rescue: a crowd of free blacks took the slave Shadrach from the custody of a deputy marshal and whisked the fugitive away to Canada. In the wake of this incident, Henry Clay introduced a resolution asking President Fillmore to report on the "alleged case of forcible resistance to the execution of . . . [the Fugitive Slave Act] in the city of Boston." Fillmore's response triggered a three-day, running debate on the Fugitive Slave Act and its enforcement. Speaking for the architects of the compromise, Clay "asserted that the law was being enforced without any uproar in Indiana, Ohio, Pennsylvania, New York City, and everywhere except at Boston." Senators Butler and Rhett believed otherwise, and on February 24 Rhett delivered a lengthy opinion on the fugitive slave issue.[109]

Rhett did not think the act could be enforced, because a "law to have its practical effect must move in harmony with the opinions and feelings of the community where it is to operate. In this case," he believed, "the feeling of the whole and entire North . . . is opposed to the institution of slavery and opposed to this law." Moreover Rhett, the faithful states-rights ideologue who "abhor[red] constructions," was unwilling to concede the federal government's authority over slavery even when that authority was to be used on behalf of the owners of runaway slaves.[110] The power to return fugitive slaves, he said, rightfully belonged only to the states; the constitution enjoined them to return such fugitives. The fact that northern states were unwilling to meet this obligation was one more sign that the Union could not endure,[111] nor could it be made to endure by the federal government's usurpation of the power and responsibility to return fugitives, a usurpation begun by the Supreme Court's "disastrous decision" in the case of *Prigg* v. *Pennsylvania* (1842). The northern states' obedience to the constitution, Rhett declaimed, was "gone, gone forever; and . . . this Union will soon come to an end."[112]

After this speech Rhett said little. The senator chosen by South Carolina's secessionists did not elaborate his views on the necessity for or the process of disunion. He delivered no ultimatum. During the Senate's special session that immediately followed the term of the Thirty-First Congress, he complained about the Senate's dilatory pace and waited impatiently to address Palmetto audiences once again. "I have done what my duty requires of me," he announced on March 11, "and as other duties call me elsewhere, I shall stay here no longer."[113]

7

Senator Rhett had not been warmly received by any of his deep South colleagues. Their views reflected intrastate divisions along a line quite different from the one that divided South Carolina's gentry. In the Palmetto State two varieties of secessionists did battle, but in Georgia, Alabama, and Mississippi defenders of the Union opposed advocates of Southern Rights. In the fall of 1850 these groups were "ostensibly pro-Compromise Union and prosecession Southern Rights parties. . . . In actuality the Southern Rights parties quickly jettisoned serious plans for secession."[114] The Georgia platform signaled the ascendancy of that state's Unionists. By 1851 only Alabama and Mississippi remained as potential allies of South Carolina in any effort to resist the compromise.

Alabama's Southern Rights activists were concentrated in the state's Southern Rights Associations. By February twenty-five of these associations had been organized in fourteen counties, and the members were summoned to convene in Montgomery on February 10. Despite encouraging words and occasional visits from members of South Carolina associations, the Southern Rights Associations of Alabama were (and remained) far less militant than those of Carolina, and the results of the Montgomery convention were disappointing to Carolinians. Neither the convention's resolutions, nor its "Address to the People of Alabama" explicitly advocated disunion. Radicals at the convention had to be satisfied with the declaration that "the question of the secession of Alabama from this government is reduced to that of time only."[115]

Moreover the convention's attempt to define policy for all of the state's Southern Rights factions succeeded only in highlighting their differences. On the one hand Alabama's most militant secessionists were soon flaying the state's most celebrated fire-eater for advising Alabamans "to abandon the idea of secession, and . . . [to accept] the Georgia Platform . . . [as] the very thing for them." On the other the conservative Southern Rights Association of Mobile not only opposed Alabama's secession but also declared "it unwise in any single state to separate herself from states with whose destiny she is and should be indissolubly connected in resistance to a common wrong. Such action would seriously jeopardize the great interests at issue."[116]

In Mississippi, meanwhile, the staunchest champion of secession had been rendered hors de combat by his legal problems; on February 3 Governor Quitman resigned his office. He had decided, finally, that the issue of Mississippi's secession should not be mingled with the issue of his alleged complicity in the López expedition against Cuba.[117] Noting Quitman's decision, the *Mercury* observed that if he had not been the leader of Mississippi's secessionists, "he would not have been troubled about Cuba." In March the federal prosecutors dropped the suits against all defendants in the López matter.[118] Quitman was free to devote himself once again to Mississippi's secession—but he was no longer Mississippi's governor.

Moreover, the state's Democratic party (in which disunion sentiment was concentrated) had fragmented on the issue of secession. By the spring of 1851 Albert G. Brown sounded much less aggrieved with the compromise than he had the previous fall; Unionist organs mercilessly taunted him as a trimmer. Jefferson Davis "favored resistance to the Compromise, but only through concerted southern action and, most important, within the Union." Quitman remained "unswerving in his belief that independent state action was the only course," and Henry Foote, leader of the new Union party, proved adept at keeping his erstwhile Democratic colleagues at odds with each other.[119]

8

South Carolina's Unionists lacked both the numbers and the morale necessary for party organization, but by the spring of 1851 they no longer lacked a Unionist organ. The first number of Perry's *Southern Patriot* appeared on February 28. The paper was warmly received and generously supported by the South's Unionists, especially those in Georgia. Inside South Carolina, too, the *Southern Patriot* found patrons willing to underwrite subscriptions for lapsed believers and, in one case, for "the hottest Secessionists in the Pedee country." In Charleston, Poinsett boasted that the new paper gave "general satisfaction to the thinking part of the community," and Petigru wrote: "I would like to correspond with you as a contributor but have not the spirit, if I had the opportunity. But I admire your courage and applaud your sentiments." Up-country subscribers were more enthusiastic, and they were more optimistic about Perry's chances of winning converts. The "good sense of the people throughout the state will sustain you and approve your course so soon as they are properly informed upon the subject," wrote Winnsboro's J. M. Rutland. "They have as yet heard but one side of the question."[120]

Claiming that less than a "third of the voters went to the polls" in February, editor Perry argued that separate secession was the goal of a tightly knit group of extremists not of the majority of South Carolina whites. Perry depicted the secessionists as mostly political novices, "a set of young enthusiasts inspired with notions of personal honor to be defended and individual glory, fame and military laurels to be acquired." Palmettodom's largest slaveholders, her oldest and most experienced leaders opposed "this new remedy of secession for redressing our wrongs, without the co-operation of the other slaveholding States." Boldly—and very loosely—Perry glossed the cooperationist position. His strategy, of course, was to widen the gap between the state's dominant political groups and to blur the distinction between cooperationists and Unionists. Cooperationist William W. Boyce responded favorably to Perry's efforts. "I would have a Southern Confederacy, but this is out of the question now, and I am utterly opposed to single isolated secession," Boyce wrote. He embraced "concert of action" between Unionists and cooperationists "to prevent secession."[121] Most cooperationists, however, objected loudly to Perry's interpretation of their views and continued to denounce Union submissionists.

Meanwhile in Washington, Secretary of the Treasury Thomas Corwin was informed that James Gadsden, superintendent of the Charleston customs house, and others "in the service of the Government" were proponents of secession. Corwin sought W. J. Grayson's advice on whether to remove these men and, more generally, on what the administration's patronage policy in South Carolina should be.[122] Since "a majority in this state . . . are willing to see the Union destroyed," Grayson replied, heavy-handed use of the patronage whip "would serve as fresh fuel to the fires of excitement." The administration should not "expect a sudden revulsion [sic] of opinion but a slow and gradual change only. . . . If the Secession party can be divided, so that a line may be drawn between the advocates of secession by the State alone, and those who, although professing . . . disunion, would postpone it," Grayson wrote, "the Country will be safe. This is not only the most expedient proceeding, but in the present State of public opinion here, the only one that can be pursued with any good effect." He recommended that only separate secessionists be excluded from government patronage. His counsel prevailed. The Fillmore administration concluded that it was wiser to encourage the schism between cooperationists and secessionists than to combat both varieties of disunionists.[123]

In the spring of 1851 the gap between secessionists and cooperationists was increasing, but it was not yet unbridgeable. In the main secessionists acknowledged that cooperationists were "resistance men," and most cooperationists proclaimed their ideological affinity with secessionists. Speaking for Cheves, Butler, Barnwell, and other cooperationist leaders, Isaac Hayne declared that Perry's "pursuit of a cherished object" had "betrayed [him] into both a perversion of general facts, and a misrepresentation of individual positions." Hoping to establish a common front for the South at large, cooperationists had certainly not forsworn one for their state. "Abolition . . . is not a placable madness . . . if let alone [it] will so kick your state & others, that resistance becomes inevitable. I am willing to wait awhile in this hope,—making in the meanwhile all possible preparations," Gilmore Simms wrote Virginia's Beverley Tucker.[124] To cooperationists patience was both a virtue and a policy, but to secessionists patience was a euphemism for indecision. This, they argued, was a fatal vice for a slaveholding society. Secessionists refused to evangelize indefinitely; they embraced the necessity of forcing their issue even at the risk of dividing the Palmetto gentry into warring camps.

Looking to the possible consequences of secession, Governor Means wrote to Hammond about the disposition of cannon that the former governor had removed "from the Old Fort near Beaufort." The Board of Ordnance, largely staffed with Means's appointees, set in motion plans to establish "a permanent manufactory of small arms in Columbia." The first of the revived brigade encampments for South Carolina militia began on March 31, and Governor Means and his military aides reviewed the encampment daily.[125]

These officials soon learned, however, that relatively modest dislocations required to prepare for secession would be accompanied by loud objections about costs and inconveniences. Charlestonians were extremely leery of the Board of Ordnance plan to construct a new magazine in their city. Even the secessionist *Mercury* opined that locating "a large Magazine of powder in the heart of a city is neither wise nor humane." Brigade encampments, too, were not universally popular with the men required to attend them or the citizens of nearby towns. "It is a notorious fact," wrote one noncommissioned officer, "that the majority of sergeants . . . are poor men. . . . A great many live forty or fifty miles . . . from the Encampments. [They] . . . will be absent from their farms at least ten days . . . their crops will be very much injured . . . and they are not compensated with a single dollar to defray their expenses. This is not only unfair, but absolutely ridiculous."[126] These grievances were not orchestrated by cooperationists, but their cause profited from them.

While Rhett was absent from South Carolina, Governor Means promoted separate secession with the help of former governors Seabrook and Richardson, Maxcy Gregg, James Adams, James Jones, J. C. Coit, Edmund Bellinger, and Edward Rhett, all of whom were delegates to the state convention.[127] Jones tried to add Hammond to the list of secessionist leaders and persisted, despite rebuffs, in plying him with secessionist arguments. Through the press and private correspondence, secessionists busily sought proselytes and denounced a lone backslider, William A. Owens, who defended his renunciation of separate secession in an "Address to the People of Barnwell District." During February and March, however, secessionist and cooperationist broadsides only rehearsed old arguments. The dispute between the two groups continued within the framework dictated by the legislature's compromise convention bill.[128]

But on April 7 Rhett made a speech that signaled a change in secessionist tactics and increased the urgency of South Carolina's internal quarrel. The occasion was the quarterly meeting of Charleston's Southern Rights Association. He acknowledged that the secessionist majority in the last legislature had agreed reluctantly to work for cooperative secession before resorting to separate secession. But "time, resistless time," he declared, "has settled at least one branch of this policy. Southern co-operation is at an end." Only Mississippi remained as a potential partner in secession, and Mississippi would not secede, according to Rhett, "She had no seaport suitable for transatlantic commerce . . . she cannot secede from the Union without her co-terminous States. . . . With the failure of

Mississippi to give us her cooperation, ends all Southern co-operation: no Southern Congress will meet." Even if a Southern Congress met, it

> would be our ruin . . . what would be its counsel? Submission.
> . . . However matters may have stood formerly, the only alter-
> native now presented to us, is submission, or secession by South
> Carolina alone. . . . [Since the co-operationists'] policy has
> become impracticable, ought they not to join with us in the last
> and only measure of redress that is left? . . . [With] their high
> regard for the honor of our State, can they counsel us to sub-
> mission? . . . Will they not rather join us . . . [in] a brave and
> united effort for redress and independence, by the secession of
> South Carolina alone from the Union?[129]

Having delivered this manifesto Rhett turned to favorite and traditional themes. After secession South Carolina should levy an ad valorem tariff of only 10 percent; with this virtual free-trade policy the state would enjoy an economic renascence. Rhett did "not believe that war of any kind . . . [would] follow as a consequence of our secession," but "if the free States use the General Government to make war on South Carolina . . . a Southern Confederacy is as sure to come as the succeeding year." The threat of a bloodless "blockade is a humbug," he said. "Blockade is war." If the blockading forces tried to obscure that fact, South Carolina "must storm the forts . . . where this aggression is carried on, and capture the ships of war employed against us. It will be war on all sides . . . which will only end in a Southern Confederacy, or the utter extinction of South Caro-lina as a State." With a revolutionary's faith Rhett could blandly contemplate such alternatives. His peroration offered both reassur-ance and benediction. Disunity in South Carolina "will alone tempt an effort at coercion. . . . When the State Convention shall deter-mine on the mode of redress—when it withdraws this State from the Union . . . unite in secession and with God's blessing, redemption is at hand for us and ours."[130]

Rhett's speech both heralded and justified a quickening in the secessionists' campaign to control South Carolina's Southern Rights Associations and their statewide convention. Envisioning "a more perfect organization" of the state's associations and hoping for "the reconciliation of conflicting opinions," the Charleston association had proposed in January that "the Southern Rights Associations throughout the State . . . send Delegates to a General Convention, to be held in Charleston" on May 5. Suspicious of this invitation from a cooperationist stronghold, secessionists countered through the Orangeburg association with a proposal that the convention be held in Columbia; the Beaufort association quickly seconded that recommendation. The Charleston site eventually proved more popular, but in one association after another secessionists were chosen as delegates to the convention. Following Rhett's speech the size of delegations increased markedly; for example Edmund Bellinger and R. A. Gantt directed a meeting of the Barnwell association which chose forty delegates. Secessionists were packing the convention, and they intended to make a proper job of it.[131]

On the same night that Rhett addressed them, the members of the Charleston association "cordially approve[d] the nomination by the Southern Rights Association of Richland District" of Senators Rhett and Butler and Congressman Joseph A. Woodward as delegates. The Charleston association proceeded to name as delegates the rest of the state's congressional delegation and the "four deputies to the proposed Southern Congress"; as its "own more immediate" representatives at the convention, the association chose an additional thirty-one men. Unhappy with these last delegates, Charleston's secessionists agitated for another meeting. Voicing the fears of fellow cooperationists, Isaac Hayne, chairman of the committee of safety, reminded secessionists of the association's chartered purpose: "To organize effectually the people of these Parishes in support of the interests of the South—to promote concert of action among this and other Southern States. . . . [S]hall the association [re]convene for the purpose of judging men by a standard and a test not acknowledged in its Constitution?" he asked.[132]

By mid-April cooperationists were hinting broadly that the convention of Southern Rights Associations might try "to limit the freedom of deliberation, or . . . to control the action of the State Convention." Secessionists piously disclaimed any such purpose. The convention of Southern Rights Associations would merely "harmonize and unite the opinions and feelings of the people . . . in whatever course her supreme authorities may see proper to take." For the convention a total of 442 delegates, representing 39 associations, gathered in Charleston. The secessionists had prepared their agenda, and they were eager "to harmonize and unite" their fellow citizens.[133]

CHAPTER VII

"The Love of Order"

1

On the afternoon of May 5, 1851, the delegates to South Carolina's convention of Southern Rights Associations assembled in Charleston's Military Hall. By the delegates' consent temporary chairman John Buchanan designated a committee of fifteen to frame the convention's rules and select its officers. This committee, in turn, chose former governor John P. Richardson as President of the convention. With Richardson presiding Maxcy Gregg moved that the chair appoint a select committee of twenty-one "to prepare and report business" and that all proposals made from the floor "be referred, without previous debate," to the committee. Gregg's motion passed; Richardson named eighteen secessionists to the committee of twenty-one. Thus the convention's machinery was swiftly in place, and swiftly it would do the work secessionists required of it.[1]

The select committee hardly needed guidance in preparing a report for the convention's endorsement, but for the sake of form secessionist resolutions were offered abundantly from the floor. All of them carried the same message: since cooperation had failed the state convention should meet as soon as legally possible and declare "South Carolina an independent state." The delegates from St. Luke's Parish, for example, saw "no possible reason for postponing secession" beyond January 1851. During this stage of the convention cooperationist dissent appeared only in a resolution from James L. Orr and a letter from Langdon Cheves. Orr's resolution affirmed that the Southern Rights Association trusted "the wisdom and fidelity" of the state's constituent convention and would not presume to dictate to it. Cheves's letter, read by George Trenholm, warned that an attempt by the Southern Rights Associations to coerce South Carolina into secession would, "among other evils, divide the people of the state into parties." But this monition did not suit the majority's mood.[2]

Immediately after Cheves's letter was laid on the table, Maxcy Gregg rose to submit the select committee's report, couched as resolutions, and an address to the state's Southern Rights Associations. The address emphasized the Palmetto State's forbearance while waiting for cooperation and concluded that South Carolinians must contend "alone, against whatever odds, for . . . [their] rights." The most pointed of the resolutions declared that "this meeting looks with confidence and hope to the Convention of the people, to exert the sovereign power of the State." The three cooperationists on the select committee revised James Orr's resolution and presented it as a minority report. The convention's managers then allowed slightly less than two days for debate on the reports. Maxcy Gregg, R. A. Gantt, James H. Adams, William F. Colcock, John A. Calhoun, Whitemarsh B. Seabrook, James A. Black, and J. B. McCall argued for secession; A. P. Butler, James L. Orr, Robert W. Barnwell, and Arthur P. Hayne pleaded for cooperation.[3]

On the afternoon of May 8 the convention voted on the reports; the secessionist resolutions passed overwhelmingly. The convention also approved the select committee's supplementary report that transformed "this meeting of Delegates from the District Associations . . . into a Central Southern Rights Association . . . under the same officers" and provided for "a Central Committee for the Southern Rights Associations of South Carolina [to] be appointed by the President of this body, to consist of nine members, whose duty it shall be . . . to promote the common cause." Secessionist leaders had orchestrated an impressive endorsement of their program, and they had secured firm control of a statewide, if primitive, party apparatus. They accompanied these successes with kind words for their cooperationist opponents and a profession of "confidence that South Carolina . . . [would] present an undivided front to her enemies." But they were, in the words of Rhett's biographer, "uneasily conscious that they might have over-reached themselves in the Charleston convention."[4]

2

By May 1851 the essential arguments for secession and
cooperation had been developed, and they were cataloged in the
speeches given at the Charleston convention. During the summer
and fall of 1851, these arguments were constantly elaborated and
endlessly repeated—but never fully systematized. Believers in secession and cooperation took the wisdom—or the folly—of separate
secession as axiomatic. But within each group spokesmen differed
(and sometimes contradicted each other) on certain hypothetical
consequences of secession. The gentry partisans of secession and
cooperation were, in the end, less concerned with the internal consistency of plural arguments than with their persuasive effect on
South Carolina's voters.

Although cooperationists were vague on the mechanism and time
for achieving southern unity, they affirmed that a southern confederacy was inevitable. Slavery "within the Southern States" was
"not only an interest . . . but . . . the very foundation of their civilization." Committed to an institution that faced "almost universal . . .
condemnation" elsewhere, the slave states were joined in the "same
destiny and fate." Slave state unity would "be brought about by
the pressure of external danger," as "all unions" from the Achaen
League to the United States had been brought about.[5]

When secessionists insisted on putting their remedy to an immediate test, cooperationists charged that their opponents had fallen
"into the error of turning the means into the end." South Carolina's
goal was "the protection of slavery." When "secession . . . expose[d]
slavery to increased danger, then certainly secession . . . [was] no
longer to be adhered to, as something excellent in itself."[6] Thus cooperationist arguments centered on the disastrous consequences of
adhering to separate secession.

The cooperationists asserted that even among their opponents
"few . . . would favor secession, if they believed that South Carolina
alone, would constitute a Republic, independent of and isolated from
the other Southern States." Yet, said the cooperationists, that would
be the precise result of South Carolina's secession, whether it was
followed by war or peace. When "prominent men in South Carolina
intimated a purpose to put the state on the track of separate secession in disregard of . . . her neighbors, they deprived . . . real friends
[elsewhere] of the power of helping" the Palmetto State. Unless
separate secession was abandoned the Southern Rights parties in
other states would "be driven to disavow" any sympathy for South

Carolina. Separate secession would draw between South Carolina
"and the other slaveholding States the deeply marked lines of a
separate national existence." Separate secession, "however accomplished," would introduce "discord, strife and permanent alienation
among those whose united force constitute[d] . . . [the] only sure
reliance for the defence of" the peculiar institution.[7]

Cooperationists warned against the facile assumption that other
states would rush to South Carolina's defense if the federal government answered secession with force. Nullifiers had expected support
from the Palmetto State's neighbors, but when an armed clash with
the federal government seemed imminent, South Carolina had not a
single ally. This outcome, the cooperationists reasoned, was "strictly
analagous" to the probable result of separate secession. The cooperationists warned, too, against underestimating the ingenuity of
South Carolina's potential adversaries. Secessionist claims to the
contrary notwithstanding, the federal government might be able to
overturn secession without landing troops on Palmetto soil. If the
United States employed a close blockade, "not a bale of cotton or a
tierce of rice could find its way into the markets of the world, nor
could a box or bale of merchandize make their ingress." South Carolina might find itself engaged in "a war of dollars and cents—a war
of custom houses—and embargoes," engaged in the sort of war that
would "not excite that sympathy from . . . sister States, which . . .
[secessionists] so much relied on to extricate" the Palmetto State
from peril. Finally, to raise the blockade, South Carolinians would
have to take the responsibility "of shedding the first blood" and
accept the moral onus of that act.[8]

The cooperationists found no comfort in the prediction that Great
Britain would not tolerate a blockade of South Carolina. James Orr
did not think that "Great Britain would hazard all the consequences
of a war with a formidable power . . . pay the heavy debts . . . [of]
war . . . and endanger the stability of the empire itself . . . for the
poor privilege of selling to 300,000 white persons the goods they
consume." Nor did Andrew Butler think so. Unable to fight the
United States at sea without the aid of Britain, an independent
South Carolina would also find difficulties in a land war. "Could we
march to Massachusetts or New York?" asked Orr. "Will we invade
the enemy's country, Georgia and North Carolina, and commence
butchering their citizens? That would be protecting our institutions
with a vengeance."[9]

Assuming that secession was not followed by a blockade, Rhett had suggested that by levying a 10 percent duty on imports South Carolina would prosper and Charleston would become the great entrepôt of the South.[10] Since the federal government exacted "thirty per cent . . . on the chief articles of importation," consumers from other states would rush to buy imports in South Carolina. To take advantage of this tariff differential, of course, United States citizens would have to smuggle their purchases out of South Carolina. But, said Rhett, that was the federal government's problem, not South Carolina's. He did not think the citizens of Georgia, for example, would long "submit to a standing army of tax collectors on their side of the Savannah River, spying, seizing, fighting them, to enforce the collection of duties their Abolition brethren of the North have laid upon them." Cooperationists, however, believed that these "bright visions of an increased and prosperous trade" were illusions.[11]

Cooperationists argued that peaceful separate secession would be followed by a drastic decline in South Carolina's trade. Since South Carolina consumed, at most, one-third of the goods she imported, her existing volume of trade could *only* be sustained by smuggling,[12] and the cooperationists poured scorn on "statesmanship . . . [that] would deliberately calculate on maintaining the commercial interests of a Republic by smuggling." Under Rhett's scheme Charleston's prosperity would "necessarily bring decay and ruin upon Savannah." Was it "reasonable to expect" that Savannah would quietly accept the destruction of "her commerce . . . by an illicit traffic?" Moreover the savings that Rhett projected for South Carolina consumers applied only to goods not produced in the United States. "But it must be remembered," observed James Orr, "that one-half . . . of the goods consumed in South Carolina . . . [was] manufactured in the New England or Middle States" and was sold duty free within the Union. Since an independent South Carolina "would levy a duty of ten per cent on all goods . . . whether coming from New England or Old England," one half of the goods consumed by the state "would cost 10 per cent more" after it seceded.[13]

Cooperationists noted further that an independent South Carolina would be impotent in foreign affairs. In an alliance she would be not a partner but a ward. Great Britain would be an especially dangerous ally. Calhoun, Robert Barnwell reminded secessionists, had favored the annexation of Texas, in part to rescue her from the "machinations" of British abolitionists.[14] Cooperationists argued, too, that nationhood involved costs that secessionists ignored or glossed: "Standing armies, foreign ministers, consuls, postal arrangements." If "federal fleets . . . cut off all import duties," then "the immense burthen of the Government would have to be raised [exclusively] by direct taxation."[15]

Increased taxation, finally, would speed the migration of whites from South Carolina. But South Carolina's slaves could not cross the state's borders once it left the Union, because the United States prohibited the importation of foreign slaves. Thus the cooperationists feared a disastrous increase in the Palmetto State's black majority. South Carolina's slave population was already "greater to the square mile than in any of the slave States," and the state's slave population would "double itself in 26 years. What . . . [would be South Carolina's] condition with such a population numbering 640,000 in 1876? Could that number be usefully or profitably employed?" To cooperationists the answers were ominous.[16]

"The idea . . . [of] obtain[ing] a Southern Confederacy by the deliberate, preconcerted, prearranged co-operation of any number of Southern States . . . [was] a most fatal delusion." On that point all secessionists agreed without qualification. Since 1832 South Carolinians had been told "to wait awhile—be patient—your neighbors will soon see the subject in the light through which you view it." Yet secessionists observed, other states still would not voluntarily confront the federal government, despite assaults on slavery which culminated in the compromise measures. If South Carolina did not employ "actual, practical organized," and, if necessary, "forcible" resistance to the compromise, if the policy of cooperationists triumphed, South Carolina would drift into submission "with the inevitable certainty of the Gulf Stream." Secession was the Palmetto State's "only alternative to submission," and the state must embrace that alternative promptly, because "a state of high excitement . . . [was] not a natural condition either in men or nations. . . . The people [would] become wearied with long continued and fruitless exertions; they [would] become fatigued into compliance, and yield a struggle that holds out no hope of immediate victory." If the South could not be forced to resist the compromise, secessionists reasoned, the South would never resist attacks on slavery. If "we are to have a Southern Confederacy," secessionists agreed, "it must, it can only, be brought about by separate State action. If secession is revolution, then the revolution must begin somewhere."[17]

Secessionists did not believe that abolitionist pressure would mold the South into a unit. In the foreseeable future there were only two actions, secessionists argued, that could conceivably drive the South into secession: abolition of slavery in the District of Columbia and repeal of the Fugitive Slave Act, but political abolitionists would not essay these measures boldly and openly. Abolition in the district would be attempted only with the consent of slaveholders there. In the district prices for slaves were falling and would be forced lower; district slaveholders would quickly accept compensated emancipation, and "the precedent of using . . . [federal] money" to purchase territory from Texas would "not be neglected in purchasing" district slaveholders' consent to the emancipation of their slaves. Neither Maryland, nor Virginia, nor Georgia, nor any other slave state would secede because of the compensated emancipation of the district's three or four thousand slaves. As for the Fugitive Slave Act, it was "already entombed." The Fugitive Slave Act, secessionists claimed, was useless to slaveowners, but it would serve abolitionists well. They would constantly denounce it as an intrusion on the rights and liberties of northern whites. Abolitionists, the secessionists warned, compassed the destruction of slavery by gradual steps that would always "stop short of uniting the South."[18]

Secessionists argued, too, that the shackles of party politics made cooperative secession impossible. Except in South Carolina southern voters had "been drawn away from the calm and unbiased consideration of great Federal questions, and have been engaged in eager strife for party ascendancy." Party politicians were "unwilling to admit into their" schemes any issue that would "disturb their chances for the control of the offices of the Government." For the disease of party secessionists "prescribe[d] a *counter irritant* as the remedy." The separate secession of South Carolina would force southerners to decide on an issue that was at once practical and philosophical. South Carolina would proclaim "her choice between slavery and the Union" by exercising a "right as dear to . . . [the other slaveholding states] as to" the Palmetto State. When "this issue . . . [was] fairly made, the great mass of the Southern people . . . [would] be found true to . . . [South Carolina] and true to themselves."[19]

Secessionists were not in complete accord regarding the federal government's probable response to the Palmetto State's withdrawal from the Union. However, in case of an armed conflict involving the right of secession and the future of slavery, secessionists were certain that "*the South . . . [would] never stand neutral.*" As for the arguments that South Carolina would not "maintain a separate existence" even if she were "permitted peaceably to secede," they were, in sum, destructive to the states-rights philosophy. To argue that South Carolina was not viable as an independent nation was to make "a fatal concession to the consolidationists." Such a concession would make the cherished doctrine of state sovereignty an "abstraction," or worse, a fiction. If South Carolinians "decline[d] to secede," because they believed their state too weak to maintain sovereignty, they would "give a death-blow to the great cause of State rights."[20]

Having noted that the cooperationists' objections to separate secession tended to subvert the states-rights philosophy, secessionists took up those objections seriatim and dismissed them as misleading or misplaced. Secessionists believed that the lure of South Carolina's staple crops on the one hand and a very low import duty on the other would insure the continuation of the state's commerce. South Carolina's markets could not "be closed by a war of custom houses." If the federal government resorted to "petty commercial restrictions," then smuggling was an appropriate response. "There . . . [was] as much dignity in the defense as in the attack,"[21] and secessionists had no fears of "a redundant black population." The inability of owners to take their slaves from South Carolina would benefit the state by forcing planters "to remain at home and cultivate . . . [South Carolina's] soil, one-sixth part of which still remain[ed] untilled."[22] Further, secessionists accused cooperationists of exaggerating vastly the size and expenses of South Carolina's post-secession government. The Palmetto State possessed "the means, and . . . [could] provide for herself the cheapest, the mildest and purest government that ever encouraged the hopes or blessed the labor of man."[23]

Secessionists argued, finally, that if South Carolinians "wait[ed] to ascertain the exact cost of every hazard in dollars and cents" they would "never resist, either separately or conjointly." Secessionists conceded that the "overthrow of any government and the establishment of another . . . [was] no holiday affair," that "pecuniary difficulties and public and private distresses [would] have to be encountered," but in "a great question of liberty or of State existence, pecuniary considerations ought not to weigh a feather." South Carolina had "already taken the initiative. . . . A Convention of the people . . . [had] been ordered . . . [and] large supplies . . . [had] been demanded." South Carolina's citizens "well understood for what purposes their money was demanded. It . . . [was], therefore, too late" to retreat. The preservation of slavery and the safety of South Carolina required that the state secede alone.[24]

3

Three days before the convention of Southern Rights Associations assembled, "a plan of action short of actual secession" appeared in the *Mercury*. Veiled in token anonymity the plan was widely known to be the work of James Hammond. Believing that separate secession was impractical and would injure prospects for a southern confederacy, Hammond proposed that South Carolina no longer "voluntarily . . . take a part in . . . [the Union's] councils, or maintain . . . any connection with it, which can be dissolved without affording plausible pretexts for violent collision." Under this plan South Carolina would cease to vote in presidential elections, cease to elect senators and representatives, and recall "those already chosen." The plan stipulated that in the future any South Carolinian who accepted a federal "office of honor, profit, or trust" would "instantly and forever" forfeit "citizenship in South Carolina"; the state would also refuse to accept federal appropriations.²⁵ Hammond was pointing a middle course between those taken by secessionists and cooperationists. But, as he conceded late in May, his plan "attracted no general attention."²⁶ Secessionists hoped that victory was in sight and wanted quietly to consolidate their gains. Cooperationists, aroused and frightened by the Charleston convention, determined to match the party organization of their opponents.

Under secessionist control the structure and function of South Carolina's Southern Rights Associations resembled the State's Rights and Free Trade Associations that nullifiers had exploited so effectively.²⁷ The members of the Southern Rights Associations' policymaking central committee were Maxcy Gregg, D. F. Jamison, John Buchanan, John Carew, A. H. Gladden, James Jones, Edmund Bellinger, Joseph Black, and William Laval. To avoid "organized opposition" to secession, the central committee instructed local associations that cooperationists should be conciliated if possible. "And with this view, unless opposition meetings should first be called in any Districts, the Central Committee . . . [believed it] unnecessary to agitate . . . or to call together the several Southern Rights Associations for the purpose of expressing their approval of the late proceedings in Charleston." The central committee requested periodic reports of local proceedings and suggested that each association extend its "organization until it shall embrace all the Resistance men in the District, leaving out none but those whose choice is submission." Finally, to speed the distribution of secessionist publications, the committee called on the local associations for help in compiling a statewide mailing list.[28]

Central committee member John Carew reflected secessionist policy in the editorial tone of his *Mercury*. The paper characterized the Charleston convention as an accurate reflection of public will, hailed the convention's "formidable influence" in favor of secession, and made light of the differences between secessionists and cooperationists. During May harsh criticism of cooperationists in the *Mercury* came only from pseudonymous contributors. The paper's editors dealt gently with cooperationist leaders; praising the civic services and personal qualities of Butler and Barnwell, the *Mercury* published their convention speeches. In the same vein Seabrook wrote Butler. The former governor implied that secession might not be necessary, if the North took South Carolina's discontent seriously and made appropriate concessions. "Take up your pen and assure the influential men of the North and South . . . that a dissolution of this union is inevitable unless our grievances are promptly redressed," Seabrook urged. "An opposition party headed by you, Orr, and Barnwell," Seabrook concluded, "is what . . . I and my friends dread." Butler replied politely but noncommittally.[29]

In caucus at the convention of Southern Rights Associations, cooperationists began to prepare their response to "the headlong movements of the secessionists." The cooperationists decided to establish their own organ in Charleston, either by acquiring the *Mercury* or by launching a new press. They agreed to publish and distribute selected speeches and letters "against separate secession by So Ca," and they planned to "get possession of the Southern Rights Associations wherever [possible]." Following the convention A. P. Aldrich had lengthy conversations with Robert Barnwell, James Chesnut, and John Manning, and reported that they were determined to check the progress of the secessionists. Aldrich found Chesnut and Manning suspicious of Rhett's motives, and he was more than willing to feed their suspicions.[30] Having concluded an informal survey of cooperationist opinion in Columbia, Aldrich talked with Maxcy Gregg. The first public meeting that denounced the Charleston convention and opposed secession, Gregg warned, would trigger a statewide party struggle.[31]

On the last day of May a public meeting to protest secession was staged at Hamburg in Edgefield District. Local cooperationists were unable to secure Hammond's endorsement, but they won support from industrialists William Gregg and Ker Boyce and enlisted W. W. Boyce and William Owen as speakers. A. P. Butler and Armistead

Burt addressed letters to the Hamburg rally. Butler reiterated his cooperationist views but was not yet ready to "mingle in such public meetings."[32] Burt, far less reticent, regretted his absence and denounced the "reckless and desperate efforts . . . to drive the people of this State" into the "suicidal measure" of secession.[33] The meeting affirmed that "the cooperation of other States in the South . . . [was] indispensable to the perpetuation of African slavery" and "request[ed] the people of South Carolina who entertain similar opinions, to assemble in all parts of the State" and speak out against separate secession.[34]

By mid-May, Charleston's Unionists perceived a growing reaction against secession, and they conveyed this impression to President Fillmore and Treasury Secretary Corwin. The city's Unionists believed that before the state convention met South Carolinians would "cool their exaggerated spirits" and reject secession.[35] Discoursing on the Charleston convention, Perry agreed with secessionists on one point: "the real issue . . . is simply secession or no secession. There is no true middle ground." Chiding cooperationists for "their clamor of resistance," the editor of the *Southern Patriot* wrote: "Let those who really oppose secession unite at least upon that ground, and by their united counsels and influence endeavor to save the State." There "may be shades of difference in our politics" announced Perry with heroic understatement, but "we will all fight under the Anti-Secession Banner—a banner under which have rallied Cheves, Butler, Barnwell, and many others of the most prominent disunionists of the South." Francis Lieber, who contributed to the *Southern Patriot* under the pseudonym "Suburanus," applauded Perry's tactics. Although Cheves had done much "to bring on all this storm . . . his anti-secessionist letters *tell*," Lieber wrote, and "one must not be over dainty in politics in storm times like this."[36]

Following the Hamburg rally Greenville Unionists held their own antisecession meeting. On the same day, June 2, the Orangeburg Southern Rights Association answered the cooperationist challenge by an endorsement of the Charleston convention's actions and by Lawrence Massillon Keitt's bellicose appeal for secession.[37] But successive rallies and counter-rallies did not take place during June. Secessionists and cooperationists were busily preparing party machinery, while each group blamed the other for initiating a partisan struggle.

The prospectus of the cooperationists' paper, *The Southern Standard*, appeared on June 9. The editor of the *Standard* was Benjamin C. Pressley, and the *Mercury* found his reasons for "laying the corner stone of a party organization" entirely unsatisfactory.[38] The *Mercury* warned cooperationists "not to let pride of opinion . . . drive them into a position they honestly abhor" and cautioned the *Southern Standard* against "imperceptibly glid[ing] into the same current of unionism and consolidationism on which the Patriot swims." The editors of the *Mercury* and the Columbia *Telegraph* disclaimed any "use of offensive epithets" or desire for "triumphs of party,"[39] but their secessionist correspondents were less charitable.[40] By late June, A. P. Butler, for one, had lost patience with secessionist appeals for harmony. "The press has perverted my views and justice has not been done to my motives. I have struggled more than any man to keep down party strife," he wrote Seabrook. On June 26 Gilmore Simms, who had not participated in the secessionist-cooperationist dispute, wrote Beverley Tucker that "[o]ne or two . . . [demonstrations] have been made by the Anti-Sec[essionists] but they have been feeble. . . . One or two [cooperationist] newspapers are about to be started. . . . We are evidently on the eve of great divisions in the State."[41]

4

In July the ballyhoo of partisan campaigns began in earnest. Secessionist and cooperationist spokesmen competed for public attention, and South Carolinians enjoyed many "a first rate Barbecue in which good mutton, and pork; and bread were washed down with . . . pure water" and various other potables.[42] Although both cooperationists and secessionists frequently held forth at the same barbecues and public meetings, the political endorsements these occasions produced were usually controlled by the local organizers of these functions. As the rival campaigns wore on and partisan feelings intensified, the faithful of each faction could little brook opposition speakers, and political rallies increasingly became exclusive party events.

The Fourth of July offered a splendid opportunity for polemics, and secessionists, cooperationists, and Unionists took full advantage of the holiday. In Greenville, Perry and three Unionist allies sponsored an "anti-Secession Celebration." The report and resolutions prepared for this rally artfully blended proslavery doctrine, antisecession argument, and a traditional up-country political grievance. Proclaiming the devotion of all white southerners to slavery, the report argued that separate secession would undermine the peculiar institution and that, following separate secession, South Carolina might "become a *black State*, a second San Domingo." The resolutions instructed Greenville District's legislators "to vote against the call of the State Convention . . . a body so revolutionary in its purposes, and so unfairly elected by a small minority." In case the convention did meet, the resolutions called for Greenville's delegates to oppose secession, to demand that any secession ordinance be submitted for popular ratification, and to sponsor at the convention a reapportionment of legislative seats "so that the people of South Carolina may be equally and fairly represented in the different sections of the State."[43]

No cooperationists chose to share the Greenville rostrum with B. F. Perry and Waddy Thompson, but cooperationists W. W. Boyce, James Chesnut, Ker Boyce, Senator Andrew Butler, and Congressmen Armistead Burt, Joseph Woodward, and James Orr were solicited as speakers. Letters from these men and from Francis Lieber, William C. Preston, and John B. O'Neall, among other Unionists, were read to the crowd at Greenville. "I have recently distributed in every part of . . . [Greenville] district, copies of the speech I . . . [made] in Charleston, in May last," Orr noted in his letter. While happy to have their arguments against separate secession broadcast, the cooperationist letter-writers were also careful to maintain their disunionist credentials.[44]

From Greenville to Charleston, Fourth of July celebrations featuring debate on secession dotted the state. Suiting their remarks to the occasion secessionists claimed to be emulating the example of American revolutionaries. "Resistance to unjust power has always been begun by minorities. They take the initiative step, and . . . the lines of division are drawn broader and deeper . . . and neutrality becomes impossible," Henry L. Pinckney, Jr., declaimed before the Seventy-Six and Cincinnati Societies of Charleston. Cooperationists, however, had their own uses for the American Revolution; they stressed the colonies' common grievances against the British government and their cooperative political and military resistance to British authority. Secessionist and cooperationist organs took up this battle of analogies and continued it through a long summer.[45]

Believing that his oratory on behalf of secession was needed more in up-country than in tidewater areas, Rhett addressed a Fourth of July rally at Rossville in Chester District. "Arm yourselves and be valiant men, and see that ye be in readiness against the morning, that ye may fight with these nations that are assembled together . . . to destroy us and our sanctuary," Richard De Treville exhorted his neighbors in Beaufort. The Fourth of July, 1851, revealed over-whelming support for secession in the parishes, and bravado was the order of the day: "South Carolina—May her patriotism be the death of many Yankees. . . . South Carolina—May she gain her independence, or perish in a blaze of glory." The *Mercury* published such Independence Day toasts for weeks.[46]

Before the echo of appeals for blood and iron had died away in the parishes, cooperationists were appealing to the purses of Charles-tonians. A business enterprise as well as a party organ, the *Standard* did its best in format and financial news coverage to appeal to the city's commercial interests, and editorial contributions to the *Standard* spelled out the alarming commercial effects of the state's potential secession. Beginning on July 7 the *Standard* ran a series of letters written pseudonymously by William Elliott, who argued that South Carolina wanted "a present, which will invite, not repel, capital and population and a future free from the hourly perils of revolution." Elliott estimated the costs of separate nationhood in detail, concluding that the venture was utterly unfeasible.[47] Once the state was "on the eve of . . . revolution," Charleston cooperation-ists warned, South Carolina bank notes would "be returned, and their redemption called for at the counters of every Bank in the State . . . the shock could not be sustained; public confidence would be destroyed, private credit ruined . . . the State, before it com-menced a revolution . . . would find itself exhausted." Capital was already fleeing South Carolina "to find *safety* and employment" elsewhere. At the end of July the *Standard* noted that Charleston's bonds were falling while Savannah's were rising. Cooperationists accompanied this chorus of woe with accusations that the secession-ists were puerile to dismiss "dollars and cents" arguments as "vul-gar trash."[48]

As evidence that secessionists were callous about Charleston's fate, the *Standard* pointed to a speech by Edmund Bellinger. A member of the Southern Rights Associations' central committee, Bellinger spoke for the secessionists at a Fourth of July barbecue in Clinton, Barnwell District.[49] According to a secessionist correspon-dent, Bellinger remarked "(partly in jest, partly in earnest) that if Charleston stood in the way of the rights and honor of the State, then the experiment of Moscow ought to be repeated." With vitriolic sarcasm the *Standard* seized on "this heroic self-sacrifice of some people, who can so coolly, in the cause of liberty, devote to the flames the whole substance and interests of—others." Secessionists un-wisely attempted to defend Bellinger's remark and in so doing allowed cooperationists to make political capital of the incident for several weeks.[50]

Henry W. Conner had once advised Calhoun that Rhett's ambition was "so exceedingly selfish . . . that he would without hesitation sacrifice . . . all the world." A number of cooperationists subscribed to that opinion and to Conner's indictment of Rhett as "a rash and ultra man in politicks, frequently bent upon extreme and desperate courses, very excitable and unstable and intollerant and contemptuous of all about him, with neither tact or discretion and without sympathy or popularity with the great mass of men."[51] These cooperationists tarred separate secession as merely the latest vehicle for Rhett's ambition. They were aided in this effort by the exuberance of Rhett's fanatical admirers.[52]

In mid-July the *Standard* took notice of a Fourth of July toast offered in St. Peter's Parish: "'Hon. R. B. Rhett—May he be the first President of South Carolina.' Sits the wind in that quarter?" asked the editors. Within a few days the cooperationist organ editorialized that Rhett's "Bluffton movement, some years since, was chiefly distinguished by a consuming zeal . . . to throw overboard Mr. Calhoun and all our other politicians. Its re-appearance in 1851 shows that the spirit of that day has only slumbered." Secessionists were soon the targets of satire and invective that depicted them as reanimated "Bluffton Boys." Cooperationists, in turn, were portrayed as cowards and submissionists in the *Mercury*'s columns, but from conviction —or for tactical advantage—cooperationists continued to identify secessionists as Rhett's cult.[53]

On July 7 secessionists in Edgefield organized a public meeting "for the promotion of union at home." The meeting attempted to enunciate a common platform for secessionists and cooperationists. The audience at Edgefield approved William H. Gist's resolution that secessionists were "not disposed to separate from those [cooperationists] who express[ed] a willingness . . . to sustain the action of the Constitutional Convention."[54] But this effort to restore South Carolina's political "harmony" died aborning, because elsewhere in the state the secessionist-dominated Southern Rights Associations demanded fidelity to the platform established by the Charleston convention.[55] The secessionists moved to remedy their lack of an effective party structure in Charleston. The central committee of the Southern Rights Associations could not rely on the cooperationist-dominated association in Charleston. Therefore the city's secessionists proclaimed that the original "Southern Rights Association of St. Philip and St. Michael, for all practical purposes of usefulness

... [was] asleep or dead" and formed an "auxiliary Southern Rights Association." The auxiliary association's liaison with the secessionist high command was quickly established. John S. Ashe, one of Charleston's state senators, was elected president of the auxiliary association. Included among the vice-presidents were Rhett's younger brother James and central committee members John Carew and William Laval.[56]

Administration was not Rhett's forte, and while Charleston's secessionists concerned themselves with party machinery, he searched for an issue that would force South Carolinians to jump to the Palmetto flag and make disunion a fait accompli. Then the only option for the state convention would be to give de jure sanction to an existing condition. An exchange of fire between South Carolina citizens and federal forces garrisoned at Charleston would present the "practical issue" Rhett so much desired. Moreover, relations between federal troops and South Carolina officials had become very tense by the summer of 1851.

In November 1850 the *Mercury* had denounced the Fillmore Administration's decision to reinforce Fort Moultrie and to garrison the long-ignored Castle Pinckney fortification. To both President Fillmore and the commanding officer at Fort Moultrie, Governor Seabrook protested vigorously that the additional troops were unnecessary.[57] In June 1851 federal officers refused to allow the Charlestonians' traditional celebration of the Battle of Fort Moultrie to be held inside the fort. The *Mercury* editorialized that South Carolina had ceded the fort to the federal government "to keep off foreign enemies," but in 1851 the fort was possessed by "an enemy ... as dangerous to the peace of our city as the British fleet ... repulsed" in 1776. At the anniversary ceremony Rhett declaimed: "Cooperation—our fathers obtained it by seizing the stamps, and by firing the guns of Fort Moultrie."[58]

Late in July, Rhett sketched for Governor Means's consideration a set of circumstances that might justify a South Carolina attack on federal strongholds. This letter has not survived, but Means's reply throws some light on Rhett's intentions. "To give a direct answer to your querries," Means wrote, "would be to give the Executive sanction to an act which would be a violation of my oath of office. . . . In fact even if it were done without my knowledge, I would not desire that the first blow should be stricken by us, & *at this time*." If the right to peaceable secession "is denied us," the governor continued, "we can then throw ourselves upon our sovereignty to assert it by force of arms. . . . But should we strike a blow without notice to the

Government to which we are now allied . . . [it would be] *treason* & the civilized world would justify the Gen Gov in treating it as such."[59]

Rhett's desire for a dramatic issue must have been heightened by evidence of the cooperationists' increasing strength. Over the signatures of approximately twelve hundred supporters, Charleston's cooperationist leaders announced a public meeting of those "in favor of Co-operation for the purpose of resist[ing] . . . aggressions of the Federal Government, but who are opposed to the Separate Secession of South-Carolina from the Union, under existing circumstances." On the rainy night of July 29, the city's cooperationist faithful assembled in Hibernian Hall.[60]

From correspondence addressed to the meeting by cooperationist notables, the letters of Langdon Cheves, James Chesnut, and James Orr were read to the audience. Orr stressed that the nascent cooperationist party must triumph or perish: the secessionists "evince a spirit of proscription and intolerance . . . [they profess harmony, but] will give us the harmony which the wolf gives to the lamb." Although ill Andrew Butler attended the meeting and spoke to it. He was followed by Robert Barnwell, who developed at length "the inability of the State to sustain herself alone, and the folly of looking to Great Britain for countenance and aid." The meeting then adopted two sets of resolutions. The first set defended the right of secession, enumerated familiar cooperationist objections to separate secession, and obscurely proposed that the state convention adopt measures enabling South Carolina officials "to take advantage of all emergencies. . . ." The second set of resolutions promised opposition to the Auxiliary Southern Rights Association and established a Committee of Vigilance and Conference and a Committee of Correspondence to manage cooperationist party affairs.[61]

Charleston's secessionists responded to the cooperationists' rally with a hastily called July 30 meeting of the Auxiliary Southern Rights Association. Rhett was the principal speaker. His speech was not recorded and he did not reconstruct it for later publication, but Rhett the fire-eater was apparently in good form that night. According to the *Standard*, Rhett declared that truces between the rival parties were ended, and he pledged to "go to the country and . . . speak upon every hill where he . . . [could] get a spot of ground to stand upon!" The *Standard*'s editors "sincerely hope[d]" for the fulfillment of that pledge. "If his intemperate zeal makes as many converts to our cause in the country as it has done in Charleston," they stated, "the result will be most fortunate for the State."[62]

In August cooperationists and secessionists waged party warfare without restraint. "[E]very day convinces me more thoroughly that our friends the Secessionists must be beat or they never can be restrained," wrote mild-mannered Robert Barnwell to James Orr. Toward that end Barnwell was anxious to increase cooperationist influence on the press. In addition to the *Standard* the cooperationist party received editorial support from the Hamburg *Republican*, Columbia *Commercial Transcript*, Erskine *Miscellany*, Charleston *Evening News*, and Charleston *Courier*.[63] Since the rest of the state's newspapers were secessionist in sympathy, cooperationists "every where ought to exert themselves," Barnwell wrote, "to have the Secession papers discontinued & their places supplied by the Standard." As for the *Southern Press*, which had become "the mouthpiece of a faction," cooperationists advised senior editor Elwood Fisher that they could not support "a Press at Washington, that . . . [advocated] seperate [*sic*] national existence for So Carolina."[64]

In their fervor to defeat separate secession, the cooperationists grew amenable to a tacit alliance with the state's Unionists. Cooperationist leaders still avowed that they opposed separate secession "as injurious to their ultimate object, the . . . formation of a Southern Confederacy," but they were willing for the "very small" number of South Carolinians who opposed secession "*in any event*" to act with the party that opposed secession "*at present*." The cooperationists were not only reaching out for tentative allies but were also proselytizing aggressively. In Charleston they set up party machinery at the ward level. Isaac Hayne, Christopher Memminger, Benjamin Pressley, and Andrew Gordon Magrath proved equally able in this work. Despite their late start the cooperationists also made progress in establishing district organizations to match the secessionist-dominated Southern Rights Associations.[65]

The campaign motifs cooperationists had sounded in July were played relentlessly in August. According to the *Standard* secessionists were a majority only in Rhett's old congressional district and the constituents there labored under the delusion that "Bluffton is the State, and the Crown Prince of Pocataligo is heir *presumptive* to the empire of South Carolina, including all the principalities of Buck Head, Scuffletown, Satkitcher and the Marshes of Colleton." Up-country cooperationists were also fond of identifying separate secession as the destructive hobby of Rhett and the residents of "Bluffton, Whippy Swamp, and sundry other swamps, branches, and ponds." In all this the cooperationists hoped to precipitate a quarrel in secessionist ranks over Rhett's leadership. The *Standard* was quick to claim that secessionist George W. Dargan, in a speech at Darlington, had "repudiated the mad fanaticism of Rhett and his party, and all affiliation with such rashness as has been recently displayed by them." Dargan vehemently denied this interpretation, but the potential for schism among secessionists had been revealed.[66]

August was not an auspicious month for Charleston's secessionists. The *Mercury* again protested loudly over the reinforcement of federal troops in Charleston, but the issue was undercut by farcical exaggeration of a minor incident. When two Charlestonians were denied permission to land at Fort Sumter, the *Mercury* waxed eloquent about tyranny and oppression, but the episode proved to be no more than the mistake of a recruit on sentry duty.[67] Ward meetings of the Auxiliary Southern Rights Association, meanwhile, suffered poor attendance and postponements. On August 25 the auxiliary association held a rally intended as a counterpoint to the cooperationists' mass meeting in July, but the secessionist rally failed as a demonstration of esprit de corps. Congressmen Wallace, Colcock, and McQueen, all of whom favored secession, were invited but did not attend; nor could Rhett be present. Maxcy Gregg and James H. Adams replaced these luminaries as speakers.[68]

True to his word Rhett began a speaking tour of the state in August, but this effort was plagued by poor scheduling and conflicting demands for Rhett's services as an orator. On his way to a secessionist rally in Yorkville, Rhett was waylaid at Chesterville by local secessionists who "pitted him" in an impromptu debate with Samuel McAiley at a meeting organized by cooperationists. In another instance Rhett inadvertently committed himself to a rally in Orangeburg and one in St. Mathew's on the same day. His up-country ally, Daniel Wallace, also made speaking engagements in haphazard fashion, disappointing various local secessionists. Moreover, in the up-country, secessionists had to contend with the popularity of Senator Butler and Congressmen Orr, Burt, and Woodward, all of whom favored cooperation. Butler, Burt, and especially Orr campaigned actively for their cause. From Charleston, Christopher Memminger and Benjamin Pressley made frequent journeys to offset the effects of Rhett's tour. At King's Tree on August 23 Rhett noted piteously that he had traveled a hundred miles to address the audience. He was dissipating his energies.[69]

5

During the summer of 1851 the divergence of Palmetto secessionists from the "resistance parties" of other states became more and more apparent. These resistance parties still pronounced the compromise an inadequate settlement, but they found secession an unacceptable political response. South Carolina secessionists argued that the course of events in other states had destroyed the rationale for cooperation—"unless . . . [South Carolina chose] to co-operate in submission."[70] Cooperationists argued that the renunciation of secession by resistance parties in the deep South demonstrated that South Carolina's secession would receive, at best, only "*barren sympathy*" from her neighbors. Moreover, they declared, South Carolina had "no moral right to force . . . [slaveholding states] into a war about a matter of common interest, without their previous assent." Cooperationists stressed that leaders of the "Southern rights parties" in Georgia, Alabama, and even Mississippi did not condone secession.[71]

Noting that secessionists had claimed Georgia's Charles J. McDonald as one of their own, the *Standard* editorialized that they were damaging his gubernatorial campaign by "drag[ging] him, though unwilling, into a participation . . . [with] their intemperance." Indeed Georgia's Unionist party, a coalition forged by Howell Cobb, Robert Toombs, and Alexander Stephens, damned McDonald's Southern Rights party by associating it with the secessionists of South Carolina. "Warn the good people of Georgia to beware of revolution—refer to France—and plant yourself against the factionists of South Carolina," wrote Stephens to Cobb, the Unionist candidate for governor. "And keep the main point prominent, that the only question now is whether we should go into revolution or not. South Carolina is for it." McDonald believed, "as . . . [did] every true Southern man, in the *right* of secession," the *Standard* observed, but he repeatedly declared that, in December 1850, Georgia had decided against secession and "that her decision ought not to be disturbed." South Carolina "cannot expect . . . the co-operation of Georgia, in any measure of resistance, against the past measures of Congress," wrote McDonald to the Charleston cooperationist rally of July 29. He suggested that it was "best [for South Carolina] to defer to the opinions of her sister States, equally wronged with herself . . . and not proceed separately and alone to a measure of at least questionable expediency." After publication of that letter the secessionists proposed no more toasts to Charles McDonald.[72]

As Oscar Lieber traveled through Alabama in July 1851, he reported to his mother that South Carolina had "not many admirers here. The other day a blacksmith accosted me: 'Capt. I say, now you'se from Sou Calina is you? Well maybe you can tell me vot she's a kicking up such a dust about. Seems to me as long as I can remember, an I aint young nether, she's been a kicking up about some Goddamn thing or other.'" South Carolina cooperationists were less salty, but they denounced the *Mercury*'s claims of extensive support for secession in Alabama. The old cry of South Carolina dictation, they warned, would help Alabama's outright Unionists defeat their opponents.[73]

Certainly South Carolina's secessionists received no comfort from Alabama's elections in August 1851. Of Alabama's seven newly elected congressmen, five were Unionists. Moreover, of the two victors who styled themselves Southern Rights candidates, one endorsed the Georgia platform and the other opposed "immediate or separate state secession." At the same time Alabama elected a legislature that "was Unionist almost two to one." These results made it apparent that Alabama would hardly be disposed to defend South Carolina from federal retaliation if the Palmetto State chose to secede alone. "Thus," proclaimed the *Standard*, were Palmetto secessionists "driving to the enemy all who . . . are not yet convinced of the necessity [for secession]. . . . Thus . . . [the secessionists] weaken and destroy the resistance party of the other States, and prepare [South Carolina] for . . . isolation and glorious littleness."[74]

South Carolina's last and best hope for an ally was Mississippi. But there, too, the probability of support for South Carolina—if she seceded—diminished dramatically. Jefferson Davis and Albert G. Brown disassociated themselves from the opinions of John Quitman. Their Democratic party, "calling itself, in response to the taunts of Foote, the Southern Rights Party, was split." At its nominating convention in mid-June it adopted the name Democratic State Rights party and a platform that included the declaration that secession "by the state of Mississippi, under existing circumstances would be inexpedient, and is a proposition which does not meet the approbation of this convention." At the convention the majority of the committee appointed to choose the party's gubernatorial candidate favored Davis, but Davis refused to accept the nomination if Quitman desired it. He did. Thus Quitman, whose views were at odds with his party's platform, opposed Foote in the gubernatorial campaign. This contest took place simultaneously with the struggle for control of Mississippi's constituent convention that was scheduled to meet in November.[75]

In late June, pressed by "an active and laborious canvass with . . . [his] wiley and adroit opponent Foote," Quitman advised Seabrook on political conditions in Mississippi. "We can not now secede alone," Quitman wrote. "We are unarmed, in debt, seriously divided and have no sea ports. . . . We can however prepare to take position promptly when other states move. This far I think this state will go, if the Southern Rights party succeed. . . . I must say," the Mississippian warned, "that I believe the destiny of the slaveholding states now depends upon the bold and prompt action of your noble state." Labeling his reply "Confidential in part," Seabrook was pleased that Quitman had "prepared . . . a suitable programme to be presented to the [Mississippi] State Convention." Seabrook claimed that "volunteers by thousands [from other states] are signifying their wish to be received into our ranks," but he conceded that "the consequences of separate state secession cannot with certainty be foretold; & a lingering hope still exist[ed] that some southern state, especially Mississippi" would declare its solidarity with South Carolina. Plaintively, Seabrook continued, "Our final course will depend much on Mississippi."[76]

Mississippi's proper course was the subject of a series of debates "between Foote and Quitman in various locations around the state. The debates were to highlight the local campaigns for the state convention." The opponents were mismatched. Quitman delivered tedious, legalistic speeches. Foote, a master of invective and buffoonery, "chose to play on the crowd's emotions, and with each success he became more daring." On July 18 in Panola County the burly Quitman, goaded to rage by his elfish antagonist, resorted to his fists. Neither man was injured in the scuffle that ensued, but Quitman decided to withdraw from the tour while Foote adhered to the original schedule and drew large crowds. On September 1 and 2 Mississippians chose their delegates to the state's constituent convention. The Democratic State Rights party carried only seventeen of the state's fifty-nine counties, and in the aggregate vote Unionists bested their opponents by 28,402 to 21,241. John Anthony Quitman, "chagrined and disappointed by his party's showing," withdrew as a candidate for governor.[77]

6

Well before Mississippi's elections in early September, secessionists and cooperationists alike knew that the Southern Congress proposed by the last South Carolina legislature would never assemble. Nevertheless the election of South Carolina delegates to such a congress had been mandated for October, and the cooperationists and their Unionist allies intended to make that election a referendum on separate secession.[78] Secessionists were forced to accept this challenge or default their claim that a majority of South Carolina citizens favored secession and would willingly abide by the consequences. Girding for the "test of strength" the secessionists called on "all State action men . . . to aid in bringing out the full force of the resistance party" on October 13 and 14.[79]

In September cooperationist and secessionist leaders busied themselves with the kind of political machinery South Carolina gentry usually considered abhorrent: party nominating conventions. In the election districts the faithful of each group gathered in party conclaves to select delegates to congressional district conventions. At these conventions each party named two candidates. In this process the cooperationists had stolen a march, and their nominations were completed before those of the secessionists. By the end of September the secessionists had fielded candidates to oppose the cooperationists' nominees in each congressional district. The cooperationists' slate included Congressman Orr and Congressman-elect William Aiken. The secessionists' slate boasted Congressman Wallace and Senator Rhett.[80]

Convinced that South Carolina's secession would lead not to a southern confederacy but to the prospect of a "desperate war . . . [to] become a separate nation," cooperationists in September and October were preoccupied with imminent catastrophe. For cooperationists the perceived dangers of immediate secession overshadowed plans for future resistance to the federal government. Their concern was reflected in party functions that were billed as "Southern Cooperation and Anti-Secession" affairs. Secessionists charged that, with this change in label, cooperationists were appearing "in the undisguised character of submissionists," in the "character of a party merely combined to prevent separate State action—to obstruct resistance." Undaunted the cooperationists adhered to their anti-secession titles. On September 20 Orr addressed the "Anti-Secession Meeting, at Cashville, in Spartanburg District," which was organized by Unionists. Perry reciprocated by urging Unionists in the second congressional district to elect "Irby and Orr for the Southern Congress . . . with a view of showing the anti-secession strength of the State."[81]

In Charleston the ward committees for cooperationist party affairs met almost weekly. On September 23 the party held a "Southern Co-operation and Anti-Secession Meeting" to install William Aiken and William Porter as the cooperationist candidates for the sixth congressional district, which included Charleston. The address prepared for this rally depicted the terrors of isolated secession in unstinting terms. Secession would put a "dark unfathomable future . . . before us, with no light to guide us, but that borrowed from the conditions of nations, too weak to invite, or too impotent to repel aggressions. . . . We stand," warned the address, "upon the verge of a revolution . . . unless *The People* will rise in their might, and arrest . . . the irrevocable and fatal step." After speeches by Christopher Memminger and Isaac Hayne, "the address and nomination[s] were . . . unanimously adopted and confirmed."[82]

In the seventh congressional district and more particularly in Beaufort and Colleton, Rhett's long-established political base, cooperationists admitted that they were "not so well organized" as they desired. Still cooperationists there were represented at open debates and held a few rallies of their own.[83] Elsewhere in the state cooperationists were increasingly confident of their strength. Christopher Memminger and Benjamin Pressley continued their speaking forays from Charleston, winning "the sincere thanks of the . . . [cooperationist] party" in the words of a Darlington rally.[84] "The two parties . . . are now nearly equally divided with a large preponderance of talent on the Co-operationist side, which is gaining ground," Hammond confided to his diary on September 7. Among new recruits in September cooperationists enlisted state-convention delegate Winchester Graham, former governor David Johnson, and Chancellor Francis H. Wardlaw. Nine of South Carolina's ten law and equity court judges opposed secession, a fact that James Orr and other cooperationists cited repeatedly.[85]

To their usual array of charges against secessionists, the cooperationists added a new one in September. The *Standard* published a letter in which James A. Lewis of Chester Grove alleged "that *although Mississippi repudiates secession* . . . General Quitman writes encouragingly to some of our secession leaders, urging them . . . to make . . . [South Carolina] secede." Lewis claimed further that "Rhett in his speech near Rossville, on the 4th of July, asserted that Quitman *had written thus to him*." Such correspondence, Lewis concluded, was a "violation of good morals" and was "calculated to deceive the people of both States . . . into a position they do not wish to occupy."[86]

"*Since my nomination* for Governor, I have no recollection of having ever written a letter to Carolina," Quitman wrote in reply to Lewis's charges.[87] Quitman conceded that, before his recent nomination for governor, "in answer to some inquiries made by several [Carolina] gentlemen . . . I may have expressed the wish that South Carolina would not recede from" her stand against the federal government. Rhett denied having ever "spoken of . . . [Quitman's] opinions on the authority of any letter from him." In a second letter Lewis yielded on some details of his allegations. Still he insisted that "Mr. R. *has* used the name of Gen. Quitman, as sanctioning and advising the policy he advocates" and that "a prominent Secessionist of Columbia, a member of the Central Committee, asserted publicly. . . 'that he had . . . a large number of letters from gentlemen in the West,' *naming General Q among the number,* 'all urging South Carolina to . . . secede, that they would sustain her.'" But in mid-September, when Quitman withdrew as a gubernatorial candidate, the question of his collaboration with Palmetto secessionists ceased to command attention, and cooperationists let the matter drop.[88]

In September secessionists freely admitted that the successive victories of procompromise parties in Alabama and Mississippi had given southern Unionism new life, and on October 7 Georgia Unionists resoundingly demonstrated their vitality: they gave Cobb an eighteen-thousand vote margin over McDonald, "secured an unprecedented majority in the legislature and elected six out of . . . eight congressmen." Secessionists took these Unionist triumphs as conclusive proof that the cooperationists' goal was unobtainable and that South Carolina must secede alone. The rest of the South must be forced to defend South Carolina's secession—or to aid in suppressing it. In October, however, the assertion that slaveholding states would inevitably support one of their own seemed less plausible than in May. As Hammond observed, "If necessary Geo. will volunteer to put down secession in So Ca."[89]

Reviews of the militia encampments by Governor Means and his party afforded speechmaking opportunities that cooperationists did not enjoy; despite cooperationist complaints that "Military Musters [were] being turned into political gatherings," secessionists continued to make the most of these occasions. Certainly secessionists needed to exploit this small advantage, for their political campaigning elsewhere revealed signs of disarray. On September 17 Charleston secessionists held a mass rally to stimulate enthusiasm for their candidates in the October election. Barely a week later a disappointed party worker wrote: "It is a matter of much regret to us that we have to complain of the inactivity of our Ward Committees. . . . We must meet together . . . take counsel together." The Southern Rights Association of St. Bartholomew announced that Senator Rhett, Congressmen Colcock, Wallace, and McQueen, central committee members Bellinger and Gregg, former Congressman Pickens, and former Governor Seabrook would address its anniversary meeting on October 6; but of these men only William Colcock managed to attend.[90]

During September cooperationists relentlessly pursued their attack on Rhett and Blufftonism. Since the "great preacher of secession" believed himself infallible, editorialized the *Standard*, "it is not surprising that his disciples should excel in the use of such classical and elegant epithets, as 'traitors,' 'cowards,' 'submissionists' and 'federal sympathisers.' " A correspondent of the *Southern Patriot* even disparaged Rhett as an outsider, a native of North Carolina. Tired and touchy Rhett not only proclaimed his South Carolina nativity but also provided a genealogy tracing his roots to "Sir John Yeamans, one of the Lords Proprietors." This elaborate response only gave more fuel to Rhett's critics. "Such a jackday exhibition of vanity I have never before seen," wrote William Elliott. "He was only called a North Carolinian, and there was no obligation on him to do more than deny it. If the People have an ounce of brain left, it must damn him." Battered by personal attacks and exhausted by his speaking schedule, Rhett reached the limit of his endurance in late September. The *Mercury* reported that he was "unable from serious indisposition, to meet the engagements he had made to address the people, in several Districts of the upper country, and that . . . he . . . [would] probably be unable to make any future engagements." Before the election Rhett departed for England to recoup his health.[91]

Worried by the growing strength of their opponents, some secessionists attempted to disrupt cooperationist rallies. Secessionists occasionally attended cooperationist meetings to offer hostile or obstructionist resolutions. When antisecession rallies were announced, secessionists "either proclaim[ed] a meeting of their own party at the same place on the same day," Perry complained, "or . . . they muster[ed] in strength enough to interrupt [their rivals] by clamor and noise." As examples of these tactics he cited incidents at Spartanburg, Edgefield, Darlington, Cashville, and Greenville. On October 6 Memminger addressed a cooperationist rally in Marion;

his speech "was twice interrupted . . . by the Secessionists, who marched past, first on one side and then on the other, all the while beating their drums and shouting."[92] The secessionists' desperation was revealed, too, in an eleventh-hour accusation "that money has been offered to the Co-operation party from the Federal government." On the day that South Carolina voters went to the polls, the *Mercury* was forced to concede that its informant "mistook the purport of a conversation in which the matter was mentioned."[93]

On October 15 two sentences in the *Mercury* told the story of the election: "the vote is the largest ever polled. . . . The Co-operationists have given to their ticket a large majority, and though it will be diminished by the Parishes, it cannot be overcome." Indeed the low country again justified its reputation for preferring militant political solutions; the secessionists carried all but three of the parishes.[94] In tiny St. Thomas's they polled 100 percent of the vote. But the secessionists carried only one congressional district—the seventh. Cooperationists obtained their largest margins in the second congressional district, which included the Unionist stronghold of Greenville, and in the sixth congressional district, which included Charleston.[95] Cooperationists won clear victories in twenty of South Carolina's twenty-nine judicial districts. They won in all the districts where whites outnumbered slaves, and they won in ten of the nineteen districts where slaves were in the majority. The two parties were virtually even in Edgefield. Secessionists won the remaining eight judicial districts.[96] In the state's aggregate vote cooperationists defeated secessionists by approximately 25,062 to 17,617.[97] Secessionists conceded that their defeat was decisive.

7

"Secession is dead. . . . We have been damnably defeated," mourned James Jones. Yet most secessionist leaders intended to make the cooperationists redeem their pledges to resist the compromise by some means "short of secession." Toward that end, Jones and the other members of the central committee of the Southern Rights Associations caucused on October 24. In a circular for the "members of the Secession Party," the committee attributed the party's defeat to "an ignominious panic" brought on by "alarms and falsehoods . . . disseminated . . . with every appearance of systematic operation." The circular warned that many cooperationists professed disunionism but desired instead to defeat "all resistance to past wrongs." The central committee urged secessionists "to arouse a sense of responsibility" in the "resistance wing" of the cooperationist party. To remind cooperationists of their duty the central committee recommended that the secessionist party's organization should be maintained.[98]

Seeking a program that would begin "practical resistance" and lead to "disunion at the earliest possible moment," a program that both secessionists and cooperationists could embrace, John Cunningham, James Jones and Maxcy Gregg corresponded with Hammond about his "plan of state action."[99] These secessionists explained

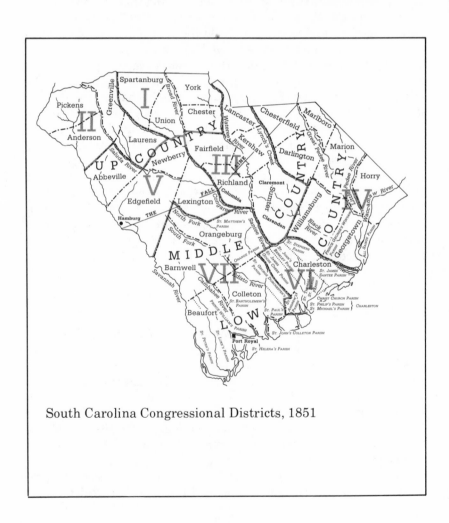

South Carolina Congressional Districts, 1851

to Hammond that their party, "having been defeated in . . . [its] favorite scheme will fall back and fight manfully in the line next to . . . [its] own. Your plan furnishes the basis of that line." Cunningham advised Hammond that the "Secession party are aware that Rhett's leadership cannot give it success," and Gregg wrote: "Should you consent to come forward as a Leader . . . you would be hailed with enthusiasm by the truest, the staunchest, the most Carolinian Party which has ever existed in the State." Hammond, however, responded warily. He was more than willing for others to sponsor his plan, but he would not affiliate himself with the secession party, nor would he lead an attempt to form a new coalition.[100]

In the wake of their victory cooperationists were increasingly embarrassed by pronunciamentos from Benjamin Perry. "The recent election *was an anti-secession, and not a co-operation, victory.* The people voted against secession, and not in favor of co-operation," he claimed early in November. In taking this position Perry forfeited any possible place in cooperationist party councils. The cooperationist leaders, while determined to ostracize Unionists, were reluctant to pursue their announced goal of a southern confederacy. "In my opinion," wrote Isaac Hayne, "*no* very decisive step can be taken at this time. *The occasion has been lost,* and cannot be recovered." As enunciated by the *Standard* the program of the cooperationist party was extremely vague: "by agitation, appeals, conciliation . . . and particularly discussion, [cooperationists intend] to develope some effectual measure of resistance, in which the whole Southern rights party may agree *to unite, and by which they are to gain the majority in each or several States.*"[101]

Early in November cooperationist leaders met in Charleston; they could agree on nothing more than to caucus again when the state's legislators assembled in Columbia. Cooperationist A. P. Aldrich, meanwhile, could drum up very little support in his party for Hammond's plan. The *Standard* dismissed the plan as unworkable. Aldrich also warned his mentor that a cooperationist rapprochement with the secessionists would require "a great deal of caution and skill. . . . For instance, I will not consent to act with any party having Mr. Rhett as its leader and the Mercury as its exponent."[102]

Meeting in caucus on November 25 and again two days later, the leaders of the cooperationist party revealed deep hostility toward not only Rhett but also Gregg, who was chiefly responsible for the secessionist circular of October 24. Believing that any proposal with secessionist connections might be designed to sow dissension among the victors, the cooperationists were not inclined to support Hammond's plan or "any proposition which savor[ed] of separate state action." The cooperationists attending the caucus meetings were of different minds on the wisdom of holding the state convention authorized by the previous legislature. Aldrich, Chesnut, and Hayne thought the convention offered an opportunity to reunite a badly divided gentry. Cheves, Memminger, Burt, and Orr, among others, did not want the convention to assemble. The caucus, however, shared Orr's inclination to place the whole burden of calling the convention upon the secessionists, unless they "would give up . . . [party] organization and drop secession entirely."[103]

At its second meeting the cooperationist caucus referred the decision on calling the state convention "to a committee of seven to report on" November 29. That committee was also empowered to formulate a cooperationist platform. On the convention issue the committee remained as divided as the caucus, agreeing only that any attempt to further secession at the convention would violate "the clear declaration of the public will." The committee affirmed the necessity of cooperative resistance to "abolitionism [and the] encroachments of the federal government," rehearsed South Carolina's "deep and indignant sense of . . . grievances," pleaded for harmony between cooperationists and secessionists, and recommended, lastly, "that the organization of those who desire to promote co-operation should be preserved."[104]

Robert F. W. Allston, who presided over the secessionist caucus, told his colleagues that their "thorough and decisive" defeat required them to accept "republican subordination." He believed that "the Secessionists, as a party, should abandon their organization; or so materially" alter it as to include all "who recognize the good old doctrine of State's Rights." Militant secessionists no longer marshaled a cohesive party.[105]

Secessionists did agree, however, that the state convention must meet. In "justice to ourselves, in good faith to our constituents, to each other & to the country, we are bound . . . to appoint a day for its meeting," said Robert Allston. Secessionists, including Governor Means, saw no reason to continue brigade encampments or other preparations for secession, but they felt that those "who have discovered a better remedy for [South Carolina's] wrongs than secession . . . [should] bring it forward." Despite half-hearted cooperationist opposition led by Memminger, a bill that provided for the state convention to assemble on April 26, 1852, passed both houses of the legislature with ease.[106]

With his party fragmented and his leadership covertly attacked,

Rhett endured a harrowing winter. In the Senate, Henry Foote and Jeremiah Clemens denounced the campaign for disunion that Rhett had led. In a speech on December 15, he reaffirmed his commitment to the secessionist cause, lost though it was. He was ill and absent from the Senate in late January and February, but his past course remained under assault, especially by Clemens.[107]

On February 27 Rhett replied to Clemens's taunts with an exposé on the Alabamian's changed attitude toward the compromise he had once condemned. In the exchange that followed this speech, Clemens courted a duel: he denied having called Rhett a knave and a traitor, but "if I had done so," he said, "the subsequent course of that Senator justifies me in adding the epithet of coward." Refusing to challenge Clemens, Rhett said, in part, "For twenty years I have been a . . . [Christian]. I cannot, and will not, dishonor my religious profession. . . . I fear God; and . . . I fear him more than man." The *Standard*, loosely paraphrasing Clemens's final rejoinder, reported the Alabaman as saying that "if he [Rhett] had put his sword on the Bible, he should apprentice his tongue more closely to the peace establishment." Despite his established reputation for piety, Rhett's Christian restraint in his quarrel did not enhance his standing with those South Carolinians who believed strongly in the code duello.[108]

For Gregg, as for Rhett, the winter and spring of 1852 was a trying time. The secessionist party was fast approaching "irretrievable confusion," but Gregg, with Rhett's blessing, continued his attempt to shape Hammond's plan into a compromise platform for cooperationists and secessionists. Cooperationists, however, wanted their defeated opponents to accept the proposition that "[separate] secession is not the policy of South Carolina for existing grievances," and militant secessionists balked at giving such a pledge. As Gregg confessed, "If I consented to renounce the right of secession—or what comes to the same thing, to declare that it must never be exercised separately, I should feel that I was abandoning the political faith of my whole life." In view of this impasse A. P. Aldrich, by April 1852, "had long since despaired of getting any effectual support for the Plan from either party," and he so informed Gregg.[109]

Assembling on Monday, April 26, the delegates organized the state convention by electing the governor to preside. The choice was in keeping with precedent, but the nearly unanimous vote for Governor John Means signaled "a conciliatory spirit on the part of the Cooperation Party."[110] Cooperationists found Means's response entirely satisfactory. On the next day, when the convention approved Langdon Cheves's motion for a committee of twenty-one to report on the convention's essential business, Means appointed twelve cooperationists, eight secessionists, and a single Unionist to the committee.[111]

The secessionist caucus, meanwhile, suggested to its cooperationist counterpart that differences between the groups be resolved by a committee of conference. This conference committee met on the night of April 27 but broke up in confusion. In a caucus meeting that followed this failure, secessionists were hopelessly divided. Gregg moved that Rhett address the meeting. According to Aldrich's information "Drayton Nance immediately said I hope not, we are twenty-one years old and capable of making up our own minds." Gregg withdrew his motion, and the caucus "then voted down all the violent propositions which had been made to the committee of conference." Amid recriminations the meeting sputtered to an end.[112]

Anxious for the convention to adjourn as soon as possible, Langdon Cheves, who chaired the committee of twenty-one, secured two uncontroversial measures as the committee's majority report.[113] The first was a resolution affirming that the federal government's "encroachments upon the reserved rights of . . . States . . . especially in relation to slavery, amply justify" secession by South Carolina and that the state "forbears the exercise of this manifest right . . . from considerations of expediency only." The second measure was "An Ordinance to declare the right of this State to secede from the Federal Union." In deciding on sufficient cause for secession, the ordinance proclaimed, South Carolina "is responsible alone, under God, to the tribunal of public opinion among the nations of the earth."[114]

On the floor of the convention die-hard secessionists moved, as a counterproposal, that the legislature be empowered to ordain secession by a two-thirds majority. The motion was laid on the table by a vote of 96 to 60.[115] Other proposals from Edmund Rhett and Benjamin Perry fared worse. The convention then approved the majority report 136 to 19 and adjourned sine die,[116] but in less than a decade a South Carolina convention found sufficient cause to ordain secession, and the Palmetto State ventured disunion to preserve its peculiar order.

8

Secessionist Maxcy Gregg, writing in retrospect to James Hammond, saw "clearly the enormous obstacles interposed against the Secession of South Carolina by what you have termed with a

happy euphemism, the *love of order*. That same *love of order* was
a great obstacle to the Revolution of '76—and to Nullification in
1832." The interpretation that Gregg imbibed from Hammond was
sketched more fully in Hammond's Diary:

> Order is a prime necessity in every community, especially an
> Agricultural one & most especially a slave-holding one. To the
> great body of the Southern People, the Union is the only
> tangible & appreciable representative of Order, & it is solely on
> this account that they love & sustain it. Its oppressions must be
> grievously *felt* before they will violate Order to resist them.
> They must be enlightened so as to appreciate these oppressions
> & all its dangers in future. . . . And pari passu steps must be
> taken to carry on resistance and insure the rupture of the
> Union, *which do not in the first instance involve any violation of
> Order*. Thus & thus only can the Great Revolution be gradually
> carried forward & ultimately accomplished.[117]

Secession might have a revolutionary political impact on the federal Union, but South Carolina secessionists intended to accomplish
disunion by orderly and, according to their lights, profoundly legal steps. Having resolved to resist "Congressional aggression and
northern fanatacism, that resolve ought to be carried into effect
with calmness and great discretion by a united people," wrote Governor Whitemarsh Seabrook. His successor John Means also spoke
for secessionists when he insisted that the constitution would never
be terminated in South Carolina except by proper republican and
constitutional machinery. Within South Carolina's borders federal laws would only be "*abrogated and annuled*" by "this State in
Convention assembled," wrote central committee member James
Jones.[118] Thus far, and in theoretical terms, cooperationists agreed
with secessionists.

It was in a willingness, at least before the fact, to accept disunion's
consequences that secessionists and cooperationists parted company.
Secessionist propaganda contained its share and more of vainglori-
ous declarations regarding the outcome of a war triggered by disunion. From the "nature of our population and territory, we could
keep in check at least 1,000,000 men that might be sent to invade
us," wrote one polemicist.[119] But the secessionists' appetite for confrontation was stimulated less by vanity than by a romantic and
revolutionary faith. After the October election Maxcy Gregg conceded that "the multitude has not the heart to encounter . . . the
perils and sacrifices" of secession; but he would not concede "that

the age has passed for maintaining the rights of small communities by force. I look upon the readiness to maintain them by force as the only safeguard for them," he said.[120]

"If the State be saved, and Constitutional liberty be placed upon a sure basis," declaimed Daniel Wallace, "it must be done by the brave." This theme was constantly on the lips of secessionists, and for a model of bravery, they unabashedly chose Hotspur. When co-operationists taunted their opponents with Hotspur's end, secessionists replied that "Harry Percy failed . . . not because he misjudged himself or his cause, but because in the hour of action" his kinsmen and allies lacked his faith. "If in spite of all the resistance we can make we are finally overwhelmed by superior physical force, *what have we lost?*" asked secessionist James Jones. "We are now in a hopeless minority in the government; we are fenced round by non-slave States. . . . the measures of a hostile majority . . . [will] drain us of our wealth . . . and finally . . . free our slaves and drive us from our homes. If we succeed in the attempt to secede, we check the current of events. . . . If we fail, we have saved our honour *and lost nothing.* We shall still be in the same political condition . . . [as] now . . . and will then have left to us the last alternative—*Submission.*"[121]

Cooperationists fully agreed with secessionists that only in disunion could the South Carolina fashioned by the gentry find safety. But the cooperationists, acutely aware that outside the South slavery faced "an almost universal sentiment of condemnation," were unwilling for South Carolina to reach alone like Hotspur for the flower safety.[122] Without an assurance of slaveholding allies, without a near certainty that disunion would be followed by a southern confederacy, cooperationists judged the risks of secession to be prohibitive, and those risks involved more than bloody conflict with external foes. "Not only did secession have the potential to spark a terrible civil war, but it would surely release disrupting social and political forces."[123] Separate secession conjured, in the minds of cooperationists, visions of revolution, of primal disorder. Deep "is the danger which follows that condition in a people, when they change their form of Government. All the balances which regulate society are removed, and confusion, in a greater or lesser degree, attends the transition. . . . The elements which are let loose may . . . carry dire ruin in their course, until restrained by superior force. . . . and it may be, that no measures afterward adopted could repair the evils and restore to us, what will be lost."[124] Thus from separate secession "the ripples of potential social disorder spread beyond racial security to threaten the unique character of government and society" in South Carolina.[125]

When secessionists began agitating "to dissolve a political connection of near a century, without a definite idea of any league or treaty to supply its place," cooperationists were merely dismayed. But when secessionists placed a higher value on implementing their policy than on maintaining consensus rule by the state's gentry, and when secessionists—in violation of the state's political mores— formed a party, cooperationists were shocked into counter-organization. Temporarily and in the heat of party battle, cooperationists perceived the secessionists as misguided revolutionaries, as Jacobins who did not scruple "to enlist the sons in a proscriptive crusade against their own fathers." Pursuing this analogy the cooperationists decided they "must inflict upon the Secessionists a Waterloo defeat."[126]

Unionists in South Carolina were as thoroughly committed to slavery as secessionists and cooperationists. Unionists of the up-country as well as the low-country stripe embraced slavery as an essential and sacrosanct institution in South Carolina.[127] As his *Letters of Curtius* demonstrated, W. J. Grayson moved easily and rapidly from defending slavery to denouncing secession.[128] Unlike secessionists and cooperationists, South Carolina's Unionists did not accept the postulate that slavery was, or inevitably would be, relentlessly assaulted by a hostile northern majority. The "friends of law and order" in the North were "more numerous and determined" than free "negroes and abolitionists," Grayson had written in October 1850, and the state's Unionist leaders asserted that belief with increasing urgency in 1851. John B. O'Neall assured his fellow citizens that there was "virtue and patriotism enough in the great body of the American people, in the executive and judicial officers of the United States . . . to maintain and enforce . . . [the constitution] to our benefit." In the *Southern Patriot* and on the hustings, Perry insistently proclaimed that "it is untrue, utterly untrue, that there is any respectable portion of the Northern people in favor of emancipating our slaves by means of the Federal Government."[129]

"I object to the secession movement," John O'Neall declared, "because it is the very thing sought by the Abolitionists. They wish to divide slave owners from the glorious stars and stripes of '76." Perry regarded "the Union of these States as the strongest protection that slavery can have. . . . We now have, under the Union constitutional guarantees for slavery, which we could not have if this Union were dissolved."[130] The state's Unionists agreed. The Union was an aegis that protected American liberties—including the liberty of South Carolinians to hold slaves. Union and slavery were not alternatives to Palmetto Unionists; slavery was, to them, an inseparable part of the orderly, republican government that the constitution guaranteed to members of the federal system. As Grayson warned in his open letter to Governor Seabrook, the choice facing South Carolinians was Union or turmoil and war, and in the tumultuous aftermath of disunion slavery might not survive.

APPENDIX

NOTES

BIBLIOGRAPHY

INDEX

Note

Tables 1–3 are presented not for the sake of absolute numbers, but to show comparative values and to demonstrate changes over time. The percentages have been rounded from four decimal places to two, therefore, the total population of each district will equal 100 ± .01 percent. No attempt was made to go beyond the data published in the census returns, but those data were checked for internal consistency before computing percentages.

The figures for 1790 are given separately, because of the great change between 1790 and 1800 in the number and boundaries of districts as well as in the system of enumerating them. Smaller changes of the same kind continued throughout the antebellum period. In all three tables the districts are arranged in tiers along a southwest-to-northeast line. The first tier (the low country) bordered the coast; subsequent tiers lay progressively inland (see map of South Carolina on page xiii).

Table A-1

Percentage of South Carolina's Population Slave (s),
*Free Black (fb)*ᵃ*, and White (w) by District, 1790*

	s	fb	w
Low Countryᵇ:			
Beaufort	75.91	0.82	23.27
Colleton	81.43	0.86	17.71
Charlestonᶜ	73.63	1.63	24.75
Georgetown	59.36	0.51	40.13
Up-Country:			
Orangeburg	59.85	0.56	39.59
Sumter	39.08	0.00	60.92
Marlboro (Cheraw)	30.16	0.55	69.29
Edgefield	27.23	0.49	72.28
Newberry	12.25	0.13	87.63
Richland	36.56	0.36	63.08
Fairfield	19.48	0.00	80.52
Lancaster	21.74	1.07	77.18
Abbeville	18.10	0.29	81.60
Laurens	12.00	0.07	87.93
Union	15.79	0.62	83.58
Chester	13.66	0.68	85.65
York	13.98	0.44	85.58
Pendleton	8.72	0.03	91.25
Greenville	9.32	0.14	90.54
Spartanburg	9.84	0.31	89.85

Source: *Fifth Census . . . of the United States, 1830: To Which Is Prefixed a Schedule of . . . 1790, 1800, 1810, 1820* (Washington: Printed by Duff Green, 1832). Titles and publishers of the antebellum censuses vary; hereafter they will be cited only by number.

a. In 1790 free Negroes were enumerated under the census category "All other free persons." In 1800 this rubric was changed to "All other free persons except Indians not taxed." In 1810 and thereafter "Free Colored Person" constituted a separate census category. In the First through Eighth Federal Censuses the number of free blacks listed was probably less reliable than the totals for whites and slaves.

b. The low country, while an indispensable concept in South Carolina's history as well as geography, has proved exceedingly difficult to define. "The most convenient distinction is that the low country benefited from malapportionment of the state legislature while the up country suffered from it" (Brady, "Slave Trade and

Sectionalism," p. 604n). Thus the term has been frequently used "more in a socioeconomic than in a geographical sense, to denote the swampy coastal area of the large rice and sea-island cotton plantations" (Freehling, *Prelude to Civil War*, p. 7n). In Tables 1–3 low country denotes the districts bordering the Atlantic—Beaufort, Colleton, Charleston, Georgetown—plus Williamsburg, which was carved out of the old Georgetown District. Although bordering the coast, Horry District was marked off from the low country by a different climate and a poorer soil. (For more precise geographic divisions of the low country and of the entire state, see Wallace, *South Carolina*, pp. 3–4.)

c. Through 1840 Charleston District, as defined in the federal census, included the city (St. Michael's and St. Philip's) plus the following surrounding parishes: St. James, Goose Creek; St. Andrew's; St. John's, Colleton; St. Thomas's and St. Denis's; St. Stephen's; Christ Church; St. James, Santee; St. John's, Berkley.

Table A-2

Percentage of South Carolina's Population Slave (s),
Free Black (fb), and White (w) by District, 1800–1820

	1800			1810		
	s	fb	w	s	fb	w
Low Country:						
Beaufort	78.48	0.97	20.56	80.79	0.70	18.51
Colleton	82.20	0.15	17.64	82.92	0.80	16.28
Charleston	72.97	2.02	25.01	71.84	2.82	25.34
Georgetown	72.23	0.41	27.36	88.44	0.65	10.91
Williamsburg	—	—	—	65.75	0.68	33.56
Up-Country:						
Barnwell	23.20	1.52	75.28	33.82	1.29	64.89
Orangeburg	33.98	0.60	65.43	49.62	0.20	50.19
Sumter	50.09	2.30	47.62	61.08	1.51	37.41
Darlington	30.61	0.42	68.97	30.19	0.63	69.18
Marion	31.17	1.99	66.84	31.19	1.06	67.75
Marlboro	25.55	3.29	71.17	34.41	1.69	63.89
Horry	—	—	—	32.15	0.41	67.44
Edgefield	27.61	0.34	72.05	37.03	0.65	62.32
Newberry	18.36	0.79	80.85	28.69	0.79	70.52
Lexington	—	—	—	28.78	0.26	70.97
Richland	49.75	2.21	48.04	58.03	3.56	38.42
Fairfield	19.51	0.23	80.26	34.02	0.31	65.67
Kershaw	34.47	1.42	64.11	49.12	0.79	50.09
Chesterfield	22.01	1.40	76.59	29.46	1.04	69.50
Abbeville	21.87	0.30	77.83	31.54	0.42	68.05
Laurens	14.98	0.16	84.86	22.08	0.19	77.73
Union	16.58	0.66	82.75	25.87	0.62	73.51
Chester	14.22	0.02	85.75	23.90	0.12	75.98
York	17.60	0.26	82.13	31.54	0.40	68.06
Lancaster	17.90	0.63	81.47	26.05	5.89	68.06
Pendleton	11.09	0.34	88.57	15.22	0.21	84.57
Greenville	12.51	0.31	87.18	17.92	0.31	81.77
Spartanburg	12.10	0.38	87.52	16.77	0.23	83.00

Source: Second, Third, and Fourth Federal Censuses.

	1820	
s	fb	w
84.91	0.56	14.53
82.45	1.11	16.44
71.34	4.51	24.16
88.31	1.29	10.40
67.28	0.65	32.07
42.96	1.71	55.34
56.40	0.41	43.19
63.63	1.51	34.86
40.85	0.63	58.52
33.95	0.84	65.21
47.21	2.21	50.58
28.54	0.46	71.00
48.56	0.23	51.21
35.70	1.10	63.20
34.65	0.19	65.16
61.90	1.58	36.51
45.11	0.28	54.61
53.83	0.90	45.27
31.03	2.57	66.40
41.50	0.28	58.22
27.59	0.28	72.14
30.28	0.44	69.28
32.01	0.25	67.74
30.73	0.64	68.63
32.10	0.80	67.09
17.45	0.62	81.93
23.56	0.62	75.82
19.47	0.15	80.38

Table A-3

Percentage of South Carolina's Population Slave (s),
Free Black (fb), and White (w) by District, 1830–1860

	1830			1840		
	s	fb	w	s	fb	w
Low Country:						
Beaufort	83.43	1.34	15.22	82.92	1.29	15.78
Colleton	78.82	1.53	19.64	75.32	1.68	23.00
Charleston	71.70	4.21	24.10	70.82	3.87	25.31
Georgetown	89.24	1.07	9.68	87.52	1.03	11.45
Williamsburg	68.34	0.29	31.37	67.47	0.31	32.22
Up-Country:						
Barnwell	44.17	1.47	54.36	49.13	2.02	48.85
Orangeburg	59.24	0.03	40.73	64.26	1.43	34.30
Sumter	66.21	1.32	32.48	67.69	1.34	30.97
Clarendon	—	—	—	—	—	—
Darlington	50.36	0.74	48.91	51.00	0.63	48.37
Marion	34.46	0.39	65.15	37.70	0.61	61.69
Marlboro	50.50	0.63	48.87	48.97	1.21	49.82
Horry	32.40	0.34	67.26	27.35	0.47	72.18
Edgefield	50.31	0.67	49.03	53.38	0.89	45.72
Newberry	47.68	1.18	51.14	53.99	1.30	44.71
Lexington	41.79	0.40	57.81	38.68	0.21	61.11
Richland	63.90	3.38	32.72	65.00	2.52	32.49
Fairfield	54.54	0.44	45.02	62.02	0.36	37.62
Kershaw	61.66	1.45	36.89	65.49	2.04	32.47
Chesterfield	35.91	1.46	62.84	33.48	1.93	64.58
Abbeville	46.55	0.64	52.81	51.61	1.10	47.29
Laurens	34.71	0.27	65.01	41.30	0.47	58.23
Union	40.03	0.49	59.48	45.29	0.53	54.19
Chester	41.57	0.55	57.89	43.51	0.77	55.72
York	37.30	0.58	62.13	36.95	0.59	62.46
Lancaster	39.79	0.70	59.50	42.76	1.08	56.15
Anderson	25.79	0.22	73.99	30.73	0.34	68.93
Pickens	19.81	0.99	79.20	18.91	0.65	80.44
Greenville	30.74	0.19	69.07	29.74	0.24	70.01
Spartanburg	23.30	0.37	76.32	23.54	0.24	76.22

Source: Fifth, Sixth, Seventh, Eighth Federal Censuses and J. D. B. DeBow, *Statistical View of the United States . . . Being a Compendium of the Seventh Census . . .* (Washington: Beverley Tucker, Senate, Printer, 1854).

a. The limits of Charleston District were undefined in the Seventh and Eighth Censuses.

1850			1860		
s	fb	w	s	fb	w
83.18	1.49	15.33	81.22	2.02	16.76
79.62	0.83	18.74	77.08	0.84	22.08
60.95[a]	5.29	33.76	53.20[b]	5.17	41.64
88.41	0.97	10.63	85.00	0.86	14.14
68.35	0.30	31.35	66.23	0.28	33.49
52.65	1.17	46.19	56.60	2.08	41.32
65.24	0.33	34.43	66.61	0.82	32.57
69.43	1.03	29.54	69.92	1.34	28.74
—	—	—	65.41	1.15	33.43
59.66	0.25	40.01	58.33	0.26	41.41
43.20	0.61	56.19	46.96	1.09	51.94
51.90	1.45	46.65	55.44	1.35	43.21
27.14	0.64	72.22	29.63	0.49	69.88
57.88	0.73	41.39	60.32	0.43	39.25
62.99	1.06	35.95	65.59	0.88	33.53
42.98	0.18	56.84	39.81	0.28	59.90
64.11	2.47	33.41	60.11	2.40	37.49
66.56	0.42	33.02	70.25	0.92	28.82
66.18	1.48	32.34	59.92	1.51	38.58
36.09	2.02	61.89	36.74	1.12	62.14
59.60	1.10	39.29	63.31	1.13	35.56
51.07	0.36	48.58	55.33	0.54	44.13
52.35	0.72	46.93	55.01	0.84	44.16
54.81	0.82	44.37	59.97	0.86	39.17
41.20	0.65	58.14	46.43	0.88	52.69
45.63	1.06	53.30	47.89	0.79	51.32
34.99	0.44	64.57	36.83	0.71	62.46
21.76	0.71	77.53	21.36	0.56	78.08
33.20	0.47	66.33	32.20	0.97	66.83
30.45	0.19	69.36	30.61	0.53	68.86

The slave population of the city of Charleston declined both relatively and
utely during the 1850s. Slaves were sold to rural areas because slave prices
rising and substitute labor sources were available in the city. See Claudia Dale
in, *Urban Slavery in the American South, 1820–1860: A Quantitative History*
ago: University of Chicago Press, 1976).

Table A-4

Percentage of Total Votes Cast for Secessionists and Cooperationists by Congressional Districts

	Secession		Cooperation		Percentage of Total Votes Secession	Cooperation
First District	Wallace	Vernon	Dawkins	Rainey		
Spartanburg	1,176	1,186	1,448	1,426	45.1	54.9
Union	988	988	288	288	77.4	22.6
York	709	672	1,420	1,382	33.0	67.0
Chester	429	416	929	923	31.3	68.7
	3,302	3,262	4,085	4,019		
Total Votes	6,564		8,164		44.8	55.2
Second District	Young	Simpson	Orr	Irby		
Pickens	152	152	1,411	1,411	09.7	90.3
Anderson	436	436	1,306	1,306	25.0	75.0
Greenville	234	237	1,498	1,500	13.6	86.4
Laurens	991	955	793	810	54.8	45.2
	1,813	1,780	5,008	5,027		
Total Votes	3,593		10,035		26.4	73.6
Third District	Barnes	Owens	Preston	Chesnut		
Lancaster	290	267	627	636	30.6	69.4
Kershaw	244	218	601	639	27.1	72.9
Fairfield	694	717	387	394	64.4	35.6
Richland	634	648	706	688	47.9	52.1
Sumter	661	660	1,110	1,110	37.3	62.7
	2,523	2,510	3,431	3,467		
Total Votes	5,033		6,898		42.2	57.8
Fourth District	Wilson	Dozier	Dudley	Zimmerman		
Chesterfield	222	222	791	791	21.9	78.1
Marlborough	222	221	512	512	39.2	60.7

Place			Total			Total	%	%
Horry	12	12		734	734		01.6	98.4
Georgetown	257	257		152	152		62.8	37.2
Williamsburg	314	314		302	302		51.0	49.0
Total Votes	2,698	2,677	5,375	4,371	4,377	8,748	38.1	61.9

Fifth District

Place	Pickens	Nance	Total	Wardlaw	Summer	Total	%	%
Abbeville	825	809		1,010	943		45.6	54.4
Newberry	533	538		608	612		46.7	53.3
Edgefield	938	938		939	939		50.0	50.0
Lexington	179	179		812	812		18.0	82.0
Total Votes	2,475	2,462	4,937	3,369	3,306	6,675	42.5	57.5

Sixth District

Place	Ashe	Palmer	Total	Aiken	Porter	Total	%	%
Charleston	1,018	1,015		2,454	2,454		29.3	70.7
Goose Creek	39	39		243	243		13.8	86.2
St. James Santee	58	59		3	3		95.1	04.9
St. Stephens	89	94		10	10		90.1	09.9
St. Andrews	35	35		15	15		70.0	30.0
St. Johns Berkley	111	111		67	67		62.4	37.6
Christ Church	66	66		35	35		65.3	34.7
St. Thomas	36	36		0	0		100.0	00.0
Total Votes	1,452	1,454	2,906	2,827	2,827	5,654	33.9	66.1

Seventh District

Place	Rhett	Duncan	Total	Patterson	Lawton	Total	%	%
Orangeburg	937	937		156	160		85.6	14.4
Barnwell	856	859		924	909		48.3	51.7
Beaufort	867	866		194	193		81.7	18.3
Colleton	600	602		583	584		50.7	49.3
St. Johns Colleton	87	88		53	53		62.3	37.7
Total Votes	3,347	3,352	6,699	1,910	1,899	3,809	63.8	36.2

Source: Charleston *Mercury*, December 2, 1851. Arithmetic errors in the original have been corrected. Percentages are based on the total vote for the two secessionist candidates and the two cooperationist candidates in each district.

NOTES

ABBREVIATIONS

(DU)   Manuscript Department, Duke University Library
(LC)   Manuscripts Division, Library of Congress
(SCHS) South Carolina Historical Society
(SCL)   South Caroliniana Library, University of South Carolina
(SHC)   Southern Historical Collection, University of North Carolina

PREFACE

1. Banner, "Problem of South Carolina," p. 60.

CHAPTER I

1. Wood, *Black Majority*, pp. 86–87; see also Rendtorff, *Fundamentals of Malaria*, pp. 6, 29–32.
2. Bridenbaugh, *Myths and Realities*, p. 64.
3. Sheridan, "Africa and the Caribbean in the Atlantic Slave Trade," pp. 21, 26, 29; see also Bennett, *Bondsmen and Bishops*, pp. 44, 53–61 passim.
4. Wood, *Black Majority*, pp. 19–20.
5. Jordan, *White Over Black*, pp. 66–85.
6. Curtin, *Atlantic Slave Trade*, pp. 143, 145.
7. Wood, *Black Majority*, pp. 36, 149–50, 145.
8. Meriwether, *Expansion of South Carolina*, p. 24.
9. Higgins, "Geographical Origins," pp. 41, 43. "Currency" meant "current money" in South Carolina, not pounds sterling.
10. Bureau of the Census, *Historical Statistics of the United States*, Part 2, p. 1154.
11. Higgins, "Geographical Origins," p. 41; Meriwether, *Expansion of South Carolina*, p. 243.
12. Wallace, *South Carolina*, p. 219.
13. Farley, *Growth of the Black Population*, p. 17; Bureau of the Census, *Historical Statistics of the United States*, Part 2, p. 1168; Potter, "Growth of Population in America," p. 661.
14. During this same period the legislature in rapid succession enacted and repealed prohibitions of the domestic slave trade to South Carolina (Brady, "Slave Trade and Sectionalism," pp. 601–8).
15. Wallace, *South Carolina*, pp. 219–20; Brady, "Slave Trade and Sectionalism," pp. 618–19, 601–3.
16. Ibid., pp. 606–7, 612, 616. Gins purchased from Whitney were less common than pirated models based on his design. The first of the improved cotton gins appeared in Newberry District as early as 1796 and rapidly converted farmers to the economic merits of short-staple cotton (Pope, *History of Newberry County, 1749–1860*, pp. 112–13).

17. Brady, "Slave Trade and Sectionalism," pp. 618–19.

18. See Appendix, Tables 1 and 2.

19. See Appendix, Tables 2 and 3.

20. For the percentages of slaves, free blacks, and whites in each district, 1790–1860, see Appendix, Tables 1–3.

21. Curtin's close study accepted the conclusion that "whatever the number of illegal imports during this period, it was too small to influence the demography of the Afro-American population" (*Atlantic Slave Trade*, p. 74).

22. Farley, *Growth of the Black Population*, pp. 22, 40; Eblen, "Growth of the Black Population, 1820–1860," p. 284; Fourth through Eighth Federal Censuses.

23. Smith, *Economic Readjustment*, p. 22.

24. See Appendix, Table 1, note c.

25. Ricards and Blackburn, "Demographic History of Slavery: Georgetown County," p. 216; Rogers, *History of Georgetown County*, p. 328.

26. Berlin, *Slaves Without Masters*, pp. 46–47, 49, 396–99.

27. Bureau of the Census, *Negro Population of the United States*, p. 51.

28. Wood, *Black Majority*, p. 103; Berlin, *Slaves Without Masters*, pp. 3, 47.

29. Jordan, *White Over Black*, pp. 347–49; Berlin, *Slaves Without Masters*, p. 49.

30. The slightly higher percentage (1.7) for 1790 given by Berlin (*Slaves Without Masters*, p. 47) is based on the erroneous total for slaves published in the 1790 Census (see note c).

31. Berlin, *Slaves Without Masters*, pp. 47, 137, 35–36.

32. Wood, *Black Majority*, p. 46.

33. DeBow, *Statistical View of the United States*, pp. 94–95; Schaper, *Sectionalism and Representation*, p. 155. During the 1840s and 1850s the ratio of slaveholding to nonslaveholding families in Mississippi climbed rapidly toward that of South Carolina. In both states by 1860 "approximately one-half the [white] families owned slaves" (Stampp, *Peculiar Institution*, p. 30).

34. Scarborough, *The Overseer*, pp. 11–12.

35. Freehling, *Prelude to Civil War*, pp. 18–19, 23.

36. Brady, "Slave Trade and Sectionalism," pp. 618–19; Smith, *Economic Readjustment*, p. 23. During the 1850s "there was a steady tendency for small farmers to sell at good prices to planters who were extending their operations" (Rogers, "Great Population Exodus," p. 20). See also: Miller, "Slavery and Population," pp. 53, 46–47, and Campbell, "Planters and Plain Folk," pp. 369–71, 391–92.

37. Smith, *Economic Readjustment*, pp. 20, 26, 22; Potter, "Growth of Population in America," p. 682.

38. Wooster, *People in Power*, pp. 28, 30.

39. Rogers, "Great Population Exodus," pp. 16–18.

40. Camden *Journal*, October 31, 1854, as quoted in Smith, *Economic Readjustment*, p. 26.

41. Wallace, *South Carolina*, p. 386; Rogers, "Great Population Exodus," p. 20.

42. Wallace, *South Carolina*, p. 88; Wood, *Black Majority*, p. 206; Degler, *Neither Black Nor White*, p. 82.

43. Degler, *Neither Black Nor White*, pp. 83–84.

44. Ibid., pp. 43, 89; Berlin, *Slaves Without Masters*, p. 5.

45. Henry, *Police Control of the Slave*, p. 32; Wood, *Black Majority*, p. 274.

46. Wood, *Black Majority*, pp. 222–23; Meriwether, *Expansion of South Carolina*, pp. 188, 185n, 189.

47. Wood, *Black Majority*, pp. 180, 170–71, 321.

48. Ibid., p. 317; Jordan, *White Over Black*, pp. 121–22.
49. Foner, *Black Americans*, pp. 443–44.
50. Wallace, *South Carolina*, p. 365.
51. Ibid., pp. 382–83; Freehling, *Prelude to Civil War*, p. 56. On the deadly earnestness of the Vesey Conspiracy, the author has accepted the conclusions of Freehling's *Prelude to Civil War* and Lofton's *Insurrection in South Carolina* rather than the opposing views in Wade's "Vesey Plot."
52. Freehling, *Prelude to Civil War*, pp. 61–64.
53. Petigru to Legare, January 9, 1839, Legare Papers; Genovese, *Roll, Jordan, Roll*, pp. 97–117 passim; Franklin, *Militant South*, p. 70.
54. Freehling, *Prelude to Civil War*, p. 64; Channing, *Crisis of Fear*, pp. 22, 21.
55. Tucker, "James Henry Hammond," p. 144; *Journal of the Legislature of South Carolina for the Year 1833*, p. 6, as quoted in Franklin, *Militant South*, p. 78.
56. Hammond to Tappan, July 9, 1850, Hammond Papers (LC). To study abolitionist tactics and arguments, Hammond had subscribed to several abolitionist newspapers. Tappan wrote Hammond ostensibly to inquire about the Carolinian's subscription to *The London Anti-Slavery Reporter* and other papers. This quotation is taken from Hammond's reply.
57. Channing, *Crisis of Fear*, p. 61.
58. On these articles of faith in the proslavery ideology of white South Carolinians, see: Wiltse, *John C. Calhoun, Nullifier*, p. 276; Wiltse, *John C. Calhoun, Sectionalist*, pp. 50–51; and Channing, *Crisis of Fear*, pp. 58–59.
59. Jordan, *White Over Black*, p. 114.
60. "Speech of the Hon. R. B. Rhett, delivered at the Mass Meeting at Macon, Ga., on the 22d August, 1850," Venable Scrapbook.

CHAPTER II

1. Hammond Diary, December 25, 1850 (SCL).
2. Schaper, *Sectionalism and Representation*, pp. 44, 167.
3. Douglass, *Rebels and Democrats*, pp. 33, 39, 43–44; Schaper, *Sectionalism and Representation*, p. 142.
4. In choosing delegates to draft the Constitution of 1790, the franchise was limited by existing property qualifications, and qualified voters were unequally represented. The convention's finished product was not ratified by the men who elected its authors; nor did the amending process provide for direct voter participation. All amendments, including the momentous Compromise of 1808, were made by the legislature. In brief the men who made South Carolina's organic law never accepted nor implemented "Rousseau's principle that there must be 'unanimity at least once': that everyone must consent to the law under which he was to live, even if later, when constitutional arrangements were made, a qualification was required for ordinary voting" (Palmer, *Age of the Democratic Revolution*, 1:223).
5. Schaper, *Sectionalism and Representation*, pp. 200–201.
6. See Appendix, Tables 1–3.
7. S.C. Constitution (1790) amendment ratified December 19, 1810. Under the 1790 franchise provision, voters could, technically, cast ballots in any election district where they held sufficient property. The relative size of election districts made such plural voting feasible only in the low country, where it continued occasionally after the property qualification for voting had been removed. Up-country legislators ob-

tained a joint resolution to end the practice (Schaper, *Sectionalism and Representation*, pp. 116, 202; "Resolutions on Constitutional Questions, Joint Resolution—1833," in Bryan, *A Scrapbook*, Vol. VIII).

8. S.C. Constitution (1790) art. I, sec. 4; art. II, sec. 1, 3; art. VI, sec. 1, 2; Wooster, *People in Power*, p. 92.

9. Hammond Diary, December 15, 27, 1850 (SCL); S. C. Constitution (1790) art. II, secs. 6–13; "Militia and Patrol Laws of South Carolina, December, 1841," in Bryan, *A Scrapbook*, Vol. V; Wooster, *People in Power*, pp. 49, 55; Daniel Wallace to Whitemarsh B. Seabrook, November 17, 1849, Seabrook Papers.

10. Williamson, *American Suffrage*, p. 132. Fletcher M. Green's statement (*Constitutional Development*, p. 122) that the Constitution of 1790 reduced the property qualifications set in 1778 overlooked the difference in value between pounds sterling and pounds currency of the revolutionary era.

11. Wooster, *People in Power*, pp. 34–36, 39–41.

12. Buel, "Democracy and the American Revolution," p. 189; see also: Pole, "Problem of Early American Democracy," pp. 637–38, 641, and Wood, *Creation of the American Republic*, pp. 273–75.

13. On the antebellum movement of most southern state governments in the direction of greater democracy, see: Counihan, "North Carolina Constitutional Convention of 1836," pp. 335–64; Green, *Constitutional Development*; Green, "Democracy in the Old South," pp. 3–23; Peterson, *Democracy, Liberty, and Property*; Pole, "Representation and Authority in Virginia," pp. 16–50; *Development of Southern Sectionalism*, pp. 282–91; and Wooster, *People in Power*, p. 5.

14. Boucher, "Representation and the Electoral Question," pp. 111–12; Green, *Constitutional Development*, pp. 249–50.

15. Alfred P. Aldrich to James H. Hammond, November 26 and 28, 1851 (reporting on caucuses of the cooperationist leadership), April 28 and May 3, 1852 (reporting on maneuvers within the convention), Hammond Papers (LC); *Southern Patriot*, May 6, 1852.

16. Kibler, *Benjamin F. Perry*, pp. 227–30; Boucher, "Representation and the Electoral Question," pp. 115–19; *Southern Standard*, November 29, 1851; *Journal of the South Carolina House, 1849*, pp. 67, 100, 221; *Journal of the South Carolina House, 1851*, p. 70.

17. Hammond to William Gilmore Simms, July 23, 1847, Hammond Papers (LC); "The Electoral Question, the Present System of Appointing Presidential Electors in South Carolina, Considered by One of the People," in Bryan, *A Scrapbook*, Vol. V; "Speech of the Hon. George W. Dargan, on the Bill to Give the Election of Electors to the People," in Bryan, *A Scrapbook*, Vol. V.

18. Pole, "Problem of Early American Democracy," pp. 643 ff.

19. Tucker to James H. Hammond, January 2, 1851, Hammond Papers (LC).

20. Weir, "South Carolinian as Extremist," p. 93.

21. Barnwell, "Hamlet to Hotspur," p. 252.

22. Perry, *Letters of Francis Lieber*, p. 254.

23. Kibler, *Benjamin F. Perry*, p. 231; "Speech of B. F. Perry, at the Anti-Secession Meeting, at Cashville . . . 20th September, 1851," Perry Scrapbook.

24. Column signed "Percy," *Mercury*, June 27, 1851.

25. Hammond to W. G. Simms, July 23, 1847, Hammond Papers (LC).

26. Hammond to Pickens, September 6, 1836, Hammond Letters (DU); R. O. Starke to Benjamin C. Yancey, February 3, 1850, Yancey Papers.

27. Jamison to George Frederick Holmes, October 1, 1846, and April 22, 1848,

Holmes Papers; Hammond to W. G. Simms, July 23, 1847, and manuscript entitled "From notes—occasional meditations—'somnia aegritudinatis' [sic] of J. H. Hammond," March 27, 1852, Hammond Papers (LC); Huger to W. P. Miles, January 23, 1858, Huger Letterpress Books. On Grayson's views see: Stoney, "Autobiography of William J. Grayson," 209, and Grayson, "Letter to His Excellency Whitemarsh B. Seabrook," in Bryan, A Scrapbook, Vol. IV. On Elliott's views, see: Jones, "Carolinians and Cubans," pp. 8, 40, 51, and Jones, "William Elliott," pp. 364–69.

28. Buel, "Democracy and the American Revolution," pp. 177 ff; Hammond Diary, November 25, 1846 (SCL); "Speech of Dargan on the Election of Electors," in Bryan, A Scrapbook, Vol. V.

29. "Notes—occasional meditations," March 27, 1852, Hammond Papers (LC); Huger to Dr. Benjamin Huger, September 16, 1853, Huger Letterpress Books.

30. Green, "Democracy in the Old South," p. 22; Sydnor, Development of Southern Sectionalism, pp. 279–80, 292–93; "The Electoral Question, the Present System," in Bryan, A Scrapbook, Vol. V.

31. Grimball Diary, September 5, 1832; Huger to W. P. Miles, January 23, 1858, Huger Letterpress Books.

32. Hugh Swinton Legare to his sister, June 16, 1833, Legare Papers; Stoney, "Autobiography of William J. Grayson," 28; Bass, "Autobiography of William J. Grayson," p. clxxviii; Grimball Diary, October 14, 1834; James H. Hammond to W. G. Simms, February 4, 1851, and A. P. Aldrich to Hammond, January 7, 1851, Hammond Papers (LC).

33. Mercury, August 9, September 17, October 5, and October 7, 1850; Statutes at Large of South Carolina, 1850, pp. 72–73 (this act provided a penalty of $500 and one month in jail).

34. N. B. Tucker to James H. Hammond, February 8, 1850, Hammond Papers (LC); Barnwell to Orr, August 26, 1851, Orr-Patterson Papers; Freehling, Prelude to Civil War, p. 89.

35. Green, "Democracy in the Old South," p. 18.

36. Kirby, "Early American Politics," p. 825; Banner, "Problem of South Carolina," p. 68. See also: Pole, "Problem of Early American Democracy," pp. 628, 637 ff; Eaton, "Class Differences," pp. 358, 370; and Formisano, "Deferential-Participant Politics," pp. 483–84, 486.

37. "The Electoral Question, the Present System," in Bryan, A Scrapbook, Vol. V; Journal of the South Carolina House, 1851, p. 53; "Speech of Dargan on the Election of Electors," in Bryan, A Scrapbook, Vol. V; Southern Standard, August 12, 1851 (see the statement of Edgar W. Charles, delegate to the state convention); Greenberg, "Representation and Isolation," pp. 729–31.

38. Jones, "Carolinians and Cubans," p. 8; Hammond to his wife, December 8, 1840, Hammond Letters (SHC); White, Robert Barnwell Rhett, pp. 55, 57.

39. Banner, "Problem of South Carolina," p. 83; "The Electoral Question, the Present System," in Bryan, A Scrapbook, Vol. V; Taylor, "Gentry of South Carolina," p. 114.

CHAPTER III

1. Freehling, Prelude to Civil War, pp. x, 81. On South Carolina's sensitivity to external antislavery activity and early development of proslavery arguments, see also: ibid., pp. 51, 79–81, 198–99, and Wilson, "Preview of Irrepressible Conflict," p. 187.

2. Freehling, *Prelude to Civil War*, pp. 24, 36, 86, 164–66, 258–59, 297. Freehling's interpretation has proved enormously influential, and, after a decade and a half, remains substantially unchallenged (see, for example, Latner, "Nullification and Republican Subversion," p. 19).

3. Freehling, *Prelude to Civil War*, pp. 268–70, 309, 314–19; Kibler, *Benjamin F. Perry*, pp. 159–60, 162–63; Perry Diary, April 27, June 22, July 3 and 7, 1833.

4. Freehling, *Prelude to Civil War*, pp. 320–21; Kibler, *Benjamin F. Perry*, pp. 169–70.

5. Wiltse, *John C. Calhoun, Nullifier*, p. 200; Kibler, *Benjamin F. Perry*, pp. 169, 175–76.

6. Grimball Diary, September 2 (?), 1833; Sydnor, *Gentlemen Freeholders*, p. 111; Hofstadter, *Idea of a Party System*, p. 259; see also: Stoney, "Autobiography of William J. Grayson," 25, and Perry Diary, July 3 and 7, 1833. Freehling argues that low-country Unionist leaders contributed heavily to their party's political eclipse during 1832–33 by mistaking the nullifiers for mere spoilsmen, by refusing to proselytize for their cause, by defective parliamentary strategy, and by their fatalism (*Prelude to Civil War*, pp. 236, 239–44, 313). In support of this view, see also: W. M. Smith to William Elliott, January 19, 1833, Elliott-Gonzales Papers; Charles Petigru to H. S. Legare, May 20, 1833, and Mitchell King to H. S. Legare, May 5, 1833, Legare Papers.

7. Petigru to H. S. Legare, May 31, 1835, Legare Papers.

8. Ibid. and Kibler, *Benjamin F. Perry*, p. 174.

9. Wilson, "Preview of Irrepressible Conflict," pp. 186–87. Freehling, however, emphasized that Drayton defended slavery as a "necessary evil" (*Prelude to Civil War*, p. 77).

10. Freehling, *Prelude to Civil War*, p. 197. Some slaveholders supported the American Colonization Society in the belief that it made slavery more secure by reducing the number of free Negroes in the United States. But South Carolinians generally believed it was a blind used by abolitionists, who intended successively to "regulate slavery . . . render the property equally valueless and dangerous—and then abolish it entirely" (Ibid.).

11. Wiltse, *John C. Calhoun, Nullifier*, p. 272; Freehling, *Prelude to Civil War*, p. 341; Bass, "Autobiography of William J. Grayson," p. cxliii; Kibler, *Benjamin F. Perry*, p. 175.

12. Tucker, "James Henry Hammond," pp. 225–29, 246–51; Wiltse, *John C. Calhoun, Nullifier*, pp. 281–83.

13. Wiltse, *John C. Calhoun, Nullifier*, p. 283; Freehling, *Prelude to Civil War*, pp. 351–53.

14. Wiltse, *John C. Calhoun, Nullifier*, pp. 285, 293–94.

15. Wiltse, *John C. Calhoun, Sectionalist*, p. 51; Kibler, *Benjamin F. Perry*, p. 218; see also Lander, "Calhoun-Preston Feud," p. 30.

16. On the composition of the clique and the mechanics of this scheme, see: Wiltse, *John C. Calhoun, Sectionalist*, p. 52; White, *Robert Barnwell Rhett*, pp. 21, 56; and Barnwell, "Hamlet to Hotspur," pp. 238n, 248–49n.

17. Wiltse, *John C. Calhoun, Sectionalist*, pp. 52–53.

18. Nevins, *Ordeal of the Union*, 1:213; Wiltse, *John C. Calhoun, Sectionalist*, pp. 309, 314; circular signed by Daniel E. Huger, Nathaniel Heyward, Wade Hampton, et al., dated August 1847, and I. W. Hayne to J. H. Hammond, August 25, 1847, Hammond Papers (LC).

19. Freehling, *Prelude to Civil War*, pp. 240, 269, 312–13, 317–18; Wiltse, *John C. Calhoun, Sectionalist*, pp. 290–91. Wiltse incorrectly characterized Andrew P. Butler, who was elected senator in 1846, as a "Unionist of other days" (p. 291); see: F[rancis] P[endleton] G[aines], "Andrew Pickens Butler," in *Dictionary of American Biography*, 3:355; Schultz, *Nationalism and Sectionalism*, p. 10; and Freehling, *Prelude to Civil War*, p. 230.

20. *Journal of the South Carolina House, 1848*, p. 29.

21. This distinction was not confined to South Carolina. While deploring the doctrine of nullification, the Virginia legislature in 1833 affirmed the "right of secession" (Freehling, *Prelude to Civil War*, p. 290).

22. Bass, "Autobiography of William J. Grayson," pp. lxviii, cxliii–iv; Jarrett, "Grayson's *The Hireling and the Slave*," pp. 17–18, 3–4, 40; Grayson to Hammond, November 3, 1849, Hammond Papers (LC).

23. Davidson, Introduction to Simms, *Letters*, 1: lvi, liii; Simms, *The Yemassee*, p. 358.

24. Published in 1852, *The Pro-Slavery Argument* collected and reprinted material written earlier.

25. Salley, "Simms" in Simms, *Letters*, 1: lxvii, lxxxvi.

26. Boucher, *Nullification Controversy*, pp. 226–27, 241, 262–63, 275, 284–85; White, *Robert Barnwell Rhett*, pp. 25–26; Wiltse, *John C. Calhoun, Nullifier*, p. 183; Freehling, *Prelude to Civil War*, pp. 25, 265; Latner, "Nullification and Republican Subversion," p. 19.

27. Freehling, *Prelude to Civil War*, p. 204.

28. Habersham to Elliott, September 22, 1832, Elliott-Gonzales Papers.

29. Miles, "*Worcester* v. *Georgia* and the Nullification Crisis," p. 534.

30. Ibid., pp. 535–36.

31. Ibid., pp. 538, 541.

32. Columbia *Telescope*, February 12, 1833, as quoted in Miles, "*Worcester* v. *Georgia* and the Nullification Crisis," pp. 541–42; Petigru to Legare, February 6, 1833 (photocopy), Petigru Papers, (SCL); Wiltse, *John C. Calhoun, Nullifier*, p. 185.

33. Bergeron, "Tennessee's Response," pp. 24–25, 27–28.

34. Ibid., pp. 29–31.

35. Ibid., pp. 31–32, 37, 39–40.

36. Ibid., pp. 41–42; Wyly to James K. Polk and James Standifer, January 11, 1833, in Weaver and Bergeron, *Correspondence of Polk*, 2:16; Stoney, "Autobiography of William J. Grayson," 24.

37. Freehling, *Prelude to Civil War*, pp. 205, 270.

38. The term "Carolina Doctrines" was apparently Webster's (see Wilson, "Liberty and Union," p. 334). The currency of this usage during 1830–33 and its longevity afterwards demonstrated the success of nullification's opponents in isolating the movement.

39. Freehling, *Prelude to Civil War*, pp. 265, 293; Petigru to Hugh S. Legare, February 6, 1833 (photocopy), Petigru Papers (SCL); see also: J. G. Witherspoon to William R. Hemphill, March 9, 1833, Hemphill Family Papers; Sydnor, *Development of Southern Sectionalism*, p. 218.

40. Freehling, *Prelude to Civil War*, p. 297.

41. Wilson, "Preview of Irrepressible Conflict," p. 187; Latner, "Nullification and Republican Subversion," pp. 26, 23.

42. Latner, "Nullification and Republican Subversion," pp. 24, 27.

43. Ibid., pp. 26, 28, 38. For the fusion of nationalist and state-rights elements in Jackson's policy and thought, see: Freehling, *Prelude to Civil War*, pp. 266–67, 294–95, and Wilson, "Liberty and Union," pp. 348–51, 354.

44. Perry Diary, November 19, 1833; Wiltse, *John C. Calhoun, Nullifier*, pp. 236, 277.

45. Rayback, "Presidential Ambitions of Calhoun," pp. 343–44; Coit, *John C. Calhoun*, p. 467.

46. Rayback, "Presidential Ambitions of Calhoun," pp. 344–45.

47. Hammond to W. G. Simms, March 21, 1847, Hammond Papers (LC); Nevins, *Polk Diary*, pp. 210–11; Rayback, "Presidential Ambitions of Calhoun," pp. 345, 347.

48. Coit, *John C. Calhoun*, pp. 475–78.

49. Hammond to Simms, November 17, 1847, Hammond Papers (LC); Hamilton, as quoted in Barney, *Road to Secession*, p. 115.

50. Pettigrew to James C. Johnston, February 5, April 16, and May 28, 1849, Pettigrew Family Papers. The charm displayed in private by the Charleston gentry eventually softened Pettigrew's attitude toward them, and he settled in South Carolina.

51. Johnston to Pettigrew, March 3, and June 16, 1849, Pettigrew Family Papers. For other testimony on the distaste of North Carolinians for "South Carolina Chivalry" and South Carolina politicians, see: David to Emily Outlaw, July 24 and 25, 1850, Outlaw Papers, and Henry T. Clark to Armistead Burt, September 15, 1850, Burt Papers.

52. Chesnut, *Diary from Dixie*, p. 40.

53. *Mercury*, May 28, 1851; Letter of Langdon Cheves to the Convention of Southern Rights Associations, printed in the *Mercury*, May 7, 1851; "Remarks of the Hon. R. W. Barnwell before the Convention of Southern Rights Associations in Charleston, May 1851," in Bryan, *A Scrapbook*, Vol. VII; Nevins, *Ordeal of the Union*, 1:370.

54. Barnwell, "Hamlet to Hotspur," p. 250; J. Williams to James H. Thornwell, July 14, 1851, Thornwell Papers; B. Alvord to Marcus Claudius Marcellus Hammond, September 20, 1851, and Maxcy Gregg to James H. Hammond, March 24, 1852, Hammond Papers (LC).

CHAPTER IV

1. Potter, *Impending Crisis*, pp. 18–19.

2. Ibid., pp. 19–21; Wiltse, *John C. Calhoun, Sectionalist*, pp. 287–88; Going, *David Wilmot*, pp. 130–31. Going has argued that Wilmot's purpose for seeking the floor was known beforehand; what no one could know, of course, was the reaction his amendment would provoke.

3. On the origins and authorship of the Proviso, see: Foner, "Wilmot Proviso Revisited," pp. 264–65, and Going, *David Wilmot*, pp. 122–23. The best summary of the Democratic party's factional turmoil over territorial and other issues before the introduction of the Proviso is found in Morrison, *Democratic Politics and Sectionalism*. Morrison has interpreted both introduction and subsequent agitation of the Proviso largely as functions of Democratic party factionalism. On the significance of the Proviso, see also: Rayback, *The Election of 1848*, pp. 23, 25, and Potter, *Impending Crisis*, p. 27.

4. Potter, *Impending Crisis*, pp. 22, 64–65.

5. Hamilton, *Prologue to Conflict*, p. 8.

6. Gara, "Slavery and the Slave Power," pp. 10, 17; Foner, "Politics and Prejudice," p. 239; Craven, *Growth of Southern Nationalism*, pp. 34–35.

7. Bestor, *Civil War as a Constitutional Crisis*, p. 328.

8. Thomas Hart Benton described "Wilmot's doctrine and Calhoun's doctrine . . . [as] the two blades of a pair of shears: neither blade, by itself, would cut very effectively; but the two together could sever the bonds of Union" (Potter, *Impending Crisis*, p. 62). For the general historiographical recognition of the Wilmot Proviso as thesis in the dialectic that led to Civil War, see: Potter, *Impending Crisis*, pp. 61–62; Foner, "Wilmot Proviso Revisited," p. 262; Morrison, *Democratic Politics and Sectionalism*, p. 52; Nevins, *Ordeal of the Union*, 1:12–13.

9. Potter, *Impending Crisis*, p. 84; Wiltse, *John C. Calhoun, Sectionalist*, p. 377.

10. Gettys, "To Conquer a Peace," pp. 3–5.

11. *Mercury*, December 29, 1837. See also Merk, *Slavery and the Annexation of Texas*.

12. Gettys, "To Conquer a Peace," pp. 11–13; Wiltse, *John C. Calhoun, Sectionalist*, pp. 169–70; Weinberg, *Manifest Destiny*, pp. 390–91.

13. Wiltse, *John C. Calhoun, Sectionalist*, pp. 170–71.

14. Silbey, "Calhoun and the Limits of Southern Congressional Unity," p. 63n.

15. Gettys, "To Conquer a Peace," pp. 26–27, 29; Wiltse, *John C. Calhoun, Sectionalist*, pp. 281–84; Calhoun to Anna C. Clemson, June 11, 1846, in Jameson, *Correspondence of Calhoun*, p. 695.

16. *Mercury*, May 20, 25, 1846, as quoted in Gettys, "To Conquer a Peace," p. 147; Wiltse, *John C. Calhoun, Sectionalist*, p. 284; Gettys, "To Conquer a Peace," pp. 31–32. Regarding press support for the war, see: ibid., pp. 136–38, and Lander, *Reluctant Imperialists*, pp. 58–59.

17. On this rupture between Calhoun and Pickens and the subsequent relationship between the two, see: Gettys, "To Conquer a Peace," pp. 108–12, 114–16, and Lander, *Reluctant Imperialists*, pp. 15–17, 20–21, 33–34.

18. Calhoun to Thomas G. Clemson, August 8, 1846, and Pickens to Calhoun, December 13, 1846, in Jameson, *Correspondence of Calhoun*, pp. 704–5, 1100; Gettys, "To Conquer a Peace," pp. 86–87, 127, 135.

19. See: Gettys, "To Conquer a Peace," p. 93, and Hammond Diary, December 6, 1846 (SCL).

20. Simms to Hammond, Christmas 1846, in Simms, *Letters*, 2:247. Although Simms justly complained that the southern market for literature made it difficult to earn a livelihood as a writer, he was a more successful author than planter (Simms to Hammond, December 24, 1847, in ibid., p. 385). Hammond also advised him that South Carolinians could not "believe . . . [a literary man] is *in earnest* when he becomes a candidate for any office" (Hammond to Simms, December 18, 1846, Hammond Papers [LC]). Hammond was Simms's creditor and, in politics, his patron. During this period A. P. Aldrich and, to a lesser extent, D. F. Jamison also served as Hammond's political subalterns.

21. Wiltse, *John C. Calhoun, Sectionalist*, pp. 290–91; Hammond Diary, December 9, 1846 (SCL).

22. Wade Hampton (1791–1858) was Hammond's brother-in-law. The scandal involved Hammond's "dalliance" (his word) with Hampton's teenage daughters during the time Hammond lived in Columbia and served as governor. Hammond confided his explanation of the matter to his diary. To his friend Simms, Hammond lashed out in impotent fury against "this damned age of hypocrisy. From Richardson who is dying

of the pox to Ashe who I presume sleeps every night with a mulatto, there is not a Saint in the State who does not turn up his nose at me" (December 4, 1848, Hammond Papers [LC]). Hammond made sporadic references to the scandal and its impact on his career in other letters to Simms. For a summary of the scandal's effect on Hammond's political aspirations in 1846 and afterwards, see: Eaton, *Mind of the Old South*, pp. 54–55, and Tucker, "James Henry Hammond," pp. 424–27.

23. Calhoun to Anna C. Clemson, December 27, 1846, in Jameson, *Correspondence of Calhoun*, pp. 715–16; J. Gregg to Calhoun, February 17, 1847, in Boucher and Brooks, *Correspondence Addressed to Calhoun*, p. 367; Gettys, "To Conquer a Peace," p. 178. Much influenced by the romantic nationalism of early nineteenth-century Germany, Lieber suffered mixed feelings about the war; his patriotic impulse was at odds with his academic analysis of the war. See Lieber to Samuel B. Ruggles, April 23 and May 2, 1847, Lieber Papers (LC).

24. Lander, "Thompson, A Friend of Mexico," pp. 33, 35–37; Morison, Merk, and Freidel, *Dissent in Three Wars*, pp. 38, 41. Charleston Whig James L. Petigru praised Thompson's "clean and concise view of the question" but did not campaign against the war as actively as his up-country colleague (Petigru to Thompson, July 9, 1847, Thompson Papers [LC]). Thompson and Calhoun differed on the issue of territorial indemnity, but Thompson eventually adopted Calhoun's view on this matter (Lander, "Thompson, A Friend of Mexico," pp. 40–41).

25. Gettys, "To Conquer a Peace," pp. 39–40; Wiltse, *John C. Calhoun, Sectionalist*, pp. 298–99. On the apprehension of some southern planters that the war would produce an unacceptably heavy debt and an increase in the tariff, see: James Chestney to Calhoun, November 23, 1846, Wilson Lumpkin to Calhoun, November 26, 1846, in Boucher and Brooks, *Correspondence Addressed to Calhoun*, pp. 361–62, and Boucher, "That Aggressive Slavocracy," p. 35.

26. Gettys, "To Conquer a Peace," pp. 41–42, 48–49, 70–71; White, *Robert Barnwell Rhett*, p. 93; Rhett to Calhoun, May 20, 1847, in Boucher and Brooks, *Correspondence Addressed to Calhoun*, pp. 376–77.

27. Gettys, "To Conquer a Peace," p. 60; Lander, "Thompson, A Friend of Mexico," p. 41; Rippy, *Joel R. Poinsett*, pp. 226–29; Perry Diary, February 8, 1848; Perry to Calhoun, January 24, 1848, and Johnson to Calhoun, October 26, 1847, in Boucher and Brooks, *Correspondence Addressed to Calhoun*, pp. 430, 408.

28. Hammond to Simms, February 23, March 21, and November 1, 1847, and James H. to M. C. M. Hammond, January 14, 1848, Hammond Papers (LC); Hammond Diary, July 15, 1847 (SCL); Simms to Hammond, April 4, 1847, in Simms, *Letters*, 2:298; White, *Robert Barnwell Rhett*, p. 101.

29. Collins, "Ideology of Northern Democrats," p. 105; Weinberg, *Manifest Destiny*, p. 115; Nevins, *Ordeal of the Union*, 1:5–6, 10–11, 18, 21, 154–55; Foner, "Wilmot Proviso Revisited," pp. 276–77; Silbey, "Calhoun and the Limits of Southern Congressional Unity," p. 64; Alexander, *Sectional Stress and Party Strength*, pp. 63–64; Morison, Merk, and Freidel, *Dissent in Three Wars*, p. 42; Robert Toombs to Calhoun, April 30, 1847, in Boucher and Brooks, *Correspondence Addressed to Calhoun*, p. 373. While the scholars listed above have emphasized the national roots of expansionist sentiment during the Mexican War, John Hope Franklin has emphasized proslavery imperialism (*Militant South*, pp. 97, 99, 112–13, and "Southern Expansionists," pp. 325–38).

30. Fuller, *Movement for All Mexico*, pp. 10, 118–19.

31. Morison, Merk, and Freidel, *Dissent in Three Wars*, p. 51; Fuller, *Movement for All Mexico*, pp. 61–63, 78–79, 74–75, 64, 118–19. In January 1848 the New York

State Democratic Convention and Tammany Hall also favored the annexation of all Mexico (Weinberg, *Manifest Destiny*, p. 174).

32. Simms to Hammond, March 29 and July 15, 1847, in Simms, *Letters*, 2:288–89, 332–33. Simms and, to a lesser extent, Hammond nurtured visions of annexing a conquered Mexico throughout the war (Hammond to David J. McCord, February 25, 1848, Hammond Papers [SCL]; Hammond to Simms, May 29, 1848, Hammond Papers [LC]; Simms to Hammond, May 20, 1848, in Simms, *Letters*, 2:411–12).

33. Gettys, "To Conquer a Peace," pp. 376–77; Wiltse, *John C. Calhoun, Sectionalist*, p. 304. South Carolinians also objected to annexation with arguments that combined republican ideology and racism. Continuation of the war, they charged, would unleash an antirepublican militarism, and the incorporation of Mexico would alter the representative character of United States political institutions (see: Weinberg, *Manifest Destiny*, pp. 160, 361–62; Gettys, "To Conquer a Peace," p. 365; John C. to Andrew Pickens Calhoun, December 11, 1847, in Jameson, *Correspondence of Calhoun*, p. 741; Rippy, *Joel R. Poinsett*, p. 229).

34. Gettys, "To Conquer a Peace," p. 378; Thompson to Calhoun, December 18, 1847, in Jameson, *Correspondence of Calhoun*, pp. 1130, 1151–52; Lander, "Thompson, A Friend of Mexico," pp. 38–39.

35. Fuller, *Movement for All Mexico*, p. 86; Wiltse, *John C. Calhoun, Sectionalist*, pp. 327–28; Hatcher to Calhoun, January 5, 1848, in Boucher and Brooks, *Correspondence Addressed to Calhoun*, pp. 416–17.

36. Gettys, "To Conquer a Peace," p. 380.

37. Alex Wells to Calhoun, April 7, 1846, James B. Sawyer to Calhoun, July 10, 1846, in Boucher and Brooks, *Correspondence Addressed to Calhoun*, pp. 341, 351–52; Cleveland *Plain Dealer*, June 24, 1846, as quoted in Rayback, *The Election of 1848*, p. 25.

38. Rayback, *The Election of 1848*, pp. 24–25; Hamer, *Secession Movement in South Carolina*, p. 2.

39. Potter, *Impending Crisis*, p. 64; Rayback, *The Election of 1848*, p. 60.

40. Russel, "Constitutional Doctrines," p. 470; Bestor, "State Sovereignty and Slavery," pp. 149, 161; Bestor, *Civil War as a Constitutional Crisis*, p. 351; White, *Robert Barnwell Rhett*, p. 92; Wiltse, *John C. Calhoun, Sectionalist*, p. 295.

41. Bestor, *Civil War as a Constitutional Crisis*, p. 336; Hamer, *Secession Movement in South Carolina*, pp. 3–4.

42. Bestor, "State Sovereignty and Slavery," p. 152.

43. Ibid., p. 153. This view is also supported by Russel, "Constitutional Doctrines," pp. 466–68, and by Nevins, *Constitution, Slavery, and the Territories*, pp. 105, 111–20.

44. Nevins, *Constitution, Slavery, and the Territories*, pp. 123, 101–3; Bestor, "State Sovereignty and Slavery," pp. 154–55; Wiltse, *John C. Calhoun, Sectionalist*, pp. 304–5. See also Wilson Lumpkin to Calhoun, December 17, 1846, in Boucher and Brooks, *Correspondence Addressed to Calhoun*, pp. 364–65.

45. An unnamed southern congressman, as quoted by James G. Blaine in *Twenty Years of Congress*, 1:272.

46. Ramsdell, "Natural Limits of Slavery Expansion," pp. 151–71. A substantial number of political leaders in the 1846–50 period espoused the argument that "natural laws" precluded slavery in the territories. They based their case largely on the climate, terrain, and soil of the territories but adduced other arguments as well, such as the legal uncertainties involved for slaveholders and the "timidity of property" in the face of these and other risks (Hart, "Slavery Expansion: A Test Case," pp. 125, 127).

47. Hart, "Slavery Expansion: A Test Case," pp. 120, 124.

48. Ibid., pp. 128–29, 131; Morrison, *Democratic Politics and Sectionalism*, p. 53.

49. *Mercury*, January 14, 1847. Franklin Elmore, acting for Calhoun, largely guided the *Mercury's* coverage of Calhoun's responses to free-soil doctrines (Gettys, "To Conquer a Peace," p. 153).

50. Wiltse, *John C. Calhoun, Sectionalist*, pp. 293, 305; Craven, *Growth of Southern Nationalism*, p. 39; Percy Walker to Calhoun, October 10, 1847, in Boucher and Brooks, *Correspondence Addressed to Calhoun*, p. 405.

51. In his resolutions of February 15, 1847, Calhoun "gained one of the few clear-cut successes of his career. The doctrine that Congress could neither exclude slavery from a territory itself nor grant power to a territorial government to do so became one of the cardinal tenets of southern orthodoxy and operated as one of the key elements of southern unity in the crises that were to follow" (Potter, *Impending Crisis*, p. 61). But neither unchallenged orthodoxy nor final unity were achieved until the late 1850s. In 1848 John A. Campbell, for example, who possessed a high legal reputation and was later appointed to the United States Supreme Court, wrote a long and closely reasoned opinion upholding Congress's power over slavery in the territories (Campbell to Calhoun, March 1, 1848, in Boucher and Brooks, *Correspondence Addressed to Calhoun*, pp. 431–34).

52. F. W. Byrdsall to Calhoun, June 25, 1848, and Joseph W. Lesesne to Calhoun, July 5, 1848, in Boucher and Brooks, *Correspondence Addressed to Calhoun*, pp. 444, 452–53.

53. Craven, *Growth of Southern Nationalism*, p. 40; Potter, *Impending Crisis*, p. 68.

54. Cralle, *Works of Calhoun*, 4:387–90. Calhoun was deluged with reports interpreting the free-soil movement as political demagoguery (see: letters from F. W. Byrdsall, February 14 and November 12, 1847, Elwood Fisher, August 22, 1847, J. K. Paulding, January 24, 1848, and Eustis Prescott, July 5, 1848, in Boucher and Brooks, *Correspondence Addressed to Calhoun*, pp. 394, 410, 427, 449). Some correspondents, however, assured Calhoun of the deep, genuine, and widespread antislavery "sentiment of the whole North and East" (see: H. W. Conner to Calhoun, September 28, 1848, in Jameson, *Correspondence of Calhoun*, p. 1183, and Chesselden Ellis to Calhoun, July 5, 1848, in Boucher and Brooks, *Correspondence Addressed to Calhoun*, p. 447).

55. Rayback, "Presidential Ambitions of Calhoun," pp. 338, 335.

56. Simms to Hammond, April 4, 1847, in Simms, *Letters*, 2:298; Hammond to Simms, April 19, 1847, Hammond Papers (LC). See also Tucker to Hammond, April 24, 1847, Hammond Papers (LC).

57. Rayback, *The Election of 1848*, pp. 30–32. The movement for a newspaper in Washington to "represent Southern views on . . . Slavery . . . [and] Southern Rights and Interests" survived and eventually reached fruition in *The Southern Press* (see: circular letter dated March 1847, Hammond Papers [LC], and Wiltse, *John C. Calhoun, Sectionalist*, pp. 314–15).

58. Rayback, "Presidential Ambitions of Calhoun," p. 349; Rayback, *The Election of 1848*, p. 34. Taylor's popularity increased as his military successes continued and his folksy habits were publicized. By June 1847 the scholarly Francis Lieber was unabashedly celebrating Taylor's exploits in doggerel verse (Lieber to S. B. Ruggles, June 23, 1847, Lieber Papers [LC]).

59. Rayback, *The Election of 1848*, pp. 34–35; Hamilton, *Zachary Taylor*, p. 40. Some Democrats also were eager to secure Taylor as their presidential candidate (see John H. Brinton to Calhoun, July 16, 1847, and Fitzwilliam Byrdsall to Calhoun,

July 19, 1847, in Boucher and Brooks, *Correspondence Addressed to Calhoun*, pp. 387–88).

60. Rayback, *The Election of 1848*, pp. 37–38, 42.

61. Rayback, "Presidential Ambitions of Calhoun," p. 349; James Hamilton to Calhoun, April 24, 1847, in Jameson, *Correspondence of Calhoun*, pp. 1117–19; Hammond to Simms, April 19, 1847, Hammond Papers (LC); Simms to Hammond, June 4 and July 15, 1847, in Simms, *Letters*, 2:322, 331.

62. Calhoun to Thomas G. Clemson, July 24, 1847, in Jameson, *Correspondence of Calhoun*, p. 735; Silbey, "Calhoun and the Limits of Southern Congressional Unity," p. 63; Wakelyn, "Party Issues and Political Strategy," pp. 73–74.

63. Elmore to Calhoun, May 16, 1847, and Rhett to Calhoun, May 20, 1847, in Boucher and Brooks, *Correspondence Addressed to Calhoun*, pp. 376–77; Rhett to Calhoun, June 21, 1847, in Jameson, *Correspondence of Calhoun*, p. 1120.

64. Elwood Fisher to Calhoun, August 22, 1847, in Boucher and Brooks, *Correspondence Addressed to Calhoun*, p. 394; Rayback, *The Election of 1848*, pp. 50–51.

65. Rayback, *The Election of 1848*, pp. 50–51, 53; J. D. B. DeBow to Calhoun, December 26, 1847, in Boucher and Brooks, *Correspondence Addressed to Calhoun*, p. 414; James Gadsden to Calhoun, December 9, 1847, and Campbell to Calhoun, December 20, 1847, in Jameson, *Correspondence of Calhoun*, pp. 1149, 1154.

66. Potter, *Impending Crisis*, pp. 57–58; Gettys, "To Conquer a Peace," p. 53.

67. Rayback, *The Election of 1848*, p. 72; Collins, "Ideology of Northern Democrats," p. 121.

68. Russel, "Constitutional Doctrines," pp. 472–73; Wiltse, *John C. Calhoun, Sectionalist*, p. 326; Potter, *Impending Crisis*, p. 71.

69. Gettys, "To Conquer a Peace," pp. 53–54; Potter, *Impending Crisis*, p. 58.

70. A. G. Magrath to Burt, January 30, 1848, Burt Papers; Wakelyn, "Party Issues and Political Strategy," p. 75; Hamilton, *Zachary Taylor*, pp. 74, 77, 80–82, 86.

71. Rayback, *The Election of 1848*, p. 267; Nevins, *Ordeal of the Union*, 1:194; Harlee to Calhoun, June 8, 1848, in Boucher and Brooks, *Correspondence Addressed to Calhoun*, p. 439.

72. See Rayback, *The Election of 1848*, pp. 60–77 passim.

73. Ibid., pp. 90–97, 99–112 passim; Potter, *Impending Crisis*, pp. 78–79.

74. Potter, *Impending Crisis*, pp. 79–80; Russel, "Constitutional Doctrines," p. 468.

75. Nevins, *Ordeal of the Union*, 1:211–12; Potter, *Impending Crisis*, pp. 76–77; Rayback, *The Election of 1848*, pp. 93–94, 233, 238ff.

76. E. M. Seabrook to Calhoun, July 8, 1848, in Boucher and Brooks, *Correspondence Addressed to Calhoun*, p. 453.

77. W. L. Yancey to Calhoun, June 21, 1848, in Jameson, *Correspondence of Calhoun*, p. 1177; Rayback, *The Election of 1848*, pp. 268–79; Benjamin F. Porter to Calhoun, July 17, 1848, in Boucher and Brooks, *Correspondence Addressed to Calhoun*, p. 457; Silbey, "Calhoun and the Limits of Southern Congressional Unity," p. 59; Hammond to Simms, June 20, 1848, Hammond Papers (LC).

78. Wakelyn, "Party Issues and Political Strategy," pp. 75–79, 81–82. See also W. H. Trescot to W. P. Miles, September 17, 1848, Miles Papers.

79. J. Gadsden to Calhoun, August 19, 1848 (misdated 1847), in Boucher and Brooks, *Correspondence Addressed to Calhoun*, p. 469; Hamer, *Secession Movement in South Carolina*, p. 20; White, *Robert Barnwell Rhett*, pp. 96–97; Simms to Hammond, July 20, August 10, August 29, 1848, in Simms, *Letters*, 2:419–23, 434–35, 441–42.

80. Caleb Cushing to Calhoun, August 26, 1848, in Jameson, *Correspondence of Calhoun*, pp. 1181–82; Kibler, *Benjamin F. Perry*, p. 224; J. L. Petigru to his daughter

Susan (Mrs. Henry C. King), September 11, 1848, Allston-Pringle-Hill Papers (microfilm) (SHC); Wiltse, *John C. Calhoun, Sectionalist*, p. 370.

81. Hamilton, *Zachary Taylor*, pp. 122, 124; Rayback, *The Election of 1848*, pp. 258–59; J. D. Wilson to Calhoun, August 4, 1848, in Boucher and Brooks, *Correspondence Addressed to Calhoun*, p. 462. The second Allison letter gave serious pause to a number of Taylor supporters, including James Hammond. But Hammond faulted Taylor less than Calhoun, whom he blamed for forcing the Louisianan into a partisan position (see: J. H. to M. C. M. Hammond, August 10 and September 10, 1848, manuscript article entitled "Looking One Way and Rowing Another" [September 21, 1848], and Hammond to Simms, September 22, 1848, Hammond Papers [LC]; Hammond Diary, September 22, 1848 [SCL]).

82. Cass to Elmore, September 16, 1848, Elmore Papers (LC). Cass explained that he had originally voted for the Proviso but that he began to oppose it as soon as he realized its symbolic meaning to the South and its divisive impact on the Union.

83. Wakelyn, "Party Issues and Political Strategy," p. 84; Stephenson, "Southern Nationalism in South Carolina," pp. 315–16; *Journal of the South Carolina House, Extra Session, 1848*, pp. 11, 13.

84. Hamer, *Secession Movement in South Carolina*, pp. 11–14; Kibler, *Benjamin F. Perry*, pp. 221–22.

85. Perry Scrapbook (No. 1), pp. 51 ff (Speech at Pickens, November or December, 1847).

86. Ibid.

87. Ibid.; Perry Diary, February 8 and December 24, 1848; Kibler, *Benjamin F. Perry*, pp. 223–24.

88. Hamer, *Secession Movement in South Carolina*, pp. 15–16; Johnson to Calhoun, October 26, 1847, and DeSaussure to Calhoun, January 7, 1848, in Boucher and Brooks, *Correspondence Addressed to Calhoun*, pp. 406–7, 420.

89. Hamer, *Secession Movement in South Carolina*, p. 23; Johnson to Calhoun, October 18, 1848, in Boucher and Brooks, *Correspondence Addressed to Calhoun*, p. 482; Conner to Calhoun, November 2, 1848, in Jameson, *Correspondence of Calhoun*, p. 1184. See also circular from the Charleston Committee of Correspondence, November 1848, Yancey Papers.

90. Hamer, *Secession Movement in South Carolina*, pp. 26–27; Boucher, "Secession and Co-operation Movements," p. 72.

91. Allston to Adele Petigru Allston, December 8, 1848, Allston Papers (SCHS); Craven, *Growth of Southern Nationalism*, p. 52; *Journal of the South Carolina House, 1848*, pp. 59, 95, 29–30.

92. Morrison, *Democratic Politics and Sectionalism*, p. 41; David Johnson to Calhoun, October 26, 1847, in Boucher and Brooks, *Correspondence Addressed to Calhoun*, pp. 406–7.

93. Morrison, *Democratic Politics and Sectionalism*, pp. 45–46, 48; Hamer, *Secession Movement in South Carolina*, pp. 16–17.

94. James Hamilton to Calhoun, April 24, 1847, Wilson Lumpkin to Calhoun, November 18, 1847, F. W. Byrdsall to Calhoun, July 31, 1848, in Jameson, *Correspondence of Calhoun*, pp. 1117, 1136–38, 1180; Joseph W. Lesesne to Calhoun, August 21, 1847, and H. W. Conner to Calhoun, October 6, 1847, in Boucher and Brooks, *Correspondence Addressed to Calhoun*, pp. 391–92, 403–4; Hammond to Simms, November 17, 1848, Hammond Papers (LC); Shryock, *Georgia and the Union*, pp. 192–93.

95. See above, pp. 55–56.

96. *Congressional Globe*, 30th Cong., 2nd sess., p. 216; Potter, *Impending Crisis*, pp. 83–86. See also Shryock, *Georgia and the Union*, pp. 178–85.

97. Tucker to Hammond, December 6, 1848, Hammond Papers (LC).

98. Potter, *Impending Crisis*, p. 86; J. H. to M. C. M. Hammond, March 8, 1849, Hammond Papers (LC).

99. Hamilton, *Zachary Taylor*, pp. 170–71, Nevins, *Ordeal of the Union*, 1:239–41; Wilson Lumpkin to Calhoun, January 3, 1849, in Boucher and Brooks, *Correspondence Addressed to Calhoun*, p. 493; Potter, *Impending Crisis*, p. 87.

100. Potter, *Impending Crisis*, p. 88; Hilliard M. Judge to Calhoun, April 29, 1849, in Jameson, *Correspondence of Calhoun*, pp. 1196–97; Hamer, *Secession Movement in South Carolina*, p. 31.

101. Hamer, *Secession Movement in South Carolina*, pp. 24–25, 32–33.

102. Allston to Committee of Correspondence of Richland, April 21, 1849, Allston Papers (SCHS); Calhoun to John H. Means, April 13, 1849, in Jameson, *Correspondence of Calhoun*, pp. 765–66; Hamer, *Secession Movement in South Carolina*, pp. 34–35; Kibler, *Benjamin F. Perry*, p. 240; Perry Diary, August 6, 1849.

103. Nevins, *Ordeal of the Union*, 1:248; Hearon, *Mississippi and the Compromise of 1850*, pp. 47–50; Wallace to Seabrook, June 8, 1849, Seabrook Papers.

104. Hamer, *Secession Movement in South Carolina*, pp. 36–37; Elmore to Seabrook, May 30, 1849, Seabrook Papers. On the suspicions of South Carolina whites that the Wilmot Proviso agitation had made slaves and free blacks arrogant and on increased racial tensions in Charleston during the summer of 1849, see: H. W. Conner to Calhoun, January 12, 1849, in Jameson, *Correspondence of Calhoun*, p. 90; "Preamble and Resolutions of the Public Meeting 'in regard to . . . Calvary Church' and . . . the management of the slave population," and manuscript entitled, "To the Committee of Fifty," in the Smith Papers.

105. Elmore to Seabrook, May 30, 1849, Seabrook Papers.

106. Mosley to Seabrook, May 18, 1849, Seabrook Papers; J. T. Trezevant to Calhoun, June 7, 1849, and Lumpkin to Calhoun, August 27, 1849, in Boucher and Brooks, *Correspondence Addressed to Calhoun*, pp. 509, 524; Johnson to Calhoun, July 20, 1849, in Jameson, *Correspondence of Calhoun*, p. 1198.

107. Nevins, *Ordeal of the Union*, 1:241, 245; Rhett to Calhoun, July 19, 1849, in Boucher and Brooks, *Correspondence Addressed to Calhoun*, p. 518.

108. Calhoun to Tarpley, July 9, 1849, as quoted in Hamer, *Secession Movement in South Carolina*, p. 39; Foote to Calhoun, September 25, 1849, in Jameson, *Correspondence of Calhoun*, p. 1204.

109. Perry Diary, August 6, 1849; Calhoun to Andrew P. Calhoun, July 24, 1849, in Jameson, *Correspondence of Calhoun*, p. 769.

110. Craven, *Growth of Southern Nationalism*, pp. 64–65; A. Hutchinson to Calhoun, October 5, 1849, in Jameson, *Correspondence of Calhoun*, pp. 1206–7. The convention's resolutions "were drawn up by Col. Hill," a leading nullifier "in [South Carolina's] York District in 1832," who had emigrated to Canton, Mississippi. To avoid charges of "South Carolina dictation," Hill's resolutions "were informally sent to the [steering] Committee . . . and the Convention adopted them without knowing" their authorship (Wallace to Seabrook, October 20, 1849 [endorsed "Report of Gen. Wallace, special agent to the State of Mississippi"], Seabrook Papers).

111. Wallace to Seabrook, October 20, 1849, Seabrook Papers.

112. Ibid.

113. Ibid., Wallace to Seabrook, November 7, 1849, Seabrook Papers.

114. Craven, *Growth of Southern Nationalism*, pp. 61–62; Shryock, *Georgia and the*

Union, p. 209; Abraham W. Venable to Calhoun, August 7, 1849, in Boucher and Brooks, *Correspondence Addressed to Calhoun*, p. 522; Reuben Chapman to Calhoun, October 19, 1849, in Jameson, *Correspondence of Calhoun, p. 1208.*

CHAPTER V

1. *Journal of the South Carolina House, 1849*, p. 13.
2. Ibid., pp. 14, 24. The governor could draw on this fund at his discretion, as long as he reported expenditures to the legislature during its next annual session.
3. Calhoun to Hammond, December 7, 1849, in Jameson, *Correspondence of Calhoun*, pp. 775–76; Coussons, "Thirty Years with Calhoun, Rhett, and the Mercury," pp. 353–54.
4. *Mercury*, January 5, 1850; Wiltse, *John C. Calhoun, Sectionalist*, p. 409.
5. *Statutes at Large of South Carolina, 1849*, p. 555; *Statutes at Large of South Carolina, 1848*, p. 547. This appropriation was $15,000 in 1848 and $22,500 in 1849 and was the only increase in the state's budget for military expenditures.
6. Hammond Diary, December 15–17, 30, 1849 (SCL); Simms to Hammond, December 17, 1849, in Simms, *Letters*, 2:574–75; Tucker to Hammond, December 27, 1849, Hammond Papers (LC).
7. Perkins, "Neglected Phase," p. 158.
8. Wiltse, *John C. Calhoun, Sectionalist*, p. 451.
9. Simpson, "Prelude to Compromise," pp. 391, 393; Hamilton, *Prologue to Conflict*, p. 38; Blue, *Free Soilers*, p. 192.
10. Blue, *Free Soilers*, pp. 192–93; Simpson, "Prelude to Compromise," pp. 394 ff.
11. Allston to Adele P. Allston, December 16, 1849, in Easterby, *South Carolina Rice Plantation*, pp. 98–99; Calhoun to Anna C. Clemson, February 24, 1850, in Jameson, *Correspondence of Calhoun*, p. 783. Cobb was the leader of North Georgia's Union Democrats and a strong believer in party loyalty (see: Shryock, *Georgia and the Union*, pp. 140, 182–84, 187–88, and Hamilton, *Prologue to Conflict*, p. 35).
12. Calhoun to Hammond, January 4, 1850, in Jameson, *Correspondence of Calhoun*, pp. 779–80; Coussons, "Thirty Years with Calhoun, Rhett, and the Mercury," p. 360. John Carew, editor of the *Mercury* and member of the South Carolina House, maintained a close political association with Calhoun. Carew routinely opened the columns of his paper to correspondents who reflected Calhoun's views (see: Coussons, "Thirty Years with Calhoun, Rhett, and the Mercury," pp. 231–32, 345–46, 376, and Gettys, "To Conquer a Peace," p. 76).
13. Hamilton, *Prologue to Conflict*, pp. 46–48, 16.
14. *Mercury*, January 25, 1850.
15. Hamilton, *Prologue to Conflict*, pp. 49–52.
16. Potter, *Impending Crisis*, p. 97; *Congressional Globe*, 31st Cong., 1st sess., p. 244.
17. In March 1849 the Mormons who had settled in the Salt Lake Valley drafted a constitution for the proposed "State of Deseret" and petitioned for admission to the Union. The Senate's Committee on Territories frowned on the petition, on the boundaries it proposed, and on the name Deseret. The committee eventually reported bills for Utah (Deseret) and New Mexico territorial governments (Hamilton, *Prologue to Conflict*, pp. 18–20, 50, 89).
18. As a republic Texas had levied its own import duties, but it forfeited this

considerable source of revenue upon entering the Union. And the new state was soon in default on the bonds and other debt instruments issued by the Republic of Texas. "Thus the case was made that compensation from Washington was only fair" (ibid., p. 20).

19. *Congressional Globe*, 31st Cong., 1st sess., p. 246.

20. Hamilton, *Prologue to Conflict*, p. 59; Coussons, "Thirty Years with Calhoun, Rhett, and the Mercury," pp. 367–70; *Mercury*, February 12, 20 and 26, 1850.

21. *Mercury*, January 10, 19, 21, February 7, 13, 14, and 21, 1850.

22. Ibid., February 6, 1850.

23. Hamilton, *Prologue to Conflict*, pp. 60, 66; Nevins, *Ordeal of the Union*, 1:272–73.

24. Hamilton, *Prologue to Conflict*, pp. 54–55, 64–65, 67; Potter, *Impending Crisis*, p. 97; Nevins, *Ordeal of the Union*, 1:303.

25. Hamilton, *Prologue to Conflict*, pp. 20–21. For Hamilton's assessment of the impact of the bondholders' lobby on events in Washington during 1850, see: ibid., pp. 124–32, and Hamilton, "Texas Bonds and Northern Profits."

26. *Congressional Globe*, 31st Cong., 1st sess., p. 455. Calhoun's speech did not specify the nature of this constitutional amendment. In December 1851 Henry S. Foote contended that the amendment Calhoun desired was the dual executive arrangement sketched in the *Discourse on the Constitution*. Calhoun's primary biographer has suggested, on the contrary, that Calhoun "meant by his remarks only that he wanted the agreement, if one acceptable to both parties could be reached, to be embodied in the Constitution" (Wiltse, *John C. Calhoun, Sectionalist*, pp. 466–67).

27. *Congressional Globe*, 31st Cong., 1st sess., p. 455.

28. Nevins, *Ordeal of the Union*, 1:255, 282n.

29. Wiltse, *John C. Calhoun, Sectionalist*, pp. 465–66; Hamilton, *Prologue to Conflict*, pp. 74–75, 82.

30. Hammond to Calhoun, March 5, 1850, in Jameson, *Correspondence of Calhoun*, pp. 1210–11.

31. Hamilton, *Prologue to Conflict*, pp. 76–78, 80.

32. Calhoun to Thomas G. Clemson, March 10, 1850, in Jameson, *Correspondence of Calhoun*, p. 784; *Mercury*, March 11, 1850.

33. Calhoun to H. W. Conner, March 18, 1850, as quoted in Coussons, "Thirty Years with Calhoun, Rhett, and the Mercury," p. 386; Hammond Diary, March 17, 1850 (SCL); Hamilton, *Prologue to Conflict*, pp. 68–69, 82; *Mercury*, February 21, 23, March 2, 4, 15, 16, and 22, 1850.

34. Hamilton, *Prologue to Conflict*, pp. 81–82; Coit, *John C. Calhoun*, pp. 501–2; *Mercury*, March 19, 1850.

35. Goode to Hunter, April 20, 1850, in Ambler, *Correspondence of Hunter*, p. 111.

36. *Mercury*, March 14, 1850; Hammond to Edmund Ruffin, March 27, 1850, Ruffin Papers (microfilm). See also Foster, "Webster's Seventh of March Speech," pp. 255–56.

37. Coussons, "Thirty Years with Calhoun, Rhett, and the Mercury," p. 391.

38. Ibid., pp. 391–92. Among other moves, Governor Seabrook sent copies of South Carolina's plan for representation at Nashville to all senators and representatives from the slave states (*Mercury*, January 24, 1850).

39. Shryock, *Georgia and the Union*, pp. 218–24; Calhoun to Hammond, January 4, 1850, in Jameson, *Correspondence of Calhoun*, p. 779; *Mercury*, January 17, 1850.

40. Shryock, *Georgia and the Union*, pp. 218, 223, 230–32. In caucus the legislators subsequently chose two delegates-at-large to the Nashville Convention (ibid., p. 265).

41. Alexander H. to Linton Stephens, January 21, 1850, as quoted in Murray, *Whig Party in Georgia*, p. 148; Shryock, *Georgia and the Union*, pp. 240n, 236.

42. *Mercury*, February 8, 1850; Hammond to Edmund Ruffin, February 8, 1850, Ruffin Papers (microfilm).

43. Tucker to Hammond, February 2, 1850, Hammond Papers (LC); Craven, *Growth of Southern Nationalism*, pp. 84, 86, 89; Herndon, "Nashville Convention," pp. 215–16; Foster, "Webster's Seventh of March Speech," p. 249; *Mercury*, February 12, 16, and March 12, 1850.

44. Coussons, "Thirty Years with Calhoun, Rhett, and the Mercury," p. 391; Herndon, "Nashville Convention," p. 215; Sioussat, "Tennessee and the Nashville Convention," pp. 318, 321; *Mercury*, March 9, 1850. On the attitude of North Carolina, Louisiana, and Arkansas Whigs toward the convention, see Craven, *Growth of Southern Nationalism*, pp. 85–88.

45. Coussons, "Thirty Years with Calhoun, Rhett, and the Mercury," p. 391; *Mercury*, March 5, 1850; Newbury, "Nashville Convention and Southern Sentiment," p. 264; Shryock, *Georgia and the Union*, pp. 249–50, 254, 256. By April 5 the New York *Herald* claimed to have surveyed a hundred southern newspapers and found "that a quarter of them were either indifferent or opposed to the Nashville gathering, and that . . . [most of] the remainder favored it . . . [merely] for consultation and as a warning to the North" (Nevins, *Ordeal of the Union*, 1:315).

46. Hammond to M. C. M. Hammond, February 1, 1850, and Hammond to Simms, March 26, 1850, Hammond Papers (LC); Hammond Diary, March 17, 1850 (SCL); Hammond to Edmund Ruffin, February 8 and March 27, 1850, Ruffin Papers (microfilm).

47. Calhoun to Hammond, February 16, 1850, in Jameson, *Correspondence of Calhoun*, pp. 781–82; Wiltse, *John C. Calhoun, Sectionalist*, pp. 456–58, 471–72, 475; Coit, *John C. Calhoun*, pp. 501–2, 511. From his deathbed Calhoun dictated a series of resolutions "intended . . . for use in the Senate or more probably for the Nashville Convention" (Ames, "Calhoun and the Secession Movement," p. 467).

48. *Mercury*, April 1–6, 1850; Alfred Huger to Robert Gourdin, April 2, 1850, Gourdin Papers; White, *Robert Barnwell Rhett*, pp. 100, 114; Coussons, "Thirty Years with Calhoun, Rhett, and the Mercury," pp. 341–45; Boucher, "Secession and Cooperation Movements," pp. 89–90.

49. J. G. de R[oulhac] H[amilton], "James Hamilton," in *Dictionary of American Biography*, 8:188; Hamilton to Calhoun, October 12, 1846, in Jameson, *Correspondence of Calhoun*, p. 1095; J. H. to M. C. M. Hammond, January 26, 1849, Hammond Papers (LC); Hamilton to Hammond, March 31, 1850, Hamilton Papers.

50. Hamilton, *Prologue to Conflict*, pp. 66, 128, 131.

51. Hamilton's open letter published in the Charleston *Courier*, ca. March 11, 1850 (copy in the Hamilton Papers), and Hamilton to Hammond, March 31, 1850, Hamilton Papers.

52. See above, p. 90.

53. Hamilton to Bell, April 2, 1850, Hamilton Papers. Bell's was only one of several proposals for subdividing Texas (see Hamilton, *Prologue to Conflict*, pp. 50, 57, 89).

54. Hamilton to Hammond, March 31, 1850, Hamilton Papers; Hammond Diary, April 7, 1850 (SCL); Hamilton, *Prologue to Conflict*, p. 129.

55. Seabrook to Hamilton, April 1, 4, and 6, and Hamilton to Seabrook, April 3 and 6, 1850, as published in the *Mercury*, April 8, 1850.

56. At Seabrook's request, Hayne and Perronneau subsequently submitted written opinions on the residency question (Hayne to Seabrook, April 18, 1850, and Perron-

neau to Seabrook, April 18, 1850, Seabrook Papers). See also Hamilton to Seabrook, April 6, 1850, in the *Mercury*, April 8, 1850.

57. *Mercury*, March 16, 1850; Simms to Hammond, April 4, 1850, in Simms, *Letters*, 3:26; Hammond Diary, April 7, 1850 (SCL). Simms speculated that the governor, "longing . . . for the Senate" himself, had appointed Hamilton in order to deprive stronger candidates for the position of "the advantages . . . which may result from [interim] incumbency" (Simms to Hammond, April 10, 1850, in Simms, *Letters*, 3:27). Hamilton wrote that Seabrook, not wanting to prejudice the chances of the leading candidates, had decided not to appoint an interim senator who would be a candidate in the regular election (Hamilton to Hammond, April 19, 1850, Hammond Papers [SCL]).

58. Cheves to Seabrook, April 9, 1850, Cheves Papers—West Collection.

59. Elmore to Seabrook, April 11, 1850, Elmore Papers (SHC); James H. to M. C. M. Hammond, April 9 and 16, 1850, Hammond Papers (LC). On Barnwell's reputation in South Carolina politics, see *Mercury*, March 6, 1850.

60. *Mercury*, March 21, 27, April 3, 4, 5, and 9, 1850.

61. B. C. Yancey to "Chairman of the Committee of Electoral delegates [from Abbeville]," April 20, 1850, Yancey Papers.

62. For a complete list of the delegates by congressional district, see *Mercury*, May 11, 1850. Three districts chose alternates as well as delegates, and alternates Samuel Otterson and John A. Bradley replaced David Johnson and W. C. Beatty at Nashville (Herndon, "Nashville Convention," pp. 215–16). The death of delegate-at-large Elmore on May 29 reduced the number of South Carolinians who actually attended the convention to seventeen.

63. Lieber to [Williams], January 18, 1850, and Williams to Lieber, February 12, 1850, Lieber Papers (SCL).

64. Kibler, *Benjamin F. Perry*, pp. 243–45.

65. *Mercury*, February 28, 1850; Rippy, *Joel R. Poinsett*, pp. 236–37.

66. Shryock, *Georgia and the Union*, pp. 257, 261; Craven, *Growth of Southern Nationalism*, p. 94.

67. Ames, "Calhoun and the Secession Movement," p. 43; Sioussat, "Tennessee and the Nashville Convention," p. 324; Craven, *Growth of Southern Nationalism*, p. 93.

68. *Mercury*, May 1 and 3, 1850; Hammond to Ruffin, May 17, 1850, Ruffin Papers (microfilm); A. P. Aldrich to M. C. M. Hammond, May 11, 1850, Hammond Papers (SCL); Hammond Diary, May 26, 1850 (SCL). See also Hammond to W. B. Hodgson, April 2, 1850, Hammond Letters (DU).

69. Hamilton, *Prologue to Conflict*, pp. 62, 92–95; Foote, *Casket of Reminiscences*, pp. 25–26.

70. *Mercury*, May 13, 17, 20, 23, and June 1, 1850. On the public meeting in Charleston to protest the select committee's report, see *Mercury*, May 18 and 21, 1850.

71. Perry Diary, June 6 and May 19, 1850; Allston to Adele P. Allston, May 24, 1850, Allston Papers (SCHS).

72. On June 8, 1850, the *Mercury* reported the number of accredited delegates as follows: "Virginia, 6; South Carolina, 17; Georgia, 12; Mississippi, 11; Texas, 1; Alabama, 21; Arkansas, 2; Florida, 6." For the number of delegates from Tennessee, see the *Republican Banner and Nashville Whig*, June 5 and 6, 1850.

73. Shryock, *Georgia and the Union*, pp. 264–65; Craven, *Growth of Southern Nationalism*, pp. 94–95; Newberry, "Nashville Convention and Southern Sentiment," p. 264.

74. Allston to Benjamin Allston, June 7, 1850, in Easterby, *South Carolina Rice Plantation*, p. 102.

75. Hammond Diary, August 10, 1850 (SCL). Tucker incorrectly transcribed "resent" as "resist" ("Hammond and the Southern Convention," p. 9).

76. Tucker, "Hammond and the Southern Convention," p. 9; Newberry, "Nashville Convention and Southern Sentiment," pp. 265–66.

77. Sioussat, "Tennessee and the Nashville Convention," p. 331; Newberry, "Nashville Convention and Southern Sentiment," pp. 265–66; Cole, "The South and the Right of Secession," p. 384.

78. Herndon, "Nashville Convention," p. 218; Sioussat, "Tennessee and the Nashville Convention," p. 336. Texas, having only one delegate, had only one member on the central committee.

79. Sioussat, "Tennessee and the Nashville Convention," pp. 336–37; White, *Robert Barnwell Rhett*, pp. 105–6; Huff, *Langdon Cheves*, p. 229.

80. Shryock, *Georgia and the Union*, p. 270; Newberry, "Nashville Convention and Southern Sentiment," p. 266.

81. *Resolutions and Address, adopted by the Southern Convention*, pp. 6–8. In the spring of 1850 Calhoun's plan for a proslavery organ in Washington was finally brought to fruition by a group of southern congressmen (see: James L. Orr to Joseph A. Scoville, May 5, 1850, Orr Papers; "Address to the People of the Southern States" [signed by A. P. Butler, Jackson Morton, R. Toombs, and J. Thompson, dated May 6, 1850], in Bryan, *A Scrapbook*, Vol. II; Perkins, "Neglected Phase," pp. 160–61).

82. *Resolutions and Address, adopted by the Southern Convention*, pp. 13, 16–20.

83. Herndon, "Nashville Convention," p. 226; "Minority Report" (signed by A. O. P. Nicholson, Aaron V. Brown, William M. Murphy, Arthur J. Forman, and Sam C. Roane), in Bryan, *A Scrapbook*, Vol. II; Hammond to Simms, June 16, 1850, Hammond Papers (LC); Tucker, "Hammond and the Southern Convention," p. 10; White, *Robert Barnwell Rhett*, p. 108; Sioussat, "Tennessee and the Nashville Convention," pp. 337–38. For a more detailed account of proceedings at the convention, see Jennings, "Reappraisal of the Nashville Convention."

84. *Mercury*, June 13, 1850; Hammond to Simms, June 16, 1850, Hammond Papers (LC).

85. Jamison to Barnwell District Fourth of July Celebration Committee, June 22, 1850, published in the *Mercury*, July 16, 1850.

86. "Speech of the Hon. R. B. Rhett . . . at Hibernian Hall, in . . . Charleston, June 21, 1850," published in the *Mercury*, July 20, 1850.

87. *Mercury*, June 22, 1850.

88. "Speech of June 21," *Mercury*, July 20, 1850; Sioussat, "Tennessee and the Nashville Convention," pp. 339–40.

89. "Speech of June 21," *Mercury*, July 20, 1850; White, *Robert Barnwell Rhett*, p. 108.

90. "Speech of June 21," *Mercury*, July 20, 1850.

91. Ibid.

92. Ibid.

93. Perry Diary, July 3, 1850 (see also his entries for June 23 and July 5, 1850).

94. Hammond to Simms, June 27, 1850, Hammond Papers (LC).

95. *Mercury*, July 1850, passim.

96. *Mercury*, July 9, 1850. On the Fourth of July oration as "a careful barometer of

the changing attitudes of the South Carolina aristocracy toward nationalism," see Huff, "The Eagle and the Vulture," pp. 10–22.

97. Hamer, *Secession Movement in South Carolina*, p. 63; White, *Robert Barnwell Rhett*, p. 110; *Mercury*, July 1, 1850.

98. *Mercury*, July 6, 2, and 27, 1850.

99. Robert W. Barnwell to Hammond, July 25, 1850, Hammond Papers (LC).

100. Barney, *Road to Secession*, p. 95; McCardell, "Quitman and the Compromise of 1850," pp. 246–47; Shryock, *Georgia and the Union*, p. 291.

101. Shryock, *Georgia and the Union*, pp. 289, 55–63 passim.

102. Ibid., pp. 278, 287, 273–74.

103. *Mercury*, August 1, 1850; Shryock, *Georgia and the Union*, pp. 275, 283; W. L. to B. C. Yancey, August 17, 1850, Yancey Papers.

104. "Speech of the Hon. R. B. Rhett, delivered at the Mass Meeting at Macon, Ga., on the 22d August, 1850," Venable Scrapbook.

105. Ibid.

106. Ibid.; White, *Robert Barnwell Rhett*, p. 110.

107. "Speech of the Hon. R. B. Rhett, delivered at the Mass Meeting at Macon, Ga., on the 22d August, 1850," Venable Scrapbook. On the apprehension that the Upper South was becoming progressively less committed to slavery, see also: James H. to M. C. M. Hammond, October 23, 1848, and J. W. Curd (?) to James H. Hammond, May 13, 1849, Hammond Papers (LC); Jeremiah Clemens to Calhoun, January 8, 1849, and C. R. Clifton to Calhoun, January 30, 1840, in Boucher and Brooks, *Correspondence Addressed to Calhoun*, pp. 495–96.

108. "Speech of the Hon. R. B. Rhett, delivered at the Mass Meeting at Macon, Ga., on the 22d August, 1850," Venable Scrapbook.

109. *Mercury*, August 23, 1850; Shryock, *Georgia and the Union*, pp. 285–86; Hammond to A. H. Colquitt et al., August 12, 1850, and Hammond to Samuel G. Ray, August 27, 1850, Hammond Papers (LC); Hammond Diary, August 10, 1850 (SCL).

110. "Debate on the Compromise Bill. Mr. Barnwell." *Appendix to the Congressional Globe*, 31st Cong., 1st sess., pp. 990–92; "Speech of Hon. A. P. Butler, On July 9 and 15, 1850," published in the *Mercury*, July 24 and 25, 1850; Jacob Geiger to Armistead Burt, June 28, 1850, Burt Papers. In January 1847, when the Palmetto delegation began battling the Proviso, Armistead Burt (on Calhoun's instructions) had proposed that the Missouri Compromise line be extended to the Pacific. When the House rejected this alternative to the Proviso, the South Carolinians hardened their position by introducing the common-property-of-the-states interpretation of the territories. Still they continued to hope that northern representatives might accept extension of the Missouri Compromise line—if the Wilmot Proviso proved unobtainable. The organization of Oregon as a free-soil territory, however, sharply reduced the incentive of northerners to accept the 36 degrees 30 minutes compromise. With Oregon's status already fixed, "a victory for 36 [degrees] 30 [minutes] offered far more advantage to the South, opening the area of what is now New Mexico, Arizona, and Southern California to slavery. Utah, Nevada, and Northern California would have been free." See Potter, *Impending Crisis*, pp. 65–66, 75–76.

111. *Appendix to the Congressional Globe*, 31st Cong., 1st sess., p. 992; "Speech of Butler, On July 9 and 15," *Mercury*, July 24–25, 1850; Wilson, "Ideological Fruits," p. 138. Among the South Carolinians in Congress, only William Ferguson Colcock challenged the belief that slaves "could not profitably be employed" in California. Slave labor might be exploited in mining, Colcock observed. But these remarks were

made only in passing; he did not insist that slavery would flourish in the Southwest. See: "Speech of the Hon. W. F. Colcock on the California Question," published in the *Mercury*, June 19, 1850, and Hart, "Slavery Expansion: A Test Case," p. 123.

112. "Speech of the Hon. Daniel Wallace, April 8, 1850," in Bryan, *A Scrapbook*, Vol. II; "Speech of James L. Orr, May 8, 1850," Orr-Patterson Papers, Series B, Box 7, Vol. 1; "Speech of the Hon. John McQueen, June 8, 1850," published in the *Mercury*, June 26–27, 1850; Barnwell, "Robert Barnwell and South Carolina Politics," pp. 38–39, 42, 50–52; "Speech of Butler, on July 9 and 15," *Mercury*, July 24–25, 1850.

113. "Speech of Colcock on the California Question," *Mercury*, June 19, 1850; "Speech of Wallace, April 8, 1850," in Bryan, *A Scrapbook*, Vol. II.

114. "Speech of Butler, On July 9 and 15," *Mercury*, July 24–25, 1850.

115. "Speech of Wallace, April 8, 1850," in Bryan, *A Scrapbook*, Vol. II; "Speech of James L. Orr, May 8, 1850," Orr-Patterson Papers, Series B, Box 7, Vol. 1; "Speech of Colcock on the California Question," *Mercury*, June 19, 1850; "Speech of McQueen, June 8, 1850," *Mercury*, June 27, 1850.

116. *Appendix to the Congressional Globe*, 31st Cong., 1st sess., p. 1537.

117. "Speech of Wallace, April 8, 1850," in Bryan, *A Scrapbook*, Vol. II; "Speech of McQueen, June 8, 1850," *Mercury*, June 27, 1850; "Letter of D. Wallace to the people of the First Congressional District," *Mercury*, June 5, 1850; "Speech of Butler, On July 9 and 15," *Mercury*, July 24–25, 1850.

118. Wilson, "Controversy over Slavery," p. 136; "Speech of I. E. Holmes on the Texas Boundary, September 3, 1850," in Bryan, *A Scrapbook*, Vol. II. Holmes was the only member of the Palmetto congressional delegation to elaborate this evils-of-time argument in regard to slavery's restriction.

119. "Speech of Holmes on the Texas Boundary, September 3, 1850," in Bryan, *A Scrapbook*, Vol. II.

120. Hamilton, *Prologue to Conflict*, pp. 191, 196–200.

121. *Congressional Globe*, 31st Cong., 1st sess., pp. 1279–80, 1305, 1314.

122. Perkins, "Neglected Phase," p. 162.

123. Ibid., pp. 165, 168, 171–73.

124. Hamilton, *Prologue to Conflict*, p. 103.

125. Ibid., p. 104; Potter, *Impending Crisis*, p. 106.

126. Hamilton, *Prologue to Conflict*, pp. 104–6; Potter, *Impending Crisis*, pp. 106–7; David to Emily Outlaw, July 7, 1850, Outlaw Papers; James L. Petigru to Robert F. W. Allston, July 5, 1850, Allston Papers (SCHS). Petigru and Butler together had an interview with Taylor between June 15 and June 20, 1850.

127. *Mercury*, June 12, 1850; see also Potter, *Impending Crisis*, p. 96.

128. Hamilton, *Prologue to Conflict*, pp. 107–8; *Mercury*, July 15, 1850.

129. See above, p. 102.

130. *Appendix to the Congressional Globe*, 31st Cong., 1st sess., p. 1269.

131. Ibid., pp. 1412–14.

132. Ibid., p. 1414. Ten days later Butler and Clay were involved in a similar, though briefer, exchange (see *Mercury*, August 8, 1850).

133. David to Emily Outlaw, July 25, 1850, Outlaw Papers.

134. A. P. Butler to Hammond, July 23, 1850, and N. B. Tucker to Hammond, July 30, 1850, Hammond Papers (LC); *Mercury*, July 29, August 3, 1850.

135. Potter, *Impending Crisis*, p. 108; Hamilton, *Prologue to Conflict*, p. 117.

136. Nevins, *Ordeal of the Union*, 1:340; *Appendix to the Congressional Globe*,

31st Cong., 1st sess., p. 1414; Potter, *Impending Crisis*, pp. 108–9; Hamilton, *Prologue to Conflict*, pp. 132–33, 135–36.

137. Hamilton, *Prologue to Conflict*, pp. 144, 136–37. On Grund's activities and influence as a "journalist-bondholder," see ibid., pp. 126, 132.

138. "Letter of D. Wallace to the People of the First Congressional District," *Mercury*, June 5, 1850; *Mercury*, June 29, 1850; Hamilton, *Prologue to Conflict*, pp. 126, 129, 138; Barnwell to Hammond, August 14, 1850, Hammond Papers (LC).

139. *Congressional Globe*, 31st Cong., 1st sess., p. 1573; *Appendix to the Congressional Globe*, 31st Cong., 1st sess., pp. 1535–41. On August 14 ten southerners, including Barnwell and Butler, tried to have the Senate receive and record their formal protest to passage of the California statehood bill (*Congressional Globe*, 31st Cong., 1st sess., pp. 1578, 1588).

140. *Congressional Globe*, 31st Cong., 1st sess., pp. 1573 ff.; Barnwell to Hammond, August 14, 1850, Hammond Papers (LC); Hamilton, *Prologue to Conflict*, pp. 140–41.

141. "Speech of Colcock on the California Question," *Mercury*, June 19, 1850; Hamilton, *Prologue to Conflict*, pp. 139–41.

142. Barnwell to Hammond, September 9, 1850, Hammond Papers (LC).

CHAPTER VI

1. Hamilton, *Prologue to Conflict*, pp. 160–61.

2. Hamilton, "Cave of the Winds," pp. 346–48.

3. While the "Act to suppress the Slave Trade in the District of Columbia" made it illegal "to bring into the District of Columbia any slave whatever, for the purpose of being sold, or for the purpose of being placed in a depot, to be subsequently transferred to any other state to be sold," it did not completely abolish the slave trade in the District—"if one's definition of 'trade' is comprehensive" (see Hamilton, *Prologue to Conflict*, pp. 208, 178).

4. *Mercury*, September 10, 16, and 18, 1850. Barnwell considered his presentation of Fremont's credentials a matter of courtesy; he still "entertained the strongest constitutional objections to the admission of California" (*Congressional Globe*, 31st Cong., 1st sess., pp. 1791–92).

5. [Garnett,] *The Union, Past and Future*. Garnett attempted to "count the means of resistance, the relative strength of the opponents, the value of what we must hazard" (p. 3). Published in June, 1850, his pamphlet was in the selective-statistics genre popular with both proslavery and antislavery authors.

6. Barnwell to Hammond, September 9, 1850, Hammond Papers (LC).

7. Barnwell to Quitman, September 19, 1850, as quoted in Hamer, *Secession Movement in South Carolina*, p. 71.

8. Hammond Diary, May 26, 1850 (SCL).

9. See: Hamilton, *Prologue to Conflict*, p. 167, and Nevins, *Ordeal of the Union*, 1:353–54.

10. Potter, *Impending Crisis*, pp. 112–13.

11. Holt, *Political Crisis*, p. 67; Hamilton, *Prologue to Conflict*, p. 185.

12. Barnwell to Hammond, September 9, 1850, Hammond Papers (LC).

13. *Mercury*, September 13, 1850.

14. Seabrook to Leland, September 18 and 21, 1850, Seabrook Papers. These letters were similar in content, but the first contained observations on Georgia that Sea-

brook did not want to make public. The second letter was published in the *Mercury*, September 27, 1850.

15. Seabrook to the Governors of Alabama, Virginia, and Mississippi, September 20, 1850, Seabrook Papers.

16. Shryock, *Georgia and the Union*, pp. 300–301.

17. *Mercury*, October 3, 1850 (column signed "Another Old Nullifier"); Seabrook to Towns, October 8, 1850, Seabrook Papers; Hamer, *Secession Movement in South Carolina*, pp. 69–70.

18. *Mercury*, August 19, September 28, October 4, 15, 24, 26, 30, and November 4, 1850. See also the proceedings of the "Southern Rights Meeting in Bluffton," which mimicked the Declaration of Independence (*Mercury*, October 24, 1850).

19. *Mercury*, December 17, 1850.

20. See above, pp. 81–83.

21. *Mercury*, September 5, October 4, 12, 16, 18, 21, November 1, 15, 1850; *Daily Sun*, October 5, 10, and 19, 1850; Rogers, *History of Georgetown County*, p. 372; Grimball Diary, December 5, 7, 1850.

22. *Mercury*, October 4, 1850 (constitution of the Southern Rights Association of St. Philip's and St. Michael's).

23. *Mercury*, October 8, 1850; "Sketch of Mr. Memminger's Remarks at the Mass Meeting in Pendleton," in Bryan, *A Scrapbook*, Vol. VII.

24. Perry Diary, October 10, November 7, 1850; *Mercury*, November 9, 1850.

25. Orr-Patterson Papers, Series B, Box 7, Vol. 1.

26. White, *Robert Barnwell Rhett*, p. 112; in the *Mercury*, see, for example, the articles signed "Hampden," September–October, 1850, passim.

27. Hamer, *Secession Movement in South Carolina*, pp. 63–64; *Mercury*, August 16, October 4, and 12, 1850; Aldrich to Hammond, October 10, 1850, Hammond Papers (LC).

28. *Mercury*, November 6 and 8, 1850.

29. William DuBose et al. to Seabrook, October 21, 1850, Seabrook Papers; *Mercury*, November 16 and 19, 1850.

30. *Mercury*, October 5, 1850; Hayne to Hammond, October 6, 1850, Hammond Papers (LC).

31. Perry Diary, October 10, 1850. On Frost's attitude toward nullification, see Freehling, *Prelude to Civil War*, p. 245.

32. Butler to Seabrook, October 22, 1850, Seabrook Papers.

33. *Mercury*, June 1, 1850; Freidel, *Francis Lieber*, pp. 250–51; Lieber to [George] Hillard, August 11, 1850, Lieber Papers (SCL).

34. Robert to Adele P. Allston, September 22, 1850, Allston Papers (SCHS). In Washington, Robert Barnwell heard that Petigru had "been offered a place in the Cabinet" [Barnwell to Hammond, July 25, 1850, Hammond Papers (LC)].

35. Perry Diary, August 4, 1850. While he supported the compromise as a whole, Perry felt that the "California Bill . . . [was] an outrage on the South" (ibid., August 25, 1850).

36. Ibid., September 14, 1850.

37. Ibid., September 25, October 5, 25, November 11, 17, 1850; *Mercury*, November 9, 1850; Kibler, *Benjamin F. Perry*, p. 248.

38. Rippy, *Joel R. Poinsett*, p. 238.

39. Petigru to his children, September 12, 1850, Petigru Letters (LC). In November, after he could find no other lawyer willing to accept appointment as United States Attorney for South Carolina, Petigru responded to a personal appeal from President

Fillmore and "reluctantly consented to take the office" (Fillmore to J. C. Hamilton, April 4, 1863, as quoted in Carson, *Life, Letters, and Speeches of Petigru*, p. 282). See also the *Mercury*, November 16, 1850.

40. Elliott to his wife, October 26, 1850, as quoted in Jones, "Carolinians and Cubans," p. 11; Freidel, *Francis Lieber*, p. 253.

41. Grayson, "Letter to His Excellency Whitemarsh B. Seabrook," in Bryan, *A Scrapbook*, Vol. IV.

42. Ibid.

43. Ibid.

44. Ibid.

45. *Daily Sun*, October 23, 1850; *Mercury*, October 22–23, November 14, 1850.

46. [Andrew G. Magrath,] "One of the People to the Hon. W. J. Grayson," and [B. C. Pressley,] "To the Hon. W. J. Grayson," in Bryan, *A Scrapbook*, Vol. IV. Pressley's pamphlet was a rejoinder to the second edition of Grayson's "Letter," which contained a reply to Magrath. See also Bass, "Autobiography of William J. Grayson," pp. clxxxxvi ff.

47. Hamilton, *Prologue to Conflict*, pp. 166, 179; *Mercury*, November 25, 1850; Craven, *Growth of Southern Nationalism*, p. 106; "Letter from Gen. James Hamilton," *Mercury*, October 1, November 28, 1850.

48. Shryock, *Georgia and the Union*, p. 296; Barnwell to Hammond, September 9, 1850 (see also Barnwell to Hammond, September 26, 1850), Hammond Papers (LC).

49. Shryock, *Georgia and the Union*, pp. 304–5; Barney, *Road to Secession*, pp. 115–16; Simms to Nathaniel Beverley Tucker, November 27, 1850, in Simms, *Letters*, 3:76.

50. James Hamilton made this observation in a public letter suggesting that South Carolina's reaction to the compromise was excessive and pointing out the risks of separate secession (*Mercury*, November 28, 1850). Among his old constituents, however, Hamilton's arguments were discredited by his financial interest in the compromise.

51. Milledgeville *Federal Union*, December 3, 1850, as quoted in Gardner, "Winning the Lower South," p. 118.

52. Shryock, *Georgia and the Union*, pp. 310–11, 316–17, 319; Stephens to John J. Crittenden, October 24, 1850, Stephens Papers; Gardner, "Winning the Lower South," pp. 94, 117; J. M. Alston to Hammond, November 1, 1850, Hammond Papers (LC); Hubbell, "Three Georgia Unionists," p. 318.

53. Gardner, "Winning the Lower South," pp. 181–87, 190–91; Craven, *Growth of Southern Nationalism*, pp. 105–6; J. J. Seibels to James Hammond, September 14, 1850, Hammond Papers (LC); Denman, *Secession Movement in Alabama*, pp. 37–41, 50.

54. Quitman to Seabrook, September 29, 1850, Seabrook Papers.

55. Ranck, *Albert Gallatin Brown*, p. 79; Gardner, "Winning the Lower South," pp. 234–35, 241–45. On Davis's ideas for opposing the compromise by means other than immediate secession, see ibid., pp. 246–47.

56. Broussard, "Quitman and the Lopez Expeditions," pp. 114–15. On Quitman's alleged complicity in Narcisco Lopez's first filibustering expedition against Cuba, see ibid., pp. 108–13.

57. In part the censure involved party discipline. Foote—"General Weathercock" to his detractors—had switched parties frequently in the 1830s. When elected to the Senate in 1847, however, he was a Democrat, and the Mississippi legislature in 1850 was not only hostile to the compromise but overwhelmingly Democratic (Miles,

Jacksonian Democracy, p. 164; Gardner, "Winning the Lower South," pp. 220–21, 250–52).

58. McCardell, "Quitman and the Compromise of 1850," p. 250.

59. Rhett apparently gave this letter to Seabrook. Datelined "Jackson [Mississippi,] Nov. 30, 1850" and addressed to Rhett at Columbia, the letter is now in the Seabrook Papers. A different interpretation of the delay between the legislative session and the state convention is offered by McCardell, "Quitman and the Compromise of 1850," p. 250.

60. Hammond to Simms, September 30, 1850, Hammond Papers (LC). Neither entreaties nor warnings persuaded Hammond to change his decision (A. P. Aldrich to Hammond, October 10, 1850, I. W. Hayne to Hammond, October 15, 1850, Maxcy Gregg to Hammond, November 4, 1850, and Hammond to Simms, November 11, 1850, Hammond Papers [LC]).

61. Sharkey, in fact, defended the compromise and soon joined Foote in Mississippi's Union party (Gardner, "Winning the Lower South," pp. 248–49, 253–54).

62. A. P. Aldrich to Hammond, October 10, 1850, Hammond Papers (LC); *Mercury*, November 18, 1850; Shryock, *Georgia and the Union*, p. 324; Sioussat, "Tennessee and the Nashville Convention," p. 344; Hammond to Seabrook, October 18, 1850, Seabrook to Hammond, October 23, 1850, Hammond Papers (LC); Robert F. W. to Adele P. Allston, November 25, 1850, in Easterby, *South Carolina Rice Plantation*, p. 105; Herndon, "Nashville Convention," pp. 229–30.

63. Elizabeth B. to R. B. Rhett, November 7, 1850, Rhett Collection (SCHS); Herndon, "Nashville Convention," p. 230; *Mercury*, November 18–19, 1850; Cheves, *Speech of Cheves, on November 15, 1850*, p. 15; Huff, *Langdon Cheves*, p. 231.

64. Newberry, "Nashville Convention and Southern Sentiment," p. 271; *Mercury*, November 18, 22, and 23, 1850.

65. Adger to Thornwell, September 30, 1850, Thornwell Papers; Edward M. to Louisa L. McCrady, November 26, 1850, McCrady Family Papers; Hamer, *Secession Movement in South Carolina*, p. 77; William H. Barnwell, "Discourse Delivered on the Occasion of the Day of Fasting, Humiliation, and Prayer," in Bryan, *A Scrapbook*, Vol. VIII; *Mercury*, December 27, 1850.

66. *Journal of the South Carolina Senate, 1850*, pp. 15, 22–23; *Statutes at Large of South Carolina, 1850*, pp. 57–58, 29, 33.

67. *Statutes at Large of South Carolina, 1850*, pp. 6, 1.

68. Robert F. W. to Adele P. Allston, November 30, 1850, Allston Papers (SCHS).

69. *Mercury*, September 7, 1850; Barnwell to Hammond, September 9, 1850, Hammond Papers (LC).

70. See above, pp. 103–4.

71. Robert F. W. to Adele P. Allston, December 5, 1850, in Easterby, *South Carolina Rice Plantation*, p. 107; *Journal of the South Carolina House, 1850*, pp. 133, 147; *Daily Sun*, December 14, 1850; *Mercury*, December 14, 17, 1850; Hamer, *Secession Movement in South Carolina*, p. 82.

72. *Daily Sun*, December 9, 1850; Hammond Diary, December 14, November 29, 1850 (SCL); Tucker, "Hammond and the Southern Convention," pp. 7–8; Perritt, "Rhett: Disunionist Heir," pp. 40–42; Merritt, *James H. Hammond*, p. 99.

73. Hammond Diary, November 30, December 14, 1850 (SCL); Hammond to W. H. Gist, December 2, 1850, Hammond Papers (LC); Tucker, "Hammond and the Southern Convention," pp. 11–12; White, *Robert Barnwell Rhett*, p. 113.

74. *Daily Sun*, December 19, 1850; P. Quattlebaum to Hammond, December 17, 1850, January 28, 1851, and L. M. Ayer, Jr., to Hammond, December 18, 1850,

Hammond Papers (LC); *Journal of the South Carolina House, 1850*, pp. 174, 218–19, 225; Hammond Diary, December 14, 21, 1850 (SCL); Petigru to Jane Petigru North, December 19, 1850, as quoted in Carson, *Life, Letters, and Speeches of Petigru*, p. 286; *Mercury*, December 19, 1850.

75. *Mercury*, September 24, 1850.

76. Perry Diary, November 17, 1850; James L. Petigru to Jane Petigru North, December 19, 1850, as quoted in Carson, *Life, Letters, and Speeches of Petigru*, p. 285.

77. See, for example, *Journal of the South Carolina House, 1850*, pp. 214–16.

78. Lottie P. to Sarah Yancey, December 14, 1850, Yancey Papers; *Journal of the South Carolina House, 1850*, pp. 56–57.

79. *Mercury*, December 10, 1850; *Journal of the South Carolina House, 1850*, p. 57; *Journal of the South Carolina Senate, 1850*, pp. 91, 131–32, 105, 110, 129, 124; Robert F. W. to Adele P. Allston, December 14, 1850, Allston Papers (SCL).

80. *Mercury*, December 10–13, 1850; Capers, *Life and Times of Memminger*, p. 202; Lottie P. to Sarah Yancey, December 14, 1850, Yancey Papers.

81. *Journal of the South Carolina Senate, 1850*, pp. 91, 131–32; *Journal of the South Carolina House, 1850*, pp. 106, 119–20, 131, 165–66, 188–94; P. Quattlebaum to J. H. Hammond, December 12, 17, 1850, Hammond Papers (LC); Robert F. W. to Adele P. Allston, December 17, 1850, Allston Papers (SCL).

82. *Journal of the South Carolina House, 1850*, pp. 196–99, 203, 214–16; *Statutes at Large of South Carolina, 1850*, pp. 55–57. Since a constituent convention possessed ultimate authority over organic law, the eligibility requirement for membership in this convention was far more liberal than for membership in the legislature: "white male citizens of this State, of the age of twenty-one years and upwards, shall be eligible to a seat in said Convention."

83. *Journal of the South Carolina House, 1850*, pp. 216–17, 269, 275–76; *Journal of the South Carolina Senate, 1850*, pp. 161–62, 193.

84. *Journal of the South Carolina Senate, 1850*, pp. 202, 197–98, 144; Hamer, "British Consuls and Negro Seamen," pp. 145–49; *Mercury*, December 3, 1850. In January, 1851, the New York *Evening Post* secured and published correspondence between Mathews and Means on the issue of free Negro sailors. The *Evening Post*'s revelations prompted northern charges that Great Britain was "encourag[ing] South Carolina in Rebellion" by ignoring proper diplomatic channels. On the repercussions of this episode, see Hamer, "British Consuls and Negro Seamen," pp. 150–54, and the *Mercury*, February 7 and March 17, 1851.

85. *Mercury*, December 21, 23, 1850; P. Quattlebaum to J. H. Hammond, December 20, 1850, Hammond Papers (LC); Hammond Diary, December 24, 1850 (SCL).

86. Perry Diary, December 29, 1850.

87. The *Mercury* accompanied Poinsett's letter with scathing editorial observations but printed it in full (December 5, 1850).

88. Kibler, *Benjamin F. Perry*, pp. 251, 249.

89. Hubbell, "Three Georgia Unionists," pp. 319–20; McCrary, "Authorship of the Georgia Platform," pp. 585–86; Shryock, *Georgia and the Union*, pp. 330–32.

90. *Mercury*, December 12 and 18, 1850.

91. See the articles by "Barnwell" in the *Mercury*, January 28, 20, and 22, 1851. "Barnwell" was one of a number of correspondents who developed the secessionists' case.

92. Ibid., January 28, 1851.

93. *Mercury*, February 1, 1851 (see the article signed "Vive Carolina"); Rhett to R. B. Rhett, Jr., January 13, 1851, Rhett Papers (SCL).

94. Charleston *Courier*, January 14, 1851; see the column signed "Moultrie," in the *Mercury*, January 30, 1851. "Moultrie's" articles developed the cooperationists' case.

95. *Mercury*, February 7, 1851.

96. *Mercury*, January 10, 1851; A. P. Aldrich to J. H. Hammond, January 7, 1851, Hammond Papers (LC).

97. *Mercury*, January 29, 14, and 21, 1851.

98. Ibid., January 15, 29, 30, February 4, 6, and 3, 1851.

99. Ibid., January 30, 24, 27, and February 6, 1851; Aldrich to J. H. Hammond, January 3, 25, 1851, Hammond Papers (LC).

100. *Mercury*, February 19, 1851. For a complete list of the delegates elected, see ibid., February 21, 1851.

101. Ibid., February 6 and 21, 1851. Several tickets for Charleston were announced, and they contained some duplication of names. The above statement refers to a comparison of the ticket dedicated to "resistance . . . by a combination of . . . Southern States" with the roster of delegates elected.

102. Kibler, *Benjamin F. Perry*, pp. 257–58.

103. *Mercury*, February 12, 1851; Hamer, *Secession Movement in South Carolina*, p. 85. The vote total in Charleston was, however, influenced by circumstances unique to the city: the elections were held during Gala Week of the social season; a heavy rain fell on Monday, February 10; and some Unionists avoided the polls in protest of the election's purpose (*Mercury*, February 4, 10, 11, 1851).

104. Hamer, *Secession Movement in South Carolina*, pp. 85–86; Freidel, *Francis Lieber*, p. 253; Hammond Diary, January 25, 1851 (SCL); John Russel to J. H. Hammond, February 10, 1851, and Hammond to W. G. Simms, February 14, 1851, Hammond Papers (LC).

105. Elizabeth B. to R. B. Rhett, February 5, 1851, Rhett Collection (SCHS); *Mercury*, January 7, 1851.

106. Rayback, *Millard Fillmore*, pp. 268–71, 278; Holt, *Political Crisis*, p. 90; Potter, *Impending Crisis*, pp. 121–22; Nevins, *Ordeal of the Union*, 1:380–81; White, *Robert Barnwell Rhett*, p. 115.

107. Potter, *Impending Crisis*, p. 130; Hamilton, *Prologue to Conflict*, p. 206; Pease, "Confrontation and Abolition," p. 926.

108. *Mercury*, October 17, November 4, 1850.

109. *Congressional Globe*, 31st Cong., 2nd sess., p. 596; Potter, *Impending Crisis*, p. 138; *Mercury*, February 27, March 4, 6, 1851.

110. "Remarks of Mr. Rhett, Feb. 24, 1851," published in the *Mercury*, March 4, 1851.

111. Ibid.

112. Ibid.

113. Perritt, "Rhett: Disunionist Heir," pp. 45–46; *Appendix to the Congressional Globe*, 31st Cong., 2nd sess., p. 418. The record of the special Senate session appears in this appendix, but it was technically a part of the Thirty-Second Congress.

114. Holt, *Political Crisis*, p. 92.

115. Gardner, "Winning the Lower South," pp. 194–95; *Mercury*, January 7, 1851; Denman, *Secession Movement in Alabama*, pp. 48, 54.

116. Gardner, "Winning the Lower South," pp. 198–99; Montgomery *Daily Journal*, March 15, 1851 (clipping in the Yancey Papers); Denman, *Secession Movement in Alabama*, p. 51n.

117. Broussard, "Quitman and the Lopez Expeditions," p. 115

118. *Mercury*, February 12, 1851; Broussard, "Quitman and the Lopez Expeditions," pp. 116–17.

119. Ranck, *Albert Gallatin Brown*, pp. 90–91; McCardell, "Quitman and the Compromise of 1850," pp. 253–54; Gardner, "Winning the Lower South," pp. 259–60.

120. *Southern Patriot*, February 28, 1851; Kibler, *Benjamin F. Perry*, pp. 260–62; Poinsett to Perry, March 4, 28, 1851, Petigru to Perry, April 1, 1851, and Rutland to Perry, March 17, 1851, Perry Papers.

121. *Southern Patriot*, February 28, March 7, 14, 28, April 4, 11, 18, and 25, 1851; Kibler, *Benjamin F. Perry*, pp. 262–63.

122. Grayson to Corwin, April 12, 1851, Corwin Papers. Corwin's informant on the opinions of Gadsden and others was a newcomer to South Carolina, James E. Harvey, who volunteered his own slate of replacements for federal jobholders in South Carolina (Harvey to Corwin, March 28, 1851, Corwin Papers).

123. Grayson to Corwin, April 12 and 16, 1851, Corwin Papers.

124. *Mercury*, March 19, 1851; Simms to Tucker, March 12, 1851, in Simms, *Letters*, 3:99.

125. Hammond to Means, February 20, 1851, Hammond Papers (LC); Columbia *Telegraph*, March 8, 1851; *Mercury*, April 3, 1851.

126. W. G. Simms to N. B. Tucker, April 7, 1851, in Simms, *Letters*, 3:108; *Mercury*, March 18, 20, and April 28, 1851.

127. Although a belated convert, Seabrook was a devout one (see, for example, "Synopsis of Gov. Seabrook's Remarks, Delivered before the people of John's and Wadmalar Islands," published in the *Mercury*, April 21, 1851).

128. Jones to Hammond, April 5, 1851, Hammond Papers (LC); *Mercury*, March 22, 24, 26, and April 5, 1851; "Address Delivered to the Freemen of Chesterfield District, March, 1851. By the Rev. J. C. Coit," in Bryan, *A Scrapbook*, Vol. VII.

129. "Speech of the Hon. R. B. Rhett, April 7, 1851," published in the *Mercury*, April 29, 1851.

130. Ibid.

131. Rhett to R. B. Rhett, Jr., April 13, 1851, Rhett Papers (SCL); *Mercury*, February 14, 13, 27, March 12, and April 10, 1851; *Southern Standard*, September 3, 1851; White, *Robert Barnwell Rhett*, p. 118.

132. *Mercury*, April 8, 16, 1851; I. I. Pope, Jr., to Armistead Burt, April 23, 1851, Burt Papers.

133. *Mercury*, April 15, 1851; Laurensville *Herald*, n.d., reprinted in the *Mercury*, April 29, 1851; "Meeting of Delegates from the Southern Rights Associations of South Carolina. List of Delegates," in Bryan, *A Scrapbook*, Vol. VII.

CHAPTER VII

1. *Mercury*, May 6–7, 1851; "Meeting of Delegates from the Southern Rights Associations of South Carolina," in Bryan, *A Scrapbook*, Vol. VII.

2. *Mercury*, May 7–8, 1851; Huff, *Langdon Cheves*, p. 233.

3. *Mercury*, May 7–9, 1851.

4. Ibid., May 9, 1851; Grimball Diary, May 7–8, 1851; "Meeting of Delegates from the Southern Rights Associations of South Carolina," in Bryan, *A Scrapbook*, Vol. VII; White, *Robert Barnwell Rhett*, p. 119.

5. "Remarks of R. W. Barnwell," in Bryan, *A Scrapbook*, Vol. VII; "Speech of J. L.

Orr, Before the Convention of the Southern Rights Associations," in Bryan, *A Scrapbook*, Vol. VII; "Letter From W. W. Boyce to John P. Richardson, President of the Southern Rights Associations," in Bryan, *A Scrapbook*, Vol. VII.

6. "Remarks of R. W. Barnwell," in Bryan, *A Scrapbook*, Vol. VII.

7. "Speech of J. L. Orr, Before the Convention of the Southern Rights Associations," in Bryan, *A Scrapbook*, Vol. VII; [Speech of A. P. Butler to the Convention of Southern Rights Associations] in the Orr Papers; "Remarks of R. W. Barnwell," in Bryan, *A Scrapbook*, Vol. VII; see also: "Letter from W. W. Boyce to John P. Richardson, President of the Southern Rights Associations," in Bryan, *A Scrapbook*, Vol. VII, and *Mercury*, April 12, 1851.

8. "Remarks of R. W. Barnwell," in Bryan, *A Scrapbook*, Vol. VII; [Speech of A. P. Butler to the Convention of Southern Rights Associations], in the Orr Papers; "Speech of J. L. Orr, Before the Convention of the Southern Rights Associations," in Bryan, *A Scrapbook*, Vol. VII.

9. "Speech of J. L. Orr, Before the Convention of the Southern Rights Associations," in Bryan, *A Scrapbook*, Vol. VII; [Speech of A. P. Butler to the Convention of Southern Rights Associations], in the Orr Papers.

10. Rhett recommended this tariff only on goods from states north "of the Potomac and Ohio Rivers . . . and all foreign nations" ("Speech of the Hon. R. B. Rhett, April 7, 1851," *Mercury*, April 29, 1851).

11. Ibid.; "Speech of J. L. Orr, Before the Convention of the Southern Rights Associations," in Bryan, *A Scrapbook*, Vol. VII.

12. Cooperationists cited varying figures on South Carolina's imports transshipped to other states. Butler and Barnwell said that three-fourths of the goods imported by South Carolina were consumed elsewhere; Orr put the fraction at two-thirds.

13. "Speech of J. L. Orr, Before the Convention of the Southern Rights Associations," in Bryan, *A Scrapbook*, Vol. VII; "Remarks of R. W. Barnwell," in Bryan, *A Scrapbook*, Vol. VII.

14. [Speech of A. P. Butler to the Convention of Southern Rights Associations], in the Orr Papers; "Remarks of R. W. Barnwell," in Bryan, *A Scrapbook*, Vol. VII. Unionist Francis Lieber acidly observed that "the leading Secessionists are so wicked and so asinine that they expect to ally the free and independent *nation* of South Carolina (I have proposed Rhettsylvania as the best name) with Great Britain . . . the alliance of so puny a State with so mighty a one can only be a dependency, a colonial vassalage" (Lieber to G. S. Hillard, May, 1851, in Perry, *Letters of Francis Lieber*, pp. 252–53).

15. "Speech of J. L. Orr, Before the Convention of the Southern Rights Associations," in Bryan, *A Scrapbook*, Vol. VII; "Letter From W. W. Boyce to John P. Richardson, President of the Southern Rights Associations," in Bryan, *A Scrapbook*, Vol. VII.

16. Ibid.

17. "Remarks of J. H. Adams, before the Convention of Southern Rights Associations," published in the *Mercury*, June 7, 1851; "Speech of Seabrook, before the Southern Rights Associations," published in the *Mercury*, May 23, 1851; "Speech of Colcock at the Southern Rights Convention," in Bryan, *A Scrapbook*, Vol. VII.

18. "Speech of Colcock at the Southern Rights Convention," in Bryan, *A Scrapbook*, Vol. VII; "Speech of John A. Calhoun, before the Convention of Southern Rights Associations," published in the *Mercury*, May 22, 1851; "Speech of Seabrook, before the Southern Rights Associations," *Mercury*, May 23, 1851. John A. Calhoun was John C. Calhoun's nephew.

19. "Speech of Colcock at the Southern Rights Convention," in Bryan, *A Scrapbook*, Vol. VII; "Speech of Seabrook, before the Southern Rights Associations," *Mercury*, May 23, 1851; "Speech of John A. Calhoun, before the Convention of Southern Rights Associations," *Mercury*, May 22, 1851; "Remarks of J. H. Adams, before the Convention of Southern Rights Associations," *Mercury*, June 7, 1851.

20. "Speech of Colcock at the Southern Rights Convention," in Bryan, *A Scrapbook*, Vol. VII.

21. Ibid.; "Remarks of J. H. Adams, before the Convention of Southern Rights Associations," *Mercury*, June 7, 1851.

22. "Speech of Seabrook, before the Southern Rights Associations," *Mercury*, May 23, 1851. Secessionists also denied the contention that runaway slaves could not be recovered, even from Georgia and North Carolina, after the Palmetto State seceded. Georgia and North Carolina would need to recover their own fugitives from South Carolina, secessionists insisted, and mutual accommodation or, if necessary, extradition agreements could easily be obtained. In their haste to answer each objection to separate secession, its proponents failed to observe that the cooperationists' concern over fugitive slaves was hardly consistent with the prediction of a disastrous increase in South Carolina's slave population.

23. "Remarks of J. H. Adams, before the Convention of Southern Rights Associations," *Mercury*, June 7, 1851.

24. "Speech of Colcock at the Southern Rights Convention," in Bryan, *A Scrapbook*, Vol. VII; "Speech of Seabrook, before the Southern Rights Associations," *Mercury*, May 23, 1851; "Remarks of J. H. Adams, before the Convention of Southern Rights Associations," *Mercury*, June 7, 1851.

25. *Mercury*, May 1851. Since his defeat for the senatorship, Hammond had avoided public statements. He continued, however, to play a sub-rosa part in South Carolina politics. His "plan of state action," as he styled it, was constructed with advice and criticism from W. G. Simms and N. B. Tucker and was released by his protégé A. P. Aldrich (Simms to Hammond, January 30, 1851, in Simms, *Letters*, 3:88; Tucker to Hammond, April 19, 1851, Hammond Papers [LC]; Hammond Diary, May 25, 1851 [SCL]).

26. Hammond to Simms, May 24, 1851, Hammond Papers (LC).

27. Freehling, *Prelude to Civil War*, pp. 224–25, 228–31.

28. *Mercury*, May 16, 1851; "Circular from the Central Committee to Presidents of Southern Rights Associations in So. Carolina," May 26, 1851, Yancey Papers.

29. *Mercury*, May 9, 13, 17, 27, and 28, 1851; Seabrook to Butler, May 12, 1851, and Butler to Seabrook, May 19, 1851, Seabrook Papers (LC).

30. Aldrich to Hammond, May 16, 1851, Hammond Papers (LC). Aldrich opined that Rhett and Adams did not truly desire secession, rather they expected "that the minority [which opposed secession] will be so large as [to] make secession impossible, but yet they [the secessionists] will have a majority to control the state and keep the power" (ibid.).

31. Ibid.

32. Hammond Diary, May 28, 1851 (SCL); Maxcy Gregg to Hammond, May 27, 1851, Hammond Papers (LC); *Mercury*, June 5 and 9, 1851.

33. *Mercury*, June 5, 1851. See also John J. Martin to Burt, May 21, 1851, Burt Papers, and *Mercury*, May 24, 1851.

34. *Mercury*, June 5, 1851.

35. Hamer, *Secession Movement in South Carolina*, p. 100; James L. Petigru to Jane Petigru North, May 14, 1851, as quoted in Carson, *Life, Letters, and Speeches of*

Petigru, p. 288; J. [?] H. to Corwin, May 18, 1851, Corwin Papers.

36. *Southern Patriot*, May 16 and 30, 1851; Freidel, *Francis Lieber*, p. 255; Kibler, *Benjamin F. Perry*, pp. 267-68.

37. *Southern Patriot*, June 6, 1851; *Mercury*, June 12 and 19, 1851.

38. *Mercury*, June 9, 1851. Pressley's financial partners in the *Southern Standard* were Ker Boyce and M. C. Mordecai (King, *Newspaper Press of Charleston*, p. 159).

39. *Mercury*, June 14, 1851; Columbia *Telegraph*, n.d., reprinted in the *Mercury*, June 25, 1851.

40. See, for example, *Mercury*, June 3, 4, and 17, 1851.

41. Butler to Seabrook, June 20, 1851, Seabrook Papers; Simms to Tucker, June 26, 1851, in Simms, *Letters*, 3:133.

42. *Mercury*, August 12, 1851.

43. *Southern Standard*, July 18, 1851; "Report and Resolutions Adopted at the Anti-Secession Celebration of the Citizens of Greenville and the surrounding Districts, on the Fourth of July, 1851," in Perry Scrapbook, No. I.

44. *Southern Standard*, July 16-18, 23-25, and August 1, 1851; *Southern Patriot*, July 11, 18, and 25, 1851; Freidel, *Francis Lieber*, p. 256; Orr to R. B. Duncan, V. McBee, and others, Committee, July 2, 1851, Orr-Patterson Papers, Series B, Box 7, Vol. 1. Figures on attendance at antebellum political rallies varied according to the politics of the reporting newspaper. Perry's *Southern Patriot* put the Greenville crowd at four thousand; the *Mercury* accepted a figure of not "over four baker's dozen" (*Southern Patriot*, July 11, 1851; *Mercury*, July 16, 1851).

45. Henry L. Pinckney, Jr., "Oration Delivered on the Fourth of July 1851," in Bryan, *A Scrapbook*, Vol. VII; *Mercury*, July 4, 7, 24, August 1-2, and September 15, 1851.

46. *Southern Standard*, July 29, 1851; Richard De Treville, "Substance of an Address Delivered on the Fourth of July, 1851," in Bryan, *A Scrapbook*, Vol. VII; *Mercury*, July 10 and 11, 1851.

47. *Southern Standard*, July 7, 1851. The quotation above is taken from the pamphlet edition of these letters (*The Letters of Agricola; by Hon. William Elliott*, p. 7). Although still a Unionist in 1851, Elliott was more amenable to regional cooperation in defense of certain interests than he had been in 1832 (Jones, "Carolinians and Cubans," pp. 11, 15).

48. *Southern Standard*, July 14, 15, 28, and 18, 1851.

49. Bellinger's debating opponent at this affair was A. P. Aldrich, who touted Hammond's "plan of state action" as an alternative to separate secession (*Southern Standard*, July 14, 1851).

50. *Mercury*, July 12, 17, and 19, 1851; *Southern Standard*, July 10 and 14, 1851.

51. Conner to Calhoun, May 7, 1847, in Boucher and Brooks, *Correspondence Addressed to Calhoun*, p. 374. See also Laura White's interpretation of this opinion "of many, if not most, of the leaders in South Carolina" about Rhett (*Robert Barnwell Rhett*, p. 101).

52. *Mercury*, July 7, 14, and 17, 1851. See also Hammond to Simms, May 24, 1851, Hammond Papers (LC).

53. *Southern Standard*, July 15, 19, 21, 28, and 30, 1851.

54. *Mercury*, July 15, 1851; *Southern Standard*, July 19, 1851.

55. *Southern Standard*, July 17, 1851; *Mercury*, July 12 and 19, 1851.

56. *Mercury*, July 15, 24, and 25, 1851; *Southern Standard*, July 25, 1851.

57. *Mercury*, November 28, December 20, 1850; Seabrook to Fillmore,

November 29, 1850, and Seabrook to Col. Ewing, November 29, 1850, United States Relations File, Governor Whitemarsh B. Seabrook.

58. *Mercury*, June 26, 28, and July 2, 1851; Stephenson, "Southern Nationalism in South Carolina," p. 322; White, *Robert Barnwell Rhett*, p. 121.

59. Means to Rhett, July 30, 1851, Rhett Papers (SHC).

60. *Mercury*, July 28–29, 1851; "Cooperation Meeting in Charleston, July 29th, 1851," in Bryan, *A Scrapbook*, Vol. VII. Charles J. McDonald, Southern Rights candidate for governor of Georgia, was numbered among those who wrote to applaud the meeting's purpose.

61. *Mercury*, July 30, 1851; "Co-operation Meeting in Charleston, July 29th, 1851," in Bryan, *A Scrapbook*, Vol. VII.

62. *Mercury*, August 1, 1851; *Southern Standard*, August 2, 1851.

63. Barnwell to Orr, August 26, 1851, Orr-Patterson Papers; *Southern Standard*, July 1, 1851; Boucher, "Secession and Co-operation Movements," p. 123. In September the cooperationist *Southern Rights Advocate* succeeded the secessionist Pendleton *Messenger*. Perry's *Southern Patriot* opposed secession, of course, but could not endorse the cooperationist goal of eventual disunion.

64. Barnwell to Orr, August 26, 1851, Orr-Patterson Papers; Perkins, "Neglected Phase," pp. 190–91. On the *Southern Press*, see also: *Southern Patriot*, April 4, 1851, and *Mercury*, July 10, 1851.

65. Waddy Thompson to James L. Orr, July 29, 1851, Orr-Patterson Papers; *Southern Standard*, August 13, 2, 20, 15, and 22, 1851.

66. *Southern Standard*, August 2, 4, and 12, 1851; *Mercury*, August 13, 1851; Orr to "the Committee of Invitation of the Co-operation Meeting, at Yorkville, on the 6th," Orr-Patterson Papers, Series B, Box 7, Vol. 1; "Letter from T. J. Withers to the Meeting at Yorkville, on the 6th August," in Bryan, *A Scrapbook*, Vol. VII.

67. *Mercury*, August 14–15, 18, and 21, 1851; *Southern Standard*, August 15–16, and 22, 1851.

68. *Mercury*, August 14–15, and 27, 1851.

69. *Southern Standard*, August 7, 12, 26, and 28, 1851; *Mercury*, August 7, 20, and 27, 1851; Daniel Wallace to W. B. Wilson et al., July 29, 1851, Pickens and Bonham Papers; Hamer, *Secession Movement in South Carolina*, p. 114.

70. *Mercury*, September 10, 1851.

71. *Southern Standard*, July 4, August 16, 1851; Stephenson, "Southern Nationalism in South Carolina," p. 333.

72. *Southern Standard*, July 21, 30, and 31, 1851; Phillips, *Correspondence of Toombs, Stephens, and Cobb*, p. 238.

73. Oscar to Matilda Lieber, July 16, 1851, Lieber Papers (SCL); *Southern Standard*, July 4, 1851. See also John J. Walker to Thomas Corwin, June 4, 1851, Corwin Papers.

74. Denman, *Secession Movement in Alabama*, pp. 58–60; Craven, *Growth of Southern Nationalism*, p. 106; *Southern Standard*, August 18, 1851.

75. McCardell, "Quitman and the Compromise of 1850," pp. 254–56; *Southern Standard*, July 2, 4, and 15, 1851; Nevins, *Ordeal of the Union*, 1:372–73.

76. Quitman to Seabrook, June 26, 1851, and Seabrook to Quitman, July 15, 1851, Seabrook Papers.

77. McCardell, "Quitman and the Compromise of 1850," pp. 257–59, 261, 263; *Southern Standard*, August 14, 1851.

78. See above, p. 140.

79. Boucher, "Secession and Co-operation Movements," pp. 126–27; Hamer, *Secession Movement in South Carolina*, pp. 120–21; *Mercury*, September 9, 1851.

80. *Southern Standard*, September 8, 25, and October 10, 1851; *Mercury*, September 10, 18, 27 and October 8, 1851.

The cooperationist nominees for the Southern Congress were: T. N. Dawkins, Samuel Rainey (First District); James L. Orr, James H. Irby (Second District); John S. Preston, James Chesnut, Jr. (Third District); C. W. Dudley, J. P. Zimmerman (Fourth District); J. L. Wardlaw, Preston S. Brooks (Fifth District); William Aiken, W. D. Porter (Sixth District); Angus Patterson, A. J. Lawton (Seventh District). Preston Brooks withdrew and was replaced by Henry Summer.

The secessionist nominees were: Daniel Wallace, T. O. P. Vernon (First District); H. C. Young, R. F. Simpson (Second District); William A. Owens, Dixon Barnes (Third District); J. D. Wilson, A. W. Dozier (Fourth District); F. W. Pickens, D. Nance (Fifth District); John S. Ashe, John S. Palmer (Sixth District); R. B. Rhett, J. G. W. Duncan (Seventh District).

81. Barnwell to Orr, August 26, 1851, Orr-Patterson Papers; *Mercury*, September 19 and 30, 1851; *Southern Patriot*, September 26, 1851; Kibler, *Benjamin F. Perry*, p. 271. Perry's Unionist followers asked him to become a candidate, but he declined "in order to produce no division in the anti-secession ranks" (ibid.).

82. *Southern Standard*, September 1 to October 10, 1851, passim; "Proceedings of the Southern Co-operation and Anti-Secession Meeting in Charleston, September 23, 1851," in Bryan, *A Scrapbook*, Vol. VII. Memminger's speech constituted an exception to the general tone of the cooperationist campaign during this period; he stressed the willingness of the cooperationists to resist the federal government as well as the follies of resistance by separate secession ("Speech of Mr. Memminger in Charleston, September 23, 1851," in Bryan, *A Scrapbook*, Vol. VII).

83. *Southern Standard*, October 7, 8, 13, and September 11, 1851; *Mercury*, October 8, 1851; W. A. Owens to Hammond, September 3, 1851, Hammond Papers (LC). See map of South Carolina's congressional districts.

84. *Southern Patriot*, September 26, 1851; *Mercury*, September 20, 1851; *Southern Standard*, September 11, 15, 19, 25, 12, October 8, and 14, 1851.

85. Hammond Diary, September 7, 1851 (SCL); "Speech of Winchester Graham, Sept. 5th, 1851," in Bryan, *A Scrapbook*, Vol. VII; *Southern Standard*, September 25 and 27, 1851; Orr to John T. Moore, S. Mayrant, John N. Fierson, Committee (for Sumter District cooperationist rally on October 6), September 29, 1851, Orr-Patterson Papers, Series B, Box 7, Vol. 1.

86. *Southern Standard*, September 5, 1851.

87. Ibid. In fact Quitman wrote Seabrook after that date.

88. *Southern Standard*, September 5 and 15, 1851.

89. Shryock, *Georgia and the Union*, p. 354; *Mercury*, September 23, 25, and October 8, 1851; *Southern Standard*, October 9, 1851; Hammond to Simms, October 11, 1851, Hammond Papers (LC).

90. *Southern Standard*, August 26 and September 1, 1851; *Mercury*, September 4, 18–20, 25, and October 9–10, 1851. Seabrook was unable to campaign for the secessionists after September 20 when he was injured in a carriage accident (*Mercury*, October 4, 1851).

91. *Southern Standard*, September 5–6, 12, and 15–16, 1851; *Mercury*, September 25, 1851; William Elliott to his wife, October 1, 1851, Elliott-Gonzales Papers; White, *Robert Barnwell Rhett*, p. 123. Rhett may have had plans to repair his financial situation as well as his health in England. In April, 1851, Rhett wrote to his son,

"My crop is short, the third in succession, and my debts heavy" (R. B. to R. B. Rhett, Jr., April 13, 1851, Rhett Papers [SCL]; see also Perritt, "Rhett: Disunionist Heir," p. 48).

92. *Southern Standard*, September 10, October 11, 1851; *Southern Patriot*, September 26, 1851.

93. *Southern Standard*, October 13–14, 1851; *Mercury*, October 13, 1851.

94. *Mercury*, October 15, 1851; Hamer, *Secession Movement in South Carolina*, p. 123.

95. See Appendix, Table 4.

96. See Appendix, Table 3 (1850) and Table 4.

97. These figures are taken from the *Mercury*, December 2, 1851, and are corrected for arithmetic errors. The totals printed in South Carolina's newspapers and quoted by Hamer, *Secession Movement in South Carolina* and other secondary sources are 25,045 to 17,710.

98. Jones to Hammond, October 26, 1851, Hammond Papers (LC); Hamer, *Secession Movement in South Carolina*, pp. 127–28. See also the "Preamble and Resolutions of the St. Helena Southern Rights Association, October 24, 1851," published in the *Mercury*, October 29, 1851.

99. Cunningham to Hammond, November 10, 1851, Hammond Papers (LC).

100. Jones to Hammond, November 16, 1851, Cunningham to Hammond, November 10, 1851, and Gregg to Hammond, November 14, 1851, Hammond Papers (LC); Hammond Diary, November 18, 21, and 30, 1851 (SCL).

101. *Southern Patriot*, October 23, December 4, 1851; Kibler, *Benjamin F. Perry*, p. 273; Hamer, *Secession Movement in South Carolina*, p. 133; Hayne to Hammond, November 9, 1851, Hammond Papers (LC); *Southern Standard*, November 11, 1851.

102. Hamer, *Secession Movement in South Carolina*, pp. 133–34; Aldrich to Hammond, November 10 and 11, 1851, Hammond Papers (LC).

103. Aldrich to Hammond, November 26 and 28, 1851, Hammond Papers (LC); see also *Southern Standard*, December 1, 1851.

104. Aldrich to Hammond, November 28, 1851, Hammond Papers (LC); *Mercury*, December 2, 1851; *Daily South Carolinian*, December 3, 1851.

105. "Address, on occasion of the Caucus of Members of the Legislature of So Ca held at Carolina Hall Columbia 28th Novr 1851," Allston Papers (SCHS); Robert F. W. to Adele P. Allston, November 29, 1851, in Easterby, *South Carolina Rice Plantation*, p. 109.

106. "Address, on occasion of the Caucus of Members of the Legislature of So Ca held at Carolina Hall Columbia 28th Novr 1851," Allston Papers (SCHS); *Journal of the South Carolina Senate, 1851*, pp. 18, 20, and 73; *Journal of the South Carolina House, 1851*, pp. 119–20; *Mercury*, December 8 and 10, 1851; Aldrich to Hammond, December 9, 1851, Hammond Papers (LC).

107. White, *Robert Barnwell Rhett*, pp. 124–27.

108. Perritt, "Rhett: Disunionist Heir," pp. 52–53; *Congressional Globe*, 32nd Cong., 1st sess., p. 655; R. B. to R. B. Rhett, Jr., February 27 and 29, 1852, Rhett Papers (SCL); "Correspondence of the Southern Standard, Washington, March 1, 1852" (clipping in Orr-Patterson Papers, Series B, Box 7, Vol. 1); Hammond Diary, January 8 and March 24, 1852 (SCL).

109. Aldrich to Hammond, December 9, 1851, and April 20, 1852, Gregg to Hammond, March 29 and April 14, 1852, Hammond Papers (LC); Hammond Diary, April 24, 1852 (SCL).

110. John B. to Meta M. Grimball, April 27, 1852, Grimball Papers.

111. *Journal of the State Convention of South Carolina; together with the Resolution and Ordinance*, pp. 9, 14; Capers, *Life of Memminger*, p. 225; Schultz, *Sectionalism and Nationalism*, p. 38.

112. Aldrich to Hammond, April 28 and May 3, 1852, Hammond Papers (LC); White, *Robert Barnwell Rhett*, pp. 130–31.

113. Aldrich to Hammond, May 3, 1852, Hammond Papers (LC); Huff, *Langdon Cheves*, p. 235. Perry offered a minority report as did Gregg (Kibler, *Benjamin F. Perry*, pp. 274–76).

114. *Journal of the State Convention of South Carolina; together with the Resolution and Ordinance*, pp. 18–19.

115. White, *Robert Barnwell Rhett*, pp. 130–31. As early as November 1851, Robert Barnwell had broached the idea of allowing the legislature to enact secession by a two-thirds majority of each house. At the state convention, he stipulated that he would favor this proposal only if amended to require a two-thirds majority in each house for two consecutive years (Aldrich to Hammond, April 28, 1852, Hammond Papers [LC]).

116. *Journal of the State Convention of South Carolina; together with the Resolution and Ordinance*, pp. 17–19. After the failure of all secessionist proposals "and upon the rising of the Convention," Rhett resigned from the Senate (Aldrich to Hammond, May 3, 1852, Hammond Papers [LC]; White, *Robert Barnwell Rhett*, pp. 131–33).

117. Gregg to Hammond, March 29, 1852, Hammond Papers (LC); Hammond Diary, December 6, 1851 (SCL).

118. Seabrook to John A. Leland, September 21, 1850, Seabrook Papers; Jones to Hammond, April 5, 1851, Hammond Papers (LC).

119. *Separate State Secession Practically Discussed*, as quoted in Franklin, *Militant South*, p. 227. See also Edward Bryan, "The Disunionist; or, Secession, the Rightful Remedy," in Bryan, *A Scrapbook*, Vol. IV.

120. Gregg to Hammond, November 14, 1851, and March 29, 1851, Hammond Papers (LC).

121. *Mercury*, September 9, June 10, 1851; Jones to Hammond, April 5, 1851, Hammond Papers (LC).

122. "Remarks of R. W. Barnwell," in Bryan, *A Scrapbook*, Vol. VII.

123. Channing, *Crisis of Fear*, p. 146.

124. *Southern Standard*, July 14, 1851.

125. Channing, *Crisis of Fear*, p. 146.

126. *Southern Standard*, July 2, October 6, 14, 1851.

127. See: Kibler, *Benjamin F. Perry*, pp. 219–20, 266–67, 275, 288–90; Channing, *Crisis of Fear*, p. 182; Jones, "Carolinians and Cubans," pp. 13–14.

128. This series of letters was originally published in the Charleston *Courier* during the summer of 1851 (Jarrett, "Grayson's *The Hireling and the Slave*," pp. 19–20).

129. Grayson, "Letter to His Excellency Whitemarsh B. Seabrook," in Bryan, *A Scrapbook*, Vol. IV; *Southern Standard*, July 18, 1851; "Speech of B. F. Perry, At the Anti-Secession Meeting, at Cashville, 20th September 1851," Perry Scrapbook (No. 1).

130. *Southern Standard*, July 18, 1851; "Speech of B. F. Perry, At the Anti-Secession Meeting, at Cashville, 20th September 1851," Perry Scrapbook (No. 1).

BIBLIOGRAPHY

MANUSCRIPTS

Manuscript Department, Duke University Library, Durham, North Carolina
 Eleanor J. W. Baker Journal
 Armistead Burt Papers
 Robert N. Gourdin Papers
 James Henry Hammond Letters
 Hemphill Family Papers
 George Frederick Holmes Papers
 Alfred Huger Letterpress Books
 Whitefoord Smith Papers
 Alexander H. Stephens Papers
 Abraham W. Venable Scrapbook
Manuscripts Division, Library of Congress
 Thomas Corwin Papers
 Franklin Harper Elmore Papers
 James Henry Hammond Papers
 Francis Lieber Papers
 James Louis Petigru Letters
 Francis W. Pickens and Milledge L. Bonham Papers
 Whitemarsh Benjamin Seabrook Papers
 Waddy Thompson Papers
 William Henry Trescot Papers
South Carolina Department of Archives and History, Columbia
 United States Relations File, Governor Whitemarsh B. Seabrook
South Carolina Historical Society, Charleston
 Allston-Pringle-Hill Papers
 Robert F. W. Allston Papers
 Cheves Papers—West Collection
 Robert Barnwell Rhett Collection
South Caroliniana Library, University of South Carolina, Columbia
 Robert F. W. Allston Papers
 Milledge Luke Bonham Papers
 James Chesnut, Jr. Papers
 William John Grayson Autobiography (Typescript)
 Maxcy Gregg Papers
 James Henry Hammond Diary
 James Henry Hammond Papers
 John Jenkins Papers
 Hugh Swinton Legare Papers
 Francis Lieber Papers
 McCrady Family Papers
 James Lawrence Orr Papers
 James Louis Petigru Papers

238 Bibliography

Francis Wilkinson Pickens Papers
William Campbell Preston Papers
Robert Barnwell Rhett Papers
James Henley Thornwell Papers
Southern Historical Collection, University of North Carolina, Chapel Hill
Samuel A. Agnew Diary
David Wyatt Aiken Autobiography (Typescript)
Allston-Pringle-Hill Papers (Microfilm)
John Hamilton Cornish Diary (Typescript)
John Hamilton Cornish Papers
Elliott-Gonzales Papers
Franklin Harper Elmore Papers
John Berkley Grimball Diary
Grimball Papers
James Hamilton Papers
James Henry Hammond Letters
Alexander Robert Lawton Papers
William Porcher Miles Papers
Orr-Patterson Papers
David Outlaw Papers
Benjamin Franklin Perry Diary
Benjamin Franklin Perry Papers
Benjamin Franklin Perry Scrapbooks
Pettigrew Family Papers
Robert Barnwell Rhett Papers
Edmund Ruffin Papers (Microfilm)
Waddy Thompson Papers
Benjamin C. Yancey Papers

OFFICIAL DOCUMENTS

Acts of the General Assembly of . . . South Carolina . . . 1848. Printed . . . in Conformity with the Statutes at Large. . . . Columbia, S.C.: I. C. Morgan, State Printer, 1848.

Acts of the General Assembly of . . . South Carolina . . . 1849. Printed . . . in Conformity with the Statutes at Large. . . . Columbia, S.C.: I.C. Morgan, State Printer, 1849.

Acts of the General Assembly of . . . South Carolina . . . 1850. Printed . . . in Conformity with the Statutes at Large. . . . Columbia, S.C.: I. C. Morgan, State Printer, 1850.

Acts of the General Assembly of . . . South Carolina . . . 1851. Printed . . . in Conformity with the Statutes at Large. . . . Columbia, S.C.: I. C. Morgan, State Printer, 1851.

Appendix to the Congressional Globe. Thirty-first Congress, First Session. Washington: John C. Rives, 1850.

Appendix to the Congressional Globe. Thirty-first Congress, Second Session. Washington: John C. Rives, 1851.

Congressional Globe. Thirtieth Congress, Second Session. Washington: Blair and Rives, 1849.

Congressional Globe. Thirty-first Congress, First Session. Washington: John C. Rives, 1850.

Congressional Globe. Thirty-first Congress, Second Session. Washington: John C. Rives, 1851.

Congressional Globe. Thirty-second Congress, First Session. Washington: John C. Rives, 1852.

Federal Censuses. First through Eighth. [Titles and Printers Vary]

Journals of the Conventions of the People of South Carolina, held in 1832, 1833 and 1852. Republished by order of the General Assembly. Columbia, S.C.: R. W. Gibbes, State Printer, 1860.

Journal of the House of Representatives of the State of South Carolina, being the Extra Session of 1848. Columbia, S.C.: A. G. Summer, State Printer, 1848.

Journal of the House of Representatives of . . . South Carolina . . . 1848. Columbia, S.C.: I. C. Morgan, State Printer, 1848.

Journal of the House of Representatives of . . . South Carolina . . . 1849. Columbia, S.C.: I. C. Morgan, State Printer, 1849.

Journal of the House of Representatives of . . . South Carolina . . . 1850. Columbia, S.C.: I. C. Morgan, State Printer, 1850.

Journal of the House of Representatives of . . . South Carolina . . . 1851. Columbia, S.C.: I. C. Morgan, State Printer, 1851.

Journal of the Senate of . . . South Carolina . . . Extra Session, Nov. 6, 1848, and Regular Session, Nov. 27, 1848. Columbia, S.C.: A. S. Johnston, Printer to the Senate, 1848.

Journal of the Senate of . . . South Carolina . . . 1849. Columbia, S.C.: A. S. Johnston, Printer to the Senate, 1849.

Journal of the Senate of . . . South Carolina . . . 1850. Columbia, S.C.: A. S. Johnston, Printer to the Senate, 1850.

Journal of the Senate of . . . South Carolina . . . 1851. Columbia, S.C.: n.p., 1851.

Journal of the State Convention of South Carolina; together with the Resolution and Ordinance. . . . Columbia, S.C.: Johnson & Cavis, 1852.

Resolutions and Address, adopted by the Southern Convention. Held at Nashville, Tennessee, June 3d to 12th, Inclusive, in the Year 1850. Published by order of the Convention. Nashville, Tenn.: Harvey M. Watterson, Printer, 1850.

South Carolina Constitution, 1790.

NEWSPAPERS

The Charleston *Courier*
The Charleston *Daily Sun*
The Charleston *Mercury*,
The *Daily South Carolinian* (Columbia, S.C.)
The Southern Patriot (Greenville, S.C.)
The Southern Standard (Charleston, S.C.)

PAMPHLETS

Bryan, Edward B., comp. *A Scrapbook, Containing the Pamphlets of the Day for 1850, 1851 and 1852. . . .* 10 vols. Charleston, S.C.: n.p., 1850–52.

Cheves, Langdon. *Speech of the Hon. Langdon Cheves, Delivered before the Delegates of the Nashville Convention, on Friday, November 15, 1850. Printed by Order of the House of Representatives.* Columbia, S.C.: I. C. Morgan, State Printer, 1850.

Elliott, William. *The Letters of Agricola, by Hon. Wm. Elliott, Published in the Southern Standard, June [1851].* Greenville, S.C.: Office of the Southern Patriot, 1852.

[Garnett, Muscoe Russell Hunter.] *The Union, Past and Future: How It Works, and How to Save It, by a Citizen of Virginia.* Charleston, S.C.: Walker and James, 1851.

PUBLISHED SOURCES AND MISCELLANEOUS WRITINGS

Ambler, Charles H., ed. *Correspondence of Robert M. T. Hunter, 1826–1876.* Annual Report of the American Historical Association, 1916. Washington: Government Printing Office, 1918.

Barnwell, John, ed. "Hamlet to Hotspur: Letters of Robert Woodward Barnwell to Robert Barnwell Rhett." *South Carolina Historical Magazine* 77 (October 1976): 236–56.

Boucher, Chauncey S., and Brooks, Robert P., eds. *Correspondence Addressed to John C. Calhoun, 1837–1849.* Annual Report of the American Historical Association, 1929. Washington: Government Printing Office, 1930.

Calhoun, John C. *The Works of John C. Calhoun.* Edited by Richard K. Cralle. Vol. 1: *A Disquisition on Government and a Discourse on the Constitution and Government of the United States.* Charleston, S.C.: Walker and James, 1851.

———. *The Works of John C. Calhoun.* Edited by Richard K. Cralle. Vol. 4: *Speeches of John C. Calhoun, Delivered in the House of Representatives, and in the Senate of the United States.* New York: D. Appleton and Co., 1854.

———. *The Works of John C. Calhoun.* Edited by Richard K. Cralle. Vol. 6: *Reports and Public Letters.* New York: D. Appleton and Co., 1855.

Carson, James P. *Life, Letters, and Speeches of James Louis Petigru.* Introduction by Gaillard Hunt. Washington: W. H. Lowdermilk & Co., 1920.

De Bow, J. D. B. *Statistical View of the United States . . . Being a Compendium of the Seventh Census, to Which Are Added the Results of Every Previous Census, Beginning with 1790, in Comparative Tables. . . .* Washington: Beverly Tucker, Senate Printer, 1854.

Easterby, J. H., ed. *The South Carolina Rice Plantation, as Revealed in the Papers of Robert F. W. Allston.* Chicago: University of Chicago Press, 1945.

Foote, Henry S. *Casket of Reminiscences.* Washington: Chronicle Publishing Co., 1874.

Harper, [William], et al. *The Pro-Slavery Argument: As Maintained by the Most Distinguished Writers of the Southern States, Containing the Several Essays on the Subject, of Chancellor Harper, Governor Hammond, Dr. Simms, and Professor Dew.* Charleston, S.C.: Walker, Richards & Co., 1852.

Jameson, J. Franklin, ed. *Correspondence of John C. Calhoun.* Annual Report of the American Historical Association, 1899. Washington: Government Printing Office, 1900.

Perry, Thomas S., ed. *The Life and Letters of Francis Lieber.* Boston: James R. Osgood and Co., 1882.

Phillips, U. B., ed. *The Correspondence of Robert Toombs, Alexander H. Stephens, and Howell Cobb.* Vol. 2 of the Annual Report of the American Historical Association, 1911. Washington: Government Printing Office, 1913.

Polk, James K. *Polk: The Diary of a President.* Edited by Allan Nevins. New York: Longmans, Green, and Co., 1929.

Simms, William Gilmore. *The Letters of William Gilmore Simms.* Edited by Mary C. Simms Oliphant, Alfred Taylor Odell, and T. C. Duncan Eaves. With an Introduction by Donald Davidson. 5 vols. Columbia, S.C.: University of South Carolina Press, 1952–56.

———. *The Yemassee.* Edited with an Introduction by C. Hugh Holman. Boston: Houghton Mifflin, 1961.

Stoney, Samuel G., ed. "The Autobiography of William J. Grayson," *South Carolina Historical Magazine* 50 (1949).

Weaver, Herbert, and Bergeron, Paul H., eds. *Correspondence of James K. Polk.* Nashville: Vanderbilt University Press, 1969–.

BOOKS

Alexander, Thomas B. *Sectional Stress and Party Strength: A Study of Roll-Call Voting Patterns in the United States House of Representatives, 1836–1860.* Nashville: Vanderbilt University Press, 1967.

Andrews, Columbus. *Administrative County Government in South Carolina.* Chapel Hill, N.C.: University of North Carolina Press, 1933.

Bailyn, Bernard. *The Ideological Origins of the American Revolution.* Cambridge: Harvard University Press, Belknap Press, 1967.

———. *The Origins of American Politics.* New York: Alfred A. Knopf, 1968; Random House, Vintage Books, 1970.

Banner, James M. "The Problem of South Carolina." In *The Hofstadter Aegis: A Memorial,* pp. 60–93. Edited by Stanley Elkins and Eric McKitrick. New York: Alfred A. Knopf, 1974.

Barney, William L. *The Road to Secession.* Foreword by James P. Shenton. New York: Praeger Publishers, 1972.

Bennett, J. Harry, Jr. *Bondsmen and Bishops: Slavery and Apprenticeship on the Codrington Plantations of Barbados, 1710–1838.* Berkeley: University of California Press, 1958.

Berlin, Ira. *Slaves Without Masters: The Free Negro in the Antebellum South.* New York: Random House, Pantheon Books, 1974.

Bestor, Arthur. *The American Civil War as a Constitutional Crisis.* 1964. Reprint. Indianapolis: Bobbs-Merrill Reprint Series in American History, 1964.

Blaine, James G. *Twenty Years of Congress.* 2 vols. Norwich, Conn.: Henry Bill Publishing Co., 1884–93.

Blue, Frederick J. *The Free Soilers: Third Party Politics, 1848–1854.* Urbana, Ill.: University of Illinois Press, 1973.

Boucher, Chauncey S. *The Nullification Controversy in South Carolina.* Chicago: University of Chicago Press, 1916.

Bridenbaugh, Carl. *Myths and Realities: Societies of the Colonial South.* Baton Rouge, La.: Louisiana State University Press, 1952; reprint ed., New York: Atheneum, 1963.

Capers, Henry D. *The Life and Times of C. G. Memminger.* Richmond, Va.: Everett

Waddey Co., 1893.

Carpenter, Jesse T. *The South as a Conscious Minority, 1789–1861*. New York: New York University Press, 1930.

Channing, Steven A. *Crisis of Fear: Secession in South Carolina*. New York: Simon and Schuster, 1970.

Chesnut, Mary Boykin. *A Diary from Dixie*. New York: D. Appleton and Co., 1905.

Coit, Margaret L. *John C. Calhoun: American Portrait*. Boston: Houghton Mifflin Co., 1950; Sentry Edition, n.d.

Craven, Avery O. *The Growth of Southern Nationalism, 1848–1861*. Vol. 6 of *A History of the South*. Edited by Wendell H. Stephenson and E. Merton Coulter. Baton Rouge, La.: Louisiana State University Press, 1953.

Curtin, Philip D. *The Atlantic Slave Trade: A Census*. Madison, Wis.: University of Wisconsin Press, 1969.

Davis, David B. *The Slave Power Conspiracy and the Paranoid Style*. Baton Rouge, La.: Louisiana State University Press, 1969.

Degler, Carl N. *Neither Black Nor White: Slavery and Race Relations in Brazil and the United States*. New York: Macmillan Co., 1971.

Denman, Clarence P. *The Secession Movement in Alabama*. Montgomery, Ala.: Alabama State Department of Archives and History, 1933.

Douglass, Elisha P. *Rebels and Democrats*. Chapel Hill, N.C.: University of North Carolina Press, 1955.

Eaton, Clement. *The Mind of the Old South*. Rev. ed. Baton Rouge, La.: Louisiana State University Press, 1967.

Edgar, Walter B., ed. *Biographical Directory of the South Carolina House of Representatives*. Vol. 1: *Session Lists*, 1692 to 1973. Columbia, S.C.: University of South Carolina Press, 1974.

Farley, Reynolds S. *Growth of the Black Population: A Study of Demographic Trends*. Chicago: Markham Publishing Co., 1970.

Foner, Philip S. *History of Black Americans*. Westport, Conn.: Greenwood Press, 1975.

Franklin, John Hope. *The Militant South, 1800–1861*. Cambridge: Harvard University Press, Belknap Press, 1956.

Freehling, William W. *Prelude to Civil War: The Nullification Controversy in South Carolina, 1816–1836*. New York: Harper & Row, 1965, 1966.

Freidel, Frank. *Francis Lieber: Nineteenth Century Liberal*. Baton Rouge, La.: Louisiana State University Press, 1947.

Fuller, John D. P. *The Movement for the Acquisition of All Mexico*. Baltimore: Johns Hopkins Press, 1936.

Genovese, Eugene D. *Roll, Jordan, Roll: The World the Slaves Made*. New York: Random House, Pantheon Books, 1974.

Going, Charles B. *David Wilmot, Free-Soiler*. New York: D. Appleton and Co., 1924.

Green, Fletcher M. *Constitutional Development in the South Atlantic States, 1776–1860*. Chapel Hill, N.C.: University of North Carolina Press, 1930.

Hamer, Philip M. *The Secession Movement in South Carolina, 1847–1852*. Allentown, Pa.: H. Ray Haas and Co., 1918.

Hamilton, Holman. *Prologue to Conflict: The Crisis and Compromise of 1850*. Lexington, Ky.: University of Kentucky Press, 1964; reprint ed., New York: Norton Library, 1966.

————. *Zachary Taylor: Soldier in the White House*. Indianapolis, Ind.: Bobbs-Merrill Co., 1951.

Hearon, Cleo. *Mississippi and the Compromise of 1850*. Vol. 14 of the Publications of

the Mississippi Historical Society. University, Miss.: printed for the Society,
1914.

Henry, H[owell] M. *The Police Control of the Slave in South Carolina*. Emory, Va.: n.p.,
1914.

Hofstadter, Richard. *The Idea of a Party System: The Rise of Legitimate Opposition in
the United States, 1780–1840*. Berkeley, Calif.: University of California Press,
1969.

Holt, Michael F. *The Political Crisis of the 1850s*. New York: John Wiley & Sons,
1978.

Huff, Archie V., Jr. *Langdon Cheves of South Carolina*. Columbia, S.C.: University of
South Carolina Press, for the South Carolina Tricentennial Commission, 1977.

Jordan, Winthrop D. *White Over Black: American Attitudes Toward the Negro,
1550–1812*. Chapel Hill, N.C.: University of North Carolina Press for the
Institute of Early American History and Culture, 1968.

Kibler, Lillian A. *Benjamin F. Perry: South Carolina Unionist*. Durham, N.C.: Duke
University Press, 1946.

King, William L. *The Newspaper Press of Charleston, South Carolina*. Charleston,
S.C.: Edward Perry Book Press, 1872.

Lander, Ernest M., Jr. *Reluctant Imperialists: Calhoun, the South Carolinians, and
the Mexican War*. Baton Rouge: Louisiana State University Press, 1980.

Lofton, John. *Insurrection in South Carolina: The Turbulent World of Denmark Vesey*.
Yellow Springs, Ohio: Antioch Press, 1964.

McCormick, Richard P. *The Second American Party System: Party Formation in the
Jacksonian Era*. Chapel Hill, N.C.: University of North Carolina Press, 1966.

Meriwether, Robert L. *The Expansion of South Carolina, 1729–1765*. Kingsport,
Tenn.: Southern Publishers, 1940.

Merk, Frederick. *Slavery and the Annexation of Texas*. New York: Alfred A. Knopf,
1972.

Merritt, Elizabeth. *James Henry Hammond, 1807–1864*. Baltimore: The Johns Hopkins Press, 1923.

Miles, Edwin A. *Jacksonian Democracy in Mississippi*. Chapel Hill: University of
North Carolina Press, 1960.

Morison, Samuel Eliot; Merk, Frederick; and Freidel, Frank. *Dissent in Three American Wars*. Cambridge: Harvard University Press, 1970.

Morrison, Chaplin W. *Democratic Politics and Sectionalism: The Wilmot Proviso
Controversy*. Chapel Hill, N.C.: University of North Carolina Press, 1967.

Murray, Paul. *The Whig Party in Georgia, 1825–1853*. The James Sprunt Studies in
History and Political Science, no. 29. Chapel Hill: University of North Carolina
Press, 1948.

Nagel, Paul C. *One Nation Indivisible: The Union in American Thought, 1776–1861*.
New York: Oxford University Press, 1964.

Nevins, Allan. *The Constitution, Slavery, and the Territories*. 1953. Reprint. Indianapolis: Bobbs-Merrill Reprint Series in American History, n.d.

———. *Ordeal of the Union*. Vol. 1: *Fruits of Manifest Destiny, 1847–1852*. New York:
Charles Scribner's Sons, 1947.

Palmer, B[enjamin] M. *The Life and Letters of James Henley Thornwell*. Richmond,
Va.: Whittet & Shepperson, 1875.

Palmer, R. R. *The Age of the Democratic Revolution: A Political History of Europe and
America, 1760–1800*. Vol. 1: *The Challenge*. Princeton: Princeton University
Press, 1959.

Peterson, Merrill D., ed. *Democracy, Liberty, and Property: The State Constitutional Conventions of the 1820s.* Indianapolis, Ind.: Bobbs-Merrill Co., 1966.

Phillips, Ulrich B. *American Negro Slavery.* Foreword by Eugene D. Genovese. New York: D. Appleton and Co., 1918; reprint ed., Baton Rouge, La.: Louisiana State University Press, 1966.

Pope, Thomas H. *The History of Newberry County, South Carolina.* Vol. 1: *1749–1860.* Reprint. Columbia: University of South Carolina Press, 1973.

Potter, David M. *The Impending Crisis, 1848–1861.* Completed and edited by Don E. Fehrenbacher. New York: Harper & Row, 1976.

Potter, J. "The Growth of Population in America, 1700–1860." In *Population in History, Essays in Historical Demography.* Edited by D. V. Glass and D. E. C. Eversley. London: Edward Arnold, 1965.

Ranck, James B. *Albert Gallatin Brown: Radical Southern Nationalist.* New York: D. Appleton-Century Co., 1937.

Rayback, Joseph G. *Free Soil: The Election of 1848.* Lexington, Ky.: University Press of Kentucky, 1970.

Rayback, Robert J. *Millard Fillmore: Biography of a President.* Buffalo: Buffalo Historical Society, 1959.

Rendtorff, Robert C. *Fundamentals of Malaria: A Self-Instructional Program.* Chapel Hill, N.C.: Health Sciences Consortium, 1974, 1976.

Reynolds, Emily B., and Faunt, Joan R. *The Senate of the State of South Carolina, 1776–1962.* Columbia, S.C.: Senate of . . . South Carolina, 1962.

Rippy, J. Fred. *Joel R. Poinsett, Versatile American.* Durham, N.C.: Duke University Press, 1935.

Rogers, George C., Jr. *Charleston in the Age of the Pinckneys.* Norman, Okla.: University of Oklahoma Press, 1969.

————. *The History of Georgetown County, South Carolina.* Columbia, S.C.: University of South Carolina Press, 1970.

Scarborough, William K. *The Overseer: Plantation Management in the Old South.* Baton Rouge, La.: Louisiana State University Press, 1966.

Schaper, William A. *Sectionalism and Representation in South Carolina.* Foreword by E. M. Lander, Jr. Washington: Government Printing Office, 1901; reprint ed., New York: Da Capo Press, 1968.

Schultz, Harold S. *Nationalism and Sectionalism in South Carolina, 1852–1860.* Durham, N.C.: Duke University Press, 1950.

Shryock, Richard H. *Georgia and the Union in 1850.* Durham, N.C.: Duke University Press, 1926.

Sirmans, M. Eugene. "The Legal Status of the Slave in South Carolina, 1670–1740." In *Colonial America: Essays in Politics and Social Development,* pp. 405–15. Edited by Stanley N. Katz. Boston: Little, Brown and Co., 1971.

Smith, Alfred G., Jr. *Economic Readjustment of an Old Cotton State: South Carolina, 1820–1860.* Columbia, S.C.: University of South Carolina Press, 1958.

Spain, August O. *The Political Theory of John C. Calhoun.* New York: Bookman Associates, 1951.

Stampp, Kenneth M. *The Peculiar Institution.* New York: Random House, Vintage Books, 1956.

Sydnor, Charles S. *The Development of Southern Sectionalism, 1819–1848.* Vol. 5 of *A History of the South.* Edited by Wendell H. Stephenson and E. Merton Coulter. Baton Rouge, La.: Louisiana State University Press, 1948.

_____. *Gentlemen Freeholders*. Chapel Hill: University of North Carolina Press for the Institute of Early American History and Culture, 1952.

Thorpe, Earl E. *Eros and Freedom in Southern Life and Thought*. Durham, N.C.: Seeman Printery for E. Endris Thorpe, 1967.

United States Bureau of the Census. *Historical Statistics of the United States, Colonial Times to 1970*. 2 Parts. Washington: Government Printing Office, 1975.

_____. *Negro Population of the United States, 1790–1915*. Washington: Government Printing Office, 1918.

Wade, Richard C. *Slavery in the Cities: The South, 1820–1860*. New York: Oxford University Press, 1964.

Wakelyn, Jon L. *The Politics of a Literary Man: William Gilmore Simms*. Contributions in American Studies. Westport, Conn.: Greenwood Press, 1973.

Wallace, David D. *South Carolina: A Short History, 1520–1948*. Chapel Hill, N.C.: University of North Carolina Press, 1951.

Weinberg, Albert K. *Manifest Destiny: A Study of Nationalist Expansionism in American History*. Baltimore, Md.: The Johns Hopkins Press, 1935; Quadrangle Paperback, 1963.

White, Laura A. *Robert Barnwell Rhett: Father of Secession*. New York: Century Co. for the American Historical Association, 1931.

White, Leonard D. *The Jacksonians: A Study in Administrative History, 1829–1861*. New York: Macmillan Co., 1954.

Williams, Jack K. *Vogues in Villainy: Crime and Retribution in Antebellum South Carolina*. Columbia, S.C.: University of South Carolina Press, 1959.

Williamson, Chilton. *American Suffrage: From Property to Democracy, 1760–1860*. Princeton, N.J.: Princeton University Press, 1960.

Wiltse, Charles M. *John C. Calhoun, Nullifier, 1829–1839*. Indianapolis, Ind.: Bobbs-Merrill Co., 1949.

_____. *John C. Calhoun, Sectionalist, 1840–1850*. Indianapolis, Ind.: Bobbs-Merrill Co., 1951.

Wood, Gordon S. *The Creation of the American Republic, 1776–1787*. Chapel Hill: University of North Carolina Press for the Institute of Early American History and Culture, 1969.

Wood, Peter H. *Black Majority: Negroes in Colonial South Carolina from 1670 through the Stono Rebellion*. New York: Alfred A. Knopf, 1974.

Wooster, Ralph A. *The People in Power: Courthouse and Statehouse in the Lower South, 1850–1860*. Knoxville, Tenn.: University of Tennessee Press, 1969.

ARTICLES

Bergeron, Paul H. "Tennessee's Response to the Nullification Crisis." *Journal of Southern History* 39 (February 1973): 23–44.

Bestor, Arthur. "State Sovereignty and Slavery, A Reinterpretation of Proslavery Constitutional Doctrine." *Journal of the Illinois State Historical Society* 59 (Summer 1961): 117–80.

Boucher, Chauncey S. "The Secession and Co-operation Movements in South Carolina, 1848 to 1852." *Washington University Studies* 5 (April 1918): 67–129.

_____. "In Re That Aggressive Slavocracy," *Mississippi Valley Historical Review* 8 (June–September 1921): 13–79.

Brady, Patrick S. "The Slave Trade and Sectionalism in South Carolina, 1787–1808."
    Journal of Southern History 38 (November 1972): 601–20.
Broussard, Ray. "Governor John A. Quitman and the Lopez Expeditions of 1851–
    1852." *Journal of Mississippi History* 28 (May 1966): 103–20.
Buel, Richard, Jr. "Democracy and the American Revolution: A Frame of Reference."
    William and Mary Quarterly, 3rd ser., 31 (April 1964): 165–90.
Campbell, Randolph B. "Planters and Plain Folk: Harrison County, Texas, as a Test
    Case, 1850–1860." *Journal of Southern History* 40 (August 1974): 369–98.
Cole, Arthur C. "The South and the Right of Secession in the Early Fifties." *Missis-
    sippi Valley Historical Review* 1 (December 1914): 376–99.
Collins, Bruce. "The Ideology of the Ante-bellum Northern Democrats." *Journal of
    American Studies* 11 (April 1977): 103–21.
Counihan, Harold J. "The North Carolina Constitutional Convention of 1836: A
    Study in Jacksonian Democracy." *North Carolina Historical Review* 46 (Autumn
    1969): 335–64.
Eaton, Clement. "Class Differences in the Old South." *Virginia Quarterly Review* 33
    (Summer 1957): 357–70.
Flanigan, Daniel J. "Criminal Procedure in Slave Trials in the Ante-bellum South."
    Journal of Southern History 40 (November 1974): 537–64.
Foner, Eric. "Politics and Prejudice: The Free Soil Party and the Negro, 1849–1852."
    Journal of Negro History 50 (October 1965): 239–56.
––––––. "The Wilmot Proviso Revisited." *Journal of American History* 56 (September
    1969): 262–79.
Formisano, Ronald P. "Deferential-Participant Politics: The Early Republic's Political
    Culture, 1789–1840." *American Political Science Review* 68 (June 1974):
    473–87.
Foster, Herbert D. "Webster's Seventh of March Speech and the Secession Movement,
    1850." *American Historical Review* 27 (January 1922): 245–70.
Franklin, John H. "The Southern Expansionists of 1846." *Journal of Southern History*
    25 (August 1959): 323–39.
Freehling, William W. "Spoilsmen and Interests in the Thought and Career of
    John C. Calhoun." *Journal of American History* 52 (June 1965): 25–42.
Gara, Larry. "Slavery and the Slave Power: A Crucial Distinction." *Civil War History*
    15 (March 1969): 5–18.
Green, Fletcher M. "Democracy in the Old South." *Journal of Southern History* 12
    (February 1946): 3–23.
Greenberg, Kenneth S. "Representation and the Isolation of South Carolina, 1776–
    1860." *Journal of American History* 64 (December 1977): 723–43.
––––––. "Revolutionary Ideology and the Proslavery Argument: The Abolition of
    Slavery in Antebellum South Carolina." *Journal of Southern History* 42 (August
    1976): 365–84.
Halliburton, R., Jr. "Free Black Owners of Slaves: A Reappraisal of the Woodson
    Thesis." *South Carolina Historical Magazine* 76 (July 1975): 129–42.
Hamer, Philip M. "British Consuls and the Negro Seamen Acts, 1850–1860." *Journal
    of Southern History* 1 (May 1935): 138–68.
Hamilton, Holman. " 'The Cave of the Winds' and the Compromise of 1850." *Journal
    of Southern History* 23 (August 1957): 331–53.
––––––. "Texas Bonds and Northern Profits." *Mississippi Valley Historical Review* 43
    (March 1957): 579–94.
Hart, Charles Desmond. " 'The Natural Limits of Slavery Expansion': The Mexican

Territories as a Test Case." *Mid-America* 52 (April 1970): 119–31.

Higgins, W. Robert. "The Geographical Origins of Negro Slaves in Colonial South Carolina." *South Atlantic Quarterly* 70 (Winter 1971): 34–47.

Hindus, Michael S. "Black Justice Under White Law: Criminal Prosecutions of Blacks in Antebellum South Carolina." *Journal of American History* 63 (December 1976): 575–99.

Hubbell, John T. "Three Georgia Unionists and the Compromise of 1850." *Georgia Historical Quarterly* 51 (September 1967): 307–23.

Huff, Archie V., Jr. "The Eagle and the Vulture: Changing Attitudes Toward Nationalism in Fourth of July Orations Delivered in Charleston, 1778–1860." *South Atlantic Quarterly* 73 (Winter 1974): 10–22.

January, Alan F. "The South Carolina Association: An Agency for Race Control in Antebellum Charleston." *South Carolina Historical Magazine* 78 (July 1977): 191–201.

Jones, Lewis P. "William Elliott, South Carolina Nonconformist." *Journal of Southern History* 17 (August 1951): 361–81.

Kirby, John B. "Early American Politics—The Search for Ideology: An Historiographical Analysis and Critique of the Concept of 'Deference.'" *Journal of Politics* 32 (November 1970):808–38.

Lander, Ernest M., Jr. "The Calhoun-Preston Feud, 1836–1842." *South Carolina Historical Magazine* 59 (January 1958): 24–37.

_____. "General Waddy Thompson: A Friend of Mexico During the Mexican War." *South Carolina Historical Magazine* 78 (January 1977): 32–42.

Latner, Richard B. "The Nullification Crisis and Republican Subversion." *Journal of Southern History* 43 (February 1977): 19–38.

Lowe, Richard G. and Campbell, Randolph B. "The Slave-Breeding Hypothesis: A Demographic Comment on the 'Buying' and 'Selling' States." *Journal of Southern History* 42 (August 1976): 401–12.

McCardell, John. "John A. Quitman and the Compromise of 1850 in Mississippi." *Journal of Mississippi History* 37 (August 1975): 239–66.

McCrary, Royce, ed. "The Authorship of the Georgia Platform of 1850: A Letter by Charles J. Jenkins." *Georgia Historical Quarterly* 54 (Winter 1970): 585–89.

Marshall, Lynn L. "The Strange Stillbirth of the Whig Party." *American Historical Review* 72 (January 1967): 445–68.

Miles, Edwin A. "After John Marshall's Decision: *Worcester* v. *Georgia* and the Nullification Crisis." *Journal of Southern History* 39 (November 1973): 519–44.

Miller, William L. "Slavery and the Population of the South." *Southern Economic Journal* 28 (July 1961): 46–54.

Newberry, Farrar. "The Nashville Convention and Southern Sentiment of 1850." *South Atlantic Quarterly* 11 (July 1912): 259–73.

Pease, Jane H., and William H. "Confrontation and Abolition in the 1850s." *Journal of American History* 58 (March 1972): 923–37.

Perkins, Howard C. "A Neglected Phase of the Movement for Southern Unity, 1847–1852." *Journal of Southern History* 12 (May 1946): 153–203.

Perritt, H. Hardy. "Robert Barnwell Rhett: Disunionist Heir of Calhoun, 1850–1852." *Southern Speech Journal* 24 (Fall 1958): 38–55.

Pole, J. R. "Historians and the Problem of Early American Democracy." *American Historical Review* 67 (April 1962): 626–46.

_____. "Representation and Authority in Virginia from the Revolution to Reform." *Journal of Southern History* 24 (February 1958): 16–50.

Ramsdell, Charles W. "The Natural Limits of Slavery Expansion." *Mississippi Valley Historical Review* 16 (September 1929): 151–71.

Rayback, Joseph G. "The Presidential Ambitions of John C. Calhoun, 1844–1848." *Journal of Southern History* 14 (August 1948): 331–56.

Ricards, Sherman L., and Blackburn, George M. "A Demographic History of Slavery: Georgetown County, South Carolina, 1850." *South Carolina Historical Magazine* 76 (October 1975): 215–24.

Rogers, Tommy W. "The Great Population Exodus from South Carolina, 1850–1860." *South Carolina Historical Magazine* 68 (January 1967): 14–21.

Russel, Robert R. "Constitutional Doctrines with Regard to Slavery in the Territories." *Journal of Southern History* 32 (November 1966): 466–86.

Senese, Donald J. "The Free Negro and the South Carolina Courts, 1790–1860." *South Carolina Historical Magazine* 68 (July 1967): 140–53.

Sheridan, Richard B. "Africa and the Caribbean in the Atlantic Slave Trade." *American Historical Review* 77 (February 1972): 15–35.

Silbey, Joel H. "John C. Calhoun and the Limits of Southern Congressional Unity, 1841–1850." *The Historian* 30 (November 1967): 58–71.

——. "The Southern National Democrats, 1845–1861." *Mid-America* 47 (July 1965): 176–90.

Simpson, John E. "Prelude to Compromise: Howell Cobb and the House Speakership Battle of 1849." *Georgia Historical Quarterly* 58 (Winter 1974): 389–99.

Sioussat, St. George L. "Tennessee, the Compromise of 1850, and the Nashville Convention." *Mississippi Valley Historical Review* 2 (December 1915): 315–47.

Stephenson, N. W. "Southern Nationalism in South Carolina in 1851." *American Historical Review* 36 (January 1931): 314–35.

Sydnor, Charles S. "The Southerner and the Laws." *Journal of Southern History* 6 (February 1940): 3–23.

Taylor, Rosser H. "The Gentry of Antebellum South Carolina." *North Carolina Historical Review* 17 (April 1940): 114–31.

Wade, Richard. "The Vesey Plot: A Reconsideration." *Journal of Southern History* 30 (May 1964): 143–61.

Wakelyn, Jon L. "Party Issues and Political Strategy of the Charleston Taylor Democrats of 1848." *South Carolina Historical Magazine* 73 (April 1972): 72–86.

Walters, Ronald G. "The Erotic South: Civilization and Sexuality in American Abolitionism." *American Quarterly* 25 (May 1973): 177–201.

Wax, Darold D. "Preferences for Slaves in Colonial America." *Journal of Negro History* 58 (October 1973): 371–401.

Weir, Robert M. "The South Carolinian as Extremist." *South Atlantic Quarterly* 74 (Winter 1975): 86–103.

Wilson, Major L. "The Controversy over Slavery Expansion and the Concept of the Safety Valve: Ideological Confusion in the 1850s." *Mississippi Quarterly* 24 (Spring 1971): 135–54.

——. "Ideological Fruits of Manifest Destiny: The Geopolitics of Slavery Expansion in the Crisis of 1850." *Journal of the Illinois State Historical Society* 63 (Summer 1970): 132–57.

——. "'Liberty and Union': Analysis of Three Concepts Involved in the Nullification Controversy." *Journal of Southern History* 33 (August 1967): 331–55.

——. "A Preview of Irrepressible Conflict: The Issue of Slavery During the Nullification Controversy." *Mississippi Quarterly* 19 (Fall 1966): 184–193.

PROCEEDINGS

Ames, Herman V. "John C. Calhoun and the Secession Movement of 1850." *Proceedings of the American Antiquarian Society*, n.s. 28 (Worcester, Mass: Published by the Society, 1919): 19–50.

Boucher, Chauncey S. "Representation and the Electoral Question in Ante-Bellum South Carolina." *Proceedings of the Mississippi Valley Historical Association . . . 1915–16*. Cedar Rapids, Iowa: Torch Press, 1917.

Hemphill, W. Edwin. "The Calhoun Papers Project: One Editor's Valedictory." *Proceedings of the South Carolina Historical Association, 1977*. Lancaster, S.C.: South Carolina Historical Association, 1978.

Henderson, William C. "The Slave Court System in Spartanburg County." *Proceedings of the South Carolina Historical Association, 1976*. Lancaster, S.C.: South Carolina Historical Association, 1977.

Herndon, Dallas T. "The Nashville Convention of 1850." *Transactions of the Alabama Historical Society, 1904*. Vol. 5. Montgomery, Ala.: Printed for the Society, 1906.

Tucker, Robert C. "James H. Hammond and the Southern Convention." *Proceedings of the South Carolina Historical Association, 1960*. Columbia, S.C.: South Carolina Historical Association, 1961.

DISSERTATIONS AND THESES

Barnwell, John. "Robert W. Barnwell and South Carolina Politics, 1850–1852." M.A. thesis, University of North Carolina, 1972.

Bass, Robert D. "The Autobiography of William J. Grayson." Ph.D. dissertation, University of South Carolina, 1933.

Coussons, John S. "Thirty Years with Calhoun, Rhett, and the Charleston Mercury: A Chapter in South Carolina Politics." Ph.D. dissertation, Louisiana State University, 1971.

Gardner, John C. "Winning the Lower South to the Compromise of 1850." Ph.D. dissertation, Louisiana State University, 1974.

Gettys, James W., Jr. "'To Conquer a Peace': South Carolina and the Mexican War." Ph.D. dissertation, University of South Carolina, 1974.

Jarrett, Thomas D. "William Grayson's *The Hireling and the Slave*: A Study of Ideas, Form, Reception, and Editions." Ph.D dissertation, University of Chicago, 1947.

Jennings, Thelma N. "A Reappraisal of the Nashville Convention." Ph.D. dissertation, University of Tennessee, 1968.

Jones, Lewis P. "Carolinians and Cubans: The Elliotts and Gonzales, Their Work and Their Writings." Ph.D. dissertation, University of North Carolina, 1952.

Senese, Donald Joseph. "Legal Thought in South Carolina, 1800–1860." Ph.D. dissertation, University of South Carolina, 1970.

Silver, Christopher. "Immigration and the Antebellum Southern City: Irish Working Class Mobility in Charleston, South Carolina, 1840–1860." M.A. thesis, University of North Carolina, 1975.

Tucker, Robert C. "James Henry Hammond, South Carolinian." Ph.D. dissertation, University of North Carolina, 1958.

INDEX

Abolition: South Carolina gentry's fear of, 32–33, 206 (n. 10)

Adams, James H.: campaigns for secession, 152, 173

Alabama: and elections of 1851, 175; division of secessionists in, 149; response of to passage of compromise measures, 132–33

Aldrich, Alfred P.: and cooperationist leadership, 183–84; and James H. Hammond, 183, 231 (n. 25); supports cooperation, 164; views on motives of secessionists, 231 (n. 30)

Allston, Robert F. W., 79, 102–3, 140; and Georgetown Southern Rights Association, 81; elected president of state senate, 136–37; views on secessionist defeat, 184

Ashe, John S.: campaigns for secession, 170

Barnwell, Robert W., 137; accepts interim senatorship, 100; and admission of California, 113–14, 122; and passage of compromise measures, 120; and *Southern Press*, 172; campaigns for cooperation, 171; defends Nashville Convention, 117; defends Rhett's disunionism, 117; elected delegate to Nashville Convention, 87; suggests mechanism for secession, 236 (n. 15); urges reassembly of Nashville Convention, 122; views on Texas debt and boundary bill, 119

Barnwell, William H. W., 136

Bellinger, Edmund: campaigns for secession, 152, 168

Benning, Henry L.: and Nashville Convention, 104

Boyce, W. W.: supports cooperation, 167

Brown, Albert G.: and passage of compromise measures, 133

Burt, Armistead: and Southern Convention, 78

Butler, Andrew P., 207 (n. 19); and admission of California, 113; campaigns for cooperation, 171; elected to Senate, 58; urges cooperation, 127–28

Calhoun, John C.: achieves reconciliation with Unionists, 37; and abolitionist literature, 46; and abolitionist petitions, 36; and annexation of Texas, 56; and "defensive line" policy, 59–60; and Free Soil party, 68; and John Carew, 216 (n. 12); and Southern Address, 47; and Southern Convention, 84; and Southern party, 46–47, 55, 68–69, 74; and Southern Rights Associations, 81; and Wilmot Proviso, 55, 66; apprehensive about war with Mexico, 57; death of, 97; denounces popular sovereignty, 72; formulates counter-doctrine to Wilmot Proviso, 65, 212 (n. 51); leads reconciliation with Unionists, 35; notes dangers of Mexican War, 60; opposes all-Mexico movement, 62–63; refuses to endorse Taylor or Cass, 75; responds to Clay's compromise measures, 92–93, 217 (n. 26); views on admission of California, 89; views on Howell Cobb, 89; views on Webster's Seventh of March speech, 93–94; views on Wilmot Proviso, 67, 79

California bill: and South Carolina congressional delegation, 112–13, 115, 221 (nn. 110, 111)

Campbell, John A., 212 (n. 51)

Carew, John: and Nashville Convention, 95; and support of secession by Charleston *Mercury*, 164

Carroll, William: opposes nullification, 43

Cass, Lewis: and nullification, 41; and popular sovereignty, 71; and Wilmot Proviso, 76

Catron, John: opposes nullification, 43

Chapman, Reuben: and Wilmot Proviso, 85

Charleston *Mercury*: advocates separate secession, 143; and incident at Fort Sumter, 173. *See also* Carew, John

Chesnut, James, 137, 140

Cheves, Langdon: addresses reassembled Nashville Convention, 135; and May 1851 convention of Southern Rights Associations, 155–56; and nullification, 43–44; and South Carolina state convention, 186; declines interim senatorship, 99; elected delegate to Nashville Convention, 87

Clay, Henry: and Fugitive Slave Act, 147; denounces Rhett's "treason speech," 117; introduces compromise measures, 90–91; omnibus strategy of fails, 118

Clayton Compromise, 74

Clemens, Jeremiah: insults Rhett, 185

Clingman, Thomas L., 91; opinion on South Carolina, 48

Cobb, Howell: and Unionist party in Georgia, 174; elected speaker of House, 89; supports Clay's compromise measures, 92

Coit, J. C.: campaigns for secession, 152

Colcock, W. F.: urges secession, 126–27

"Common-property-of-the-states" doctrine. *See* Calhoun, John C.; Rhett, R. B.

Compromise measures: and election of 1852, 123; become law, 122; denounced in South Carolina, 102; passage of denounced in South Carolina, 122, 125; reported as bills, 102

Compromise of 1850. *See* Clay, Henry; Compromise measures

Conner, Henry W.: and Southern Convention, 78; views on Rhett, 169

Cooperation: and Whitemarsh B. Seabrook, 124; arguments for, 144, 157–60, 231 (n. 22); increased editorial support for, 172

Cooperationists: and analogy to nullification, 158; and attack on Rhett, 169, 172–73, 180; and Charles McDonald, 174; and fears of disorder, 188–89; and increasing differences

with secessionists, 151; and Southern Rights parties, 174; and tacit alliance with Unionists, 172, 177–78; and Unionists, 150; attack speech by Bellinger, 168–69; begin party organization, 164–66; begin public campaigning against secession, 166; defined, 127; deplore tactics of secessionists, 145; disavow any relationship with Perry, 183; establish *Southern Standard*, 165–66; legislative tactics of in 1850, 139–40; nominating conventions of, 177; nominees for Southern Congress, 234 (n. 80); party organization of in Charleston, 172, 178; reaction of to victory, 183–84; relationship of with Unionists, 167; retain control of Charleston Southern Rights Association, 154; urge restraint and harmony, 127; views on alliance of South Carolina with Britain, 158–59; views on blockade of South Carolina, 158; views on legality of secession, 187; views on meeting of state convention, 184; views on ultimate necessity of secession, 188; weakness of in seventh congressional district, 178; win October 1851 elections, 181

Corwin, Thomas: and federal patronage policy in South Carolina, 150, 229 (n. 122); corresponds with South Carolina Unionists, 165

Dargan, George W.: and secessionists, 173

De Leon, Edwin: becomes editor of *Southern Press*, 115

De Treville, Richard, 167

Democratic party: and territorial expansion, 61–62

DeSaussure, W. F., 78

Dickinson, Daniel S.: and popular sovereignty, 71

Elliott, William, 129; and abolitionist petitions, 36; opposes secession, 168; Unionism of, 232 (n. 47)

Elmore, Franklin H.: accepts interim senatorship, 100; and Southern Rights Associations, 82–83; corresponds with

Lewis Cass, 76; death of, 100; elected delegate to Nashville Convention, 87; views on Taylor administration, 82; views on Zachary Taylor, 70–71
"Evils-of-time" argument: and cooperationists, 160. *See also* Holmes, I. E.

Fillmore, Millard: and abolition of slavery in District of Columbia, 75–76; asserts finality of compromise measures, 146; becomes president, 116; supports compromise measures, 116
Fisher, Elwood: becomes editor of *Southern Press*, 115
Florida: and Wilmot Proviso, 83
Foote, Henry S.: and Mississippi convention, 1849, 83; attacks Calhoun, 94; breaks with Calhoun, 93; campaigns for governorship of Mississippi, 175–76; censured by Mississippi legislature, 133, 225 (n. 57); forms Union party in Mississippi, 133; leads Union party in Mississippi, 149; relationship of with compromise opponents, 119
Forsyth, John: and nullification, 41; opposes nullification, 42
Free Soil party: convention of, 73
Frost, Edward: opposes separate secession, 127
Fugitive Slave Act: effects of, 146–47

"Georgia Platform," 148
Georgia: and Wilmot Proviso, 83; conditionally accepts compromise measures, 142–43; delegates to state convention of elected, 132; legislature of calls state convention, 95; plan for representation of at Nashville Convention, 95; procompromise forces in, 109; realignment of parties in, 96; secessionist tactics in modified, 132; secessionists in, 110; state convention of meets, 142; state convention of scheduled, 131; Unionist party in, 174
Gist, William H.: proposes political reconciliation, 169
Goode, William: views on Webster's Seventh of March speech, 94
Gott, Daniel: and abolition of slavery in

District of Columbia, 56, 80
Graham, Winchester, 178
Grayson, W. J., 189–90; and Andrew Jackson, 43; and federal patronage policy in South Carolina, 150–51; commitment to Union and slavery, 39; opposes disunion, 129–30; Unionism of attacked, 130–31
Green, Duff: defends nullifiers, 45
Gregg, Maxcy: campaigns for secession, 152, 173; urges secession, 126; views on secessionist defeat, 185–87

Habersham, Richard: views on nullification, 40–41
Hamilton, James: financial situation of, 98–99; forced to decline interim senatorship, 99; lobbying activities of, 98, 119; offered interim senatorship, 98–99, 219 (n. 57); retires from South Carolina politics, 35; supports Clay's compromise measures, 98, 225 (n. 50)
Hammond, James H., 231 (n. 25); and abolitionist petitions, 36; and Bluffton Movement, 58; and Mexican War, 58; and Nashville Convention, 88, 97, 102; and reassembly of Nashville Convention, 134; at Nashville Convention, 103, 105; delivers eulogy on Calhoun, 137; disparages Southern party, 74–75; elected delegate to Nashville Convention, 87; impact of scandal on career of, 58–59, 209 (n. 22); laments Rhett's "treason speech," 108; loses struggle for Senate seat, 138; predicts reaction against Rhett's policies, 141; privately denounces Rhett's tactics, 111; proposes alternative to secession, 163; views on abolitionist tactics, 17–18, 203 (n. 56); views on government of South Carolina, 20; views on Nashville Convention, 106; views on passage of compromise measures, 122; views on secessionist defeat, 187; views on Southern party, 69; views on Zachary Taylor, 80, 214 (n. 81)
Hayne, Isaac W., 99, 172; accuses Perry of misrepresentation, 151; urges cooperation, 127
Holmes, I. E.: and "evils-of-time" argu-

ment, 114, 222 (n. 118); and Texas debt
and boundary bill, 114
Huger, Daniel E.: elected to Senate, 37

Irby, James H., 140

Jackson, Andrew: and nullification,
44–45
Jamison, David F.: views on Nashville
Convention, 106
Johnson, David, 178; and Southern Convention, 78; and Wilmot Proviso, 78;
elected governor, 38; opposes all-
Mexico movement, 63; supports Calhoun's "defensive line" policy, 60
Jones, James: campaigns for secession,
152

Keitt, Lawrence M.: campaigns for secession, 165
King, John P.: attacks Calhoun, 46
King, Mitchell: mission of to Tennessee,
42
King, Preston: revises Wilmot Proviso,
54, 64
King, Thomas B.: mission of to California, 81

Laval, William: campaigns for secession,
170
Legare, Hugh S., 37
Leigh, Benjamin: mission of to South
Carolina, 44
Lieber, Francis, 100; and alliance of
South Carolina with Britain, 230 (n.
14); contributes to *Southern Patriot*,
165; defends compromise measures,
128; views on Mexican War, 59, 210 (n.
23), 212 (n. 58)
Lieber, Oscar, 175
Lumpkin, Wilson: and nullification,
41–42

McCrady, Edward, 140
McDonald, Charles: and reassembly of
Nashville Convention, 134; leads
Georgia secessionists, 110
McDuffie, George: elected governor,
1834, 34; retires from Senate, 58
Macon (Georgia) secessionist rally:

speeches at, 110–11
Magrath, Andrew G., 172
Manning, John, 164
Means, John H.: and plans to manufac-
ture arms in South Carolina, 151; and
South Carolina state convention,
185–86; campaigns for secession, 152,
179; elected governor, 137; rejects action against federal installations,
170–71
Memminger, Christopher G., 172; and
cooperationist tactics, 139; campaigns
for cooperation, 173, 234 (n. 82); denounces compromise measures,
125–26
Mexican War. *See* South Carolina: and
reaction to Mexican War
Mississippi: and Southern Convention,
83; decline of secession sentiment in,
175; division of Democratic party in,
149; election results for state convention of, 176; legislature of censures
Henry Foote, 133; legislature of
schedules state convention, 134; response of to passage of compromise
measures, 133; unofficial state convention in, 1849, 83–84

Nashville Convention: address adopted
by, 105; and Florida, 97; and legislature of Alabama, 96; and legislature of
Mississippi, 96; and legislature of
Tennessee, 96; and legislature of Virginia, 96; assembles in June 1850, 103;
popularity of declines in the South,
96–97, 101; proposed by Mississippi
convention, 1849, 84; reassembles in
November 1850, 135; representation of
southern states at, 103; resolutions
adopted by, 104–5; resolutions offered
at, 104; results of hailed in South
Carolina, 106; support for in southern
newspapers, 218 (n. 45); tactics of
South Carolina delegates at, 103–4;
views of delegates at, 104
"Natural limits" thesis, 66–67, 211 (n.
46)
Negro Seaman Law, 141, 227 (n. 84)
Nullification: failure of, 44
Nullifiers: hope for alliance with Geor-

gia, 40; isolation of in 1833, 40, 42, 44; isolation of, 207 (n. 38)

O'Neall, John B., 189; favors compromise measures, 128
Oregon: established as free-soil territory, 74
Orr, James L.: and May 1851 convention of Southern Rights Associations, 155–56; campaigns for cooperation, 167, 171, 177–78; urges resistance to compromise measures, 126

Perronneau, Henry W., 99
Perry, Benjamin F.: and Southern Convention, 77, 84; campaigns against secession, 150; changes opinion on Southern Convention, 100–101; defeated for Congress, 1834, 34; defeated for Congress, 1848, 77; defends compromise measures, 128; denounces Wilmot Proviso, 77; maneuvers to delay secession, 138–39; opposes reconciliation with nullifiers, 33; plans to issue Southern Patriot, 129; predicts reaction in favor of Union, 141–42; proposes alliance with cooperationists, 150; supports Calhoun's "defensive line" policy, 60; views nullifiers as disunionists, 35; views on abolition, 77; views on defeat of secessionists, 183; views on slavery and the Union, 35–36; views on Union as guarantor of slavery, 189
Petigru, James L.: and Zachary Taylor, 222 (n. 126); becomes U.S. attorney for South Carolina, 224 (n. 39); views on Mexican War, 210 (n. 24); views on Rhett's election as senator, 138
Pettigrew, James J., 208 (n. 50); and hostility toward South Carolina, 47–48
Pickens, Francis W., 137; forced into political retirement, 58; supports Mexican War, 58; supports secession, 180
Pinckney, Henry L., Jr., 167
Pinckney, Henry L.: and abolitionist petitions, 36
Poinsett, Joel R.: opposes secession, 142; promoted as delegate to Nashville Convention, 101; supports Southern

Patriot, 129
Polk, James K.: opinion on Calhoun, 46
Popular sovereignty: denounced in South Carolina, 72
Pressley, Benjamin C., 172; campaigns for cooperation, 173; edits Southern Standard, 165
Preston, John S.: and cooperationist tactics, 139
Preston, William C.: and nullification, 43

Quitman, John A.: and passage of compromise measures, 133; campaigns for governorship of Mississippi, 175–76; confers with Daniel Wallace, 84–85; corresponds with Rhett, 134, 226 (n. 59); corresponds with secessionists, 178–79; corresponds with South Carolina secessionists, 176; corresponds with Whitemarsh Seabrook, 109; resigns governorship, 149

Randolph, John: and nullification, 44
Rhett, Edward: campaigns for secession, 152
Rhett, James: campaigns for secession, 170
Rhett, R. B.: addresses Charleston Southern Rights Association, 152–53; addresses rally in Macon (Georgia), 110–11; addresses Southern Rights Associations, 126; and correspondence with Quitman, 179; and report on Nashville Convention, 106; and southern confederacy, 108, 111; and Southern Convention, 78; and "treason speech," 107–8; and Wilmot Proviso, 55; attacked by cooperationists, 169, 172, 180; breaks irrevocably with cooperationists, 152–53; campaigns for secession, 167; defeated for Senate, 37; delivers eulogy on Calhoun, 137; description of by Henry W. Conner, 169; elected senator, 138; exhausted by speaking schedule, 180; finances of in 1851, 234 (n. 91); formulates counterdoctrine to Wilmot Proviso, 64; insulted by Jeremiah Clemens, 185; leadership of challenged, 183–86; opposes continuation of Mexican War, 60;

opposes Taylor for president, 75; organizational problems of, 173; reaction
to "treason speech" of, 108–9; refuses
to duel Clemens, 185; undertakes
speaking tour, 171; urges action
against federal installations, 170–71;
views on blockade of South Carolina,
153; views on Fugitive Slave Act,
147–48; views on secession and slave
revolt, 19; views on Zachary Taylor,
71; writes Nashville Convention Address, 105
Richardson, John P.: advocates secession,
38; and May 1851 convention of
Southern Rights Associations, 155;
campaigns for secession, 152; elected
governor, 37
Ritchie, Thomas: supports Clay's compromise measures, 92
Ruffin, Edmund: and Nashville Convention, 102

Santo Domingo slave rebellion: impact
on South Carolina, 10, 15–16
Seabrook, Whitemarsh B.: and Nashville
Convention, 86; and reestablishment
of brigade encampments, 86; and Wilmot Proviso, 86; campaigns for secession, 152; elected governor, 79; proposes new militia forces, 86–87; requests increase in military budget, 87;
responds to passage of compromise
measures, 123–24
Secession: and political disorder, 187; arguments for, 143, 160–62, 231 (n. 22);
costs and inconveniences of, 152; legality of, 187; process of, 187; rationale of,
188; support for in low country, 168
Secessionists: accused of disrupting
cooperationist rallies, 180–81; and
Charles McDonald, 175; and elections
for state convention, 145–46; and fear
of an opposition party, 164; and Fort
Moultrie, 170; and Fort Sumter, 170;
and Hammond's alternative to secession, 182–83; and incident at Fort
Sumter, 173; central leadership of,
163; control central Southern Rights
Association, 156; control SRAs, 163;
dominate May 1851 convention of

SRAs, 154–56; dominate SRAs,
153–54; form new SRA in Charleston,
169–70; increasing desperation of,
180–81; legislative tactics of in 1850,
139–40; lose October 1851 elections,
181; nominating conventions of, 177;
nominees for Southern Congress, 234
(n. 80); organizational problems of,
173; party machinery of, 163–64; reaction of to defeat, 181–82; views on abolitionist tactics, 160–61; views on legality of secession, 187–88; views on
meeting of state convention, 184;
views on necessity of secession, 188;
views on process of secession, 187;
weakness of in Charleston, 180
Seward, William H.: emerges as advisor
to Taylor, 80; southern view of, 116
Sharkey, William L., 84; and reassembly
of Nashville Convention, 134
Simms, William G.: and Mexican War,
58; conversion from Unionist to secessionist, 39–40; favors annexation of
Mexico, 62; obstacles to political career
of, 209 (n. 20); supports cooperation,
151; supports Taylor for president, 70,
75
Slave revolt: and abolitionism, 17–18;
anxiety about in South Carolina,
13–17, 215 (n. 104). See also Vesey
Conspiracy
Slave trade: resumed by South Carolina,
1803–1807, 16; to South Carolina, 201
(n. 14)
Slaveholders: in South Carolina compared to other states, 11, 202 (n. 33)
Slavery: growth and development of in
South Carolina, 4–9
South Carolina gentry: and annexation
of Texas, 56–57; and Mexican territories, 54; oppose admission of
California, 90; oppose all-Mexico
movement, 61–63, 211 (n. 33); provinciality of, 49; views on Clay's compromise measures, 91; views on Webster's Seventh of March speech, 94
South Carolina: and elections for Southern Congress, 140; and elections for
state convention, 140, 228 (n. 103); and
reaction to Mexican War, 57–59; aris-

tocratic government of, 20, 22–25, 203 (nn. 4, 7), 204 (n. 10), 227 (n. 82); climate of, 3; elects delegates to Nashville Convention, 100; government of compared to other states, 24, 27; government of defended, 26–29; holds elections for state convention, 145–46; hostility toward in Georgia, 131–32; hostility toward in the South, 11, 46–48, 78–80, 85, 179, 207 (n. 38), 208 (n. 51), 215 (n. 110); political power in, 30–31; provides for representation at Nashville Convention, 87; relationship of government and slavery in, 21–22; reputation for political extremism, 45–46; state convention of adjourns, 186; state convention of assembles, 185–86

—free Negro population of: compared to other states, 10; size of, 10

—legislature of: approves brigade encampments, 136; calls for Southern Congress, 140; charters steamship company, 136; discontinues brigade encampments, 184; establishes Board of Ordnance, 136; increases military appropriation, 136; schedules state convention, 184

—slave population of: compared to Brazil's, 13–14; compared to other colonies, 6; compared to other states, 8–9; emigration to other states, 12

—white population of: commitment to slavery, 13; emigration to other states, 11–12, 202 (n. 36); percentage born in state, 12

Southern Address, 81

Southern Congress: elections for used as referendum, 177

Southern Convention: movement for, 48. *See also* Nashville Convention

Southern party: failure of in 1847, 76

Southern Patriot: begins publication, 149; supported by South Carolina Unionists, 150

Southern Press: established, 115, 220 (n. 81); origins of, 212 (n. 57); positions of disapproved by cooperationists, 172

Southern Rights Association of Charleston, 145, 154

Southern Rights Associations (SRA): centralized control of established, 156; delegates from meet in Columbia, 81; form central committee, 1849, 82; idea of revived in 1848, 81; largely captured by secessionists, 144–45; of Alabama, 148; plan to organize, 76; reanimated in 1850, 124–25; structure of, 125

Southern Rights parties: in southern states, 148, 174

Southern Standard: format and purpose of, 168. *See also* Cooperationists

Stephens, Alexander H.: and Unionist party in Georgia, 174; views on secession, 95–96

Stono Rebellion, 5, 13–14. *See also* Slave revolt

Tarpley, Collin S.: and Mississippi convention, 1849, 83

Taylor, Zachary: and California, 80–81; and Wilmot Proviso, 76; death of, 116; loses electoral vote of South Carolina, 76; popularity of in South Carolina, 69–72; popularity of in South, 70; refuses to pledge veto of Wilmot Proviso, 88; support for in Charleston, 75; urges admission of California, 90; urges admission of New Mexico, 90

Tennessee: and Wilmot Proviso, 83; legislature of opposes nullification, 42–43

Texas debt and boundary bill: and relationship to slavery, 116; lobbying activity for, 118. *See also* Holmes, I. E.

Thompson, Waddy: defends compromise measures, 126; denounces Wilmot Proviso, 77; elected to Congress, 1834, 34; lobbying activity of, 119; opposes all-Mexico movement, 62; opposes continuation of Mexican War, 59

Toombs, Robert: and Southern party, 47; and Unionist party in Georgia, 174

Towns, George W., 95

Tucker, N. Beverley: views on Zachary Taylor, 80

Union: rationale for, 189

Unionists: and fears of disorder, 190; and preservation of slavery, 189–90; and tacit alliance with cooperationists, 172, 177–78; decline of in South Carolina, 38–40; political mistakes of, 206 (n. 6); proscribed from politics by nullifiers, 33–34, 38; tactics of, 165; victories of in southern states, 179; views on slavery, 189

Van Buren, Martin: and nullification, 41
Vesey Conspiracy, 203 (n. 51)

Wallace, Daniel, 188; campaigns for secession, 173; mission of to Mississippi convention, 1849, 82, 84–85
Wardlaw, Francis H., 178
Webster, Daniel: attacks Nashville Convention, 116–17; supports Clay's compromise measures, 93
Whig party: and territorial expansion, 61

Wilmot Proviso: and fears of slave revolt, 215 (n. 104); and formation of Free Soil party, 54, 68; and perception of slavepower, 54; as perceived in South Carolina, 55, 67–68; as political innovation, 65; denounced in South Carolina, 77; reaction to in South Carolina, 64
Wilmot, David: introduces Proviso, 54, 208 (n. 2)
Woodward, Joseph A., 137
Worcester v. Georgia: and nullification, 41
Wyly, James W.: opposes nullification, 43

Yancey, William L.: and "Alabama Platform," 72–73